ecpr PRESS

Indigenous Politics
Institutions, Representation, Mobilisation

Edited by
Mikkel Berg-Nordlie, Jo Saglie
and Ann Sullivan

ecpr PRESS

Cover photo © Kenneth Hætta (http.//www.kennethhaetta.com)

First published by the ECPR Press in 2015

This paperback edition published in 2016

The ECPR Press is the publishing imprint of the European Consortium for Political Research (ECPR), a scholarly association, which supports and encourages the training, research and cross-national co-operation of political scientists in institutions throughout Europe and beyond.

ECPR Press
Harbour House
Hythe Quay
Colchester
CO2 8JF
United Kingdom

Typeset by the ECPR Press

Printed and bound by Lightning Source

British Library Cataloguing in Publication Data

A catalogue record for this book is available from the British Library

HARDBACK ISBN: 978-1-907301-66-7

PAPERBACK ISBN: 978-1-785522-35-2

PDF ISBN: 978-1-785522-39-0

EPUB ISBN: 978-1-785522-40-6

KINDLE ISBN: 978-1-785522-41-3

www.ecpr.eu/ecprpress

You may also be interested in:

Spreading Protest: Social Movements in Times of Crisis
Edited by Donatella della Porta and Alice Mattoni
ISBN 9781785521638
Which elements do the Arab Spring, the *Indignados* and Occupy Wall Street have
in common? How do they differ? What do they share with social movements of
the past? This book discusses the recent wave of global mobilisations from an
unusual angle, explaining what aspects of protests spread from one country to
another, how this happened, and why diffusion occurred in certain contexts but
not in others. In doing so, the book casts light on the more general mechanisms
of protest diffusion in contemporary societies, explaining how mobilisations
travel from one country to another and, also, from past to present times.

Constitutional Deliberative Democracy in Europe
Min Reuchamps and Jane Suiter
ISBN 9781785521454
European institutions have introduced different forms of deliberative democracy
as a way to connect citizens back in. These empirical cases are emblematic of a
possibly constitutional turn in deliberative democracy in Europe. The purpose
of this book is to critically assess these developments, bringing together
academics involved in the designing of these new forms of constitutional
deliberative democracy with the theorists who propagated the ideas and evaluated
democratic standards.

Political Violence in Context: Time, Space and Milieu
Lorenzo Bosi, Niall Ó Dochartaigh and Daniela Pisoiu
ISBN 9781785521447
Context is crucial to understanding the causes of political violence and the form
it takes. This book examines how time, space and supportive milieux decisively
shape the pattern and pace of such violence. While much of the work in this
field focuses on individual psychology or radical ideology, Bosi, Ó Dochartaigh,
Pisoiu and others take a fresh, innovative look at the importance of context in
generating mobilisation and shaping patterns of violence.

Contents

PART III: INDIGENOUS REPRESENTATION – CONCRETE CONFLICTS

List of Figures and Tables

Contributors

JOHANNES BERGH is a researcher at the Institute for Social Research in Oslo, where he works on the Norwegian Electoral Studies Program. His research interests include political participation, elections and voting: in general, as well as with respect to minorities and indigenous groups.

MIKKEL BERG-NORDLIE is a researcher at NIBR – Norwegian Institute for Urban and Regional Research. He is currently writing a history PhD at the University of Tromsø – the Arctic University of Norway. His research is mainly on political organisation, representation, governance and discourses related to indigenous peoples and other ethnic minorities particularly in, but not limited to, Russia and the Nordic countries.

EINAR BRAATHEN is a political scientist and senior researcher at the Norwegian Institute for Urban and Regional Research. His main research interests include democratisation, decentralisation, sustainable development and the politics of poverty-reduction. Recently, he has mainly worked on Brazil. He has published in several edited volumes and international journals.

RAVI DE COSTA is Associate Professor in the Faculty of Environmental Studies at York University in Canada. His research is on indigenous politics and movements and on the institutional and cultural aspects of the indigenous–settler relationship.

CÁSSIO INGLEZ DE SOUSA is a Brazilian anthropologist who has worked with several indigenous peoples and traditional communities since 1994, especially in initiatives related to applied anthropology, ethnodevelopment, sustainable projects, indigenous land-management, impact-assessment and engagement with the private sector. He has many publications related to these themes and has professional experience of government, international co-operation, NGOs, indigenous organisations and the private sector; he currently works as an Independent Consultant.

PATRIK LANTTO is a Professor of History and the Director of the Centre for Sámi Research at Umeå University, Sweden. His main research focus is on Sámi political mobilisation in Sweden, and Swedish Sámi policy, as well as indigenous education. He has published three books and articles in several edited volumes and international journals.

JOHN-ANDREW MCNEISH is Associate Professor of International Environment and Development Studies at the Norwegian University of Life Sciences and Senior Researcher at Christian Michelsens Institute (CMI). His main research interests include indigenous politics, natural-resource rights and politics, and the anthropology of development. As well as numerous journal articles he has published several co-authored volumes, including *Flammable Societies: Studies on the socio-economics of oil and gas* (Pluto Press 2012), *Gender Justice and Legal Pluralities: Latin American and African perspectives* (Routledge 2012) and *Indigenous Peoples and Poverty* (Zed Books 2005).

ULF MÖRKENSTAM is Associate Professor at the Department of Political Science, Stockholm University. His main fields of research are political theory and policy analysis with a specific focus on indigenous rights. He has written extensively on Swedish Sámi policy and on the capacity of the Swedish Sámi Parliament to safeguard the Sámi people's right to self-determination.

CIARAN O'FAIRCHEALLAIGH is Professor of Politics and Public Policy in the School of Government and International Relations, Griffith University, Brisbane. His research focuses on the inter-relationship between indigenous people and large-scale resource development; he has a particular interest in social-impact assessment and in negotiation of agreements between indigenous and mining companies. For over 20 years he has acted as a negotiator and advisor for indigenous communities in Australia, Canada and Papua New Guinea.

MARTIN PAPILLON is Associate Professor in the Département de science politique, Université de Montréal. Martin's research focuses on Aboriginal governance and Canadian federalism as well as the politics of self-determination in comparative perspective. He is the coeditor of *The Global Promise of Federalism* (University of Toronto Press), *Federalism and Aboriginal Governance* (Presses de l'Université Laval) and *Les Autochtones et le Québec* (Presses de l'Université de Montréal). His comparative work on Aboriginal politics is published amongst others in *Publius: the Journal of Federalism*, *Lien social et politiques* and *Politics & Society*.

TORUNN PETTERSEN is currently completing her PhD project at the Arctic University UiT, Norway. She holds a part-time position as a researcher at the Sámi University College in Guovdageaidnu, Norway. Her research interests include the Sámediggi elections, the living conditions of Sámi and other indigenous peoples, and the conditions for knowledge-building and opinion-formation on Sámi issues, with a special focus on (deficient) Sámi ethnicity data and statistics.

JANE ROBBINS is Associate Professor in Politics in the School of Social and Policy Studies, Flinders University in Adelaide, South Australia. She has published an edited volume on Australian politics and has contributed numerous chapters and articles to books and international journals, including *Ethnicities*. Her research interests focus on indigenous policy, particularly political representation and political rights, international indigenous movements and international law and on Australian welfare and social policy.

JO SAGLIE is Research Professor at the Institute for Social Research, Oslo, Norway and Adjunct Senior Researcher at the Sámi University College in Guovdageaidnu, Norway. His main research interests include party organisations and intra-party democracy, local elections and local democracy, as well as indigenous politics.

ANN SULLIVAN is a member of the northern Ngapuhi tribe of New Zealand. She has a PhD in political science and is Associate Professor and Head of Māori Studies and co-Head of Te Wānanga o Waipapa/School of Māori Studies and Pacific Studies, University of Auckland. Her main research interests are Māori electoral behaviour, Māori development, representation and indigenous public policy issues. Her teaching covers a range of areas of Māori and comparative indigenous development with an emphasis on public policy.

Preface

In April 2011, researchers from three continents gathered to discuss the realities of contemporary indigenous politics in different countries around the world. The occasion was a workshop at the European Consortium for Political Research (ECPR) Joint Sessions in St Gallen, Switzerland, where nineteen authors with backgrounds from political science, indigenous studies, social anthropology and history presented papers on the subject Indigenous Politics: Mobilisation, Representation, Internationalisation. Topics that were discussed included: how an indigenous people can achieve self-determination without having a sovereign state; problems of gaining political empowerment under conditions of land loss and lack of economic and other resources; what defines an indigenous people; what are some of the formalities and realities of consultation, organisation and representation of indigenous peoples; what are some of the international developments between and among indigenous peoples; and what are some of the frameworks that may be used to further their goal of self-determination.

In the aftermath of this successful workshop, we have produced an anthology on modern indigenous politics. Eight of the chapters in this book originate from papers presented at the St Gallen workshop. In addition, we sought and included three further chapters (de Costa, Braathen and Inglez de Sousa and McNeish) on topics and geographical areas that were insufficiently covered by our workshop.

Many individuals and institutions have provided valuable help and comments during the process. We would especially like to thank those workshop participants whose papers had to be omitted from this anthology, for reasons of thematic unity and geographic variation. All the participants at the St Gallen workshop made valuable contributions to the discussions, from which this book has sprung. We wish to thank the contributors to the book for all the work they have done in rewriting their conference papers into chapters for this book, and for their valuable comments to the introductory chapter. Our thanks also go to the ECPR Press, and especially our editor, Alexandra Segerberg, for comments, support and encouragement.

Finally, we would like to thank our respective home institutions: the Norwegian Institute for Urban and Regional Research (NIBR), Oslo, Norway; the Institute for Social Research (ISF), Oslo, Norway; the University of Auckland, New Zealand; and the University of Tromsø – Arctic University of Norway. Thanks are also due to the Research Council of Norway, which financed some of the projects that led to the both the conference and the production of this book – *The Norwegian Sámi Election Study* (Sámi University College, Norut Alta and ISF); and *Russia in pan-Sámi politics* (NIBR and NUPI).

Mikkel Berg-Nordlie, Jo Saglie and Ann Sullivan
Oslo and Tromsø/Romsa; Oslo; Auckland/Tamaki Makaurau
June 2015

Chapter One

Introduction: Perspectives on Indigenous Politics

Mikkel Berg-Nordlie, Jo Saglie and Ann Sullivan

Over the last fifty years, indigenous politics has become an increasingly important field of study. Indeed, as a result of successful mobilisation and lobbying, the political and legal recognition of indigenous rights has been given widespread support by international organisations and nation-states around the world. Indigenous struggles are shaped by historical and social circumstances particular to their nations but there are, nevertheless, many shared experiences. This book seeks to identify some of the commonalities, similarities and differences that currently exist in modern indigenous politics.

The ratification of human and indigenous rights treaties and declarations, and the corresponding legal duties of states, are having an impact on domestic policies. Indigenous peoples are being empowered by the advent of a discourse on indigenous rights and the internationalisation of that discourse. They are now debated as previously ill-treated rights-holders, towards whom the encroaching states are duty-bearers. Increasing availability of information and new communication technologies have enhanced indigenous movements' abilities to mobilise at the local, national and international level of politics. Still, although indigenous politics today is heavily internationalised, it is the individual states that effectively respond to indigenous demands – and they respond in very different ways (see Hocking 2005; Nettheim *et al.* 2002; Wessendorf 2001).

In some cases, states have created separate institutions to ensure that the political voice of indigenous peoples is heard by national governments – such as the Sámi Parliaments of Finland, Norway and Sweden. In other cases, indigenous peoples such as the New Zealand Māori have dedicated seats in their national parliament. A number of Native American tribes are self-determining 'nations within nations', with some limited legislative, judicial and regulatory powers (Fleras and Elliott 1992). In Russia, the umbrella organisation RAIPON tries to provide a voice for indigenous interests at the federal level of government; while at the local or regional level there are a large number of small state-based and civil-society-based groups seeking to represent indigenous interests.

This variation in indigenous political arrangements will be a key area of focus for this anthology. Both the institutional framework and the actual use of these institutions will be taken into consideration. For example, although the Māori of New Zealand have had separate seats in parliament since 1867, positive policy changes only began post-1970, following a decade of activism challenging the state to recognise a multitude of grievances relating to broken treaty promises (Walker 2004; Sullivan 2009, 2010).

This first chapter of the book is divided into three sections. Firstly, an introduction to the anthology's subject: indigenous political institutions, representation and mobilisation. Here we present our approach and how this contributes to the literature on indigenous politics, and we account for some of the commonalities in indigenous politics as well as differences between indigenous peoples and between states. The purpose is to describe some of the variations in the world of indigenous politics – within which our case studies take place – as well as the similarities. We then turn to discuss briefly the question of defining 'indigenous peoples'. The second part constitutes an overview of the book and its chapters; in the third part we present some thoughts about problems in contemporary indigenous politics and the research of this subject, based on insights from the book's chapters.

Indigenous politics: Commonalities and variations

Indigenous cultures have long been a subject of study for anthropologists, historians and linguists. Such studies have often been culture-focused, in the sense that they have a particular interest in traditional social structures and the clash between those structures and the states that have incorporated indigenous peoples and lands. Hence, such studies often emphasise policy issues such as assimilation, exclusion and marginalisation. During the latter half of the 1900s, this tradition of research expanded to include the emergent indigenous political movements.

As the ratification of human rights agreements intensified post-World War II, we saw the development of a corpus of academic writing focused on legal frameworks for individual human rights. Law-focused indigenous studies have emphasised indigenous rights within the field of human rights, initially concentrating on individual civil and political rights before moving on to include the duty and responsibilities of states to recognise individual socio-economic rights, such as education, shelter, food and clothing. As collective indigenous rights have become increasingly recognised internationally, most notably through ILO Convention 169 on Indigenous and Tribal Peoples (ILO 169, 1989) and the United Nations Declarations on the Rights of Indigenous Peoples (UNDRIP 2007), that subject has naturally become central in law-focused indigenous studies.

As the attention shifted to collective rights, an academic literature focused on the normative foundation of collective rights has emerged. While some argue that indigenous peoples do not possess rights beyond those enjoyed by the group members as individuals (see, for example, Kukathas 1992), it has become an increasingly accepted point of view in political-philosophical writings that recognition of past injustices is required; that collective rights must be recognised even within a context of democratic liberalism; and that the rights of indigenous peoples cannot be reduced to assimilated, undifferentiated individual rights (Kymlicka 1995, 1998; Tully 1995, 2000).

Such philosophical, legal, and ethnographic studies of indigenous peoples and indigenous rights are valuable entry points into indigenous politics. However, in our opinion there is too little explicit focus on political structures and the practicalities within them – there is too little indigenous political science. This anthology seeks to amend this by providing a political-science-based and comparative dimension, gathering academic writings that focus explicitly on the political institutions, systems and structures that indigenous peoples negotiate in their ongoing struggle for representation and participation within the political structures and processes of their nation-states. The book treats indigenous politics and indigenous governance not as examples that may be drawn upon to illustrate philosophical or legal points – nor as context that enable us to better understand indigenous cultural practice – but as the main area of study.

Indigenous peoples are not undifferentiated collectives but include individual political actors who may have diverse agendas. It is important, therefore, to pay attention to how different movements, tribal organisations and individuals promote and represent the interests of their peoples. The structures used by indigenous activists to engage with their own people need to be robust, in order for them to legitimately represent their group *vis-à-vis* decision-makers in local, regional, state and federal governments. Likewise, the channels for influence offered by state structures must be able to communicate indigenous grievances in an uncensored manner and to the appropriate authorities. The ways in which indigenous peoples organise, and the types of official structures for indigenous representation established by states, are of core interest to indigenous-oriented political science. The case studies in this anthology illustrate differing goals, differing strategies and differing state responses to indigenous demands.

Indigenous mobilisation and internationalisation

Indigenous mobilisations in various countries are not isolated events; rather, they are frequently influenced by the general internationalisation of grassroots politics. Links have been forged between indigenous activists in many different countries through a range of regional and global networks (see, for example, Niezen 2000, 2003; de Costa 2006; Minde 2003, 2008). Though there are great distances in both culture and geography between indigenous peoples, most seek some measure of control over their social, cultural, economic and political development and they desire a measure of influence and input over the use and management of their ancestral territories. For indigenous peoples, four types of internationalisation can be identified. Firstly, there is the construction of a global indigenous identity, which unites very diverse peoples in a global community based on perceptions of common historical experiences and political interests. Secondly, many indigenous peoples draw inspiration from the experiences of other indigenous nations. Thirdly, indigenous peoples have, during the last four decades, increasingly entered into trans-border networking – through loose networks, NGO umbrella organisations, regional state co-operations, and bodies within the UN system. Finally, the developing corpus of indigenous-oriented international law has changed the playing field fundamentally, because indigenous movements can now appeal to authorities that transcend the state level.

The Sámi people of Finland, Norway, Russia and Sweden may exemplify the significance of a long-standing indigenous trans-border co-operation (Berg-Nordlie 2013; Henriksen 1999; Varsi 2007). Their ancestral lands are divided between four countries, a situation Robbins (2007) describes as 'imposed internationalism'. Their collective co-operation accelerated in the 1970s following the Norwegian government's controversial decision to site a large hydro-electric power project on core Sámi lands. Sámi indigenous rights became part of the political agenda both nationally and internationally. Sámi parliaments have established an international co-operation regime centred on the Sámi Parliamentary Council, which promotes trans-border Sámi co-operation and solidarity and the standardisation of Sámi policies. The Sámi Council, a unitary, border-transcending NGO umbrella organisation, also gives political expression to the Sámi aspiration of not being divided by imposed borders.

Internationalisation is not limited to those indigenous peoples who are divided by national borders. Indeed, the emergence of indigenous movements on the international scene has happened parallel to, and influenced by, increasing contact between different indigenous peoples across borders and continents. Minde (2003: 81–7; 2005: 17–19; 2008: 58–60) and Nyyssönen (2007) describe how connections with representatives of the North American Indigenous Movement became important for the formation of Sámi activists' discourses and strategies. Inspiration also came from non-indigenous movements, such as the 1960s American civil rights movement. In Australia, voting for the national parliament was only extended to the total Aboriginal population in 1962 and it was not until 1967 that discriminatory clauses were removed from the Australian Constitution. Similar to the civil rights freedom rides in the South of the United States, bus rides promoting Australian Aboriginal rights were used to draw national attention to Aboriginal issues. International indigenous co-operation has become institutionalised through the International Working Group for Indigenous Affairs (IWGIA, 1968–present), the World Council of Indigenous Peoples (WCIP, 1975–1996), the UN Working Group on Indigenous Populations (WGIP, 1982–2006), and the work towards the adoption of International Labour Organisation Convention 169 on the Rights of Indigenous and Tribal Peoples (ILO 169, 1989) (Minde 2005, 2008).

During the process of indigenous internationalisation since the 1960s, international laws and conventions that address indigenous rights have been created, most notably ILO 169 but also and most recently the United Nations Declaration of the Rights of Indigenous Peoples (UNDRIP). ILO 169 recognises that indigenous peoples have the right to maintain and develop their identities, languages, and religions; and it contains provisions that advance indigenous cultural integrity, land, and resource rights. It also requires that signatories take affirmative steps to assist indigenous peoples in preserving their culture and uphold their right to travel freely within tribal lands. Customary international norms are reflected in several documents. Article 3 of the UNDRIP acknowledges that indigenous peoples have the right to self-determination and by virtue of that right they freely determine their political status and economic, social and cultural development. Furthermore, both the 1945 United Nations Charter and the 1948 Universal Declaration of Human Rights recognise the fundamental rights of all peoples, and the Genocide Convention guarantees the right of cultural survival. Other documents of importance include the UNESCO Declaration of Principles of Cultural Cooperation, the Helsinki Document, and the Vienna Declaration and Program of Action.

With the new paradigm of indigenous rights, coupled with the international treaties and conventions to which their nation-states are signatories, indigenous peoples are now able to seek support beyond their domestic arrangements and national governments. Indigenous movements that have been in conflict with states are able to take that conflict beyond their borders and appeal to international institutions such as the United Nations to recognise governments' breaches of the various international declarations, treaties or conventions to which they are signatories. Although states are sovereign, international exposure and the 'shaming' of a government can add considerable weight to the struggles of indigenous peoples. For example, in Canada, many First Nations women lost their Native status and right to live on tribal land (as did the children from such unions) when they married a non-Native. Sandra Lovelace, a Maliseet woman from New Brunswick, took her case to the United Nations Human Rights Committee. The Committee upheld her claim and the Canadian government was forced to repeal the discriminatory legislation (see *Sandra Lovelace v Canada*, Communication No. 24/1977: Canada 30/07/81, UN Doc. CCPR/C/13/D/24/1977). When the New Zealand government denied Māori the right to go to court to get a determination on whether Māori had customary rights to the foreshore and seabed, Māori activists appealed to the United Nations to recognise that such actions were inconsistent with the government's international legal obligations. In 2005 and again in 2010, the United Nations Special Rapporteur visited New Zealand to assess Māori grievances. The New Zealand government was subject to criticism by United Nations treaty bodies, including the Committee on the Elimination of Racial Discrimination.[1] For Māori, the internationalisation of their struggle strengthened their determination to seek further changes in the law, which resulted in legislative changes in 2011.[2] The endorsement of UNDRIP by 148 States means there will be an increasing international focus on how states behave towards their indigenous peoples.

Nevertheless, indigenous rights may be recognised in international discourse and international law but it is at the state level that policies affecting indigenous people are enacted and implemented. This anthology demonstrates how states have responded to indigenous movements' demands for inclusion, representation and participation rights in very different ways. It provides comparative insight

---

1. See A/HRC/18/XX/Add.Y The situation of Māori people in New Zealand. Report of the Special Rapporteur on the rights of indigenous peoples to the Human Rights Council of the United Nations.

2. The discriminatory Foreshore and Seabed Act 2004 was repealed and replaced with the slightly less discriminatory Takutai Moana Act 2011.

into how indigenous organisations are developing their resources to overcome historical losses of land and economic resources and how states are meeting and responding to those challenges.

In the following two sections, we will briefly discuss some factors that may influence the character of indigenous politics in different cases. We group these factors into two categories: *characteristics of the indigenous peoples* and *characteristics of the states* in which they live. This list of differences to 'watch out for' is, of course, not exhaustive but it includes some of the major variables.

Different indigenous peoples

The *demographics* of indigenous peoples vary enormously, and this obviously has an impact on an indigenous people's relationship with the state. But to what extent does size matter? In Bolivia, 55 per cent of the people are Amerindian and an additional 30 per cent are described as 'mixed' (CIA World Factbook 2012). This has contributed to recent developments in Bolivia regarding the political influence of indigenous peoples (*see* McNeish Chapter 11 in this volume). In Nepal, the groups considered to be Adevasi Janajati (aboriginal nationalities) together make up 36.3 per cent of the population, while the dominant castes Brahmin and Chhetri constitute 30.8 per cent together (Ranjan 2009; Sharma 2007). The Adevasi Janajati, though internally divided into smaller peoples, are the largest social category in Nepal. In a context of post-revolutionary democratisation like that of Nepal, percentages can be an asset. On the other hand, Brazil has a large indigenous population but it is small in comparison to the total population. In this context, sheer numbers have not been enough. Indigenous lands have been protected in Brazil since 1986 but the actual rights of the peoples are still very much in contest. In New Zealand, Māori are approximately 15 per cent of the total population – a large percentage in indigenous terms. This combined with their proportional representation in parliament gives them heightened potential for political influence. Meanwhile, Australian Aboriginal and Torres Strait Islanders are less than 3 per cent of the total population and, as Robbins shows in her chapter, they have suffered appalling race-based policies of exclusion that have denied them the most basic privileges of citizenship. In Russia, the *korennye maločislennye narody* (native, small-numbered peoples) category of ethnic groups number about 250,000 in a population of about 143 million – and are, as one might expect, not among the most influential indigenous populations on the globe. Demographics are not necessarily a good indicator of difference, however – if so, the Sámi and Inuit of the Arctic would be among the world's least empowered indigenous populations, but they are not.

Access to *economic resources* is usually central to the fate of any nation, indigenous or not. Most indigenous peoples have been marginalised and their socio-economic positioning tends to be poor because their lands, forests, fisheries, waterways and subterranean assets have been alienated by their colonisers. Traditional lands and environmental resources have been acquired by colonisers through unjust confiscation, excessive and illegal land sales, state interventions and acquisitions. Resources have been, and are being extracted from traditional lands but the resulting wealth is channelled to corporate entities, private and international conglomerates, social classes and geographical regions in which indigenous peoples are poorly represented. Many indigenous activists aim specifically at preventing further resource-exploitation by having tribal ownership or guardianship of ancestral lands and resources recognised by the courts. However, the extent of economic marginalisation varies between indigenous groups. Indigenous peoples in the Nordic countries and Canada, for example, are positioned to reap economic benefits that are withheld from the indigenous groups of less affluent countries. Royalties paid to the Arctic Inuit are creating space for indigenous self-determination and development. In countries with universal social-welfare arrangements, individuals are guaranteed a minimum standard of living far above the situation of those in countries such as Brazil, where the welfare system is less developed and social-class divides run deep. Other indigenous peoples have been able to develop economic resources through entrepreneurial development, such as Native American casino ownership (see The Harvard Project on American Indian Economic Development 2008), or land-compensation packages provided by Treaty of Waitangi settlements in New Zealand (see Hayward and Wheen 2004). There is even one group among Nepal's 63 indigenous peoples, the Newars, that rate higher than the national average on economic indicators (Aasland and Haug 2008; Berg-Nordlie and Schou 2011). Economic resources are a most significant variable in the struggle to maintain one's social, cultural and political integrity but economic resources alone may not overcome cultural discrimination and marginalisation, which may very well be present even when economic marginalisation is not.

Organisational resources are another factor, closely linked to economic resources. Unjust, illegal or excessive acquisitions of indigenous natural resources often leads to protracted periods of negotiation for compensation. The New Zealand government has negotiated settlements with a number of tribes since the 1990s through its Waitangi Tribunal and treaty settlement processes. Indigenous organisations need to create representative structures and have the necessary infrastructures in place to be able to effectively and efficiently negotiate with government officials for recognition of their grievances.

The extent of marginalisation or inclusion can be influenced by the extent of an indigenous people's *integration* into the dominant group's social order. A tribal community living at the fringes of the national community may be more easily able to retain its separate and distinct indigenous cultural practices and values but may also have less potential for political influence than indigenous groups that are more integrated into the majority's culture and political system. Eriksen (1993; *cf.* Overland and Berg-Nordlie 2012) has suggested that 'the leaders of a dominated group must master the cultural codes of the dominant group in order to present their case efficiently'. The Sámi have mastered the social norms of the dominant culture as have Māori in New Zealand. The paradox is that social integration can simultaneously increase the threat to cultural survival – the danger of total cultural assimilation is more imminent.

Finally, *internal cohesion* as a collective is obviously an important component to engaging with the state successfully. The extent to which the leadership of a group can mobilise grassroots support is considered in several of the chapters. In some states, there may be only one, relatively homogenous, indigenous people, whereas in others there can be multiple indigenous nations or tribal groupings that may have a history of conflict with each other. The latter can provide the state with fertile soil in which to sow seeds of discord, using the tactics of divide and rule. The experience of stronger marginalisation seems to have caused stronger internal cohesion among the Adevasi Janajati of Nepal than what is found among the more homogenous Sámi of Norway, suggesting that cultural homogeneity may be less important for some indigenous movements than a shared experience of harsh suppression (*cf.* Berg-Nordlie and Schou 2012).

Different states

A highly relevant difference between the states that indigenous movements need to work with is *how internal pressure groups are treated*. States have varying traditions regarding the extent to which, and the ways in which, they allow stakeholder groups access or input to policy-formation processes. There are, for example, considerable differences between the Scandinavian *Rechtstaats* characterised by 'decentralisation' and 'a strong participation ethic' (Rhodes 2000: 70) on the one hand and the Russian tradition of a top-down hierarchy, where policy formulation is determined to a much larger extent without, or with very limited, input from civil society (*cf.* Berg-Nordlie, this volume). There are observable variations also between countries that have 'traditions of pluralism' (Rhodes 2000: 70): some governments are more inclusive and consensus-seeking in their relationship with civil-society groups; others are more heavy-handed. This will vary not just between countries but also over time within countries, reflecting political, institutional and structural changes. States are not static.

Nation-states also differ when it comes to their *national ideological basis*. On the one hand, a state that is considered multicultural or multi-ethnic may recognise and accept its indigenous peoples' demands to ensure their cultural survival, along with special measures for representation, although this is no guarantee of the acceptance of indigenous self-determination rights. On the other hand, governments in nation-states built upon the culture and interests of one single *ethnos* may work actively against the idea of a multi-ethnic statehood and promote policies of integration or assimilation. However, such national ideologies may change over time. The example of Norway's eventual recognition of Sámi rights reflects the ability of states to accept indigenous values and cultural practices into its governing framework – also when said state was originally built around a nation-state ideology.

In addition to government ideology, the popular attitude of the dominant group towards the indigenous population is also relevant here. If their historical interrelations are characterised by hostility, demands from the indigenous peoples are likely to be met with scepticism or even fear – whereas if the tradition is more one of paternalism, the situation may be less likely to become 'securitised' and lead to sharp confrontation (*cf.* Kaufman 2001).

The economy of the state is also an important variable, as fulfilling indigenous rights costs money. Some states may be financially secure enough to finance representative organs and indigenous institutions and compensate groups that lose their lands to extraction projects. Other states may not consider themselves in a position to do so, being in an economic situation that leads politicians to primarily think about foreign investment, economic development and extracting the resources they have. For countries in a dire economic predicament, finding the money to set up indigenous councils will perhaps not be seen as a priority by the (non-indigenous) decision-makers. Of course, elites in wealthy countries may also choose to give business priority over indigenous peoples.

Finally, *the impact of internationalisation* may vary between states. The international networks, organisations and institutions created to assist indigenous peoples in their struggle for cultural and political survival may be called on by activists to assist them when in conflict with their states – but here, too, the nature of the state in question is relevant. Some states respond to international pressure, as shown in the above-mentioned case in which a Maliseet Indian woman from Canada took a case of gender discrimination to the United Nations Human Rights Committee. Subsequently the Canadian government amended its discriminatory Indian Act. Other states are not so concerned.

There is also the matter of relationships between states – criticism from states perceived as antagonistic is not likely to be taken very seriously. This mechanism is also valid when states decide which types of indigenous governance they are to establish: they are likely to look at ways in which countries they co-operate with or compare themselves to have solved similar issues – and less likely to take inspiration from states perceived as somehow qualitatively different, or belonging to rival blocs. For example, the idea of a Sámi Parliament could easily be transferred between the Nordic countries of Finland, Norway and Sweden but it was much less acceptable to the authorities in Russia (*cf.* Berg-Nordlie 2013).

In short, despite the development of international standards for state–indigenous relations and international networks for indigenous activism, it is the interplay between indigenous groups and states that determines the outcome. In this anthology, we will go through examples of such interplay.

Who are the indigenous peoples?

In this book, one of the first chapters (de Costa) will offer a comprehensive discussion of states' definitions of indigenousness. Nevertheless, it is proper to briefly address that subject in this introductory chapter as well. The term 'indigenous peoples' is today, across the globe, commonly used when referring to original peoples, sometimes stateless, often a minority and frequently marginalised. A single, universally recognised definition of the term does not exist but a very commonly cited one is found in ILO 169. That definition states that a group needs to retain some of its 'social, economic, cultural and political institutions'[3] and descend from the populations that inhabited the state prior to 'conquest or colonisation or the establishment of present state boundaries'. Furthermore, the group needs to self-identify as indigenous.[4]

While other definitions of indigenousness may focus on other elements, like aboriginality, ruralness, specific cultural traits, or small numbers, the ILO definition does not. The most striking dissonance between the ILO definition and the common understanding of the term 'indigenous' is probably the limited emphasis on aboriginality: according to the ILO definition, an indigenous or tribal group may not even be the oldest identified group to occupy its present homelands – but still be indigenous if, following its immigration into the area, it was forcibly incorporated into some other, colonising nation's state. An example of the latter is the Sherpa of Nepal, who arrived in their present homeland during the 1500s – but since the Nepalese state incorporated that area at a later point in history, they are considered indigenous. Conversely, the Brahmin and Chhetri castes are not considered indigenous groups. They have an older history of presence in certain areas of Western Nepal than the Sherpa have in their part of the country but they are the dominant groups that have created, defined, expanded and controlled the state – and hence cannot be considered 'indigenous' according to this definition (cf. Berg-Nordlie and Schou 2011).

The question of definition becomes even more difficult in states that have been established by an outsider group and subsequently left to the local population. Take, for example, Kenya, a state established by the British. Should one consider all other peoples than the remnant minority of *Wazungu* ('Whites') to be Kenya's 'indigenous population'? That would be a difficult conclusion to reach, seen in light of the post-colonial dominance of the largest ethnic group, the Kikuyu – their position in Kenya today is hardly comparable to those of the peoples identified as 'indigenous' elsewhere in the world (Hornsby 2012). IWGIA talks about certain Kenyan 'peoples that identify with the indigenous movement', notably 'pastoralists and hunter-gatherers' and have as such seemingly fallen back on a culture- or rurality-based definition. The problem of defining indigenous groups is valid not only for Kenya: the universality of the concept of indigenousness is generally challenged when discussing Africa.[5] Pre-colonial interrelations between certain African peoples sometimes have

---

3. The word 'institution' is here applied in a broader sense than it commonly is. A 'cultural institution' can, for example, be a language, etc.

4. http://www.pro169.org/res/materials/en/general_resources/Manual%20on%20ILO%20 Convention%20No.%20169.pdf (accessed 18 December 2014); http://www.ilo.org/wcmsp5/ groups/public/—ed_norm/—normes/documents/publication/wcms_100897.pdf (accessed 18 December 2014).

5. http://www.achpr.org/mechanisms/indigenous-populations/about/ (accessed 18 December 2014); http://www.iwgia.org/iwgia_files_publications_files/African_Commission_book.pdf (accessed 18 December 2014): 89; http://www.iwgia.org/iwgia_files_publications_files/0573_THE_ INDIGENOUS_ORLD−2012_eb.pdf (accessed 18 December 2014): 421.

relationships that in other parts of the world would indeed be identified as dominant people/indigenous people relationships – and these relationships tend to have carried over into post-colonial times. In African contexts such peoples are, however, rarely discussed as 'indigenous', although that may be beginning to change.

The 'ILO definition' remains the most authoritative definition of indigenous peoples and does provide a number of characteristics that contribute to the definition of being 'indigenous'. Applying this definition, a significant similarity between indigenous peoples is their historical and/or contemporary experiences of marginalisation, oppression or suppression by authorities established by an immigrant people. This is the common fate of the Ashaninka of Brazil and Peru, the Métis of Canada, the Māori of New Zealand, the Newars of Nepal, the Sámi of Northern Europe and many other indigenous peoples who are culturally different and occupy very different parts of the world. Some were hunter-gatherers, some nomadic herders, some were involved in small-scale agriculture, some based their economy around fishing resources and some lived in large and complex cities – but the history of conquest unites them.

Overview of the book

The contributions to this volume approach the general theme of indigenous representation and self-determination in different ways. The first section of the book consists of *comparative studies of institutional arrangements*. The second section consists of *case studies that provide country-specific examples* of institutional arrangements. The third section consists of chapters dealing with *processes of representation* – how indigenous people mobilise in specific policy processes, how alliances are formed and conflicts arise.

Part I: Institutional arrangements – international comparison

In the first chapter of this volume, Ravi de Costa discusses the complexities of defining the concept of 'indigenous peoples'. He carries out a comprehensive overview of the legal status of indigenous peoples in a wide range of countries. The 'status' of an individual or community as indigenous was originally an administrative marker: it designated those who were entitled to access particular programmes or subject to certain rules. The issue of indigenous rights, however, raises questions of demarcation: which peoples are regarded as indigenous and which individuals are regarded as members of these indigenous peoples? De Costa shows that demarcation criteria in fact vary considerably between countries. States define indigeneity as a matter of descent, cultural requirements, self-definition or a combination of these. The dynamism within indigenous communities has led these definitions to change. This was first done in ways that suited evolving state purposes, while more recent shifts have included devolution of the matters of identification and membership to indigenous peoples themselves. This does not, however, guarantee radical changes in approach.

The comparative approach is continued in Jane Robbins' analysis of indigenous political representation in seven liberal-democratic countries: Australia, Canada, Finland, New Zealand, Norway, Sweden and the USA. Her starting point is Sally Weaver's (1983a, b) comparative study of indigenous representative institutions, ranging from government-appointed advisory bodies to publicly supported indigenous 'pressure groups'. Weaver concluded that the level of independence of the representative body, its relationship to government and to its indigenous constituents and the adequacy of its resources and administrative support are important for the success and effectiveness of indigenous representative bodies. Robbins revisits and develops Weaver's analysis and investigates the characteristics of indigenous representation in each of these seven countries. Her chapter reflects on the political opportunities as well as the limitations associated with each model as a vehicle for indigenous self-determination; it demonstrates that the lessons of the past provide valuable insight into the strengths and weaknesses of different models of representation.

Martin Papillon compares two of Robbins' countries, Canada and the United States, more closely, to assess the specific impact of federalism. Both countries are federal systems, in which sovereignty is already divided along borders of territorially based governments. In both countries, federalism has adapted to indigenous autonomy through the development of multi-level governance regimes that are layered over the division of powers and intergovernmental relation systems. Papillon nevertheless points to some differences between the two cases. In the United States, tribes are only loosely integrated into the federal system. As extra-constitutional entities with residual sovereignty, tribal governments in the United States assume their jurisdictional authority and, in many cases, compete with states to extend it, often engaging in interest-group-type lobbying. Canadian First Nations, by contrast, have engaged in negotiations to have their jurisdictional rights recognised within the parameters of the Canadian constitution. The outcome is a more formal, but arguably more limited, regime of self-government, grounded in a mixture of constitutional rights and federal legislation.

Part II: Institutional arrangements – country studies

The first of our single-country studies deals with the case of New Zealand – a country with dedicated seats for the Māori population in the national parliament. Ann Sullivan compares Māori representation in national and local government. In New Zealand, the right of Māori, the indigenous peoples, to participate and be represented on central and local government councils is a fundamental right. However, the practical effect of the electoral system at the local government level of politics inhibits the effective and active participation of Māori. Some of the initiatives being pursued by Māori to increase the engagement of local Māori tribes with local governments provide insight on the importance of indigenous peoples being part of decision-making councils as of right.

In many cases, indigenous peoples have been divided by state borders and had to adapt to different states' political and legal entities to achieve the same goals – whilst simultaneously working to keep contact across the political divide cut through their lands. That is the case of the Sámi in Sweden, Finland, Norway and Russia. Due to variations at the state level – despite the general view that the Nordic states are rather similar – the Sámi of Norway, Sweden and Finland constitute three very different cases of indigenous representation and self-government. In Russia, the Sámi must operate in an entirely different type of political, social and economic state structure compared to their Nordic kin.

In their chapter, Patrik Lantto and Ulf Mörkenstam analyse the strategies of the Sámi movement in Sweden since 1900. The Swedish Sámi movement developed from small local Sámi societies aided by the creation of Sámi newspapers during the first half of the century, to the formation of the first national organisation in 1950 and the creation of a Sámi Parliament in 1993. The Swedish Sámi movement experienced many problems and setbacks during its history, due to internal problems and resistance from Swedish authorities. For instance the institutionalisation of legislation which divided the Sámi people into two different legal categories: reindeer-herders and non-reindeer-herders. Lantto and Mörkenstam provide an analysis of the different strategies used by the Swedish Sámi movement to overcome these obstacles in order to understand the contemporary discussion of Sámi self-determination in Sweden.

Two chapters go in-depth into the Norwegian Sámi Parliament. Torunn Pettersen follows up the question of delimitation previously raised by de Costa, and discusses the importance of the electoral roll of the Norwegian Sámi Parliament. Sámi who have chosen to register on the Sámi electoral roll are eligible and entitled to vote. Pettersen gives an overview over how this electoral roll has developed through its 20 years of existence and discusses two challenges: First, not all people who meet defined membership criteria may choose to identify themselves as members. Second, internal and/or external disagreement about indigenous affiliation in general and indigenous rights in particular, have challenged the legitimacy of certain arrangements and outcomes. Since the first Sámi Parliament election in Norway was held in 1989, the number of registered voters has nearly trebled, causing significant shifts in the geographical distribution of the roll. Pettersen suggests that the general growth can be related partly to increased support of the Sámi Parliament as a political body but that it is also due to changes in how Sámi ethnic affiliation is dealt with by individuals and in local communities.

Johannes Bergh and Jo Saglie explore the political significance of the idea of self-determination in elections to the Norwegian Sámi Parliament. Using data from the first Norwegian Sámi Election Study, conducted in connection with the 2009 election, they analyse voter behaviour. They find that the two largest parties, the Norwegian Sámi Association (NSR) and the Labour Party, are, in practice, indistinguishable along many conflict lines. What separates the voters of the two parties seems to be their ideas about the role and future of the Sámi political system. The NSR voters favour an extension of the power and jurisdiction of the Sámi Parliament; the Labour party voters represent the middle-of-the-road position; whereas the voters of the right-wing populist Progress Party are against any policy that moves in the direction of Sámi self-determination. Their findings suggest that Sámi politics is defined – to some extent – by a conflict over the role of the Sámi political system itself. The creation of an indigenous parliament does not put a stop to the debate about indigenous political influence and self-determination; rather, these debates are incorporated into the electoral politics of such institutions.

The Russian chapter deals with the political representation of the Kola Sámi, those of the border-transcending North-European nation who are native to Russia. Mikkel Berg-Nordlie accounts for attempts to reform Sámi representation in Murmansk Province 1992–2014. The development of Russian Sámi politics takes place in a complex political landscape in which key roles are played by the provincial authorities, the increasing number of local Sámi civil-society formations and a number of Western actors, prominently featuring the Sámi of the Nordic countries. Berg-Nordlie discusses developments in Murmansk Province's Sámi policy and the changing network of government structures, focusing particularly on the issue of representation.

The subject of Einar Braathen and Cássio Inglez de Sousa's chapter is indigenous semi-autonomy in Brazil. The Brazilian constitution of 1988 granted the indigenous peoples the right to establish indigenous territories (*Terra Indígena* or TI) with exclusive rights of residence and sustainable use of natural resources. However, the land and its subterranean resources (such as minerals) were declared federal state property. This chapter discusses the emergence of this new and complex system for indigenous self-organisation and representation in Brazil. Consolidation of leadership and differing interests at local, regional and national levels have been among the major challenges for the indigenous peoples. Other challenges include the issues of territorial control, lack of capacity and sustainability of the indigenous territories and the poor quality of healthcare and other basic public services. Federal projects for hydropower generation, mining and other economic purposes represent a real threat to Brazilian indigenous peoples, particularly in the Amazon. The indigenous relationship with the Brazilian state is characterised by institutional fragmentation, as indigenous peoples have to deal with three constitutional tiers (municipal, federated state and federal union) as well as checks-and-balances arrangements between legislative, executive and judicial authorities. Hence, the ambiguity and limits of indigenous territorial autonomy in Brazil today demonstrates the semi-autonomous position of its indigenous peoples. Still, the indigenous movement has shown its capacity to defend the victories of the 1980s and to address the new challenges.

Part III: Indigenous representation – concrete conflicts

The final chapters of the volume deal with *processes of representation*, rather than representative institutions. Land rights and natural resources often feature prominently in indigenous peoples' drive for self-determination. Natural-resource extraction is the theme of the chapter by John-Andrew McNeish, which takes us to Bolivia and the case of the 2011 TIPNIS march – a protest march against plans to build a road through an indigenous territory. The fact that a member of the indigenous population is the elected leader of the country has not prevented indigenous–state conflicts. McNeish argues that current confrontations between indigenous peoples and the state over natural resources in Bolivia are complex. The chapter shows that state, private economic and political interests – as well as internal conflicts and tensions between indigenous people – have contributed to public scenes of confrontation. McNeish suggests that events such as the TIPNIS march are part of a difficult but necessary process, in which conflicting norms and values related to modernity and use of the environment continue to be worked through.

Similar issues arise in Ciaran O'Faircheallaigh's chapter on indigenous control over development in Australia, which uses the processing of natural gas in Western Australia to address the issue of how the growing recognition of indigenous rights can be translated into indigenous control over developments, with a share of the benefits going to the indigenous peoples. In 2006 the State Government said that gas development would only occur with the 'informed consent and substantial economic participation' of Aboriginal Traditional Owners. The traditional owners and their regional organisation mobilised their people and, by combining customary law with 'modern' forms of representation and communication, were able to assert substantial control over the process of selecting a location for a natural gas processing hub. A change of State Government in 2008 rejected the principle of indigenous informed consent. This required a different form of political mobilisation to negotiate an acceptable project configuration with the state and industrial interests while, at the same time, countering environmental groups opposed to any form of commercial development.

Cross-cutting themes

Indigenous movements have applied and adapted a range of strategies when attempting to strengthen their position on key issues such as language survival; protecting traditional economic activities; improving their socio-economic situation; regaining ownership of traditional territories or customary usage rights to those territories; resource management and rights to self-determination. Throughout the anthology we find considerable variation in such strategies, but also certain recurring themes, which could be explored in future research on indigenous politics.

Internal indigenous disagreement

A major recurring theme in the chapters is how indigenous peoples deal with challenges regarding internal cohesion. Earlier in this chapter we have identified internal schisms as a potential weakness for indigenous peoples, when facing external pressure. However, this implicitly constructs an ideal situation in which the indigenous population is in agreement about what their main problems are and how these should be met. The chapters show that this ideal situation rarely exists: there are often fundamental disagreements within indigenous populations regarding what strategies should be chosen to deal with their challenges; and sometimes there are also disagreements regarding what constitutes the basic nature of the problem.

In both chapters that concern representation in concrete political processes, we observe that internal antagonisms come forcefully into play. O'Faircheallaigh describes how 'serious and protracted internal conflict' among local Australian Aboriginals manifested in the midst of negotiations; and shows how this impacted all indigenous claims negatively. McNeish discusses the opposition between members of the Bolivian Aymara and Quechua, who have settled in Lowland Bolivia mainly as coca-growers, and the hunter-gatherer communities that are indigenous to the area. He furthermore highlights the internal political fragmentation caused by contrasting visions of development and modernity within the Lowland Bolivian indigenous communities involved in the TIPNIS case. We also observe this phenomenon in several of the single-case studies. Braathen and Inglez de Sousa describe the parallel existence of traditional and modern leaders in Brazil's indigenous communities and the complexity of Brazilian indigenous civil society. Likewise, Berg-Nordlie shows the fragmentation of Russian Sámi civil society and the parallel existence of groups that have different political desires and ambitions – and how these differences came to the fore during discussions about the establishment of a Nordic-type Sámi Parliament, the institutions that Bergh and Saglie, Pettersen, Lantto and Mörkenstam, and Robbins write about. The Sámi Parliaments are institutionalisations of political disagreement – simultaneously a Sámi platform to speak to the state authorities and an arena in which internal disputes can find expression. Bergh and Saglie focus on the main political cleavages present in Parliament, whereas Pettersen discusses internal disagreements regarding who should be allowed to vote for these representative organs. Lantto and Mörkenstam discuss Swedish Sámi history up to the establishment of the Sámi Parliament, commenting on oppositions that have carried into modern times. In the New Zealand case, Sullivan describes how more than 50 per cent of all Māori choose to register on the Māori electoral roll while the rest make a political decision to register on the general electoral roll. De Costa, like Pettersen, explores a different aspect of internal opposition: he delves into the divide between those who have access to official indigenous status and those who have problems obtaining such status. When the former wish for a more conservative definition than the latter, this constitutes the most fundamental intra-indigenous conflict: who belongs to the people, and who do not?

This anthology moves beyond the traditional narrative of 'indigenous *v* state and big business', which is an over-simplification of very complex relationships. A more nuanced understanding of indigenous peoples' political arrangements, institutions and organisations will be fruitful. By failing to acknowledge or understand internal conflicts relating to their indigenous populations, political scientists continue to make the indigenous voice inaudible, or fail to recognise that there is often more than 'one' indigenous viewpoint that should be taken into account. Internal conflicts should be viewed as an integral component of indigenous politics. On the one hand, disagreement within an indigenous community does make it difficult for outsiders and governing bodies that desire a single voice to represent the indigenous people. On the other hand, an open discussion, in which conflicting positions are voiced and debated until a decision is reached, is also an important aspect of democracy. The important question, therefore, may be how this internal debate is organised.

Indigenous representation – who represents whom?

This brings us to another lesson found in this book: awareness about who represents whom and how representation is organised. Any political actor can *call* themselves a representative of their people but this claim should not be taken at face value. Indigenous peoples have internal divisions just like any other sector of the population. These may be based on linguistic difference, ideology, religion, geographic location, political affiliation, gender, generation, ancestry or cultural subgroup. Such differences need to be taken into account when the activities of (self-proclaimed or state-authorised) indigenous representatives are discussed.

Processes for representation found among indigenous peoples are not necessarily the same as those of the dominant group. In some cases, individuals considered as leaders or representatives may have been selected on culturally specific criteria based on ancestry, rather than through democratic elections. Indigenous political processes may – just like the processes of the dominant group – be questioned and discussed. Relevant questions could be, for example: are there barriers to the representation of certain subgroups? Are there structural mechanisms in place to ensure that representatives speak for the general interest of their peoples, rather than just the subgroups they belong to? Do the people have any opportunity to regularly evaluate or remove their representatives, and how are these processes organised?

In short, there is no single indigenous perspective, voice or representative. Indigenous politics are no less complex than other politics.

Robbins points to a basic difference between systems for indigenous representation: some are established by the state, others are non-governmental. Pettersen, Lantto and Mörkenstam and Bergh and Saglie explore the Sámi Parliaments, which are examples of state-based institutions that nevertheless have mechanisms that aim to ensure that indigenous representatives are responsive to their people. A closer look at the Norwegian and Swedish *Sámediggis*, however, reveals considerable differences in how these two institutions work. The historical split (partly created by government policy) between reindeer-herding Sámi and other Sámi in Sweden seems to have left a mark on today's Swedish Sámi Parliament. The difference between Norway and Sweden nevertheless seem insignificant when the *Sámediggis* of these two countries are compared with the Russian Sámi. Berg-Nordlie shows how a protracted conflict in Russian indigenous politics led to the establishment of two parallel systems for indigenous representation – one state-based, one non-governmental.

The question of how indigenous representation is organised reappears in the chapters that discuss processes of representation, rather than institutions. O'Faircheallaigh's contribution shows how a process of collective decision-making, incorporating customary law with 'modern' forms of representation and communication, provided Australian indigenous peoples with some influence over development on their traditional lands. In contrast, this kind of inclusive process is strikingly lacking in the Bolivian case-study, even though Bolivia is a democracy with an indigenous majority, a President who is also indigenous and a legal structure that ostensibly supports 'free, prior and informed consent'.

Multi-level politics

The chapters presented in this book showcase the need to identify the various *levels* of government – national, regional and local – that indigenous communities have to deal with. One recurring topic is what Papillon calls indigenous multi-level governance regimes, in which indigenous self-government is added to the existing federal system. Papillon's chapter demonstrates that there are considerable differences between the federal systems of Canada and the US, regarding the relationship between federal and state governments on the one hand and indigenous peoples on the other. Indigenous multi-level governance is also a central topic in Braathen and Inglez de Sousa's chapter, in which the authors discuss how the semi-autonomous indigenous territories fit into the Brazilian federal state. A contrasting situation is found in Bolivia, where McNeish shows how a conflict between Bolivia's central state elites and certain regional elites is woven together with state–indigenous (and intra-indigenous) conflict. Multi-level politics are, however, not limited to federal states. Research on multi-level governance tends to focus on the national level (and federal level, in federal states) while local government gets less attention. Looking into the case of the unitary state of New Zealand, Sullivan demonstrates systemic differences in approach to indigenous representation at the local and central level.

The internationalisation of indigenous politics is a major theme in several chapters in this book. However, the contributions to this book also point to the importance of different levels *within* the states, in addition to the international level. We hope to enhance the discussion on the interplay between indigenous peoples and institutions at various levels within the individual state. There are many important questions to explore in this regard. What characterises the attitude to indigenous policy of the different levels of the state and the different institutions found there? What characterises the relationships between the state-based actors involved? What levels of the state do various indigenous groupings prefer to appeal to, and why?

Concluding remarks

The field of indigenous politics is complex. The chapters presented in this book represent only some of the challenges facing indigenous peoples. The complexity of indigenous politics makes it a challenging field of specialisation. Insight into international indigenous institutions, law and organisation also requires an understanding of domestic political realities, which often reflect the international indigenous rights' discourse rather poorly. In some cases it has had no measurable impact apart from being treated by certain actors as an ideal towards which to strive. What holds true in all cases is that researchers need to learn about local history, law and politics in order to produce a good analysis. Hence, 'indigenous politics' is an area of research that demands researchers to transcend disciplines. The study of indigenous politics requires collaborative efforts, in which researchers from different fields, as well as indigenous representatives, work together to ensure that the research being carried out is for the benefit of both the indigenous peoples and academia.

References

Aasland, Aa. and Haug, M. (2008) 'Social exclusion in Nepal – stronger or weaker?', *NIBR Working Paper* 2008: 115, Oslo: Norwegian Institute of Urban and Regional Research.

Berg-Nordlie, M. (2013) 'The Iron Curtain through Sápmi. Pan-Sámi politics, Nordic cooperation and the Russian Sámi', in K. Andersson, (ed.) *L'image du Sápmi II, Études comparées. Humanistica Oerebroensia. Artes et linguae,* Örebro: Örebro University.

Berg-Nordlie, M. and Schou, A. (2011) 'Who are indigenous – and how should it matter? Discourses on indigenous rights in Norway and Nepal', *Ethnopolitics Papers* No. 13. Exeter Centre for Ethnopolitical Studies/ PSA Specialist Group on Ethnopolitics.

de Costa, R. (2006) *A Higher Authority. Indigenous Transnationalism and Australia,* Sydney: UNSW Press.

Eriksen, T. H. (1993) 'The epistemological status of the concept of ethnicity', The Anthropology of Ethnicity Conference, Amsterdam, December 1993.

Fleras, A. and Elliott, J. L (1992) *The 'Nations Within': Aboriginal–state relations in Canada, the United States, and New Zealand,* Toronto: Oxford University Press.

Harvard Project on American Indian Economic Development (2008) *The State of the Native Nations,* New York: Oxford University Press.

Hayward, J. and Wheen, N. (2004) *The Waitangi Tribunal,* Wellington, NZ: Bridget Williams Books.

Henriksen, J. B. (1999) *Saami Parliamentary Cooperation. An analysis,* IWGIA Document No. 93. Nordic Sámi Institute and IWGIA: Guovdageaidnu and Copenhagen.

Hocking, B. A. (2005) (ed.) *Unfinished Constitutional Business. Rethinking Indigenous Self-Determination,* Canberra: Aboriginal Studies Press.

Hornsby, C. (2012) *Kenya: A history since independence.* New York: I. B. Tauris.

Kaufman, S. J. (2001) *Modern Hatreds: The symbolic politics of ethnic war,* New York: Cornell University Press.

Kukathas, C. (1992) 'Are there any cultural rights?', *Political Theory,* 20(1): 105–39.

Kymlicka, W. (1995) *Multicultural Citizenship*, Oxford: Oxford University Press.
— (1998) *Finding Our Way: Rethinking ethnocultural relations in Canada*, Toronto: Oxford University Press.
Minde, H. (2003) 'The challenge of indigenism: the struggle for Sami land rights and self-government in Norway 1960–1990', in S. Jentoft, H. Minde and R. Nilsen (eds) *Indigenous Management and Global Rights*, Delft: Eburon Academic Publishers.
— (2005) 'The Alta case: from the local to global and back again', in G. Cant, A. Goodall and J. Inns (eds) *Discourses and Silences. Indigenous peoples, risks and resistance*, Christchurch, NZ: University of Canterbury.
— (2008) 'The destination and the journey: indigenous peoples and the United Nations from the 1960s through 1985', in H. Minde (ed.) in collaboration with H. Gaski, S. Jentoft and G. Midré, *Indigenous Peoples: Self-determination, knowledge, identity*, Delft: Eburon Academic Publishers.
Nettheim, G., Meyers, G. D. and Craig, D. (2002): *Indigenous Peoples and Governance Structures: A comparative analysis of land and resource management rights*, Canberra: Aboriginal Studies Press.
Niezen, R. (2000) 'Recognizing indigenism: Canadian unity and the international movement of indigenous peoples', *Comparative Studies in Society and History* 42(1): 119–48.
— (2003) *The Origins of Indigenism: Human rights and the politics of identity*, Berkeley, Los Angeles, CA: University of California Press.
Nyyssönen, J. (2007) *Everybody Recognized That We Were Not White*, PhD thesis, history, University of Tromsø.
Overland, I. and Berg-Nordlie, M. (2012): *Bridging Divides. Ethno-political leadership among the Russian Sámi*. New York and Oxford: Berghahn Books.
Ranjan, P. (2009) *Nepalese Minority Groups. Struggle for identity and representation*, Kathmandu: Support Nepal.
Rhodes, R. A. W. (2000) 'Governance and public administration', in J. Pierre (ed.) *Debating Governance. Authority, steering and democracy*, Oxford: Oxford University Press.
Robbins, J. (2007) 'Home and away: indigenous peoples and international politics', paper presented at the Northern Europe's Indigenous Minorities Conference, University of New South Wales, July 2007.
Sharma, P. (2008) *Unravelling the Mosaic. Spatial aspects of ethnicity in Nepal*, Kathmandu, Litapur: Himal Books.
Sullivan, A. (2009) 'Māori Participation', in R. Miller (ed.) *New Zealand Government and Politics* (5th edn), Melbourne: Oxford University Press.
— (2010) 'Democracy and minority indigenous representation', in M. Mulholland and V. Tawhai (eds) *Weeping Waters: The Treaty of Waitangi and a Constitution for Aotearoa New Zealand*, Wellington, NZ: Huia Publishers.

Tully, J. (1995) *Strange Multiplicity: Constitutionalism in an Age of Diversity*, Cambridge: Cambridge University Press.

— (2000) 'The struggles of indigenous peoples for and of freedom', in D. Ivison, P. Patton and W. Sanders (eds) *Political Theory and the Rights of Indigenous Peoples*, Cambridge: Cambridge University Press.

Varsi, M. O. (2007) (ed.) *The Nordic Sámi Convention. International Human Rights, self-determination and other central provisions, Gáldu Cálá – Journal of Indigenous Peoples' Rights* No. 3/2007, Guovdageaidnu: Gáldu.

Walker, R. (2004) *Ka Whawhai Tonu Matou: Struggle without end* (revised edn), Auckland: Penguin.

Weaver, S. (1983a) *Towards a Comparison of National Political Organizations of Indigenous Peoples: Australia, Canada and Norway*, lecture series, Institute of Social Sciences, University of Tromsø.

— (1983b) 'Australian Aboriginal policy: Aboriginal pressure groups or government advisory bodies?, Part I, *Oceania* 54(1): 1–22; Part II, *Oceania* 54(1): 85–108.

Wessendorf, K. (2001) (ed.) *Challenging Politics. Indigenous people's experiences with political parties and elections*, IWGIA document No 104, Copenhagen: IWGIA.

PART I

INSTITUTIONAL ARRANGEMENTS – INTERNATIONAL COMPARISON

Chapter Two

States' Definitions of Indigenous Peoples: A Survey of Practices[*]

Ravi de Costa

Introduction

One of the enduring legacies of colonialism is the designation of particular individuals and communities as indigenous (or a host of analogous terms, such as Aboriginal, American Indian or Tribal). This 'status' – identifying those entitled to access particular programmes or subject to certain rules – originated largely during the nineteenth century with colonial administrations seeking to rationalise management of lands and populations.[1] A prevailing assumption was that indigenous populations would soon die out, overwhelmed by superior European cultures; the failure of these dreams of deracination and assimilation means difference persists and, consequently, the status remains, with administrative efficiency still its primary purpose. The fact that these systems are deeply resented in many places or, contrarily, that affected communities have taken control of the rules of definition, does not diminish the fact that 'status' is a tool of state reason and administrative efficiency.[2]

As a consequence, simply *being* Māori, Sámi, Munda or Tuareg, for example, is not a qualification for indigenous status in New Zealand, Norway, India or Mali. States do not aggregate the self-defined memberships of all communities who pre-date the arrival of colonists or the coming of modernity. Both directly – through policies such as 'enfranchisement' (the granting of citizenship to natives who were deemed to be 'civilised' by abandoning communal ties and identity) – and indirectly, through policies such as forcible relocation – states have interfered with the ways indigenous communities identify themselves. Identity and status are very much distinct.

Moreover, the notion of a *prior* community (inherent in words like 'aboriginal' or *adivasi*) is highly fraught in many parts of the world. Though 'priority' has greatest coherence and relevance in states colonised by Europeans from the early

[*]   An earlier version of this chapter has been published in the journal *Aboriginal Policy Studies.* Thanks to Rauna Kuokannen, Andrew Erueti, Tim Rowse, Mikkel Berg-Nordlie, Jo Saglie and Len Smith for suggestions and comments. Particular thanks to Sonia Singh, for assistance with the Latin American section and translation of Spanish-language texts. Any errors are those of the author.

1.   The term 'status' will be used as shorthand, denoting all state-sanctioned categorisations of indigenous peoples.

2.   Some of the words are used in other contexts, such as 'indigenous knowledge'.

modern period on, many parts of the world do not have a '1492 moment' to act as an initial distinction. This leads to a broader observation, one supported by the recent analysis of Francesca Merlan (2009), that being indigenous and the very concept of indigeneity are the culmination of collective political projects of the original inhabitants of European colonies, chiefly those of Britain but also of the Spanish colonies in Latin America. International instruments and associated discourses are a reflection of the transnationalism and solidarity of those particular indigenous peoples, beginning in the 1960s (de Costa 2006). This may give indigeneity a paradoxical eurocentrism.

However, status is growing in importance, as states on all inhabited continents refine their systems of definition, narrowing and expanding in response to demographic, legal and political pressures. In its boundaries, its entitlements and its operation, status varies considerably across the range of nations that use it. One scholar generalises that in the European settler states, policies of negotiation with indigenous peoples define potential claimants either according to a 'race' model of definition that prioritises ancestry or to a 'nation' model that foregrounds membership in a tribe (Gover 2011: 10–11).

This is useful but is limited to states engaged in negotiations with corporate indigenous entities over land and resources. A global survey of state practices of definition for a variety of policy goals is better framed by three broad characteristics: *descent* (calculated in a variety of ways that require a demonstrable relation between present-day claimants and some prior, unquestioned indigenous community); *cultural requirements* (language use, for example, or 'participation' in community life or certain economic practices); and *self-definition* (where states have devolved to indigenous communities the power to manage their own membership rules). These are not exclusive; indeed, many indigenous self-definitions use descent or cultural standards. Moreover, state impositions can be highly arbitrary (such as numerical size), can be inter-subjective (requiring recognition by non-indigenous communities living around claimants) or can seek to approximate indigenous practices of recognition.

The intent of this chapter is to survey this variety and to consider policy challenges: practicalities such as pressures on status-holders and states from demographic trends; shifting cultural norms; and legal and institutional change, including the passage of the United Nations Declaration on the Rights of Indigenous Peoples (UNDRIP). Before turning to the series of cases, some discussion of the parameters of the paper is warranted.

The chapter starts with a survey of those states where debates and legal frameworks of indigenous status are most developed: Australia, New Zealand, Scandinavia, Canada and the USA. It was in these countries (and, to a lesser degree, in Latin America), that the greatest significance was placed on status as a means of defining entitlements and authority as colonial settlement expanded. It is in these countries, moreover, that indigenous peoples have been most politically effective. They also resemble each other in social and economic arrangements: high levels of intermarriage/intercultural mixing; widespread penetration of capitalist modes of economy/livelihood; high levels of urbanisation; rapid population/

identification growth of indigenous peoples in the last 30–40 years; and persistent marginalisation of those groups in social and economic indices. Also comparable are the liberal and democratic legal and political frameworks in which debates and policy-making take place.

However, this chapter also examines state modes for defining indigeneity in Asia, Africa and Russia, discussing over 20 states in all. This is obviously not comprehensive but reveals both patterns and debates of wider relevance. For example, the success of the global indigenous movement has created discursive and some institutional change in particular nation-states.

Some limits have been imposed on the types of definition included in the survey, for reasons of space. The approach taken here is to identify institutions at the highest level of government and administration that define and maintain direct relationships with individuals and communities designated as indigenous. Therefore the focus is on constitutional and legislative clauses and on administrative rules setting out terms of eligibility for public programmes. In some cases, these arrangements have been shaped by jurisprudential change. Census standards and data are used largely to develop the context of comparison.[3]

Survey of cases

USA

Since the US Supreme Court judgement in *Cherokee v Georgia* (1831), the federal government has had a 'trust' relationship with indigenous peoples of the United States.[4] This has underpinned a long and complex series of federal actions to intervene in Native peoples' lives, often in ways that effectively redefined who they were. Practice in the USA now varies according to jurisdiction and agency. As the American Indian Policy Review Commission concluded in a 1977 report to Congress, '(t)he Federal government, State governments and the Census Bureau all have different criteria for defining "Indians" for statistical purposes, and even the Federal criteria are not consistent among Federal agencies' (Gonzales 1998: 207).

However, there are three criteria of eligibility for services provided by the Bureau of Indian Affairs (BIA). An individual must either: be a member of a federally-recognised tribe; have one-half or more of blood of a tribe indigenous to the US; or must, for some purposes, be of one-fourth or more Indian ancestry. The most commonly used definition of 'tribe' is that of the *Indian Self-Determination Act* 1963, which states: '"Indian tribe" means any Indian tribe, band, nation, or

---

3. For a critical survey of censuses' approaches to measuring indigenous populations, see Peters 2011. Morning (2008) surveyed 141 national censuses, noting that only 15% included questions on indigenous or tribal identity. It should be stressed that state censuses have been part of colonial history and therefore both absolute numbers as well as population trends need to be seen within a matrix of the forces of assimilation.

4. *Cherokee Nation v Georgia*, 30 U.S. 1, 12, 5 Pet. 1, 17 (1831).

other organised group or community ... which is recognised as eligible for the special programs and services provided by the United States to Indians because of their status as Indians.'[5] (Garroutte 2003: 25).

Past federal recognition of a tribe occurred through treaties, Acts of Congress, executive actions or decisions of the Federal Court. Since 1978, the US Department of the Interior has administered the Federal Acknowledgment Process (FAP) to determine claims by tribes for recognition (the overarching regulations of the FAP are known as 25 C.F.R. Part 83 and were last revised in 1994).[6] In 1994, Congress also passed the *Federally Recognised Indian Tribe List Act* (FRITLA), which set out the only three formal pathways by which a tribe could receive federal recognition: by Act of Congress, through the FAP, or through the decision of a United States court.[7]

Quinn has summarised these criteria as follows:

> ... a single Indian group has existed since its first sustained contact with European cultures on a continuous basis to the present; that its members live in a distinct, autonomous community perceived by others as Indian; that it has maintained some sort of authority with a governing system by which its members abide; that all its members can be traced genealogically to an historic tribe; and that it can provide evidence to substantiate all of this (Quinn 1990: 152).

As of April 2011, 350 applications for recognition had been received;[8] 71 cases had been resolved with 17 acknowledged through the federal process and 32 denied, while nine received passage or restoration of specific federal legislation by Congress.[9]

FRITLA also created a Federal Register of Indian Tribes, which must be published annually by the Secretary of the Interior.[10] Typically, members of such tribes hold Indian identity or tribal citizenship cards or Certificates of Degree of Indian Blood. The authority of tribes to determine their own membership rules was first established in US law in 1905, in *Waldron v United States*.[11] Garroutte

---

5. 25 U.S.C. § 450b(e) (1963), amended by Act of Oct. 5, 1988, 102 Stat. 2285 (1988).

6. Abbreviated Form of 25 CFR Part 83 Criteria http://www.bia.gov/idc/groups/public/documents/text/idc-001115.pdf.

7. US Department of the Interior, Indian Affairs, 'Why tribes exist today in the United States – How is federal recognition status conferred?': http://www.bia.gov/FAQs/index.htm.

8. See 'Letters of intent received as of April 29, 2011': http://www.bia.gov/idc/groups/xofa/documents/text/idc013622.pdf.

9. See 'Status summary of acknowledgment cases' (April 29, 2011): http://www.bia.gov/idc/groups/xofa/documents/text/idc013624.pdf.

10. 'Indian entities recognised and eligible to receive services from the United States Bureau of Indian Affairs' (List of Federally Recognised Indian Tribes, FR 75-60810), 1 October 2010: http://www.bia.gov/idc/groups/xofa/documents/document/idc012038.pdf.

11. Garroutte notes that a few tribes are required to have certain criteria determined by the federal government (2003: 168). Where tribes' constitutions reserve a power to pass future ordinances regarding membership rules, in some cases these are 'subject to review' by the Secretary of the Interior. For an extensive collection of tribal constitutions setting out membership rules, see http://thorpe.ou.edu/const.html.

(1998: 15) discusses the range of ways that recognised tribes define membership, noting that 'blood quantum' is relevant in two-thirds of cases and that the most common quantum is 25 per cent, that is, one full-blood grandparent.

Generally, an individual seeking membership must provide genealogical documentation proving lineal descent from someone included on the 'base roll' of a recognised tribe or be in a relationship with a tribal member who descended from someone named on the base roll. A base roll is an original list of members set out in a tribal constitution or other document that formalises enrolment criteria – such documents need to be approved by the BIA (Thornton 1997: 35). However, it should be noted that these rolls are highly contested in some cases. Many Indians with a determination to maintain their own traditions of identification strongly resisted these practices of registration, refusing to be enrolled. This has resulted in many descendants of such 'traditionalists' finding that they cannot demonstrate their Indian identity for federal purposes today (Garroutte 2003: 22; Otis 1973: 40–6). Some tribes have membership rules that stress matrilineal or patrilineal descent, residence in tribal communities, political involvement in or ongoing contact with the community.[12] In 1987, Thornton found that tribes that are based primarily in reservation communities are significantly more likely to use blood quanta in their membership criteria (Thornton 1997). More recently, Gover found that since the beginning of the 'self-determination era' of US Indian policy in 1970, tribes have increasingly used descent and blood quantum in their membership rules (2011: 112).

According to the government's regulations, 'acknowledgement of tribal existence by the Department is a prerequisite to the protection, services, and benefits from the Federal Government available to Indian tribes' (O'Brien 1991: 1469). Yet several categories of Native Americans who do not or cannot meet criteria for recognition by the federal government, in certain cases remain eligible for certain programmes. These include 'terminated tribes', 'non-recognised tribes' and 'state-recognised tribes'. An extended discussion of these categories is in O'Brien (1991: 1470–7).

Recognition of individuals is equally variable. The federal government defines and identifies individual Indians for the purposes of numerous specific programmes such as those legislated by the Indian Child Welfare Act (1978), as well as preferential employment in Indian agencies such as the BIA (Garroutte 2003: 17–18). Additionally, particular programmes (ranging from housing and pensions for – railroad workers to environmental protection and small business development) are open to members of 'underrepresented minority' populations, for whom the federal government has a special responsibility, including Alaskan Natives. Indigenous peoples in US possessions and protectorates, such as Guam and American Samoa, are also eligible for certain forms of federal entitlement (O'Brien 1991: 1477–9).

---

12. US Department of the Interior, Indian Affairs, 'Guide to tracing your American Indian ancestry', pp. 3–4 http://www.bia.gov/idc/groups/public/documents/text/idc002656.pdf; see also Garroutte 2003: 15–16.

Native Hawaiians, who were not formally acknowledged as 'Native American' for the purposes of federal programmes until the 1970s, have been most active in reforming status rules. In 2011, Native Hawaiians began co-ordinated legislative change with regard to their status and relationship to the federal government of the US.[13] That bill would formalise the federal government's trust responsibility to Native Hawaiians (making Native Hawaiians eligible for federal programmes), as well as creating a 'Native Hawaiian governing entity ... [and] a government-to-government relationship.'[14]

Almost simultaneously, the Hawai'i State Legislature recognised Native Hawaiians as 'the only indigenous, aboriginal, maoli population of Hawai'i' and created a Native Hawaiian Roll Commission (NHRC), to create and publish a roll of 'Qualified Native Hawaiians'.[15] Those qualified will elect officials to a convention to constitute a governing entity acknowledged both by Hawai'i and the United States. The enabling legislation does not instruct the NHRC as to the criteria for eligibility but its initial report discusses the 'mission and spirit' of their task, placing indigenous understandings in the foreground.[16]

When juxtaposed with enrolment in recognised-tribes, US census data contextualises some of the demographic shifts in indigenous populations. In 2000, the census first allowed respondents to identify as belonging to more than one 'race'.[17] It also broke down American Indian/Alaskan Native (AIAN) respondents into nearly 40 tribal identifications, from Aleut to Yuman. Those claiming only AIAN identity increased 18.4 per cent between 2000 and 2010. The number of

---

13. In the Congress, see (S.675) and (H.R. 1250): 'A bill to express the policy of the United States regarding the United States relationship with Native Hawaiians and to provide a process for the recognition by the United States of the Native Hawaiian governing entity' http://akaka.senate. gov/upload/S675.pdf . Both are in committee at the time of writing. http://thomas.loc.gov/cgi-bin/ bdquery/z?d112:HR01250:|/bss/112search.html.

14. The bill includes the need to establish a roll of electors and processes for elections as well as a constitution (*ibid.*: 23).

15. Act 195, Session Laws of Hawai'i 2011.

16. '(C)reating a vessel for Native Hawaiians to sign on to an official register has historical and cultural importance and is not just a bureaucratic act ... (previous administrative) processes have divided Hawaiians, and the commission is resolved for this to be a process of *lōkahi* – unity ... The Commission understands that their *kuleana* – responsibility – is to publish a roll of qualified Native Hawaiians with the intent to facilitate the process under which Native Hawaiians may independently commence the process of Nationhood ... The Commission understands that there are varied views as to how the process of Nationhood should be achieved. The Commission respects these views with the values of *aloha, hō'ihi* (respect), *mālama* (to care), and *ike pono* (to understand what is fair). The Commission believes that in order to achieve its mission, it is important to strive for *laulima* (cooperativeness), *lōkahi* (unity), to be *onipa'a* (steadfast) and to do what is *pono* (right), with the support of *ohana* (family, including ancestors).' Native Hawaiian Roll Commission, 'Report to Governor Abercrombie and the Hawai'i State Legislature, as required by Act 195, Session Laws of Hawai'i 2011 (December 28, 2011) http://www.oha.org/ images/stories/files/pdf/NHRC/1211nhrc_report_web.pdf.

17. US Office of Management and Budget, 'Revisions to the standards for the classification of federal data on race and ethnicity', Federal Register Notice October 30, 1997: http://www.whitehouse. gov/omb/fedreg_1997standards.

those claiming AIAN 'alone or in combination with one or more other races' was, in 2000, approximately 4.1 million persons. Those claiming AIAN identity 'alone' was, in 2000, under 2.5 million persons.[18] By contrast, according to the BIA, total reported 2001 tribal enrolment (that is, in recognised tribes) was 1,816,504.

Canada

The 1867 constitution of Canada gave legislative power over 'Indians, and Lands reserved for the Indians' exclusively to the federal government. 'Indians' have been defined by the Canadian state since 1876, under the wide-ranging Indian Act, (although a Register of Indians, which used descent to define status, was held by the colonial government as early as 1850).[19] The Register continues, as well as a policy of issuing status cards (Secure Certificates of Indian Status).

Beginning with the strident indigenous reaction to the abortive White Paper of 1969, which sought to erase indigenous identity as a subject of public policy, the mode of definition has moved steadily away from paternalism and assimilation.[20] The entrenchment of Aboriginal and treaty rights, extended to 'Indians, Inuit and Métis', was a feature of the patriation of the Canadian constitution from Great Britain in 1982 (the cases of the Inuit and Métis are dealt with below). This marked a shift in administrative policy and practice towards acknowledging indigenous difference. However, the growing appreciation of human rights in a context of culturally-specific entitlements required the overhaul of membership-control regimes, rather than their abandonment.

Critical to this shift was the case of Sandra Lovelace, a Maliseet woman from New Brunswick, who had been denied federal recognition as Indian after she had married a non-Indian man.[21] In the view of the UN Human Rights Committee, this violated Lovelace's right to enjoy her culture, protected by Article 27 of the International Covenant on Civil and Political Rights. That finding in 1981 led, after lengthy negotiations between the Canadian government and indigenous organisations, to the passage of Bill C-31, which did not protect rights to culture in the Indian Act but, rather, removed gender discrimination in its operation. The period revealed distinct indigenous concerns about membership, with the push for human rights and gender equality presented by some as undermining indigenous autonomy and self-determination (Innes 2007; Grammond 2009).

---

18. 'Census 2000 demographic profile highlights: selected population group: American Indian and Alaska Native alone' and 'Census 2000 demographic profile highlights: selected population group: American Indian and Alaska Native alone or in combination with one or more other races', US Bureau of Census, Fact Sheets http://factfinder.census.gov/home/saff/main.html?_lang=en.

19. Aboriginal Affairs and Northern Development Canada, 'The Indian Register' (January 2011) http://www.aadnc-aandc.gc.ca/eng/1100100032475.

20. This section draws heavily on Sebastien Grammond's *Identity Captured by Law* (2008: 106–49), which is the most thorough study of the Canadian context done in recent years; it focuses on the relationship of definitions to principles of human rights.

21. It should be noted that challenges to the gender discriminations in the law dated back to 1971: see McIvor 2004.

Put simply, the reforms created two forms of indigenous identity for administrative purposes, splitting Indian 'status' off from membership in 'bands' (communities defined under the Indian Act). So federal benefits, including scholarships and tax exemptions, are enjoyed by those who hold status, as defined by the federal government; having been freed from gender discrimination, status is now determined by descent. The benefits of Band membership – participation in the political life of the community, land-holding on Indian reserves, access to housing – are enjoyed by those who are members of Bands, determined by rules drawn up by Bands themselves, albeit within state-prescribed norms. This was driven by the government's concern to limit its financial obligations: the self-definition process allocates benefits which are granted by the federal government to Bands as lump sums, while status benefits are accorded to indigenous individuals.

Descent is paramount in the revised Indian Act, which abolished gender discrimination (section 12(1)b) and 'enfranchisement' (the voluntary renunciation of status), and reinstated those who had been enfranchised. Grammond estimates that the changes led to 115,000 reinstatements between 1985 and 2000 (2009: 112). The reforms also created two categories of Indian status, in order to end status after two successive generations of marrying out – the so-called 'second-generation cut-off rule'. A '6(1) Indian' has full rights to transfer status to his/her children because both his/her parents held status; she or he can have children with a non-Indian and their children will have status. However, a '6(2) Indian' only has partial rights – the other parent cannot be a non-Indian if the children are to hold status. Effectively, a person must have at least two status Indian grandparents in order to hold status himself or herself.

However, the introduction of the changes effectively maintained gender discrimination because, in 1985, the wives of status men who had married out had automatically gained status under the old rules, while the husbands of women who had been reinstated after 1985 did not. This meant that the children of male and female siblings were treated differently. Sharon McIvor began litigation in 2001 to address this ongoing discrimination and the case was resolved in her favour by the Court of Appeal for British Columbia in 2009.[22]

In January 2011, the federal government brought into law the Gender Equity in Indian Registration Act. This simply enabled the grandchildren of women who had lost their status as a result of marrying non-Indian men to be entitled to registration.[23] As part of those reforms the government also held an 'Exploratory

---

22. *McIvor v Canada (Registrar of Indian and Northern Affairs)*, 2009 BCCA 153 http://www.courts. gov.bc.ca/jdb-txt/CA/09/01/2009BCCA0153err2.htm; (accessed 16 December 2014); however, the distinguished legal scholar Mary Eberts has lamented the narrowness of the court's ruling, calling it 'a risk management device, presenting to the government a small and discrete task of legislative repair' (Eberts 2010: 40).

23. Aboriginal Affairs and Northern Development Canada, 'Gender equity in Indian Registration Act' http://www.aadnc-aandc.gc.ca/eng/1308068336912/1308068535844.

Process on Indian Registration, Band Membership and Citizenship', which funded 20 indigenous organisations to consult their constituencies and report to government on further areas requiring reform.[24]

Treaty-making has, since the 1970s, been another route towards self-definition in Canada, the idea being to devolve land, resources and governance power to communities defined according to indigenous understandings of identity, territory and belonging. However, it is heavily constrained, such that the federal interest in limiting its financial obligations prevents expansion of membership to those not covered by land-claims agreements.

Grammond notes two broad 'models' of membership, one applying in treaties with First Nations – where membership is transmitted via descent – and another adopted in treaties with Inuit communities – where Inuit custom defines membership. Inuit communities were never administered under the Indian Act and so had no experience with the problems of 'marrying out' that the Act had created (2009: 132–4).

Inuit people were first brought into definitions of entitlement through the comprehensive claims process, which formulated modern treaties; these agreements devolved membership control to communities and thereby largely ended status. The Nunavut Agreement (1993) defines an Inuk as a person who meets customary rules, as well as both self-identifying and having links to an Inuit community; it avoids reference to descent. Other Inuit outside Nunavut are adopting similar approaches. Here there is greater emphasis on 'relational' models of definition, where a community applies their own criteria, such as residence or participation in a community, on a case-by-case basis. Some entitlements can be suspended if members have not lived in the community for lengthy periods (Grammond 2009: 135)

The membership codes provided for communities under Bill C-31 – that is, those communities not party to modern treaties – remain problematic to many. Firstly, there is no requirement that Bands publish their codes, nor even allow members to consult the rules; according to Grammond only about 50 of 250 membership codes are public (135; see also Gover 2011). Notwithstanding the law, the thousands of mostly women who had been reinstated were also effectively unable to participate in the drafting of the new codes, because of band election rules preventing those who lived off reserves from voting. On the other hand, the new provisions protected the 'acquired rights' of those reinstated by guaranteeing them membership; but children of those women were not given those protections until after two-year transition period, thereby enabling some Bands to pass membership codes that excluded them. Some Bands reacted strongly to these impositions, continuing to exclude reinstated women and their children in various ways in violation of the law (McIvor 2004: 119).

---

24. Aboriginal Affairs and Northern Development Canada, 'The exploratory process on Indian Registration, Band Membership and Citizenship', http://www.aadnc-aandc.gc.ca/eng/1308584070908/1308584221643 (accessed 16 December 2014).

The codes themselves prioritise descent, though this varies considerably in the degree of ancestry required, some adopting a strict rule whereby both parents would have to be members in order for a child to have membership. As Grammond points out, this appears to place a racial justification on descent rather than a cultural one. Other codes are less stringent but do retain criteria of 'blood quantum'. In the case of adoptions, courts have found that biological requirements do not infringe constitutional rights to equality. The discretionary parts of the code, which applicants to membership must use, are based on descent but also may adopt quite arbitrary cultural requirements or standards of personal conduct or they may depend upon the availability of band resources to support an individuals' membership (Grammond 2009: 140–4).

The case of the Métis is complex and highly dynamic. Beginning with constitutional recognition in 1982, the Métis – a community descended from unions of indigenous and French-Canadian individuals – have sought and been granted certain forms of recognition. The federal government dealt with two organisations – the Métis National Council (who represent the Métis of the western provinces[25]) and the Congress of Aboriginal Peoples (who represent not only Métis in other parts of Canada but also off-reserve Indians and other non-status groups) – as a way of channelling services to these communities; they did not recognise those organisations as the official representatives of the communities. In 2013, the Federal Court decided that the latter group of people (approximately 200,000 Métis and 400,000 'non-status Indians' for whom the federal government provides some services but not full recognition) are in fact 'Indians' for the purposes of section 91(24) of the constitution.[26] This means that even more diversity needs to be accommodated within the federal approach.

The MNC as well as other organisations now have their own criteria, with the MNC, for example, adopting a definition of Métis people in 2002 that combined descent, self-identification, communal recognition and distinctiveness from other Aboriginal peoples.[27]

Meanwhile the Supreme Court's 2003 decision in *Powley*[28] not only set out principles for Métis definition, including self-definition, but also indicated a range of principles that must be adhered to in any future framework the Métis might adopt, including authenticity (durable attachments to a Métis community and some evidence of indigenous ancestry), fairness and clarity (Grammond 2009: 122–3). The matter of communal attachment or recognition is more rigid in the Court's approach than in the MNC definition, requiring membership-granting organisations to demonstrate their representativeness and

---

25. Manitoba, Saskatchewan, Alberta and British Columbia.

26. *Daniels et al. v The Queen*, 2013 FC 6.

27. There is a range of organisations now offering membership as identification of Métis identity. See http://www.aboriginalcanada.gc.ca/acp/site.nsf/en-frames/ao35055.html (accessed 4 November 2013).

28. *R. v Powley*, S.C.C. 2003.

coherence. In effect the Court has 'assumed the power to recognise specific Métis communities and to assess whether individuals may legitimately claim membership in them.' (Grammond 2009: 125) A further area of difficulty concerns the distinction between status Indians and Métis, communities with high rates of intermarriage, because holders of any other indigenous status cannot be Métis. The Métis Settlements Act of 2004 was devised to address the situation but it has been subject to repeated court challenges.

Australia

The Commonwealth of Australia is a federal union of six colonies. Each colony (later state) had varied and overlapping practices for defining who was an 'Aborigine', an 'Aboriginal person' or a 'member of the Aboriginal race'. McCorquodale records at least 67 different definitions since colonisation began in 1788 (1987).

The 1901 constitution explicitly denied the federal government any legislative authority over indigenous peoples, in stark contrast to the Canadian arrangement. It was not until 1967 that this was altered by referendum; a *concurrent* authority now exists. State government departments and legislation continue to use a variety of formulations (ALRC 1986: 88). This is the case even within one jurisdiction (ALRC 1986: 93). After 1967, a definition relying on descent came into use in federal legislation, declaring that an 'Aboriginal person ... was a member of the Aboriginal race of Australia'. This was, for example, the approach of the Racial Discrimination Act of 1975 (Gardiner-Garden 2003: 5). That began to shift with an internal administrative document of 1981, which noted: 'Assessments of degree of descent were generally considered unreliable and capable of giving offence. Such definitions also failed to take sufficient account of concepts of self-identification and community acceptance'.[29] This gave rise to a three-part definition of an Aboriginal or Torres Strait person as someone who:

1. is of Aboriginal or Torres Strait Islander descent;
2. identifies himself or herself as an Aboriginal person or Torres Strait Islander; and
3. is accepted as such by the indigenous community in which he or she lives.

The relative weight and clarity of each of these three criteria has been subject to interpretation and controversy and, in fact, courts have become the most significant institutions in the process of reforming status in Australia. During the 1990s, a series of judicial rulings pointed to a more flexible definition, one that could expand and contract according to context. The first case concerned individuals whose deaths were to be investigated as part of the Royal Commission

---

29. Department of Aboriginal Affairs, 'Report on a review of the administration of the working definition of Aboriginal and Torres Strait Islander', unpublished, Canberra, 1981, 1, cited in ALRC Report 1986: §91.

into Aboriginal Deaths in Custody, the federal court ruling in 1990 that even someone who did not identify nor was recognised by a community could be included in the investigations of the Commission (Gardiner-Garden 2003: 4).

Then came two cases pertaining to eligibility criteria for standing for and voting in elections to the Aboriginal and Torres Strait Islander Commission. In 1995 the federal court further strengthened the idea that descent could be interpreted as a matter of degree, in light of the strength of the other two criteria: 'The less the degree of Aboriginal descent, the more important cultural circumstances become in determining whether a person is "Aboriginal".'[30] Then, in *Shaw v Wolf*, the Federal Court found that descent might be established via the other two means:

> Aboriginal identification often became a matter, at best, of personal or family, rather than public, record. Given the history of the dispossession and disadvantage of the Aboriginal people of Australia, a concealed but nevertheless passed on family oral 'history' of descent may in some instances be the only evidence available to establish Aboriginal descent.[31]

Since the 1992 High Court decision in *Mabo* and subsequent passage of the Native Title Act, the Commonwealth government has recognised certain indigenous peoples as native-title holders.[32] Claimants must meet a 'registration test' set out in the Act:

> identification of the area subject to the native title claim; a sufficient description to identify the persons in the native title claim group; a clear description of the native title rights and interests claimed; a sufficient factual basis for the assertion that the claimed native title rights exist, including the native title claim group's continuing association with the area and continuing observation of traditional laws and customs; a current or previous traditional physical connection by at least one member of the native title claim group with any part of the area.[33]

In practice, it is a rigid framework for limiting membership of the entitlement group (Gover 2011: 174–5) and is quite distinct from the approach to status for the purposes of social policy.

Tasmania remains the site of most bitter controversy about Aboriginality in an administrative context.[34] In the early 2000s the Federal government sought

---

30. *Desmond Gibbs v Lyle Capewell, Australian Electoral Commission and Minister of Aboriginal and Islander Affairs* [1995] FCA 1048; (1995) 128 ALR 577 (1995) 54 FCR 503 (3 February 1995).

31. *Edwina Shaw & Anor v Charles Wolf & Ors* [1998] FCA 389 (20 April 1998), §8–11.

32. *Mabo and Others v Queensland* (No. 2) (1992) 175 CLR 1, [1992] HCA 23.

33. National Native Title Tribunal, 'The Registration Test', http://www.nntt.gov.au/News-and-Communications/Publications/Documents/Brochures/The%20registration%20test.pdf

34. In the colonial imagination as well as in contemporary popular culture, Tasmania is where Aborigines became 'extinct', with a fetish made of Truganini, the last 'full-blood' to die in 1876; it is a story in many ways resonant of the history of Beothuk people in Newfoundland.

to create an indigenous electoral roll for the state, which generated further controversy and litigation. Briefly, the independent commission charged with determining eligibility for the roll considered using DNA research drawn from the Human Genome Project to establish descent, in addition to archival and genealogical data, though this proposal was abandoned after vigorous criticism (see Gardiner-Garden 2003: 10).[35]

A problem throughout Australian history has been how to identify the descendants of unions between indigenous and settler peoples. The colonial imagination and policy approach prior to the post-WWII period assumed that the less Aboriginal blood an individual had, the less Aboriginal they were. The Australian history of the 'Stolen Generations', similar in some respects to Canada's history of Residential Schools, had an explicit emphasis on coerced and forcible removal from Aboriginal families of children of mixed descent. This creates serious ethical and practical difficulties for a status system predicated on communal recognition and descent as criteria of Aboriginality.

As early as the 1970s, once the first substantial piece of land-rights legislation had been enacted in the Northern Territory, the Aboriginal Land Commissioner could write that 'there is nothing in the Act to compel the view that a person who is descended from both Aboriginal and non-Aboriginal ancestors cannot be considered an Aboriginal'.[36] Moreover, recent recognition of the realities of the Stolen Generations has given rise to a range of programmes intended to allow indigenous peoples to reconnect with their identities and, where possible, their families. This adds further complexity to practices of definition.

It should be noted that popular culture in Australia has great difficulty acknowledging the Aboriginality of those with mixed antecedents (Sweeney and Associates 1996; Reconciliation Australia 2010: 32).[37] In the circumstances, argues Gardiner-Garden, 'the three part definition has generally been found to help protect individuals from the tendency among "mainstream Australians" to consider "real" indigenous people as people living somewhere else and others as manipulating the system'. (2003: 15) Interestingly, when the Australian Law

---

35. Genetic testing of claimants to indigeneity has been advocated and carried out in New Zealand as well as Australia, though not with significant outcomes for state policy. In 2000, the state legislature of Vermont sought to introduce Bill H.809, which would have required DNA proof of American-Indian identity in the provision of services. However, these measures failed in the face of widespread disapproval; many see such uses of genetic material as simply offensive and linked with past crimes of eugenics, as well as irrelevant as a marker of contemporary social identity. It does not seem an approach that states should or will take.

36. Aboriginal Land Commissioner, Report, AGPS, Canberra, 1981, §119–21, referring to *Uluru (Ayers Rock) National Park and Lake Amadeus/Luritja Land (Claim)*, AGPS, Canberra, 1980, §114–6, cited in ALRC 1986 at §94.

37. However, a recent case found a high-profile newspaper columnist guilty of racial vilification in a series of columns called 'White is the new black' and 'It's so hip to be black', which criticised individual indigenous whom he did not think had the right skin-colour to be considered Aboriginal; see http://blogs.news.com.au/heraldsun/andrewbolt/index.php/heraldsun/comments/column_white_is_the_new_black (accessed 16 December 2014).

Reform Commission investigated the recognition of indigenous customary laws in 1986, it concluded that, 'it is not necessary to spell out a detailed definition of who is an Aborigine, and that there are distinct advantages in leaving the application of the definition to be worked out, so far as is necessary, on a case by case basis.' (ALRC 1986: 95).

Censuses in Australia taken every five years since 1981 have inquired into the size of the indigenous population and a significant rise in the last four censuses has been attributed both to a greater willingness amongst individuals to identify themselves as well as the willingness of children of mixed marriages to identify themselves as indigenous. However, the phrasing of the question does not allow respondents to identify themselves as both indigenous and non-indigenous (Gardiner-Garden 2003: 11). The 2006 census estimate of indigenous persons was 517,000.[38]

Aotearoa/New Zealand

For Māori people, it is *whakapapa* that establishes ones identity as Māori. The term roughly means genealogy, or the story of belonging. However, statutory definitions of indigenous identity in New Zealand (Māori) use descent as a definition of eligibility. Subsequent legislation in NZ has adopted the same self-referential descent approach used in Australia. According to the Māori Affairs Restructuring Act 1989 No 68, 'Māori means a person of the Māori race of New Zealand; and includes a descendant of any such person'. This is also the case for the Māori Electoral Roll.[39]

However, tribal membership is, for many, the critical issue: not only does it confer access to tribally based social services such as on-reserve (*marae*) housing or tertiary scholarships but it also reasserts *hapu* and *iwi* (sub-tribal and tribal) identities as the basis of identity, rather than the pan-tribal idea of Māori that emerged after colonisation (Kukutai 2004: 93–4). This is not universal, however, as organisations such as Te Whānau O Waipareira have elided the *iwi* and *hapu* bases of Māori identity, preferring a different way of establishing their client community: 'whānau (family) are at the centre of everything we do ... (it) empowers whānau to choose their own direction and outcomes.'[40]

Gover has recently examined tribal membership rules under the Treaty of Waitangi process, which is the framework in which indigenous peoples pursue

---

38. Australian Bureau of Statistics. 'Experimental estimates of Aboriginal and Torres Strait Islander Australians', June 2006: http://www.abs.gov.au/AUSSTATS/abs@.nsf/ProductsbyCatalogue/9E3 34CF07B4EEC17CA2570A5000BFE00?OpenDocument (accessed 16 December 2014).

39. 'The Electoral Act defines Māori as "a person of the Māori race of New Zealand"; and includes any descendant of such a person. This includes Chatham Island Māori.' Elections New Zealand, *Maori Electoral Option* – FAQ, http://www.elections.org.nz/maori/enrolment/maori-option-faq. html (accessed 4 November 2013).

40. Te Whānau O Waipareira, http://www.waipareira.com/ (accessed 16 December 2014); thanks to Andrew Erueti for pointing this out.

their claims against the state, and requires greater institutional clarity of tribes' corporate identities. NZ policy is only to negotiate with 'large natural groupings' of Māori, and requires claimant groups to produce a Deed of Mandate, then a constitution for the new Treaty Settlement Entity, with matching rules for membership and beneficiary eligibility, both of which require ratification by majority vote (Gover 2010: 167–9).

Clearly, there is both variety and dynamism in what constitutes status in NZ. This probably reflects community values. Chapple, in a widely-cited paper from 2000, argued that Māori identity was 'multiple rather than singular, evolving rather than primordial, and fluid rather than rigid' (Chapple 2000: 101). As Kukutai notes, 'ancestry is often treated as an objective basis for identity and serves a gatekeeping function, albeit that the process of recalling ancestry has subjective elements' (2004: 91). Indeed, the New Zealand census has, since 1991, enabled the counting of three characteristics which can be used differently to ascertain overall population numbers: ancestry, ethnicity (particularly language-use) and *iwi* membership. The latter criterion was included because tribal authorities had lobbied for it (Chapple 2000: 91). If adherence to all three criteria (ancestry, ethnicity and tribal affiliation) is counted, the 2001 census showed a 'core Māori' population of just under 400,000; this increases to over 600,000 if descent is the sole criterion (Kukutai 2004: 92–5).

Scandinavia (Norway, Sweden, Finland)

The Sámi are an Arctic indigenous people, whose traditional territory of Sápmi comprises northern and central Scandinavia (Norway, Sweden and Finland) as well as sections of the Kola Peninsula (*see* Russia section, below). The total population is roughly estimated at 70,000–100,000 people, 40,000–60,000 of whom reside in Norway, 15,000–20,000 in Sweden, 9,000 in Finland and 2,000 in Russia (UNHRC 2011: 4).[41]

Each of the three Scandinavian countries has a Sámi parliament, which combines representative and administrative roles; while in many respects these are autonomous political institutions, each was created by state legislation and depends entirely on state funding. Much of that is designated for specific purposes to do with Sámi language, education and culture.

There is significant overlap across the three countries in determining eligibility to vote in Sámi parliamentary elections: self-identification plus language and/or descent are the key criteria. For example, in Sweden, the Sámi Parliament Act 1992 (2006) defines a Sámi as a person 'who considers him/herself to be a Sámi' and who meets one of the following criteria: he/she

---

41. It should be stressed that these estimates are subject to criticism, both for being conservative and for exaggerating the relevant numbers. *See* Pettersen, Chapter 7 for a careful discussion of the statistical debates on the Sámi population and Peters 2011 for a wider discussion about indigenous peoples and census data internationally.

can demonstrate a probability that he/she has or has had Sámi as the language in the home, or … can demonstrate a probability that one of his/her parents or grandparents has or has had Sámi as the language in the home, or … has a parent who is or has been included on the electoral register for the Sámi Parliament, without this subsequently being decided otherwise by the county administrative board.[42]

The Swedish government has decided that it is up to each individual to decide what constitutes use of the Sámi language 'in the home'. However, a 2004 amendment allows for anyone on the electoral roll to challenge the status of anyone else on the roll (Beach 2007: 11–13). Additionally in Finland, the legislation makes eligible anyone who is a 'descendent of a person who has been entered in a land, taxation or population register as a mountain, forest or fishing Lapp' (which Sámi consider to be a condescending word).[43] The definition in these laws is used for other more recent legislation. For example, the Finnish *Sámi Language Act* (1086/2003), defines a Sámi as an 'individual as referred to in section 3 of the Act on the Sámi Parliament'.[44]

Each Parliament Act provides for a Sámi register but there is some evidence that participation in the registration system is not as widespread as may have been expected based on rough population estimates: in Norway, only around 14,000 out of the 50,000–65,000 Sámi are registered; in Sweden, the number is about 7,000 out of 17–20,000; and in Finland around 5,200 out of 8,000.[45] Beach argues that

some Saami fear that apathy already causes many Saami to refrain from joining the Saami electorate, and that if Saami language skills decline further over the generations, the potential electorate, not to mention those who actually register, will decrease severely (Beach 2007:11).

A quite different argument is that non-participation is a sign of diversity and resistance within the Sámi population. However, enrolment is increasing: in

---

42. This is an English translation of the Act, available at http://www.sametinget.se/9865 (accessed 16 December 2014). While in Norway, §2.6 of the Sámi Act (1987) which established the Sametinget, describes the Sámi electoral register: 'All persons who make a declaration to the effect that they consider themselves Sámi, and who either have Sámi as their domestic language, or have or have had a parent, grandparent or great-grandparents with Sámi as his or her domestic language, or are the child of a person who is or has been registered in the Sámi electoral register may demand to be included in a separate register of Sámi electors in their municipality of residence.' Act of 12 June 1987 No. 56 concerning the Sameting (the Sámi Parliament) and other Sámi legal matters (the Sámi Act): http://www.regjeringen.no/en/doc/laws/Acts/the-sami-act-.html?id=449701 (accessed 16 December 2014).

43. The unofficial English translation is at http://www.finlex.fi/fi/laki/kaannokset/1995/en19950974.pdf (accessed 16 December 2014). See also Skogvang, Susann Funderud: 'Samerett', Oslo: Universitetsforlaget, 2009. Thanks to Mikkel Berg-Nordlie for these sources.

44. *Sámi Language Act* (1086/2003) s.3.2.2, http://www.ciemen.org/mercator/butlletins/58-03.htm (accessed 16 December 2014).

45. IWGIA: 30.

Norway, from 5,500 at the time of the first election in 1989 to almost 14,000 in the autumn of 2009 and in Sweden from 5400 in 1993 to over 7800 in 2009.[46] Participation by those enrolled in elections appears to fluctuate between 65–75 per cent and appears to be sensitive to contemporaneous legislative initiatives affecting Sámi rights. The gender ratio of those enrolled as well as the age profile is also skewed, towards older males (Selle and Strømsnes 2010: 69).

Constitutional change in Sweden meant that, as of January 2011, the Sámi are acknowledged as a distinct 'people of Sweden'. Section 17 of the Finnish constitution recognises the Sámi as an indigenous people, acknowledging the right to cultural autonomy within the Sámi homeland.'[47] Article 110a of the Norwegian constitution on 'Minority Rights of the Sámi' declares, '(i)t is the responsibility of the authorities of the State to create conditions enabling the Sámi people to preserve and develop its language, culture and way of life.'[48]

Additionally, legislation conferring rights and entitlements distinguishes between types of Sámi, according to whether or not they practise reindeer-herding on designated lands. In its original versions, passed in the late nineteenth and early twentieth centuries, this legislation was designed to restrict reindeer-herding (perceived to be a backward economic practice) to limited areas, while protecting the responsible and productive agricultural enterprises of non-Sámi settlers from damage by reindeer herds. This legislation now gives rise to resentment amongst some Sámi who are excluded not only from the right to keep reindeer herds but also from the associated rights to hunt and fish understood in the Sámi conception of 'husbandry' (Beach 2007: 5).

In Sweden, the Reindeer Husbandry Act (1971) formalised territorial divisions for administering reindeer-husbandry, now known as *samebys*, each unit having an allotted reindeer quota to be distributed amongst *sameby* members. Their original purpose was 'to provide a legally responsible entity for paying compensation to farmers whose property was damaged by reindeer herds.' Revised in 1993, the law now makes anyone who has Sámi ancestry eligible for membership in a *sameby*, but this does not guarantee membership, which, in practice, is restricted because the addition of new members reduces the value of the reindeer quota. Effectively, the legislation also makes non-reindeer-herding activities on *sameby* lands more difficult.[49] In Norway, the Reindeer Herding Act (1978, revised 2007) determines that only those 'who

---

46. Statistisk sentralbyrå (2009). 'Sametingsvalet, 2009', http://www.ssb.no/sametingsvalg/ (accessed 16 December 2014) and cited in Selle and Strømsnes 2010: 69; Lantto and Mörkenstam (this volume). As Pettersen (this volume) observes, one must consider the subtle dynamics of identification along lines like gender and geography, if measured by electoral enrolment.

47. IWGIA: 34; UN Sámi Report: 7. In Finland, the Sámi homeland is narrowly defined and only includes the northern part of Lapland province.

48. http://www.servat.unibe.ch/icl/no00000.html (accessed 16 December 2014)

49. Beach 2007: 5–9; International Centre for Reindeer Husbandry 'Reindeer husbandry in Sweden – rights to own reindeer and "sameby"': http://icr.arcticportal.org/index.php?option=com_content&view=article&id=176&Itemid=56&lang=en&limitstart=1 (accessed 16 December 2014).

have the right to a reindeer earmark can conduct reindeer husbandry in the Sámi reindeer herding area. The right to a reindeer earmark requires that the person is a Sámi and themselves, their parents or their grandparents have or had reindeer herding as their primary occupation.'[50] By contrast, Finland's legislation regulates reindeer-herding by any resident of a herding district and is not reserved for Sámi at all.

Scandinavian state practice lacks all-encompassing definitions of Sáminess but, in the particular contexts of voting and reindeer-herding, draws on aspects of all three approaches used in defining indigenous peoples. Eligibility requirements for the electoral rolls combine the obligations of individual self-identification with a demonstration of descent and/or a cultural standard of language. Simultaneously, state definition applies to a subset of the Sámi who are in the reindeer economy, revealing the multi-generational interactions of descent and cultural standards.

Latin America

The constitutions of Latin American states are primary defining documents for the region's indigenous peoples. Broadly speaking, these offer rich and varied formulations that draw both on descent and cultural difference.[51] There has also been considerable reform of these and related texts in recent years, reflecting the growing place of indigenous peoples in political debate.

For example, in **Bolivia**, the revised constitution of 2009, sets out in Article 30 the characteristics of indigeneity found in other countries (such as priority, cultural difference) joining these with the term 'peasant':

> The indigenous peasant nation and people are the collectivity of people who share identity, language, historical tradition, institutions, territory and world vision ... whose existence pre-dates the colonial Spanish invasion.[52]

Legislation further specifies this category: The Regulation of Base Territorial Organisations, of the Law of Popular Participation describes

> the collectivity of people who descend from populations who pre-date the conquest and colonisation, and who are located within the current borders of

---

50. International Centre for Reindeer Husbandry, 'Reindeer husbandry in Norway – rights to own reindeer', http://icr.arcticportal.org/index.php?option=com_content&view=article&id=175&Itemid=117&lang=en&limitstart=1 (accessed 16 December 2014).

51. It should be noted that there is a significant body of literature on Latin America assessing the limited forms of state recognition that are widespread through the continent, employing terms such as 'neoliberal multiculturalism' (Assies *et al.* 2006: 40; Hale 2002; Stavenhagen, 2008). A common view is that while cultural difference has been recognised, often in sophisticated ways, it is not matched by implementation of the social, political, legal and economic rights that should attend that recognition.

52. Chapter 4, Derechos de Las Naciones y Pueblos Indígena Originario Campesinos. http://pdba.georgetown.edu/Constitutions/Bolivia/bolivia09.html (accessed 16 December 2014).

the state; possess history, organisation, language or dialect or other cultural characteristics ... recognising themselves as belonging to the same socio-cultural entity, maintain a territorial link in the function of administration of their habitat and social economic, political and cultural institutions.'[53]

Recent legislative reforms give greater autonomy to indigenous peoples, particularly in local law and justice matters, in what Barrera (2011: 7–8) describes as a 'plurinational state model', in which all ethnic communities 'freely decide the course of their development, based on their own values, norms, and identities'.. Sixty-two per cent of Bolivians identified as belonging to an indigenous group in the 2001 census. Consequently, the question of group definition or status has devolved to communities and organisations. This is visible in the jurisdiction indigenous legal institutions hold over individuals: 'indigenous law shall apply to all individuals who are bound by a specific relationship to an indigenous group or who are considered members thereof.'[54] Precisely what this means is likely to emerge in the coming years.

The constitution of **Colombia** did not define who indigenous peoples were (Correa 2008: 7) but legislation promulgated in 1995 revised the prior definition of an 'indigenous community or group' as follows:

a group or group of families with Amerindian ascendency, who have awareness of identity and share values, characteristics, cultural customs, as well as their own forms of government, management, social control or normative systems that distinguish them from other communities, whether or not they have property titles, or can be recognised legally or whether their *resguardos* [indigenous territorial reserves] were dissolved, divided or declared vacant.[55]

Where doubt exists about a particular community, the Institute for Agrarian Reform of Colombia requests the Ministry of the Interior to conduct ethnological research to determine compliance. Correa describes this law as retrograde, however, shifting the power to define indigeneity back towards state actors (2008: 8).

The constitution of **Peru** recognises indigenous peoples as well: Article 89 declares, 'Native and *campesino* communities have a legal existence and are juridical persons.'[56] Again, it is in legislation that an operating definition is

---

53. El Reglamento de las Organisaciones Territoriales de Base, de la Ley de Participación Popular, cited in Comisión Económica para América Latina y el Caribe (CEPAL) (2005), 'Los pueblos indígenas de Bolivia: diagnóstico sociodemográfico a partir del censo del 2001', Santiago de Chile: 2005: 18: http://www.eclac.org/publicaciones/xml/3/23263/bolivia.pdf (accessed 16 December 2014); original: http://www.legislacionmunicipal.fam.bo/Archivo/Docs/Decretos/DS_23858.pdf (accessed 4 November 2013).

54. Art. 191 of the Bolivian constitution and Arts 8–11 of the Bolivian Law on Jurisdictional Delimitation, cited in Barrera 2011: 12.

55. Decreto 2164 de 1995, cited in Correa 2008: 7 original: http://www.presidencia.gov.co/prensa_new/decretoslinea/1995/diciembre/07/dec2164071995.pdf

56. *Campesino* refers to peasant or traditional farming communities.

provided: the Law on indigenous People's Right to Prior Consultation (2010), sets out, in Article 7, objective and subjective criteria:

> The objective criteria are the following: 1) Direct descent from the original populations of the national territory; 2) Way of life and spiritual and historical links and with the territory that has been traditionally used and occupied; 3) Social institutions and distinct customs; 4) Cultural patterns and ways of living that are distinct from other sectors of the national population. The subjective criteria are to be related to the awareness of the collective group of possession of an indigenous or first nations identity. Peasant or Andean communities and native communities or Amazonian peoples can also be identified as indigenous or first nations peoples, as per the criteria laid out in this article.[57]

Peru also has a law 'to protect isolated indigenous and first nations peoples and in situations of initial contact', which considers indigenous peoples as 'those who self-identify as such, maintain a distinct culture, are found in possession of an area of land, are part of the Peruvian state as per the constitution. These include isolated indigenous people or indigenous people in a situation of first contact.'[58]

Article 56 of the 2008 constitution of **Ecuador** declares that 'indigenous communities, peoples and nationalities', along with other distinctive Ecuadorian communities, are recognised as having an inherent status in Ecuador. According to the Instituto Interamericano de Derechos Humanos (IIDH), self-definition is the key principle in the constitution:

> In exercise of this right and invoking their ancestry, indigenous people have self-defined themselves as nationalities – cultural nations – each with evidence of its distinct traits, including linguistic ones ... The exercise of this right of self-definition is the fundamental pillar of the political project of indigenous nationalities in Ecuador that constitutes the foundation for the construction of a pluri-national state. (IIDH 2009: 59).

At the end of the military dictatorship in **Brazil**, various articles in the new 1988 constitution reserved for the federal government exclusive legislative power over Indians (Articles 20, 22, 49 and 109), while Chapter VIII set out the rights of Indians in detail. Article 1 of that Chapter gives further context:

---

57. Ley de Consulta Previa a los pueblos indígenas (2010), Artículo 7, Criterios de identificación de los pueblos indígenas u originarios http://servindi.org/pdf/AutografaLeyConsulta23Ago2011.pdf (accessed 16 December 2014).

58. Ley para la protección de pueblos indígenas u originarios en situación de aislamiento y en situación de contacto inicial LEY N° 28736. Artículo 2, Definiciones http://www.legislacionambientalspda.org.pe/images/stories/normas/Normasfinales/Parte3/PueblosIndigenas/BaseLegal/Ley28736.pdf http://www.legislacionambientalspda.org.pe/images/stories/normas/Normasfinales/Parte3/PueblosIndigenas/BaseLegal/Ley28736.pdf (accessed 4 November 2013).

Lands traditionally occupied by Indians are those on which they live on a permanent basis, those used for their productive activities, those which are indispensable to preserve the environmental resources required for their well being and those necessary for their physical and cultural reproduction, according to their uses, customs, and traditions.[59]

However, no formal definition is provided in the constitution itself.

The state agency designed to implement the constitutional protections, Fundação Nacional do Índio (FUNAI), identifies

that portion of the population that has problems of adaptation to Brazilian society, motivated by the preservation of customs, habits or mere loyalties to a pre-Columbian tradition. Or, more broadly, any individual Indian recognised as a member for a pre-Columbian community who identifies and is considered so by the Brazilian population with whom they are in contact.[60]

This interpretation combines both self-identification and local recognition.

However, in the last decades the population identifying as indigenous has increased dramatically: in the lower Amazon it now appears to encompass communities hitherto regarded (somewhat pejoratively) as *caboclo* – a type of *mestizo* 'without value'.[61] Similarly, in the north-east of the country, over 40 new tribes have been recognised by the state since the 1970s. In the view of one ethnographer, these are 'composed primarily of African-descended individuals who possess few of the traditional cultural diacritics, who speak only Portuguese and whose Indianness is not always evident from their physical appearance but who nonetheless self-identify as indigenous' (French 2011: 1). Much of this dynamism is attributed to the clause in the 1988 constitution according rights to the inhabitants of the former *quilombos* or hiding places of fugitive black slaves.

The constitution of **Mexico** contains extensive recognition and definition of indigenous peoples in Article 2, which sets out the nation's

pluricultural composition, sustained originally in its indigenous peoples ... who are descendants from the populations who lived in the territory of the country at the start of colonisation and who maintain their own social, economic, cultural and political institutions ... Self-awareness of their indigenous identity must be a fundamental criterion ... [indigenous]

---

59. Brazil – Constitution 1988 http://www.servat.unibe.ch/icl/br00000_.html, (accessed 16 December 2014).

60. Approximate translation of 'O que é ser índio', FUNAI, 'Povos Indígenas' http://www.funai.gov.br/index.html (accessed 4 November 2013).

61. Bolanos (2010: 65–6) discusses the complexities of these new forms of identification and claiming.

Communities ... are those who form a social, economic and cultural unit, established in a territory and recognise their own authorities according to their customs and traditions.[62]

Consequently, the constitution makes a distinction between indigenous *peoples*, who can show descent and maintain their own institutions, and indigenous *communities*, which are given official recognition on the basis of the above as well as their establishment in a given territory governed by those institutions.[63]

Article 66 of the constitution of **Guatemala** asserts that the state is composed of

diverse ethnic groups, amongst whom are indigenous groups of Mayan descent. The state recognises, respects and promotes their ways of life, customs, traditions, forms of social organisation, use of indigenous dress by men and women, languages and dialects.[64]

In 1995, as part of the conclusion of the conflict in the country, the government and the guerrillas of the Unidad Revolucionaria Nacional Guatemalteca reached an 'Agreement on the Identity and Rights of Indigenous Peoples', which set out in detail the five characteristics fundamental to the identity of the Maya (the indigenous peoples of Guatemala):

I) direct descent from the ancient Mayas; II) Languages which contain a common Maya root; III) A world vision ... based in the harmonic relations of all elements of the universe, and in which the human being is only another element, the earth is mother of life, and corn is a sacred symbol, central core of their culture ... transmitted from generation to generation through material production and writing and ... oral tradition, in which women have played a determining role; IV) A common culture based in ... Mayan thought, a philosophy, a legacy of scientific and technological consciousness, artistic conception and aesthetics, collective historical memory, a community organisation based in solidarity and respect ... ethical and moral values; and V) self-identification.

---

62. Constitución política de los Estados Unidos Mexicanos, Articulo 2 http://www.diputados.gob.mx/LeyesBiblio/pdf/1.pdf (accessed 16 December 2014).

63. Comisión Nacional Para El Desarrollo de Los Pueblos Indígenas, Conceptos Generales Sobre Pueblos Indígenas: http://www.cdi.gob.mx/index.php?option=com_content&view=article&id=272&Itemid=58 (accessed 16 December 2014). However, this distinction has been criticised for creating potential conflicts between specific Indi communities and larger indigenous peoples to whom they belong, as well as incoherence in the way the law defines a 'community'. See the discussion in Zolla and Zolla Márquez 2004.

64. Seccion Tercera: Comunidades indígenas, Artículo 66, Protección a grupos (translation in Sieder, 2011: 253).

This multifaceted definition, including an appreciation of culture and religion in indigenous terms, makes the Guatemalan context unusual amongst states in this survey. However, a range of reforms on indigenous peoples' rights that would strengthen the commitments contained in the agreements was put to a national referendum in 1998 but defeated (Sieder 2011: 252–3).

Russia

Article 69 of the Russian constitution of 1993 now recognises 'the rights of the indigenous small peoples according to the universally recognised principles and norms of international law and international treaties and agreements of the Russian Federation'.[65] Indigenous peoples are defined in Russian legislation as *korennye malochislennye narody* or 'numerically-small indigenous peoples' (Shapovalov, 2005), under the Federal Law on the Guarantees of the Rights of Indigenous Numerically Small Peoples of the Russian Federation (1999) (Petrov 2008). Shapovalov notes that the law applies to those who:

(1) live in territories traditionally inhabited by their ancestors, (2) maintain traditional ways of life and economic activity, (3) number less than 50,000 people, and (4) identify themselves as separate ethnic communities (Shapovalov 2005: 438).

The number 50,000 has been subject to debate. The rationale seems to be that many other relatively small communities, with populations of 50–100,000, have their own 'titular republics', which are able to identify and protect their own populations. Originally the cut-off was 35,000. Shapovalov notes a discourse in Russia driven by 'certain ethnographic studies showing that ethnic groups numbering less than 50,000 cannot self-develop and thus require special support from the State' (Shapovalov 2005: 438). Newcity notes that such numerical criteria have a long history and were an important principle of Soviet nationalities policy (Newcity 2008: 370).

What entitlements does recognition as a 'numerically small indigenous people' bring? Guarantees include group and individual rights to 'land and renewable natural resources in the territories which they have traditionally occupied and where they engage in traditional economic activities'; self-government bodies 'in places of compact settlement'; the right to education in keeping with tradition; compensation for industrial damage to their environment; and customary legal rights that do not require enactment through additional statutes (UNHRC 2010a: 7). Quotas in local governing bodies exist, but require further legislation to become effective (Murashko 2005: 26; Xanthaki 2004: 79).

---

65. The constitution of the Russian Federation in English translation is available at http://www.constitution.ru/en/10003000-04.htm.

The Russian government keeps the official Unified List of Numerically Small Indigenous Peoples of the Russian Federation, which initially totalled 26 peoples. According to IWGIA's 2011 global survey: '41 are legally recognised as "indigenous, small-numbered peoples of the North, Siberia and the Far East"; others are still striving to obtain this status' (IWGIA 2011: 38). Sokolovskiy points out that those added after the initial 26 have tended to stretch the definition, as they 'do not practice hunting, herding, or fishing as subsistence economic activities'. The list is further complicated by exemptions: the Republic of Dagestan is allowed to make its own rules under the law and its official list (included in the Unified List) includes communities of more than 100,000 in both Dagestan and the Russian Republic itself, including, oddly, ethnic Russians themselves (Newcity 2008: 372–3). Shapovalov estimates a total indigenous population of 350,000: 'Calculations based on the data obtained during the 2002 census show that as of 2002 there were about 350,000 people belonging to numerically small indigenous peoples' (Shapovalov 2005: 439; see also Petrov 2008: Table 1). According to Sokolovskiy, in the way the census is framed, all that the phrase 'peoples of Russia' provides is a founding sense of indigeneity, while further layers emerge through the category of 'small-numbered peoples', which are officially listed (2007: 74).

Africa

Africa is probably the least institutionally developed region in terms of indigenous peoples' status, rights and administrative frameworks. A 2005 report for the African Commission on Human and Peoples' Rights, found that 'very few African countries recognise the existence of indigenous peoples in their countries. Even fewer do so in their national constitutions or legislation.' (ACHPR Report 2005: 47). It notes exceptions such as South Africa, where

> the Khoe and San are generally acknowledged as the aboriginal and indigenous people who occupied the land long before the Bantu-speaking people did so. There is, however, yet to be a South African norm as to the meaning of 'indigenous peoples' and who qualifies for such status in South Africa.

A 2009 survey of legislative provisions for indigenous peoples done for the ILO found that while many states recognised the ethnic diversity of their populations, 'the term 'indigenous peoples' is not officially used in national legislation'. Only one state, Cameroon, referred to 'indigenous populations' in its constitution. However, the report noted 'a positive trend' in making provision for peoples who might be considered so. (ILO Report 2009: 17–22). What are visible in such instruments are both ideas of descent and strong notions of cultural difference, including isolation and exclusion.

Botswana is a diverse country in which one tribal grouping, the Tswana, has historically dominated, to the exclusion of other smaller tribal communities, including the Basarwa or San people, who number approximately 50,000 (UNHRC 2010b).[66] However, the government has long considered all communities as 'indigenous' and so differences in status are strongly tied to variations in social and economic need and claims. However, a long period of legislative discrimination favouring Tswana in political institutions came to an end in 2008, with the passage of the Bogosi Act, which sought to regularise the recognition of traditional tribal governing institutions. The Act includes a broad power for ministerial recognition of tribes in Part 2:

> (1) The Minister, after consulting a tribal community ... may recognise that tribal community as a tribe. (2) In deciding whether a tribal community shall be recognised as a tribe, the Minister shall take into account the history, origins, and organisational structure of the community, and any other relevant matters.[67]

In 2010, the **Democratic Republic of Congo** became the first country to adopt a comprehensive law on the rights of indigenous populations, who are distinguished as follows: 'populations who are different from the national population by their cultural identity, lifestyle and extreme vulnerability'.[68] Also in the DRC, the Forest Code refers to local communities that have specific rights under the Code. The Code defines 'local communities' as 'populations traditionally organised on the basis of custom and united by ties of clan or parental solidarity ... they are also characterised by attachment to a specific territory'.[69]

The 2010 constitution of **Kenya** does not recognise indigenous peoples *per se* but recognises 'marginalised communities' in ways that are in accord with international standards on indigenous rights (IWGIA 2011: 406):

> (a) a community that, because of its relatively small population or for any other reason, has been unable to fully participate in the integrated social and economic life of Kenya as a whole; (b) a traditional community that, out of a need or desire to preserve its unique culture and identity from assimilation, has remained outside the integrated social and economic life of Kenya as a whole; (c) an indigenous community that has retained and maintained a traditional lifestyle and livelihood based on a hunter or gatherer economy; or (d) pastoral persons

---

66. Report of the Special Rapporteur on the Situation Of Human Rights and Fundamental Freedoms of Indigenous People, James Anaya, Addendum: The situation of indigenous peoples in Botswana: http://daccess-dds-ny.un.org/doc/UNDOC/GEN/G10/139/68/PDF/ G1013968.pdf?OpenElement (accessed 4 November 2013).

67. Government of Botswana, Chapter 41: 01 Bogosi, http://faolex.fao.org/docs/pdf/bot91578.pdf (accessed 16 December 2014).

68. Act No. 5-2011 of 25 February 2011, On the Promotion and Protection of Indigenous Populations: http://www.iwgia.org/images/stories/sections/regions/africa/documents/0368_congolese_ legislation_on_indigenous_peoples.pdf.

69. Cited in ILO Report 2009: 20–1.

and communities, whether they are (i) nomadic; or (ii) a settled community that, because of its relative geographic isolation, has experienced only marginal participation in the integrated social and economic life of Kenya as a whole.[70]

Asia

Asia has an estimated 100 million indigenous persons, many belonging to groups that cross state borders. State practices vary considerably in terms of recognition as well as terminology used, revealing a variety of emphases on continuity/descent as well as on cultural difference, often understood as isolation. The terms 'tribals', 'tribal people', 'hill tribes', 'scheduled tribes', 'natives', 'ethnic minorities', 'minority nationalities' are common, in addition to country-specific terms such as *Adivasis* (original inhabitants) in India and Bangladesh, *Orang Asli* (original peoples) in Malaysia, or *Adevasi Janajati* in Nepal (UNHRC 2007: 5).

Numerous countries in the region have explicitly rejected the emergent category of indigenous peoples, most notably **China**, which avers:

> indigenous issues ... are the result of the colonialist policy carried out in modern history by European countries in other regions of the world, especially on the continents of America and Oceania. As in the case of other Asian countries, the Chinese people of all ethnic groups have lived on our own land for generations. We suffered from invasion and occupation of colonialists and foreign aggressors. Fortunately, after arduous struggles of all ethnic groups, we drove away those colonialists and aggressors. In China, there are no indigenous people and therefore no indigenous issues.[71]

China does, however, recognise 'minority nationalities' in its constitution of 1982 (Article 4) for purposes of social and economic development; some of these would meet criteria associated with indigenous peoples in other countries.

Constitutional provisions for tribal peoples in **India** date from the early moments of Indian independence and sought to achieve the two goals of tribal protection and development. So-called 'Scheduled Tribes' (STs) are one of the two categories of 'Backward Classes' in India (the other being Scheduled Castes). Section 342 of the constitution empowers the President to 'specify the tribes or tribal communities or parts of or groups within tribes or tribal communities which shall for the purposes of this constitution be deemed to be Scheduled Tribes'.[72] Elsewhere, the constitution provides for the reservation of seats for Scheduled Tribes in India's House of People (Article 330), and in the Legislative Assemblies

---

70. Constitution of Kenya 2010, Chapter 18: 162–3.

71. Adviser of the Chinese delegation Long Xuequn, 1 April 1997, 53rd Session of the United Nations Commission on Human Rights: http://www.china-embassy.ch/eng/ztnr/rqwt/t138829.htm (accessed 4 November 2013).

72. Constitution of India, Section 342(1): http://lawmin.nic.in/olwing/coi/coi-english/Const.Pock%202Pg.Rom8Fsss(22).pdf (accessed 16 December 2014).

of the states (Article 332), as well as provisions for 'Scheduled Areas' or lands designated for STs (Schedule Five). The 2001 census showed over 84 million Scheduled Tribes, 8.2 per cent of the national population.[73]

According to the Indian Ministry of Tribal Affairs, the key criteria for Scheduled Tribes are 'primitive traits, distinctive culture, geographical isolation, shyness of contact with the community at large, and backwardness ... (this is) not spelt out in the constitution but has become well established'. Most ST designations were made shortly after Indian independence, , with eight additional declarations (comprising multiple STs) made since, the most recent in 1989. India also issues a Scheduled Tribes Certificate to individuals, the guidelines specifying that,

> Where a person claims to belong to a Scheduled Tribe by birth it should be verified: (i) That the person and his parents actually belong to the community claimed; (ii) That the community is included in the Presidential Order specifying the Scheduled Tribes in relation to the concerned State. (iii) That the person belongs to that State and to the area within that State in respect of which the community has been scheduled. (iv) He may profess any religion. (v) That he should be permanent resident on the date of notification of the Presidential Order applicable in his case.[74]

Taiwan promulgated its Indigenous Peoples Basic Law in 2005, 'for the purposes of protecting the fundamental rights of indigenous peoples, promoting their subsistence and development and building inter-ethnic relations based on co-existence and prosperity'. The legislation includes several key definitions, firstly of indigenous peoples:

> the traditional peoples who have inhibited in Taiwan [sic] and are subject to the state's jurisdiction, [12 tribes are listed], and any other tribes who regard themselves as indigenous peoples and obtain the approval of the central indigenous authority upon application. 'Tribe' refers to 'a group of indigenous persons who form a community by living together in specific areas of the indigenous peoples' regions and following the traditional norms with the approval of the central indigenous authority.[75]

The Basic Law provides a range of rights and protections that deepen the state's categorisation of indigenous peoples, including:

---

73. http://www.censusindia.gov.in/Census_Data_2001/India_at_Glance/scst.aspx (accessed 16 December 2014).

74. India, Ministry of Tribal Affairs, Definition – Article 342 Scheduled Tribes: http://tribal.nic.in/index3.asp?subsublinkid=303&langid=1 (accessed 4 November 2013).

75. Taiwan, Council of Indigenous peoples, Executive Yuan, 'The Indigenous Peoples Basic Law' (2005): http://www.apc.gov.tw/portal/docDetail.html?CID=74DD1F415708044A&DID=3E651 750B4006467D4B40DD3AC1D7378 (accessed 16 December 2014).

Hunting wild animals; Collecting wild plants and fungus; Collecting minerals, rocks and soils; Utilising water resources … [all of which] can only be conducted for traditional culture, ritual or self-consumption.

A further 2001 law covers other questions of indigenous status in Taiwan, including inclusive approaches to the extension of status in the case of intermarriage with non-indigenous persons, children of such couples and adoption.[76]

Discussion

In the background to these changes in states' practices for defining indigenous peoples, one can find the steadily more effective activism of indigenous groups. As noted earlier, politicisation began in the European settler states and had many strands: the emergence of state-level human-rights standards and institutions in the post-war period; the accessibility of courts; increases in social programmes for indigenous peoples; improvements in communications and transportation; urbanisation; significant shifts in broader social attitudes to cultural difference; and the intensification of the global economy (de Costa 2006).

Such forces have contributed in most countries to a problematic consolidation of state and non-indigenous assumptions about an homogenous or only partly differentiated indigenous community or population; that is a major institutional and imaginative obstacle for those that would return to pre-colonial identities based in the particular sovereignties of indigenous nations. The very structure of this paper – focused on state definitions that generalise numerous tribes and nations into 'indigenous' or 'Aboriginal peoples' – both reveals and reproduces that problem.

Yet it is through these changes that states have come to appreciate the importance of enabling indigenous peoples to define themselves according to their own values and practices; this may often mean the devolution of existing definitions. However, few have abandoned completely a role for racial/ genealogical ideas of 'descent', while arbitrary cultural standards, including a perceived lack of sophistication, degree of isolation and numerical size, remain widespread. The ways in which these approaches interlock in real life are likely to be highly varied. It is somewhat misleading to suggest, as Beach has argued recently, 'states [will] gradually abdicate nationally unique classificatory regulation in favour of indigenous self-ascription with an attempt at global harmonisation of principles' (Beach 2007: 1).

Some are worried about the potential and actual injustices that may arise in processes of self-definition (Snipp 1986; Kukutai 2004). The matter of self-definition of membership rules produces extraordinary complexity and

---

76. Taiwan, Council of Indigenous peoples, Executive Yuan, 'Status Act for Indigenous Peoples' (2001): http://www.apc.gov.tw/portal/docDetail.html?CID=74DD1F415708044A&DID=3E651 750B400646776702AECEC7630DD (accessed 16 December 2014).

inequity; this is the case for indigenous Tasmanians electors, children of a single Native American parent and Sámi reindeer herders. As Beach asks, 'who are the Saami who should decide who is a Saami?' (Beach 2007: 1–2). Corporate *indigenous* institutions, like all institutions, are subject to a variety of forces shaping their decision-making about entitlements, including capture by particular sub-communal groups. Furthermore, self-definition or community recognition standards for claimant individuals can put those charged with determinations in an invidious position, given the historic disruptions to indigenous communities. Forced removals and the destruction of traditional economies set in train dislocating effects that could never be 'resolved' simply by the greater empowerment of indigenous people whose indigeneity states find least problematic.

Moreover, it may seem to the casual observer that the term indigenous peoples is a basic descriptor, consistent all over the world; but indigeneity is contested in many places, in its boundaries and its basis. Sometimes the contest is between claimants of indigeneity and state arbiters of that status; other times the contest is amongst those who hold or claim indigenous status; while non-indigenous societies frequently contest the indigeneity of some claimants.

It is also clear that confidence in coherent communities of 'indigenous' and 'other' distinguished by priority is absent in some regions, the distinguishing lines so blurred or contested that seeking an administrative resolution is unwise and undesirable. In much of Asia and Africa, state governments reject the term's applicability to their own inhabitants:[77] Indigeneity, they argue, is a function of European settler-colonialism; it is the status that now characterises the situation of those original inhabitants of the Americas and Oceania (and a few other places) who were overwhelmed by European invaders and settlers from the fifteenth century on. Such peoples are now non-dominant minorities with historical claims. Elsewhere, they aver, indigeneity would apply to everyone and is therefore irrelevant.

In the African context, for example, some human-rights advocates are encouraging a different approach, moving away from an emphasis on 'aboriginality' as priority demonstrated by descent:

We should put much less emphasis on the early definitions focusing on aboriginality, as indeed it is difficult and not very constructive ... to debate this in the African context. The focus should be on the more recent approaches focusing on self-definition as indigenous and distinctly different from other groups within a state; on a special attachment to and use of their traditional land whereby their ancestral land and territory has a fundamental

---

77. For example, Morning argues that 'Indigeneity seems to serve as a marker largely in nations that experienced European colonialism, where it distinguishes populations that ostensibly do not have European ancestry (separating them from mestizos, for example, in Mexico) or who inhabited the territory prior to European settlement. The indigenous status formulation was not found on any European or Asian censuses.' (2008: 247–8).

importance for their collective physical and cultural survival as peoples; on an experience of subjugation, marginalisation, dispossession, exclusion or discrimination because these peoples have different cultures, ways of life or modes of production than the national hegemonic and dominant model. (ACHPR Report 2005: 92–3).

Such a shift may have the effect of widening, not narrowing, eligibility.

Anthropologists appear to have particular concerns about such trends. In Brazil, one scholar notes the 'larger, flexible, international context ... made available for theorising indigeneity by the lack of definition in the United Nations Declaration'. This, she argues, jeopardises the moral grounding of state action on behalf of marginalised groups:

> is it conceptually defensible from both an ethical and legal perspective of justice to include in a single category both people who have a clear claim to 'difference' and have struggled for generations to gain even limited political autonomy, and those who have just recently discovered their claim to indigeneity under an expansive view of indigenous peoples? (French 2011: 242).

In India, Karlsson decries the 'abstraction' of the global category (2003), while Ghosh argues that the global movement appears to create instances of isolated authenticity (2006). Shah observes the 'dark side' that attends these features of indigeneity, fearing it may provide intellectual cover for Hindu extremism (2007).[78]

Regardless of its precise aegis, the emergence of an international standard for the rights of indigenous peoples remains an extraordinary development. It creates but does not define two distinct categories of human community and experience in the world: indigenous peoples and, by default, all others. There are precedents in international law, for example the 'minorities' arrangements set out after the First World War (de Costa 2006); in those cases, though, each group was clearly identified.[79]

However, there is a piece of text that has been widely used at the international level for some time. The Cobo Report of 1986 spelt out the experiences of indigenous peoples in general terms:

> Indigenous communities, peoples and nations are those which, having a historical continuity with pre-invasion and pre-colonial societies ... consider themselves distinct from other sectors of the societies now prevailing in those territories ... They form at present non-dominant sectors of society and

---

78. It could also here be noted that the extreme right in Europe has adopted some of this rhetoric. For example, see the British Nationalist Party's invocation of 'Aboriginal Britons' during the 2010 election campaign: http://www.youtube.com/watch?v=4iKfrY9l2kY (accessed 16 December 2014).

79. The history of international instruments of indigenous rights is too long to be taken up here, with the ILO a key actor in the development of both standards and definitions. For a narrative of events and further sources, see de Costa 2006.

are determined to preserve, develop and transmit to future generations their ancestral territories, and their ethnic identity, as the basis of their continued existence as peoples, in accordance with their own cultural patterns, social institutions and legal systems.[80]

Though it provides no definition, UNDRIP has many ramifications for state policies of definition. Article 3 of the Declaration endorses indigenous peoples' rights of self-determination; subsequent articles declare that this encompasses the rights to autonomy and self-governance, to their own political institutions and to a nationality. Article 9 prohibits discrimination against indigenous peoples' right to belong to an indigenous community, 'in accordance with the traditions and customs of the community or nation concerned'. Articles 18–20 entrench a right to indigenous institutions. Most critically, Article 33 provides that,

> indigenous peoples have the right to determine their own identity or membership in accordance with their customs and traditions. This does not impair the right of indigenous individuals to obtain citizenship of the States in which they live ... (and that) indigenous peoples have the right to determine the structures and to select the membership of their institutions in accordance with their own procedures.

In the aspirations set out in UNDRIP and endorsed by most states, there would seem to be little role for the state in *defining* who was or was not an indigenous person.

However, this assumes a relatively straightforward adoption of international standards in domestic legislation and policy. That is rarely true in practice and, for UNDRIP, a Declaration of the General Assembly rather than a formal convention (with its own institutions for monitoring compliance), its influence will be rather harder to predict. In a separate paper I have taken up this issue in detail (de Costa 2011), drawing on developments in states that are signatories to UNDRIP. Since its passage, it would seem that legislation in states with large indigenous populations, such as Bolivia, is conforming to its prescriptions, though this was the path that country was on in any case. Elsewhere, the influence has been jurisprudential. Certain jurisdictions have seen rulings draw on UNDRIP as a source of customary international law. No doubt such cases will continue, driven by indigenous litigants seeking protection and relief from state or corporate intrusions, but the process of 'legal transnationalism', by which these international standards come to be operational in municipal settings is, at this moment, far from clear (de Costa 2011: 66–9).

---

80. Jose R. Martinez Cobo, Special Rapporteur of the Sub-Commission on Prevention of Discrimination and Protection of Minorities, 'Study on the problem of discrimination against indigenous populations', UN Doc. E/CN.4/Sub.2/1986/7 and Add. 1–4. Moreover, a set of conventions exists within these institutions such that some policing is possible (as in the refusal of indigenous delegates to interact with members of the Rehoboth Baster community, who sought indigenous status at an international meeting in the 1990s).

Indigenous activism will likely be crucial to the unfolding of events, and will influence to some extent the principles that emerge most readily from the international domain. However, even full adoption of UNDRIP as domestic law would not relieve all the pressures welling up around indigenous status. Whether states collect and administer registers of indigenous persons or not, or whether indigenous communities themselves do it, the realities of mobility and intermarriage will continue to delimit existing practices: proving descent will remain as fraught and fragmented as before; while strong cultural standards may be equally arbitrary or open to abuse, potentially restricting individual and communal choice. The question of whether and how indigenous individuals participate in such identities as they evolve is also open, particularly given the changing landscape of benefits accruing to indigeneity, perceived and actual.

The origins of status were in attempts by colonising or modernising states to manage what were thought of as unchanging indigenous populations. These colonial definitions were racist, arbitrary and imposed with little or no input from the people subject to them. In the face of tremendous dynamism within indigenous communities and through greater interaction with wider populations, these definitions were first changed in ways that suited evolving state purposes. More recent shifts have included some devolution of the matters of identification with and membership of indigenous peoples, though this has not guaranteed radical changes in approach, nor a global uniformity of definition. It may be that the only real driver for universal definition may be the consolidation of international laws concerning indigenous peoples.

References

African Commission on Human and Peoples' Rights (2005), *Report of the ACHPR Working Group of Experts on Indigenous Populations/Communities*.

Assies, W. and Sevilla, L. R. (2006) 'Autonomy rights and the politics of constitutional reform in Mexico', *Latin American and Caribbean Ethnic Studies* 1(1): 37–62.

Australian Law Reform Commission 1986, *Recognition of Aboriginal Customary Laws*, Australia.

Barrera, A. (2011) *Turning Legal Pluralism into State-Sanctioned Law: Assessing the implications of the new constitutions and laws in Bolivia and Ecuador*, Hamburg: GIGA German Institute of Global and Area Studies.

Barrios, R. M. and Pinto, A.V. (2007) *Los Derechos de los Pueblos Indígenas en Bolivia: Una introducción a las normas, contextos y procesos*, La Paz: CEBEM.

Beach, H. (2007) 'Self-determining the self: aspects of Saami identity management in Sweden', *Acta Borealia* 24(1): 1–25.

Berg-Nordlie, M. (2011) 'Striving to unite. The Russian Sámi and the Nordic Sámi Parliament model', *Arctic Review on Law and Politics* 2(1): 52–76.

Bolanos, O. (2010) 'Reconstructing indigenous ethnicities: the Arapium and Jaraqui Peoples of the Lower Amazon, Brazil', *Latin American Research Review* 45(3): 63–86.

Chapple, S. (2000) 'Maori socio-economic disparity', *Political Science* 52(2): 101–15.

Correa, F. (2008) *Desencializando lo 'Indigena' en las Categorías Jurídicas del Estado Colombiano*, Colombia, Universidad Nacional de Colombia http://www.docentes.unal.edu.co/grnemogas/docs/11_Correa_tr.pdf (accessed 29 May 2015).

de Costa, R. (2006) *A Higher Authority: Indigenous transnationalism and Australia*, Sydney: University of New South Wales Press.

— (2011) 'Implementing UNDRIP: developments and possibilities', *Prairie Forum* 36 (Fall 2011): 55–77.

French, J. H. (2009) *Legalizing Identities: Becoming Black or Indian in Brazil's northeast*, Chapel Hill, NC: University of North Carolina Press.

— (2011) 'The power of definition: Brazil's contribution to universal concepts of indigeneity', *Indiana Journal of Global Legal Studies* 18(1): 241–61.

Gardiner-Garden, J. (2003) *Defining Aboriginality in Australia*, Canberra: Department of the Parliamentary Library, Parliamentary Research Service.

Garroutte, E. M. (2003) *Real Indians: Identity and the survival of Native America*, Berkeley, CA: University of California Press.

Ghosh, K. (2006) 'Between global flows and local dams: indigenousness, locality, and the transnational sphere in Jharkhand, India', *Cultural Anthropology* 21(4): 501–34.

Gonzales, A. (1998) 'The (re)articulation of American Indian identity: maintaining boundaries and regulating access to ethnically tied resources', *American Indian Culture and Research Journal* 22(4): 199–225.

Gover, K. (2011) *Tribal Constitutionalism: States, tribes, and the governance of membership*, Oxford: Oxford University Press.

Grammond, S. (2009) *Identity Captured by Law: Membership in Canada's indigenous peoples and linguistic minorities*, Montreal: McGill-Queen's University Press.

Hale, C. R. (2002) 'Does multiculturalism menace? Governance, cultural rights and the politics of identity in Guatemala', *Journal of Latin American Studies* 34(3): 485–524.

Innes, R. A. (2007) 'United Nations Human Rights Committee and The Bill C-31 Amendment to the Indian Act', Canadian Native Studies Association Conference, June 2007.

Instituto Interamericano de Derechos Humanos (IIDH) (2009) *Acceso a la Justicia y Derechos Humanos en Ecuador*, San Jose, Costa Rica: http://www.iidh. ed.cr/BibliotecaWeb/varios/Documentos.Interno/BD/Acceso%20a%20 la%20justicia%20ECUADOR.pdf (accessed 29 May 2015).

International Labour Organization and African Commission on Human and Peoples' Rights (2009) *Overview Report of the Research Project by the International Labour Organization and the African Commission on Human and Peoples' Rights on the Constitutional and Legislative Protection of the Rights of Indigenous Peoples in 24 African Countries*, Geneva: http://www.ilo.org/wcmsp5/groups/public/—ed_norm/—normes/documents/publication/wcms_115929.pdf (accessed 29 May 2015).

International Work Group for Indigenous Affairs (IWGIA) (2011) *The Indigenous World 2011* (ed. K. Wessendorf), Copenhagen: IWGIA and Edison NJ: Transaction Publishers http://www.iwgia.org/iwgia_files_publications_files/0454_THE_INDIGENOUS_ORLD-2011_eb.pdf (accessed 29 May 2015).

Karlsson, B. G. (2003) 'Anthropology and the indigenous slot', *Critique of Anthropology* 23(4): 403–23.

Kukutai, T. (2004) 'The problem of defining an ethnic group for public policy: who is Maori and why does it matter?', *Social Policy Journal of New Zealand/Te Puna Whakaaro* 23: 86–108.

McCorquodale, J. (1987) *Aborigines and the Law: A digest*, Canberra: Aboriginal Studies Press.

McIvor, S. D. (2004) 'Aboriginal women unmasked: using equality litigation to advance women's rights', *Canadian Journal of Women and the Law* 16(1): 106–36.

Merlan, F. (2009) 'Indigeneity: global and local', *Current Anthropology* 50(3): 303–33.

Morning, A. (2008) 'Ethnic classification in global perspective: a cross-national survey of the 2000 census round', *Population Research and Policy Review* 27(2), 239–72.

Murashko, O. O. (2005) 'Introduction – the International Roundtable on an Indigenous Parliament', in K. Wessendorf (ed.), *An Indigenous Parliament? Realities and Perspectives in Russia and the Circumpolar North*, Copenhagen: IWGIA, pp. 22–7.

Newcity, M. (2008) 'Protecting the traditional knowledge and cultural expressions of Russia's "numerically-small" indigenous peoples: what has been done, what remains to be done', *Texas Wesleyan Law Review* 15: 357–414.

O'Brien, S. (1991) 'Tribes and Indians: with whom does the United States maintain a relationship?', *Notre Dame Law Review* 66: 1461–94.

Ortiga, R. R. (2004), *Models for Recognizing Indigenous Land Rights in Latin America*, Washington, DC: World Bank Environment Department.

Otis, D. S., (1973[1898]) *The Dawes Act and the Allotment of Indian Lands*, Normal, OK: University of Oklahoma Press.

Pathy, J. (2005) 'Tribe, region, and nation in the context of the Indian state', in P. M. Chacko (ed.), *Tribal Communities and Social Change*, New Delhi and Thousand Oaks, CA: Sage Publications: 30–45.

Peters, E. J. (2011) 'Still invisible: enumeration of indigenous peoples in census questionnaires internationally', *Aboriginal Policy Studies* 1(2): 68–10.

Petrov, A. N. (2008) 'Lost generations? Indigenous population of the Russian north in the post-Soviet era', *Canadian Studies in Population* 35(2): 269–90.

Porter, F. W., III (1990) 'In search of recognition: Federal Indian policy and the landless tribes of western Washington', *American Indian Quarterly* 14(2): 113–32.

Quinn, W. W., Jr. (1990) 'The southeast syndrome: notes on Indian descendant recruitment organizations and their perceptions of Native American culture', *American Indian Quarterly* 14(2): 147–54.

Reconciliation Australia, (2010), *Australian Reconciliation Barometer 2010: Comparing the attitudes of indigenous people and Australians overall*: https://www.reconciliation.org.au/wp-content/uploads/2014/05/Australian-Reconciliation-Barometer-2010-full-report1.pdf (accessed 29 May 2015).

Selle, P. and Strømsnes, K. (2010) 'Sámi citizenship: marginalisation or integration?', *Acta Borealia* 27(1): 66–90.

Shah, G. (2004) *Social Movements in India: A review of the literature*, (2nd and enlarged edn), New Delhi and Thousand Oaks, CA: Sage Publications.

Shapovalov, A. (2005) 'Straightening out the backward legal regulation of "backward" peoples' claims to land in the Russian north: the concept of indigenous neomodernism', *Georgetown International Environmental Law Review*, 17(3): 435–69.

Sieder, R. (2011) ' "Emancipation" or "regulation"? Law, globalization and indigenous peoples' rights in post-war Guatemala', *Economy and Society* 40(2): 239–65.

Snipp, C. M. (1986) 'Who are American Indians? Some observations about the perils and pitfalls of data for race and ethnicity', *Population Research and Policy Review* 5: 237–52.

Sokolovski, S. V. (2000) 'The construction of "indigenousness" in Russian science, politics and law', *Journal of Legal Pluralism and Unofficial Law* 45: 91–114.

— (2007) 'Indigeneity construction in the Russian census 2002', *Sibirica* 6(1): 59–94.

Stavenhagen, R. (2008) 'Los pueblos indigenas', Mexico, D.F.: UNESCO Mexico.

Sweeney, B. and associates (1996) *A New Beginning: Community attitudes towards Aboriginal reconciliation*, Canberra: Aboriginal Reconciliation Unit, Australia.

Thornton, R. (1997) 'Tribal membership requirements and the demography of "old" and "new" Native Americans', *Population Research and Policy Review* 16,(1–2): 33–42.

United Nations Human Rights Council (2007) *Report of the Special Rapporteur on the Situation of Human Rights and Fundamental Freedoms of Indigenous People, Rodolfo Stavenhagen*, Addendum: 'General considerations on the situation of human rights and fundamental freedoms of indigenous peoples in Asia'.

— (2010) *Report of the Special Rapporteur on the Situation of Human Rights and Fundamental Freedoms of Indigenous People, James Anaya*, Addendum: 'The situation of indigenous peoples in Botswana'.

— (2010) *Report of the Special Rapporteur on the Situation of Human Rights and Fundamental Freedoms of Indigenous People, James Anaya*, Addendum: 'The situation of indigenous peoples in the Russian Federation'.

— (2011) *Report of the Special Rapporteur on the Situation of Human Rights and Fundamental Freedoms of Indigenous People, James Anaya*, Addendum: 'The situation of the Sami people in the Sápmi region of Norway, Sweden and Finland'.

Walsh, J. F. (1985) 'Settling the Alaska Native Claims Settlement Act', *Stanford Law Review* 38: 227–63.

Xanthaki, A. (2004) 'Indigenous rights in the Russian Federation: the case of numerically small peoples of the Russian north, Siberia, and Far East', *Human Rights Quarterly* 26(1): 74–105.

Zolla, C. and Zolla Márquez, E. (2004) *Los Pueblos Indígenas de México, 100 preguntas*, Mexico: Universidad Nacional Autónoma de México/National Autonomous University of Mexico (UNAM).

Chapter Three

Indigenous Political Representation in Liberal-Democratic Countries: A Comparative Analysis

Jane Robbins

Introduction

The United Nations' adoption of the Declaration on the Rights of Indigenous Peoples (UNDRIP) in 2007 sets a new benchmark for the recognition of indigenous rights to self-determination. Article 3 of the Declaration expresses this right:

> Indigenous peoples have the right to self-determination. By virtue of that right they freely determine their political status and freely pursue their economic, social and cultural development (UN 2007).

While the Declaration is not prescriptive about the form that self-determination should take, several of its articles elaborate important principles in relation to the rights of indigenous peoples to realize their political autonomy and identity (see the discussion in Allen and Xanthaki 2011). While some indigenous authors have argued that the Declaration simply perpetuates a false 'paradigm of domination' (Newcomb 2011: 579–607), many believe that it establishes indigenous rights to a robust form of political autonomy. Importantly, this includes the right to establish indigenous representative processes according to principles of their own choosing. Governments are required to consult and co-operate with indigenous representative bodies as the political voice of their peoples in seeking consent for proposals that affect their interests. For this reason, the adoption of the Declaration provides a new imperative for an examination of the diverse forms of indigenous political representation that have developed over recent decades.

Processes of indigenous representation vary not only in form but also in purpose. Some indigenous representative institutions exist for the purpose of local or internal governance within the indigenous community. Other political representative structures have the purpose of voicing a unified indigenous agenda to the wider community and engaging with the broader institutions of national governance. It is this latter function that will be the main focus of this chapter. This is not to discount the importance of local and regional indigenous political structures or to suggest that national political arrangements are more significant in the attainment of goals of self-determination than those that operate at local level. To the contrary, there are many reasons why local indigenous governance structures can be seen as strongly embedded in traditional cultural practices.

The chapter begins with a discussion of the concept of indigenous self-determination in the context of recent developments in international law. It considers the importance and nature of indigenous political representative bodies as instruments for achieving indigenous aspirations for self-determination. In a second section, the chapter explores Weaver's differentiation of different models of indigenous representation (publicly funded pressure groups and government advisory bodies) considering the potential of each to provide a basis for self-determination. Subsequent sections then describe examples of indigenous representative bodies in a number of countries: Australia, Finland, Norway, Sweden, Canada, the US and New Zealand. In a concluding section Weaver's analysis of the different models of indigenous representation provides a basis for reflections on the comparative experiences of the indigenous representative bodies in the countries previously described. The final section stresses the importance of culturally appropriate political representation for the achievement of an authentic form of indigenous self-determination.

Indigenous aspirations for self-determination and political representation

The Declaration on the Rights of Indigenous Peoples was the product of a long process of deliberation and negotiation within the UN. It is important that indigenous representatives played a key role in its development (Stavenhagen 2009). The Declaration makes clear references to indigenous representation as one of the fundamental planks of the attainment of self-determination (see particularly Articles 18 and 19, 32). In this context it is worth considering what indigenous leaders mean by the term self-determination.

In some contexts, self-determination can be understood in a similar way to sovereignty as the exercise of exclusive political authority within a defined territory (Pritchard 1998: 8). However, many indigenous leaders specifically discount the relevance of this interpretation, especially any connotations it may imply about secession from the nation-state (Robbins 2011: 46). Indigenous Australian lawyer Larissa Behrendt, for example, writes of indigenous concepts of sovereignty encompassing 'a new relationship with the Australian state with increased self-government and autonomy, not through the creation of a new country' (2003: 102). This leads to a conceptualisation of self-determination as a shared form of sovereignty, in which indigenous people control a formal sphere of political authority within the framework of a single nation (O'Sullivan 2007: 4). Stavenhagen suggests that 'the right to self-determination should be interpreted as an internal right, that is, within the framework of an established independent state, especially where this state is democratic and respectful of human rights' (2009: 364–5). Nevertheless it would be wrong to understand indigenous peoples' rights to self-determination as an *inferior* form of self-determination. James Anaya, UN Special Rapporteur on the Situation of Human Rights and Fundamental Freedoms of Indigenous Peoples, argues that:

...[s]uch a notion, that *full* self-determination necessarily means a right to choose independent statehood, ultimately rests on a narrow state-centered vision of humanity and the world, that is, a vision of the world that considers the modern state – that institution of Western theoretical origin – as the most important and fundamental unit of human organization. This framework of thinking obscures the human rights character of self-determination, and it is blind to the contemporary realities of a world that is simultaneously moving towards greater interconnectedness and decentralization, a world in which the formal boundaries of statehood do not altogether determine the ordering of communities and authority (2009: 188–9).

This frequent willingness to work within the framework of a single nation does not mean that all indigenous scholars accept that their rights should be bestowed or assigned by the wider state within which they exist. Some argue that they should be seen as rights that are 'not merely derivative from the state, but rather are justified in relation to their own political theories and practices' (Ivison 2007: 615).

In the conceptualisation of indigenous self-determination as a form of shared sovereignty, the role of indigenous representative bodies becomes particularly important as a key component of institutional arrangements through which indigenous authority intersects with non-indigenous governance systems.

Weaver: a political analysis of national indigenous representative bodies

A good starting point for reflection on the nature of indigenous political representation is the work of Canadian social anthropologist Sally Weaver, who, in the 1980s, began a comparative study of the institutional arrangements through which indigenous peoples achieved a political voice in Canada, Australia and Norway (Weaver 1983a). Unfortunately this project was curtailed by her untimely death in 1993. Weaver identified a number of different models, ranging from government-appointed advisory bodies to publicly supported indigenous 'pressure groups' (Weaver 1983b). She linked the development of these organisations in the post-war era to a mobilisation of indigenous activists seeking the 'power to define themselves, the issues of importance to them, and the policies and programs governments dispensed' (1983a: 1).

In the 1980s, Weaver located the development of national indigenous representative bodies in Canada, Australia and Norway within a wider context of evolving colonial relationships. This approach is supported by Beckett, who pointed out that in the post-war era, world-wide attitudes to race were changing, influenced by social movements and the development of international human-rights instruments (Beckett 1987: 173–4). In this new global context of decolonisation, the relationship between the nation-state and indigenous minorities began to change in most western liberal democracies. In Beckett's view: '[t]he ideological constraints under which colonialism now ha[d] to work oblige[d] it to seek the consent of its clients, giving rise to the need for representation and a new kind of politics' (Beckett 1987: 17). Weaver also identified this period as the era when indigenous nationalism 'took firmer hold' and became identified with the goal of self-determination (Weaver 1993: 53). 'In short, they sought to establish a new political regime, one in which they were the architects of their own institutions' (1993: 54). While indigenous cultural and political identity was often localised and regional in character, Weaver suggests that activists, particularly from the younger generation, 'saw the need for national organizations to represent their interests to the nation-state because policies emanated from the national level, policies they were determined to influence' (1993: 55).

Weaver also addressed what she saw as the opportunities and challenges that shaped the effectiveness of the representative bodies that emerged in countries such as Australia and Canada. She argued that unprecedented demands for the introduction of indigenous self-determination (from both indigenous and non-indigenous pressure groups) challenged national governments, which had no prior experience of dealing with the rights-based claims of indigenous minorities. In this controversial political space, what Weaver called indigenous 'representivity' (perhaps best understood as the legitimate right to speak for a people) became a politically contested attribute that governments frequently challenged (1985: 120) When indigenous representative bodies were established in these two countries, indigenous 'representivity' became a political resource that governments attempted to manage or assign for their own purposes but which, at the same time, indigenous leaders could also manipulate in pursuit of their interests (Weaver 1985: 113–50). This is perhaps one of Weaver's most valuable insights.

Weaver emphasised that there was an important distinction between a publicly funded pressure group (that is, an indigenous-devised and -controlled organisation that might be supported by government funding) and a government advisory body, defined and legitimated by government (1983b: 106). She believed that the more autonomous pressure groups were 'more powerful instruments than advisory bodies because they provide Aboriginals the opportunity to broker their own internal differences and define their common "interests" ... and because they facilitate independent and more effective political action by Aboriginals' (1983b: 106). However Weaver acknowledged the problems faced by independent indigenous representative bodies: without stable resourcing it is very difficult to develop and articulate policy positions or political strategies or even to effectively communicate with constituents through travel and meetings (1983b: 107). This is particularly pertinent in countries of vast size such as Australia and Canada, in which the 'tyranny of distance' can create a frustrating obstacle to consultation involving remote communities.

The key points that can be drawn from Weaver's body of work are that she believed that crucial determinants of the capacity of indigenous representative bodies to achieve their political agendas for self-determination are the level of independence of the representative body (especially its ability to define and control the process of representation): the efficacy of the body's relationship to government and to its indigenous constituents; and the adequacy of its resources and administrative support (1983b). These issues are still relevant today and can be used as the basis of a useful critique of the development of national indigenous representative bodies in the last forty years.

Institutions of indigenous political representation

Australia

At the national level, Australia has experimented with a number of different forms of indigenous representative bodies since the 1970s and a new body, the National Congress of Australia's First Peoples (NCAFP) has recently been created. This long-standing commitment to the principle of indigenous representation belies what Weaver, in the 1990s, believed to be the institutionalised 'practice of government intervention and control of national political organizations for Aboriginals' (1993: 70).

Historically, Australian indigenous people experienced some of the worst policies of race-based exclusion from the privileges of citizenship. Under the historical control of the state governments, most indigenous people lived as 'citizens without rights' (Chesterman and Galligan 1997) for the first half of the twentieth century, subject to intrusive and paternalistic controls that limited their freedom of movement and excluded them from most of the developing civil, political and social rights extended to other citizens. This affected their right to political participation, both directly and indirectly. Restrictions on indigenous voting were not completely removed until the 1960s. This history of formal race-based exclusion from political representation makes an interesting backdrop to the development of special indigenous representative bodies from the 1970s onwards.

The National Aboriginal Consultative Committee (NACC)

In the late 1960s and early 1970s, an indigenous political movement emerged based primarily on demands for the recognition of land rights. In the national election of 1972, the Australian Labor Party won office after more than two decades of government by the Liberal Coalition parties. The new Prime Minister, Gough Whitlam, was committed to an agenda of Aboriginal development, including recognition of land rights and the promise of an indigenous representative body (Robbins 2011: 49). The new government called this policy 'self-determination' and in many ways it was the beginning of a new era.

The national ALP government was in power for a relatively short time but, nevertheless, began a number of important initiatives that changed the foundations of race relations in Australia. One of the most important of these was the creation of the National Aboriginal Consultative Committee (NACC), the first elected national indigenous representative body. The NACC consisted of 41 representatives, directly elected by indigenous voters (Weaver 1983b: 3). The government made grandiose statements about political autonomy that raised indigenous expectations about the role that was intended for this indigenous body (Robbins 1994: 128–30). Unfortunately, these hopes were not to be realized: the government was quite unprepared for the scale of demands made by the elected representatives and the relationship soon turned sour as the national Minister attempted to limit the NACC's ambitions and impose on it the role of an advisory body (Robbins 1994: 157–62). The NACC declared that it wished to become a 'Congress', take over the national Aboriginal Affairs budget and make the Department into its secretariat (Robbins 1994: 159). This was beyond anything the government had envisaged and its relationship with the NACC fell into chaos and acrimony. In Weaver's assessment, this was an attempt to become an independent political authority, independent of government, a type of publicly funded pressure group (Weaver 1983b: 3). Inevitably, in these circumstances the NACC made little headway with any policy proposals and, by the time the Whitlam ALP government fell from power at national level, it had achieved few lasting gains.

The National Aboriginal Conference (NAC)

The Fraser Coalition government that followed was more aware of the potential tensions in establishing a representative body. After an inquiry, the NACC was disbanded and, in its place, a new body was established. The National Aboriginal Conference (NAC) was also elected but its responsibilities were carefully defined and controlled by government. It was to be an advisory body with limited resources and no statutory basis, so its continuing existence depended on ministerial approval. It had no right of access to the Minister, who could refer matters to it as he/she saw fit (Robbins 1994: 198). During this era the national government failed to refer many contentious indigenous policy issues to the NAC for advice. Given this history, it is not surprising that Weaver saw the NAC as weak and ineffective, a structure 'designed to reflect and serve government values and purposes, not those of Aboriginals' (Weaver 1983b: 106).

A new Labor (ALP) national government in 1983 initially suggested restructuring the organisation. However, government support quickly evaporated when factional dysfunction in the NAC was highlighted by differences of opinion about what its role should be (Weaver 1993: 60–3). The NAC engaged in public criticism of the ALP government's land-rights proposals, exacerbating a difficult policy controversy (Beresford 2006: 197–206). The Minister issued instructions for it to be closed down on 30 June 1985. Its former chairman's views were voiced in a press release in the same year:

> The NAC was created as window dressing to placate critics of Australia's treatment of Aboriginal people. Quite deliberately it was never provided with the funding or the recognition needed to ensure it operated effectively and efficiently … it was because the NAC had maintained an independent stand in the face of Government threats and bullying that it was disbanded (Riley 1985).

Aboriginal and Torres Strait Islander Commission (ATSIC)

In 1987, a completely new portfolio structure was announced, which rewrote the model of indigenous representation in Australia. The Aboriginal and Torres Strait Islander Commission (ATSIC) was an extraordinary departure from what had been in place before – not only did it incorporate elected regional councils and a national board of Commissioners but it was also given executive powers, in that it took over the national portfolio budget responsibilities from the Department of Aboriginal Affairs. In other words ATSIC became responsible for spending that portion of the Commonwealth budget on indigenous programmes that had formerly been controlled by the national minister. It is important to note that this was not the full range of indigenous expenditure carried out by all government agencies – but approximately 50 per cent (Rowse 2002: 183). At the same time, ATSIC was tightly accountable to government – deliberately so. Not only did the minister have the power to approve its financial decisions but an internal office of evaluation and audit, which reported directly to the minister, was incorporated into ATSIC's structure (Robbins 2011: 52–3). Parliament was assured that 'there is no other department or statutory authority in existence in the Commonwealth which will be as accountable as the Aboriginal and Torres Strait Islander Commission' (Hand 1989: 2734).

ATSIC was a strange combination – a government-designed organisation that was intended to deliver both strong accountability to government and self-determination for indigenous peoples. It is not surprising that ATSIC had a troubled and controversial history and struggled to satisfy the competing demands of its electorate and the government. Coe, for example, argued that the boundaries of regional councils were inappropriate for the traditional lands of indigenous nations and tribes – 'so that we are treated as a group of individuals within Australian society, as opposed to a collection of distinct, separate societies within Australia' (Coe 1994: 36). This is not to dismiss ATSIC lightly – there were many important achievements over the one and a half decades of its existence. Perhaps one of the most important was its status as an NGO in the UN and its enthusiastic participation in the development of an international indigenous movement. Many of the ATSIC regional councils used their capacity to fund local development projects in innovative ways to begin addressing the disadvantage of their people.

Yet there were frequent reminders of the ability of government to impose its decisions on ATSIC – in the 1995 budget, ATSIC was stripped of responsibility for health programmes, for example (Tickner 2001: 298–301). Perhaps the most serious challenge to ATSIC came with the election of the Coalition government in 1996. Under the leadership of Prime Minister John Howard, the policy of self-determination was abandoned and a 'special auditor' was appointed by the Minister, John Herron, to examine and control ATSIC's funding decisions. ATSIC mounted a legal challenge which eventually led to the Federal Court's decision that the Minister had exceeded his powers in the Act (Ivanitz 2000: 7) This acrimonious beginning to the relationship between the Howard national government and ATSIC set the tone for long period of disputation that eventually led to ATSIC's termination.

The Prime Minister, John Howard, had strong personal views about indigenous rights – he believed in the primacy of national unity and a common identity, assessing differentiated indigenous institutions as a threatening 'separatism' (Bradfield 2006: 80). He had opposed the creation of ATSIC back in 1989 and had committed his party to its termination (Howard 1989: 1328).

ATSIC's agenda of achieving a treaty and its criticism of government policy, particularly in international forums such as the United Nations, antagonised the government (Zifkac 2003: 38). From 1999, with the election of Geoff Clark as chairman of ATSIC, relations deteriorated even further; he pursued an activist agenda of indigenous rights that did not sit easily with the government's own policy of 'practical reconciliation' – an emphasis on improvements in indigenous socio-economic outcomes (Pratt 2003: 7). Clark was the first elected chairman – previously, government had appointed the position. When Clark became embroiled in a number of court cases about his personal behaviour, the government moved to suspend him from office (Robbins 2004). Eventually, none of these cases against the chairman were upheld by the court but the controversy cast ATSIC in an unfavourable light and this lost it crucial public support. In the Australian Parliament, this led to a decisive decision by the leader of the opposition, Mark Latham. He declared that he supported the closure of ATSIC and recommended its replacement with a reformed body on the grounds that it had 'lost the confidence of much of its own constituency and the wider community' (cited in *ATSIC News* 2004: 6). The government moved immediately to abolish ATSIC, despite the recommendations of a review it had commissioned, which recommended restructuring ATSIC to strengthen the regional councils (Hannaford, Huggins and Collins 2003). The Prime Minister attempted to draw a line under the idea of indigenous representative bodies by declaring that 'the experiment in separate representation, elected representation for indigenous people has been a failure' (cited in *ATSIC News* 2004: 4). ATSIC's portfolio responsibilities were relocated in mainstream government agencies and an appointed indigenous body (the National Indigenous Council) was set up to advise government on policy decision.

The termination of ATSIC was greeted with mixed reactions. For many it had never fulfilled its promise of providing indigenous people with a real level of political autonomy. For others, it was too radical and represented a dangerous form of separatism with the potential to damage national unity and identity. ATSIC was always faced with impossible tensions of reconciling accountability to government and to its indigenous electors. Many believed that its joint responsibility for service-delivery and policy and monitoring were an impossible combination (Behrendt, Cunneen and Libesman 2009: 293). Prominent indigenous leader Noel Pearson reflected that ATSIC was set up to be 'an Indigenous-affairs ghetto away from the main game' (2007: 367). These difficulties may explain its poor voter turnout, although it is also possible that the lack of compulsory voting requirements in ATSIC elections influenced voter-turnout in a country in which parliamentary elections involve compulsory voting.

The National Congress of Australia's First Peoples (NCAFP), 2009

In 2007 the Coalition government lost power and a new ALP government was established with a new approach to indigenous policy. The Prime Minister, Kevin Rudd, formally announced Australia's endorsement of the Declaration on the

Rights of Indigenous Peoples in April 2009, retreating from Australia's original opposing vote in the UN (McQuire 2009).

The ALP government established a process to set up a new representative body that has taken a very different form to its predecessors. Firstly, the government invited the Australian Human Rights Commission's Aboriginal and Torres Strait Islander Commissioner for Social Justice to set up a steering committee of indigenous representatives to propose a model. This was to be an indigenous-controlled body, designed through a process of indigenous consultation. However, the government did set some guidelines of its own that set parameters for the indigenous proposal:

- The Government would not create another ATSIC;
- There should not necessarily be separate elections for the body;
- The body would have urban, regional and remote representation (FaHCSIA 2008: 1).

The new institution that was proposed after the consultations was a radical departure from the past. Rather than being a government statutory authority or portfolio body, NCAFP is incorporated as a company. Unlike previous representative bodies, which were chosen on the basis of individual voting in geographical regions, NCAFP has three categories of membership – peak organisations and national body members; other indigenous organisations and experts; private individuals and community members. These members are organised in three 'Chambers', each of which is represented by delegates at the National Congress. In the case of individual members (Chamber 3) delegates to the National Congress are appointed by the National Board. The National Board is appointed by the National Congress and has male and female co-chairs (AHRC 2009a: 3–4). A unique feature of this body is the Ethics Committee, which has responsibility for overseeing the activities of the company and must 'apply a merit based process and diligence test to the National Congress and National Executive candidates' (AHRC 2009a: 3). One might speculate that this 'ethics monitoring' is an attempt to overcome the bad press attracted by past leadership in previous representative bodies.

In explaining the new model, the Steering Committee acknowledged a number of tensions that needed to be balanced: the first relates to representation and the need to achieve 'political legitimacy' whilst at the same time being 'streamlined, cohesive and expert' (AHRC 2009b: 18). A second tension identified by the Steering Committee is its relationship with government – how to be independent but still influential? This is one of the issues highlighted by Weaver as a crucial determinant of effectiveness. The NCAFP has made a calculated choice and has opted for independence as a company, which places it more firmly in the category Weaver called a 'pressure group' rather than that of a formal advisory group. One of the main challenges for the NCAFP is whether it will be capable of asserting the level of political autonomy and influence that is desired. One important detail will be its ability to raise funding independently – it has only a modest amount of establishment funding from government and then it is expected to become independent, relying on 'partnerships with business, industry and philanthropic bodies to fund its work' (Jopson, 2010: 1). Of course, the biggest question is whether government will respond in the manner desired by the NCAFP and enter into a co-operative and consultative relationship on matters of indigenous policy.

This history of indigenous representative bodies in Australia shows only too clearly the impact of the issues identified by Weaver. The NACC, NAC and ATSIC were creations of government rather than organic expressions of indigenous political initiative. Each was defined, controlled and bound to government by imposed accountability, resourced by government and, ultimately, unilaterally dismissed without any consultation or consent from the indigenous population. These circumstances appear to fall significantly short of the standards expressed in the Declaration on the Rights of Indigenous Peoples. The new NCAFP is a much more independent body but it has yet to make its mark.

The Nordic countries

Like Australia, the Nordic countries of Norway, Sweden and Finland have indigenous populations that challenge their governments with their agenda for political recognition. Commonly used estimates that there are 70,000–100,000 Sámi in Norway, 15,000–20,000 in Sweden, 6,500 in Finland and 2,000 in the Kola Peninsula of Russia (Henriksen 1999: 24) are now considered to be vastly inaccurate (see Pettersen 2011). There are differences between each of the countries in the way Sámi are eligible for voting and there are not always reliable processes, such as censuses, to identify exactly who is a Sámi (Lehtola 2010: 10). Pettersen argues that 'it is not possible to provide precise answers to any questions about the number, distribution or composition of the Sámi people', as there is no institution responsible for systematic data-collection (2011: 187).

The Sámi have lived in these regions for thousands of years (Solbakk 2006: 14) and, over time, their populations have become divided by the boundaries established by the expansion of modern nation-states (Lantto 2010). From the mid nineteenth century, Sámi were increasingly subjected to assimilationist policies, especially in Norway, where their religion was suppressed and their leaders persecuted (Olsson and Lewis 1995: 149–58). This led many Sámi to abandon their language and cultural practices (Josefsen 2011: 33). In the early twentieth century, the establishment of small, local Sámi organisations in Norway and Sweden signalled a nascent political movement. An important development took place in 1906, when Isak Saba became the first Sámi member of the Norwegian Parliament. This Sámi leader stood as a Labour Party candidate but was elected 'largely on the basis of a Sámi election programme and as a result of a Sámi mobilization' (Josefsen, Mörkenstam and Saglie 2015: 36). In 1956, another significant event took place: the founding of the Nordic Sámi Council to represent the indigenous populations of Norway, Sweden and Finland (Beach 1994: 187). This body became an important focus for Sámi political activism, both in domestic issues and in international forums, and it was a participant in the development of the Declaration on the Rights of Indigenous Peoples in the UN (Henriksen 1999: 28). In 1992, the Russian Sámi joined the organisation which then became known as the Sámi Council (*Sámiraddi*). It is funded by the Nordic Council of Ministers (Josefsen 2001: 78).

The success of the Sámi Council in promoting Sámi political interests has been complemented by the development of national representative bodies in Finland, Norway and Sweden. Each will be considered briefly in turn and key characteristics will be discussed.

Finland

Finland was the first of the group of nations to establish a Sámi Parliament. This emerged from two Sámi organisations' attempts, in the 1940s, to protect cultural traditions and livelihoods, especially concerning the needs of reindeer-herders (Beach 1994: 194). A Commission was set up to investigate the question and its recommendations eventually led to the establishment of what was originally called the Sámi Delegation in 1973, by presidential decree (Solbakk 2006: 210). This name was intended to emphasise that it had no legislative mandate (Nyyssönen 2011: 86).

In 1995, the Finnish government recognised the Sámi as an indigenous people in its constitution, guaranteeing cultural and language protection as well as self-determination within their homeland (Vars 2008: 69). Additionally, new legislation was enacted to provide a statutory basis for the Sámi Parliament (*Sámediggi*) and extend its jurisdiction (Solbakk 2006: 216). Voting is open to anyone who is defined as a Sámi on the basis of being able to speak Sámi or has a parent or grandparent who speaks Sámi as a first language. Some controversy has arisen about the manner in which the Finnish Sámi electoral register is controlled by the Sámi Parliament. Joona provides evidence of inconsistencies in the treatment of applications, even between members of the same family (2012: 158–64). Seurujärvi-Kari suggests that the Sámi Parliament's position is intended to prioritise the protection of Sámi language and culture, rather than descent alone (2011: 51). This is a particularly sensitive issue as Sámi identity is seen in Finland as 'closely connected to and … dependent on whether a person is registered or not' (Joona 2012: 164). It suggests that the Sámi register is not a comprehensive list of Sámi cultural membership in Finland, just as similar registers in Norway and Sweden are not seen as defining Sámi ethnicity.

Voting takes place by direct elections for nominated candidates, without any party affiliations (Solbakk 2006: 210–18). The Sámi Parliament is intended to perform the function of an advisory body to government on economic, cultural and social issues that affect the Sámi (Robbins 2011: 60). However the legislation did not confer the right for the Sámi Parliament to make recommendations to government, unlike the previous Sámi Delegation (Nyyssönen 2011: 87).

While on the face of it, these political gains seem to provide significant levels of political influence, many Sámi analysts deprecate the Finnish state's recognition of Sámi rights. Nyyssönen argues that Finland's political culture is essentially egalitarian and this tends to make 'special rights for Sámi appear as an encroachment on the rights of other groups and those of other Finnish citizens, and thus against the dogma of equality' (2011: 89). As a result, constitutional provisions have not resulted in the recognition of Sámi rights to the extent that might be expected. The obstacles to Sámi advancement can be subtle – often they take the form of bureaucratic obstruction of Sámi policy agendas, preference for other interest groups and the limitation of resources on the basis of financial stringency (Nyyssönen 2011). Eriksson claims that co-option of Sámi activists into conservative bureaucracies stifled independent political activism (cited in Josefsen 2001: 79). As Nyyssönen puts it, 'the Sámi in Finland, enveloped by institutionalized political structures, found themselves entrapped in bureaucratic dysfunctions and official Finnish ambivalence' (2011: 87). As a result, the Finnish Sámi Parliament has limited independence and, in practice, acts more in the role of a broker or negotiator between the Finnish Parliament and the Sámi people, rather than exercising self-determination in its own right as a partner with the government (Robbins 2011: 61).

Norway

The Norwegian Sámi were subject to assimilation policies which lasted from the middle of the nineteenth to the middle of the twentieth centuries. Many Sámi lost their language and identity during this period (Josefsen 2011: 33). In the 1950s, a cultural movement began to develop that challenged the view that Sámi were integrated into mainstream society and this led, in 1964, to the appointment of an 'expert' Sámi Council to advise the government on Sámi issues (Solbakk 2006: 172). In the late 1970s and 1980s, an issue arose that is commonly seen as a turning point in terms of Sámi political ethno-genesis. This was the Norwegian government's decision to dam the Alta River for a hydroelectric power station, with a proposed loss of Sámi reindeer pasture and a village (Robbins 2011: 62). The subsequent high-profile political protest saw Sámi activists confronting the police and making a case for recognition of their rights in terms that had never been heard before in Norway. Although the dam went ahead on a revised plan that saved the village, the protest it sparked had a lasting legacy – the mobilisation of Sámi leaders and the evolution of a new sense of political identity on the one hand, and a growing government awareness of the entitlements of an indigenous minority on the other (Josefsen 2011: 33).

The Alta dam protests coincided with a public debate about indigenous rights under international law that was taking place in Norway. According to Minde (2003: 89) a public report asserting that Sámi are an indigenous people helped to change public perceptions. The government set up a Sámi Rights Commission in 1980 to investigate the situation of the indigenous minority in the light of its international treaty obligations. This led, in time, to the establishment of a national representative body and an amendment to the Norwegian constitution. In 1988, a new clause was added to the constitution: 'It is the obligation of the State authorities to create the conditions necessary for the Sámi to protect and develop their language, their culture and their society' (Nettheim, Meyers and Craig 2002: 215).

The Sámi Parliament or *Sámediggi* was created on a statutory basis in 1987 and was opened by the King in 1989. It consists of 39 representatives elected by Sámi voters in seven electorates, using a proportional representation system and with elections held concurrently with the general Norwegian parliamentary elections. Voting is optional but voters must be identified as Sámi (Josefsen 2011: 33–4; Robbins 2010). Eligibility to register on the Sámi electoral roll is on the basis of self- identification as a Sámi, plus a parent, grandparent or great-grandparent who spoke Sámi or a parent registered on the Sámi roll. The number of registered Sámi voters is increasing and there are currently nearly 14,000 on the list; however, ambiguities persist about the relationship between the register and the true size of the Sámi population (Pettersen, this volume).

The candidates for election are organised in 'lists' for this purpose on the basis of party or association allegiance. After the representatives are chosen, they elect, in turn, an executive council and president. Voting turnout is generally good, with a rate of 72 per cent in 1997; however, this was lower than the Norwegian turnout for the general Parliamentary elections. (Hætta 2008: 75). In contrast to Australia, where party affiliations have not entered the indigenous representative bodies, they are embedded in the Norwegian Sámi Parliament. Mainstream parties such as Labour have a Sámi section while other parties are based on Sámi organisations such as the Norwegian Sámi Association (NSR) or regional interests. The NSR was the dominant party in the *Sámediggi* until 2007, when the Sámi Labour party was able to form a governing coalition (Josefsen 2011: 34).

It is interesting to consider the impact of this development on the capacity of the Sámi Parliament to represent the diverse views and interests of its Sámi constituents (*see* Bergh and Saglie, Chapter 8). Weaver argues that representation can be as much a problem for indigenous delegates as it is for government (Weaver 1985). In political theory, one of the functions performed by political parties is to offer competing policy platforms to the electorate. This function may be as relevant to indigenous voters as it is to the wider electorate and, as a result, political parties may help provide a more effective channel of communication in making voting choices.

In 2008 the Sámi Parliament's budget was around NOK 306 million, with approximately two-thirds of this ring-fenced for use on designated programmes such as language-support, cultural activities and Sámi industry development. Tasks may also be delegated by the Norwegian Parliament (Josefsen 2011: 34). Over time, there have been significant expansions in the role of the Sámi Parliament, which have, arguably, transformed its role from an advisory body to one in which it has expanded functions of decision-making. This has taken place through transfer of responsibility by the Norwegian government but also, according to Josefsen, because 'the Sámi Parliament became a vehicle for producing new perspectives on Sámi rights and transforming these into political demands' (2011: 36). In this way, she argues, the Sámi Parliament has capitalised on the opportunities it was given for consultation and has transformed them into new responsibilities.

A good example of this is the process leading up to the creation of the Finnmark Estate Board – an authority which now manages the land that comprises the Finnmark Estate, part of the Finnmark Region in the north. This is an area with a strong Sámi tradition, although the Sámi have become a demographic minority (Josefsen 2011: 37), at least in terms of self-identification, although not necessarily by descent. The Sámi Parliament played a crucial role in the process that led to the legislation, including an unprecedented level of consultation in the development of the Act by the Norwegian Parliament's Justice Committee (Smith 2011: 27). The legislation that was enacted gave the Sámi Parliament control of half the seats on the management board of the Finnmark Estate (Josefsen 2011: 38). Through a relationship of dialogue and growing trust, the Norwegian Sámi Parliament appears to have had some success in evolving a co-operative partnership with government. This has been consolidated with a 2005 agreement between the Norwegian and Sámi parliaments that explicitly gives Sámi the right to be consulted on matters that affect them (Smith 2011: 27). Despite this, the political authority of other Sámi organisations, especially those based on reindeer-herding and other sectoral interests, is also acknowledged by the Norwegian government, which has stated that it 'may also be obliged to consult with other Sámi interests in addition to the Sámediggi' (Norwegian Ministry of Labour and Social Inclusion 2008). The Sámi Parliament's status is contested within the Sámi community (Semb 2005: 534), despite its developing political influence.

Sweden

Like the other Nordic countries, Sweden has established a Sámi representative body. However, its authority as a representative voice is weak, with many Sámi choosing to express their views through other means. This has been explained as the result of past government policies that defined only reindeer-herders as Sámi and thus created a rift between groups of Sámi (Josefsen 2001: 82). Government policy emphasised segregation for reindeer-herder groups but assimilation for other Sámi (Josefsen 2001: 181). In the past, through a series of measures originating with the Reindeer Grazing Act of 1886, reindeer-herding Sámi were required to live a traditional nomadic life or lose their Sámi status (Mörkenstam 2005: 438–9). Importantly, this legislation also effectively converted any individual land-ownership into collective grazing rights (Lantto and Mörkenstam 2008: 30). A specific government body was established to take responsibility for Sámi matters: the Lapp Administration (*see* Lantto and Mörkenstam, Chapter 6). Historically Sámi had been subjected to formal discrimination, especially in relation to state housing loans, but, by the 1950s, this was largely removed (Solbakk 2006: 191). Nevertheless, old policies leave their legacies and many of the most contested political issues centre around the rights of reindeer-herders.

Swedish Sámi activism began in the early years of the twentieth century, largely as protests against the restrictions of the Reindeer Grazing Acts, but soon adapted into 'a more organized ethno-political mobilization' on the basis of ethnic identity

(Lantto and Mörkenstam, this volume). In the 1950s, the formation of the first national Sámi organisation in Sweden was a turning point. The National Union of Swedish Sámi (SSR) focussed largely on the protection of reindeer-herders' interests in its initial campaigns (Lantto and Mörkenstam 2008: 33–7); but later, in the 1960s, this was modified to embrace a broader and more inclusive concept of Sámi cultural diversity (*see* Lantto and Mörkenstam, Chapter 6).

The high-profile Tax Mountains Case initiated by the SSR (originally submitted in the 1960s) was a test of Swedish Sámi land rights; the Swedish Supreme Court dismissed the case. A further investigation of the case in the 1980s eventually led to a Sámi Rights Report, which resulted in the establishment of the Sámi Parliament in 1993 (Robbins 2011: 64–5).

The Swedish Sámi Parliament has a single electoral district and voting is open to Sámi who identify themselves as Sámi and speak Sámi themselves or have a parent or grandparent who did (Solbakk 2006: 195). However, its role as an advisory body to government is emphasised by the fact that the government appoints its chair (the only full time member of the Sámi Parliament), albeit on the recommendation of the Sámi Parliament. The 31 elected members meet three times a year in plenary sessions and on a day to day basis business of the Sámi Parliament is carried out by an elected Board or executive (Josefsen 2005: 197). The government has laid out the responsibilities of the Sámi Parliament, which are, essentially, to support language and culture. Its autonomy is strictly limited – the government prohibits it from acting as 'an organ of self-rule' (Josefsen 2001: 174). It is widely regarded as a government agency rather than a political voice for the Sámi people (Vars 2008: 70). Moreover, it has serious structural problems – it is hard to get attendance at plenary meetings and the relationship between the Board and the general assembly (the plenary meetings) is dysfunctional, principally because the role of the Board is not clearly specified (Hætta 2008: 78) and tensions have emerged when the Board has failed to put forward the views of the majority of the plenary (Josefsen 2005: 197–8). However, there are also some factors which might suggest a potentially more positive view: Lantto and Mörkenstam (this volume) cite increasing number of votes in recent elections (although percentage turnout is down), together with an increased number of people on the Sámi register. Overall, though, the Swedish Sámi Parliament is severely compromised as an authoritative voice in its role as a national representative body and it has been accused of becoming a 'structural obstacle to Sámi self-determination' (Lawrence and Mörkenstam 2012: 207).

Canada

The political status of indigenous Canadian First Nations has been shaped by a very different colonial history. From the seventeen to early nineteenth centuries, British colonial powers accepted the need to negotiate treaties with the peoples of North America, acknowledging their right to govern themselves (Russell 2005: 171–2). This was acknowledged in the Royal Proclamation of 1736, which declared: 'Possession of such Parts of Our Dominions and Territories as not having been ceded to or purchased by us are reserved to them' (cited in Russell 2005: 172). However, Russell points out that the Royal Proclamation assumed, at the same time, that sovereignty over indigenous lands lay with the British Crown (2005: 172). Not all the indigenous peoples who now live within the Canadian nation negotiated treaties but, in many ways, the existence of treaties has provided a context that has shaped the broad direction of modern Canadian policy towards its indigenous peoples.

In later eras, under domestic Canadian rule, governments assumed control of the 'internal affairs' of First Nations peoples and tried to assimilate them (Russell 2005: 173). The main legislative tool for this purpose was the Indian Act of 1876, which, amongst other things, defined Indian status (Maaka and Fleras 2005: 160). It was this legislation that expanded the reserve system and provided for Indian Band governance (Nettheim, Meyers and Craig 2002: 83). Under the Indian Act, self-government as a lived experience was a sham: the government defined who was an Indian and who could access reservation-based services. Aboriginal people were unable to vote in federal elections until 1960 (Maaka and Fleras 2005: 189), even though it was the federal government that had constitutional responsibility for Aboriginal policy. Imai describes this as 'a dark century when government policy was aimed at destroying their cultures and taking away their lands', an experience common to indigenous populations in Australia, New Zealand and the United States (2009: 287).

The National Indian Brotherhood (NIB)

In 1969, a turning point came as a result of what initially appeared to be a final adversity and led to what Weaver called a 'new paradigm' in Aboriginal policy: from 'preoccupation with law, formality, and control' to 'justice, adaptation and workable inter-cultural relations' (1990: 15). The catalyst was a government White Paper on Indian Policy that proposed to terminate the Indian Act, transfer responsibility for Aboriginal issues to the provinces and withdraw Indian reserves and special services. The philosophy behind this was to 'reintegrate by desegregating' (Maakas and Fleras 2005: 190) – in other words, assimilation. First Nations leaders reacted angrily – they wanted change but not of this kind. The White Paper stimulated a national surge of First Nations' political activity intended to achieve recognition of their unique status as indigenous peoples.

In 1966, the federal Indian Affairs branch had set up an Indian Advisory Board comprising First-Nations-appointed delegates from regional advisory boards. This body lacked support amongst First Nations communities as it was not seen as accountable to grassroots views and it was expected to follow a government agenda. Dissatisfaction with the government advisory bodies was widespread and, when a small amount of government funding was made available, regional organisations were set up. The National Indian Brotherhood (NIB) emerged as the national voice of a loose federation of bodies over a period from 1968–70 (Weaver 1985: 122–3; 125–7). In the ensuing debates, the government changed its approach to one that was more cognisant of indigenous demands for self-determination (Maakas and Fleras 2005: 190).

In the 1980s, Weaver described the record of the NIB and its presidents as 'persistently outspoken critics of government policy', noting that, despite its modest funding from Ottawa, it appeared to have a strongly independent base. Indeed, in her view, its position was often too radical for some of the more conservative First Nation leaders and this led to doubts that it was truly representative. It often had difficulty persuading its member organisations to follow its advice and struggled to find the resources to prepare submissions and responses to government policy positions. On the government side, officials were distrustful of the NIB's claim to represent all First Nations interests and they routinely consulted directly with other organisations that did not participate in the NIB. (Weaver 1985: 126–9).Yet, on other occasions, especially if it wanted endorsement of a particular initiative, government would accept the NIB's credentials. In this way, Weaver argued, 'the government assigne[d] representivity to the NIB on the basis of its own self-interest' (1985: 129).

Assembly of First Nations

By 1978, First Nations leaders were keen to create a new structure to represent their political interests more effectively, with an executive more accountable to grassroots membership. Important momentum for change came from the government's announcement that it was embarking on a process of constitutional reform by 'repatriating' the constitution from Britain (Weaver 1985: 134). A major concern of First Nations peoples was that the recognition of their special status would be lost in this process (AFN, no date). Another challenge came with an announcement that the Indian Act would be reviewed. A central concern here was a new government emphasis on empowerment of local and regional Band organisations, rather than the national level (Maaka and Fleras 2005: 191). In response to these new developments, the NIB underwent a major transformation in 1982 – renamed the Assembly of First Nations, it brought together the leaders or chiefs of First Nations regional governments. The NIB now became a secretariat that supported the assembly. The strength of this new arrangement was the direct link from local to national level and the improved breadth of its representation. (AFN, no date). In 1978, it represented 573 chiefs (Weaver 1992: 114); however, it should be noted that it did not represent the Inuit or Métis.

The AFN played a major role in the constitutional debates that took place in 1980s. In a series of First Minister Conferences, AFN representatives discussed their interpretation of Aboriginal and treaty rights that are recognised and protected in section 35 (1) of the Canadian Constitution. Although the AFN was unable to convince the provincial and federal governments to entrench recognition of the inherent right of First Nations to self-government in the constitution, they were, nevertheless, successful in preserving the existing treaty and Aboriginal rights against fierce opposition from several provincial governments (AFN, no date). Some years later, in 1992, agreement was eventually reached on a proposal for entrenching the 'inherent right to Aboriginal self-government' (the Charlottetown Accord), but this was defeated in a public referendum (Walters 2009: 33). Despite this setback, many gains have been made politically – in 1995 the government accepted the principle of Aboriginal self-determination and adopted a framework of modern treaty-making as a means to negotiate this with First Nations representatives (Walters 2009: 33–4). Perhaps the most outstanding example of this is the creation of the new Canadian territory of Nunavut in 1999 by dividing the North West Territories, to give the Inuit population self-government in that region (Russell 2005: 180).

While the AFN has achieved considerable respect, there remain some questions about its role as a national representative body. Maddison points out that it only represents 'Status First Nations People' (that is, those recognised as Indians under the Act), not Inuit, Métis or non-status Indians; as a result, other representative bodies have proliferated (2010: 16). She raises questions about the funding of the AFN and suggests that that there is some evidence that the government has used the power of its purse to indicate its disapproval of the AFN. The Aboriginal representative bodies, on their part, express concern about the level of 'red tape and complexity that surrounded their funding agreements with government' (Maddison 2010: 18). Representation is a contested issue, too – the National Chief is elected by other chiefs rather than by Aboriginal voters at large. Maddison reports concerns that it operates as a chiefs' rather than a mass organisation. In some communities, the chief is chosen by the provisions of the Indian Act while in others the chief is simply the hereditary leader. Similarly, there is discussion around the current electoral arrangement of 'one chief, one vote, one tribal community, one vote' and consideration of the principle of proportional representation (2010: 19).

While these issues constitute serious concerns, especially the sectional focus of the AFN's representative base, it appears to have established a place for itself in the negotiating space between government and Aboriginal peoples of Canada and it seems to have the capacity for reflective development towards an improved role as a representative body.

The United States

The legal foundation of indigenous self-determination in the US is based on the recognition of the 'inherent sovereignty' (Richardson 2009: 53) of indigenous peoples. This was affirmed in a number of Supreme Court cases in the nineteenth century, which, in effect, while acknowledging the right of the federal government to control Indian nations, confirmed that the 'political authority of tribes is inherent since it derives from aboriginal sovereignty' (Harvard Project 2008: 38). This has been legally described as a 'domestic dependent nations' status (Imai 2009: 293) and is taken to mean that tribes retain authority to the extent that Congress does not act to curtail it.

As in Canada, Native American tribes have a mixed experience of treaty-making. Many treaties were signed with the British government prior to the

War of Independence and the practice was continued by the US government until 1871, when it was banned. Treaties were initially seen by Congress as a way of maintaining peaceable relationships with Indians. Gradually, with a firmer hold on the government of the nation from the 1830s onwards, Congress came to believe that the objective of Indian policy should be to remove indigenous people from key regions to facilitate the expansion of settlement (Richardson 2009: 59). This ushered in a dismal period of containment on reservations for many Native American tribes or, in some cases, such as the Sioux nations, a costly resistance. In 1887, the Dawes or General Allotment Act was intended 'to destroy Native American governments, privatise tribal land, and assimilate Indians into American society' (Richardson 2009: 63). It was argued that breaking up communal lands into private ownership would enable Native Americans to better integrate into local economies. In many cases, however, it brought great hardship and poverty: and, of course, it also made it easier for non-Indians to purchase land (Harvard Project 2008: 4).

By the 1920s, the condition of Native Americans had become so desperate that a national report blamed the government for the poor health and deplorable living conditions on many reservations. Congress responded with the Indian Reorganization Act of 1934, which favoured the re-establishment of tribal governance (Harvard Project 2008: 4). However, many of the processes of governance contained in the Act and foisted on tribal governments were far from traditional practices and this legacy persists today.

In the 1940s and 1950s federal policy swung back in favour of assimilation. Public Law 280, passed in 1953, allowed State governments to acquire jurisdiction over Native Americans and reservation lands, thus ending their special relationship with the federal government and ending their entitlement to assistance. More dramatically, under the policy of 'termination', the federal government began de-registering tribes as recognised entities and encouraging individuals to relocate to cities (Harvard Project 2008: 4). This was also designed to encourage assimilation and to reduce the level of federal government funding.

By the late 1950s, there was a growing public awareness of the parlous state of Indian reservations and in the 1960 presidential election both candidates supported a change in policy (Debo 1995: 405). This trend continued, with Lyndon Johnson declaring in 1968 that 'We must affirm the rights of the first Americans to remain Indians while exercising their rights as Americans. We must affirm their rights to freedom of choice and self-determination' (cited in Pevar 2004: 12). In a famous speech announcing the end of the termination policy in 1970, President Nixon recognised that the policy of assimilation was not working and advocated greater self-determination. President Reagan also confirmed the principle of self-determination: 'This administration intends to restore tribal governments to their rightful place among governments of this nation and to enable tribal governments, along with State and local governments, to resume control over their own affairs' (cited in Pevar 2004: 12). In effect, this launched a new era of tribal sovereignty, through 'contractual delegation of federal authority' (*see* Papillon, Chapter 4).

The National Congress of American Indians

The intrusive policies of the 1940s and 50s set the scene for a growing Indian political movement, fuelled by the evolving civil rights movement in the wider community. Self-determination became one of the most important political demands of Native American leaders. A number of representative bodies formed to articulate demands to government with a national voice; amongst them, the National Congress of American Indians (NCAI) stands out for its influence and longevity. It is important to recognise, however, that these organisations are not seen as potential mechanisms of governance in their own right, which is different to the role of bodies such as ATSIC in Australia or the Sámi parliaments. In the US, Native American self-determination is firmly understood to be based on local tribal governance.

The NCAI was originally established in 1944, at the time of the termination policies. It now represents over 250 member tribes (Wilkins and Stark 2011: 194). This is just under half of the number of registered tribes in the US (565) (Maddison 2010: 38). NCAI membership is restricted to Native Americans and recognised tribes with non-voting associate membership. Member tribes are allocated votes on the basis of the size of the tribe and choose delegates who represent tribal interests. All tribes have a representative on the Executive Council and, unlike in the AFN arrangements, this is not necessarily the chief (Maddison 2010: 35–6).

The NCAI has promoted an agenda of treaty rights and tribal sovereignty and has acted as a high-profile lobby group. The NCAI has also been prepared to support individual tribes with issues at local and regional level and has managed to steer a moderate pathway between the more extreme and conservative viewpoints of Indian leaders and to maintain a reasonable level of consensus. One of its most important roles is to support tribal governments in their efforts to establish appropriate bases for self-determination. This may mean engaging in lobbying activity or legal cases to support tribal rights; appearing at government inquiries; producing policy papers and submissions; and generally raising the profile of tribal authorities.

It has developed some innovative ways of achieving political influence. A good illustration is the 'native vote' campaign run by NCAI, which encourages American Indians to enrol and vote in general elections, reinforcing public perceptions of their political weight (Harvard Project 2008: 61). In recent years, NCAI has operated a State–Tribal Relations Initiative – a programme that 'educate[s] state government officials on tribal sovereignty' (Johnson 2008: 373). This can include training on Indian law and building relationships with tribes. NCAI offers technical assistance to state governments engaging in negotiation with tribal governments and 'offers model documents of state–tribal agreements that demonstrate effective solutions to issues surrounding law enforcement or welfare' (Johnson 2008: 374). This is part of a wider commitment to raising public awareness about Native American issues.

The NCAI faces a number of questions in its role as a national representative body. The first is the fact that not all tribes are members, including the largest tribe, the Navaho nation. According to Maddison, the Navaho 'maintain that they can represent their own interests more effectively than any organisation' (2010: 38). Despite this, the NCAI does not operate in a closed fashion but includes all tribes in its information-sharing. A further challenge is to maintain credibility as the united voice of enormously diverse tribes. It strives to achieve this by offering a forum in which consensus can be negotiated in the face of a common commitment to tribal authority and self-determination. Another concern is the balance between tribal interests and individual viewpoints. The practice of offering individual membership and voting rights has been an effective way to attract urban members into the organisation but the danger is that tribal government interests could be overwhelmed in the deliberations of the organisation. To counter this possibility, the NCAI has introduced a voting formula that ensures that tribal perspectives will be prioritised (Maddison 2010: 39–44).

One of the great strengths of the NCAI is its independent funding base. It receives the majority of its income from membership fees, with only a small amount from government. This is seen as an improvement from past practice, when the Bureau of Indian Affairs provided funding and was believed to use this as a tool for control (Maddison 2010: 42). In short, the NCAI is much closer in structure and practice to Weaver's concept of a representative body acting as a 'pressure group', with a much greater degree of autonomy from government than government-created bodies elsewhere.

Aotearoa New Zealand

Finally, it is worthwhile to consider a very different approach to establishing a national political voice for an indigenous minority – one that has been in place for over a century in Aotearoa New Zealand. Rather than creating a separate national representative body for the expression of Māori views, New Zealand has reserved Māori seats in the national Parliament.

The Treaty of Waitangi

The European settlement of Aotearoa New Zealand had a different style to that of its neighbour Australia in many important aspects. The original colonisation was not an act of imperial expansion: rather, it was 'an unplanned and scattered European (principally British) occupation' from the 1770s (Armitage 1995: 138). Māori society was organised into *hapu* and *iwi* (the equivalent of Native American bands and tribes) and political authority was localised. Disputes over land became common and were exacerbated by the introduction of muskets to the Māori, after which they not only used them against each other but also against the colonists. In this context, there was a push from missionaries, some Māori and the more reputable of the settlers to persuade the British government to set up a government and colonial administration 'to protect Māori from unscrupulous entrepreneurs' (Durie 2005: 14) In 1840, Captain William Hobson was sent to sign the Treaty of Waitangi on behalf of the British Crown. On the Māori side, more than 500 chiefs signed the Treaty (*te Tiriti o Waitangi*). Unfortunately the content of the Treaty has been the subject of continuous controversy ever since: the problem arises from the fact that there were two versions – a Māori one and an English one. The dispute is over the precise meaning of the words in each version. In the English version, Māori are described as ceding sovereignty to the Crown in return for the exclusive possession of their lands, forests, fisheries. In the Māori version, they agree to cede governance to the Crown but retain *tino rangatiratanga* (sovereignty) over their *taonga* (treasures) (Ruru 2009: 114). The Crown was given exclusive right to purchase land and the Māori were given the same status as British citizens living in Aotearoa New Zealand. From a Māori perspective, this was a power-sharing partnership but the British understanding was that the Crown had acquired a new colony (Fleras and Spoonley 1999: 13).

The Treaty proved to be no protection for Māori rights. With the introduction of self-government in 1853, settler interests became focused on land acquisition. Many Māori lost their land in coerced or fraudulent land deals and some was confiscated as a result of Māori protest. Without personal property, Māori were unable to vote, further adding to their marginalisation in the political arena. These tensions erupted in warfare in the 1860s, which lasted for many years. In 1862, the Native Lands Act established a court which began one of the most destructive phases of Māori policy. The court's aim was to transform Māori communal property rights to individual freeholds, which could be sold. (Ruru 2009: 117). By the turn of the century, Māori land-holdings were reduced to one-tenth of what they were at the time of the Treaty and fishing and mineral rights had been assumed by the Crown (Durie 2005: 14).

Māori parliamentary seats

In 1867, four Māori seats were created in the New Zealand Parliament, elected directly by Māori registered on a Māori electoral roll (Armitage 1995: 143). While modern Māori sentiment is to regard this as the expression of Māori political rights, the historical reasons for the measure were to limit Māori political participation to four designated seats (Ruru 2009: 118). This allocation of four seats for 40,000 to 50,000 Māori – compared to 72 general seats for 220,000 non-Māori – was patently unfair (Xanthaki and O'Sullivan 2009: 191). In 1876, it was decided that the seats should be extended indefinitely, largely because the settlers feared that they would be dramatically outvoted if Māori were accepted on to the general roll (Iorns Magallanes 2005: 109–110). As Fleras writes: 'Māori representation arose as a politically deceptive strategy of indirect control which co-opted the Māori population while simultaneously conveying the illusion of democratic power sharing' (1985: 558).

Over time, reforms have improved the political equality of Māori. From the 1930s, the political parties began to extend their electoral base to the Māori seats, drawing them into a wider political arena; in 1975, Māori were given the choice of joining either the general or the Māori roll (Iorns Magallanes 2005: 110). A notable change came with the general reform of the New Zealand electoral system by the Electoral Act of 1993. Initially, the recommendation of the Royal Commission on the issue was to disestablish the Māori seats on the grounds that it provided an unequal political base for Māori (Xanthaki and O'Sullivan 2009: 191). However, Māori protested loudly that this was 'an important symbol of their distinctive constitutional position as indigenous peoples' (Xanthaki and O'Sullivan 2009: 192). Accordingly, with the adoption of the Mixed Member Proportional (MMP) proportional representation system of voting in 1996, Māori seats have been made proportional to the number of Māori registered on the Māori roll. Under these arrangements, the number of Māori seats increased to five and subsequently to seven of the 120 seats in the parliament. MMP has provided Māori with political representation equal to their proportion of the population for the first time (Sullivan 2006: 611–2). Indeed, in 2005 election, Māori, who are 15 per cent of the population, won 17 per cent of the seats (Lloyd 2009: 6).

Assessing the political efficacy of designated parliamentary seats is not easy. Lloyd suggests that 'Māori seats have acquired, for Māori, a particular significance in relation to the Treaty of Waitangi. They have come to be seen as a means of recognition, and continued faith with the terms of, the Treaty' (Lloyd 2009: 7). In other words, there is an important symbolic value in the seats as an act of recognition. While this positive interpretation may be true in contemporary times, it is important to remember that for many years, the Māori seats arrangements restricted Māori political representation to a lower level than equity demanded.

Another question is whether a presence in parliament necessarily translates into political power? Some have argued that separating Māori seats from general seats could encourage non-Māori MPs to ignore Māori issues. There is also a view (especially valid in the years when Māori seats were restricted to four) that the numerical inequality of the Māori seats in parliament creates a 'political cul de sac' that entrenches Māori ineffectiveness in a system of majority rule (Fleras 1985: 566–7). However, the reforms to the New Zealand electoral system introduced a 'two-vote' arrangement that means that mainstream parties cannot afford to disregard Māori views because they need to attract their support on the 'party' vote (Xanthaki and O'Sullivan 2009: 195). In addition, where Māori MPs have become ministers, they have had genuine opportunity for decision-making. In 1972, Matiu Rata was appointed Minister of Māori Affairs in a Labour government and was able to implement sweeping changes to Māori language education and the promotion of a policy of bi-culturalism (Fleras 1985: 586). Xanthaki and O'Sullivan believe that the dual system of general and Māori electoral rolls overcomes an important problem: ' [t]he division of Māori voters between the Māori and the general electorates seems to maintain a difficult balance between inclusion of Māori in the general life of the state and recognition of their distinctiveness' (2009: 195).

Ultimately, it is not clear whether the dedicated Māori seats in the New Zealand Parliament have actually increased Māori political effectiveness over and above that which they might access through the mainstream electoral system. It is also important to understand Māori seats as one measure in a wider spectrum of significant gains in the recognition of Treaty rights and the implementation of greater measures of tribal autonomy and compensation. What is clear, however, is that this measure provides a means to express the inherent bi-culturalism of Aotearoa New Zealand as a nation and makes formal acknowledgement of the principles of the Treaty of Waitangi. This, for many Māori, is the real point.

Indigenous representation – a discussion of the issues

In the preceding accounts, a diverse range of approaches to indigenous political representation has been explored. The purpose of this inquiry is to examine the characteristics of these various models in the light of the entitlement of indigenous peoples to develop their own political arrangements that is expressed in the Declaration on the Rights of Indigenous Peoples. What has become clear is that contemporary practices of indigenous representation arise out of the specific historical and political context of each nation and are one factor in the ongoing negotiation of the colonial relationship between state and indigenous first nations.

In this chapter, only models of national indigenous representation have been considered. It is necessary to reiterate that this is not intended to discount the importance of other forms of representation at local or regional level as significant expressions of the indigenous right to self-determination. Many nation-states have developed layered approaches to indigenous self-government that can only be appropriately understood if considered in totality.

In the 1980s and 90s, Weaver identified a number of important issues that, in her view, presented challenges for indigenous peoples seeking to develop some form of political engagement with government in pursuit of their desire to achieve recognition of their inherent rights to self-determination (1983b; 1984; 1985; 1990; 1992; 1993). Weaver suggested that a number of tensions could be observed – in the level of autonomy and means of engagement of indigenous bodies with the institutions of the state, in the management of processes of representation and in the level and independence of funding and resources available. Each of these will now be discussed in turn.

Level of autonomy: Political engagement, representation and resourcing

Weaver compared the development of representative bodies in Australia and Canada and suggested that there were two main models that had emerged: one was a government-initiated advisory body and the other was a publicly funded pressure group (1983a; 1983b; 1993). It is not necessary to engage with the niceties of Weaver's definition here: rather, her important observation is that the nature of the relationship between the indigenous representative body and the state is an important determinant of the capacity of the representative body to act as a vehicle for indigenous political empowerment.

Where the state itself has initiated and defined the process of formation of an indigenous representative body for its own purposes (as in the development of the NAC in Australia), such a body may reflect the values and priorities of the state, rather than those of indigenous peoples themselves. In Weaver's words, this strategy runs the risk of 'fostering Aboriginal organizations in which neither [governments] nor Aboriginals have confidence' (1983b: 1). Government-designated indigenous representative bodies may also be vulnerable to dismissal or restructuring at the caprice of government. The Australian history of representative bodies reveals a tendency for representative bodies to be dismissed by unilateral decisions of government – NACC, NAC and ATSIC were all terminated without the agreement of the Aboriginal and Torres Strait populations.

A related issue is the willingness of the state to engage in meaningful consultation with indigenous representative bodies. As the Australian NAC discovered, it could be side-lined or simply not consulted on crucial issues because its role as an advisory body was designated by government. For this reason, indigenous minorities may seek to negotiate some legal or constitutional foundation to protect and embed their right to a political voice. This may involve constitutional confirmation of a general principle of their right to be consulted. In the case of Norway, the Sámi achieved an agreement with the Norwegian Parliament in 2005 that gives Sámi the right to be consulted on matters that affect them (Smith 2011: 27).

Evidence from the examples presented here indicates that indigenous minorities have sought to gain security and certainty in the relationship between the national representative bodies they have developed and the mainstream processes of government. Moreover, they seek to find ways to formalise and compel engagement on the part of relevant government authorities, either through their representative bodies or through other means – such as the Norwegian Sámi agreement mentioned above. The history of the Norwegian Sámi Parliament demonstrates that this can take place as a developmental process, with the evolution of a co-operative relationship between an indigenous representative body and government.

An alternative model of political representation appears to have emerged in the US and Canada and, more recently, in Australia. This is what Weaver calls the 'pressure group' approach. Here, indigenous representation is a function that is developed, controlled and authenticated by indigenous peoples themselves. The Canadian AFN and the US's NCAI are examples of this model. While this leads to a significant level of indigenous autonomy, there are some obvious difficulties. One is the maintenance of appropriate levels of funding to be effective; another, shared with the government-created representative bodies, is the capacity to ensure governments engage in a systematic and meaningful way with the representative body. The NCAI has been fortunate in securing an adequate level of funding, underpinned by the improving economic development of many tribal members (Maddison 2010). However, in Australia, the newly formed NCAFP recognised that independent funding was likely to be a major problem that could compromise its effectiveness. Short-term funding has been approved by the government but, in the long term, this is a difficulty that will need to be resolved (Calma and Dick 2011: 187).

Finally, Weaver alerts us to the importance of control of representation in the development of the indigenous organisations that implement indigenous rights to self-determination. Article 18 of the Declaration on the Rights of Indigenous Peoples says:

> Indigenous peoples have the right to participate in decision-making in matters which would affect their rights, through representatives chosen by themselves in accordance with their own procedures, as well as to maintain and develop their own indigenous decision-making institutions.

Where governments have themselves decided the nature and structure of indigenous representation, there is the risk that the essential nature of the representation achieved might be inappropriate or culturally inauthentic. The Declaration gives a new authority to indigenous demands for a form of representation that reflects their own cultural and social values and these may not be identical to Western-influenced notions of electoral processes.

Conclusion: An imperative for a new model of indigenous representation?

Indigenous peoples around the world have struggled to achieve recognition of their rights as First Nations with an entitlement to self-determination. Their struggle has been rewarded to different extents and has been shaped by the particular historical and social circumstances of the individual contexts. More recently, this struggle has become an international movement, with a focus on the commonalities of shared indigeneity and an increasing engagement with instruments of international law (Niezen 2003). The achievement of some form of indigenous representative process is now seen as an essential part of the attainment of self-determination as laid out in the Declaration of the Rights of Indigenous Peoples.

Indigenous peoples are entitled to the same basic human rights as other peoples, including the right to self-determination. The Declaration has spelled this out in words that are unequivocal. What remains to be achieved is the implementation of this principle in ways that meet the cultural and political aspirations of each indigenous people and are legitimated by them. There is no simple recipe for a uniform model of appropriate indigenous representation – it must arise out of an agreed process of negotiation of an acceptable form of self-determination. The lessons of the past provide invaluable insight into the strengths and weaknesses of different approaches and demonstrate that the structure and control of the processes of indigenous representation shape the nature of the engagement between indigenous and non-indigenous political authority. An understanding of these lessons will, it is hoped, enable indigenous peoples to move forwards with a clear understanding of what they wish to achieve.

References

AFN (Assembly of First Nations) no date, *Our Story*, http://www.afn.ca/index. php/en/about-afn/our-story (accessed 11 March 2011).

AHRC (2009a) *Our Future in Our Hands: Creating a sustainable National Representative Body – a community guide,* http://www.hreoc.gov.au/ social_justice/repbody/report2009/community_guide.html (accessed 20 March 2011).

AHRC (2009b) *Our Future in Our Hands: Creating a sustainable National Representative Body: Report,* http://www.hreoc.gov.au/social_justice/ repbody/report2009/index.html (accessed 20 March 2011).

Allen, S. and Xanthaki, A. (2011) (eds) *Reflections on the UN Declaration on the Rights of Indigenous Peoples,* Oxford and Portland, Oregon: Hart Publishing.

Anaya, S. J. (2009) 'The right of indigenous peoples to self-determination in the post-Declaration era', in C. Charters and R. Stavenhagen (eds), *Making the Declaration Work: The United Nations Declaration on the Rights of Indigenous Peoples,* Document 127, Copenhagen: International Work Group for Indigenous Affairs, pp. 184–99.

Armitage, A. (1995) *Comparing the Policy of Aboriginal Assimilation: Australia, Canada and New Zealand,* Vancouver: University of British Colombia Press.

ATSIC News, 'The end of the experiment', June 2004, pp. 4–9.

Attwood, B. and Marcus, A. (1997) in collaboration with D. Edwards and K. Schilling, *The 1967 Referendum or When Aborigines Didn't Get the Vote,* Canberra: Aboriginal Studies Press.

Beach, H. (1994) 'The Saami of Lapland', in Minority Rights Group (ed.) *Polar Peoples: Self-determination and development,* London: Minority Rights Publications, pp. 147–232.

Beckett, J. (1987) *Torres Strait Islanders: Custom and colonialism,* Cambridge: Cambridge University Press.

Behrendt, L. (2003) *Achieving Social Justice: Indigenous rights and Australia's future,* Annendale, NSW: Federation Press, Leichhardt.

Behrendt, L., Cunneen, C. and Libesman, T. (2009) *Indigenous Legal Relations in Australia,* South Melbourne: Oxford University Press.

Beresford, Q. (2006) *Rob Riley: An Aboriginal leader's quest for justice,* Canberra: Aboriginal Studies Press.

Bradfield, S. (2006) 'Separatism or status-quo? Indigenous affairs from the birth of land rights to the death of ATSIC', *Australian Journal of Politics and History* 52 (1): 80–97.

Calma, T. and Dick, D. (2011) 'The National Congress of Australia's first peoples: changing the relationship between Aboriginal and Torres Strait Islander peoples and the state?', in S. Maddison and M. Brigg (eds) *Unsettling the Settler State: Creativity and resistance in indigenous settler-state governance,* Sydney: Federation Press, pp. 168–88.

Chesterman J. and B. Galligan (1997) *Citizens without Rights: Aborigines and Australian citizenship*, Cambridge: Cambridge University Press.

Coe, P. (1994) 'ATSIC: self-determination or otherwise', *Race and Class* 35(4): 35–9.

Debo, A. (1995) *A History of the Indians of the United States*, London, Pimlico: Random House.

Durie, M. (2005) *Ngā Tai Matatū: Tides of Māori endurance*, Melbourne: Oxford University Press.

FaHCSIA (Department of Families, Housing, Community Services and Indigenous Affairs) (2008) *Report on the Outcomes of the First Phase of Consultation for a National Indigenous Representative Body (NIRB)*: http://www.humanrights.gov.au/social_justice/repbody/outcomes.html (accessed 20 March 2011).

Fleras, A. (1985) 'From social control towards political self-determination? Māori seats and the politics of separate Māori representation in New Zealand', *Canadian Journal of Political Science* 18(3): 551–76.

Fleras, A. and Spoonley, P. (1999) *Recalling Aotearoa: Indigenous politics and ethnic relations in New Zealand*, Auckland: Oxford University Press.

Hætta, O. M. (2008) *The Sámi – An Arctic indigenous people*, Karasjok: Davvi Girji.

Hand, G. (1989) Commonwealth Parliamentary Debates, House of Representatives, 23 May 1989: 2734.

Harvard Project on American Indian Economic Development (2008) *The State of the Native Nations: Conditions under US policies of self-determination*, New York: Oxford University Press.

Hannaford, J., Huggins, J. and Collins, B. (2003) *In the Hands of the Regions – A New ATSIC: Report of the review of the Aboriginal and Torres Strait Islander Commission*, Canberra: Commonwealth of Australia, Review Panel.

Henriksen, J. B. (1996) 'The legal status of Sámiland rights in Finland, Russia, Norway and Sweden', *Indigenous Affairs* 2: 4–13.

Henriksen, J. B. (1999) *Saami Parliamentary Co-Operation: An analysis*, IWGIA Document No. 93, Guovdageaidnu and Copenhagen: Nordic Sámi Institute and International Work Group for Indigenous Affairs.

Hocking, B. A. (2005) 'Commenced constitutional business? Reflections on the contributions of the Saami parliaments to indigenous self-determination', in B. A. Hocking (ed.) *Unfinished Constitutional Business: Rethinking indigenous self-determination*, Canberra: Aboriginal Studies Press, pp. 248–76.

Howard, J. (1989) Commonwealth Parliamentary Debates, House of Representatives, 11 April 1989.

Iorns Magallanes, C. J. (2005) 'Indigenous political representation: identified parliamentary seats as a form of indigenous self-determination', in B. A. Hocking (ed.) *Unfinished Constitutional Business: Rethinking indigenous self-determination*, Canberra: Aboriginal Studies Press, pp. 106–17.

Imai, S. (2009) 'Indigenous self-determination and the state', in B. Richardson, S. Imai and K. McNeil (eds) *Indigenous Peoples and the Law: Comparative and Critical Perspectives*, Oxford and Portland, Oregon: Osgoode Readers and Hart Publishing, pp. 285–314.

Ivanitz, M (2000) 'The demise of ATSIC? Accountability and the coalition government', *Australian Journal of Public Administration* 59(1): 3–12.

Johnson, J. (2008) 'Defending tribal sovereignty', in Harvard Project on American Indian Economic Development, *The State of the Native Nations: Conditions under US policies of self-determination*, New York: Oxford University Press, pp. 372–5.

Joona, T. (2012) *ILO Convention No. 169 in a Nordic Context with Comparative Analysis: An interdisciplinary approach*, Juridica Lapponica 37, Rovaniemi: Lapland University Press.

Jopson, D. (2010) 'Indigenous group pledges different approach', *Sydney Morning Herald*, May 3.

Josefsen, E. (2001) 'The Sámi and the national parliaments: direct and indirect channels of influence', in K. Wessendorf (ed.), *Challenging Politics: Indigenous peoples' experiences with political parties and elections*, Copenhagen: International Work Group for Indigenous Affairs (IWGIA), pp. 64–93.

Josefsen, E. (2005) 'The experience of Sapmi', in K. Wessendorf (ed.) *An Indigenous Parliament? Realities and perspectives in Russia and the circumpolar North*, Copenhagen: International Work Group on Indigenous Affairs (IWGIA), pp. 178–209.

Josefsen, E. (2011) 'The Norwegian Sámi Parliament and Sámi political empowerment', in G. Minnerup and P. Solberg (eds), *First World, First Nations: Internal colonialism and indigenous self-determination in Northern Europe and Australia*, Eastbourne: Sussex Academic Press, pp. 31–44.

Josefsen, E., Mörkenstam, U. and Saglie, J. (2015) 'Different institutions within similar states: the Norwegian and Swedish *Sámediggis*', *Ethnopolitics* 14(1): 32–51.

Lantto, P. (2010) 'Borders, citizenship and change: the case of the Sámi people, 1751–2008', *Citizenship Studies* 14(5): 543–56.

Lantto, P. and Mörkenstam, U. (2008) 'Sami rights and Sami challenges', *Scandinavian Journal of History* 33(1): 26–51.

Lawrence, R. and Mörkenstam, U. (2012) 'Självbestämmande genom myndighetsutövning? Sametingets dubbla roller', *Statsvetenskaplig Tidskrift*, 114(2): 207–39.

Lehtola, V.-P. (2010) *The Sámi People – Traditions in transition*, (4th edn), translated by L. W. Müller-Wille, Aanaar-Inari: Kustannus-Puntsi Publisher.

Lloyd. B. (2009), *Dedicated Indigenous Representation in the Australian Parliament*, Research Paper no 23, 2008–9, Canberra: Politics and Public Administration Section, Parliamentary Library, Australian Parliament.

Maaka, R. and Fleras, A. (2005) *The Politics of Indigeneity: Challenging the state in Canada and Aotearoa New Zealand*, Dunedin, NZ: University of Otago Press.

Maddison, S. (2010) *To Study Indigenous Representative Organizations in Canada and the United States*, Report to the Winston Churchill Memorial Trust of Australia, Churchill Fellow, 2009 September: https://www.churchilltrust.com.au/media/fellows/2009_Maddison_Sarah.pdf. (accessed 20 March 2011).

McQuire, A. (2009) 'Rudd government endorses UN Declaration on the Rights of Indigenous Peoples', *National Indigenous Times*, April 3.

Minde, H. (2003) 'The challenge of indigenism: the struggle for Sámi land rights and self-government in Norway 1960–1990', in S. Jentoft, H. Minde and R. Nilsen, (eds) *Indigenous Peoples: Resource management and global rights*, Delft, Netherlands: Eburon Academic Publishers, pp. 75–106.

Mörkenstam, U. (2005) 'Indigenous peoples and the right to self-determination: the case of the Swedish Sami People', *Canadian Journal of Native Studies* XXV(2): 433–61.

Nettheim, G., Meyers, G. D. and Craig, D. (2002) *Indigenous Peoples and Governance Structures*, Canberra: Aboriginal Studies Press.

Newcomb, S. T. (2011) 'The UN Declaration on the Rights of Indigenous Peoples and the paradigm of domination', *Griffith Law Review* 20(3): 579–607.

Niezen, R. (2003) *The Origins of Indigenism: Human rights and the politics of identity*, Berkeley, CA and Los Angeles, CA: University of California Press.

Norwegian Ministry of Labour and Social Inclusion (2008) 'Consultation duty in Sámi matters': http://www.regjeringen.no/en/dep/aid/Topics/Sámi-policy/midtspalte/consultation-duty-in-Sámi-matters.html?id=86931 (accessed February 2009).

Nyyssönen, J. (2011) 'Principles and practice in Finnish national policies towards Sámi people', in G. Minnerup and P. Solberg (eds), *First World, First Nations: Internal colonialism and indigenous self-determination in Northern Europe and Australia*, Eastbourne: Sussex Academic Press, pp. 80–96.

O'Sullivan, D. (2007) *Beyond Biculturalism: The politics of an indigenous minority*, Wellington: Huia Publishers.

Olsson S. E. and Lewis, D. (1995) 'Welfare rules and indigenous rights: the Sámi people and the Nordic welfare state', in J. E. Dixon and R. Scheurell (eds) *Social Welfare with Indigenous Peoples*, London: Routledge, pp. 149–85.

Pearson, N. (2009) 'A two-way street', reproduced in *Up From the Mission: Selected writings*, Melbourne: Black Inc.

Pettersen, T. (2011) 'Out of the backwater? Prospects for Sami demography in Norway', in P. Axelsson and P. Sköld (eds), *Indigenous Peoples and Demography: The complex relation between identity and statistics*, New York and Oxford: Berghahn Books, pp. 185–96.

Pevar, S. L. (2002) *The Rights of Indians and Tribes*, New York: New York University Press.

Pratt, A. (2003) *Make or Break? A Background to the ATSIC Changes and the ATSIC Review*, Current Issues Brief no 29, 2002–03, Canberra: Parliament of Australia, Parliamentary Library.

Pritchard, S. (1998) 'The significance of international law', in S. Pritchard (ed.), *Indigenous Peoples, the United Nations and Human Rights*, Leichhardt: Zed Books, The Federation Press, pp. 2–17.

Richardson, B. (2009) 'The dyadic character of US Indian law', in B. Richardson, S. Imai and K. McNeil (eds), *Indigenous Peoples and the Law*, Oxford and Portland, OR: Osgoode Readers, Hart Publishing, pp. 51–79.

Riley, R. (1985) press release, printed as Attachment A in *Department of Aboriginal Affairs, Meeting of Major National Aboriginal Organisations*, Canberra 12/4/85, NAC Records held at the Australian Institute of Aboriginal and Torres Strait Islander Studies, accessed 1992.

Robbins, E. J. (1994) *Self-Determination or welfare colonialism: Aborigines and federal policy-making*, PhD thesis, Adelaide: Politics Department, Flinders University of South Australia.

Robbins, J. (2004) 'The failure of ATSIC and the recognition of indigenous rights', *Journal of Australian Indigenous Issues* 7(4): 3–17.

Robbins, J. (2010) 'Norwegian Sámi Parliament elections', *Arena Magazine* 103 joint issue (12) 2009 and (1) 2010: 9–11.

Robbins, J. (2011) 'Indigenous representative bodies in Northern Europe and Australia', in G. Minnerup and P. Solberg (eds), *First World, First Nations: Internal colonialism and indigenous self-determination in Northern Europe and Australia*, Eastbourne: Sussex Academic Press, pp. 45–79.

Rowse, T. (2002) *Indigenous Futures: Choice and development for Aboriginal and Islander Australia*, Sydney: University of New South Wales Press.

Ruru, J. (2009, 'Māori encounter with Aotearoa: New Zealand's Legal System', in B. Richardson, S. Imai and K. McNeil (eds), *Indigenous Peoples and the Law: Comparative and critical perspectives*, Oxford and Portland, Oregon: Osgoode Readers, Hart Publishing, pp. 111–33.

Russell, P. H. (2005) 'Indigenous self-determination. Is Canada as good as it gets?', in B. A. Hocking (ed.) *Unfinished Constitutional Business: Rethinking indigenous self-determination*, Canberra: Aboriginal Studies Press, pp. 170–89.

Semb, A. J. (2005) 'Sámi self-determination in the making?' *Nations and Nationalism* 11(4): 531–49.

Seurujärvi-Kari, I. (2011) '"We took our language back" – the formation of a Sámi identity within the Sámi movement and the role of the Sámi language from the 1960s until 2008', in R. Grünthal and M. Kovács (eds), *Ethnic and Linguistic Context of Identity: Finno-Ugric minorities*: Helsinki: Uralica Helsingiensia 5: 37–78.

Smith, C. (2011) 'The development of Sámi rights in Norway from 1980 to 2007', in G. Minnerup and P. Solberg (eds.), *First World, First Nations: Internal colonialism and indigenous self-determination in Northern Europe and Australia*, Eastbourne: Sussex Academic Press, pp. 22–30.

Solbakk, J. T. (2006) *The Sámi People: A handbook*, Norway: Davvi Girji OS.

Stavenhagen, R. (2009) 'Making the Declaration work', in C. Charters and R. Stavenhagen (eds), *Making the Declaration Work: The United Nations Declaration on the Rights of Indigenous Peoples*, Document 127, Copenhagen: International Work Group for Indigenous Affairs, pp. 352–371.

Sullivan, A. (2006) 'Māori policy and politics', in Raymond Miller (ed.), *New Zealand Government and Politics*, 4th edn, South Melbourne: Oxford University Press, pp. 605–15.

Tickner, R. (2001) *Taking a Stand: Land rights to reconciliation*, Crows Nest, NSW: Allen and Unwin.

United Nations General Assembly (2007) Resolution 61/295 United Nations Declaration on the Rights of Indigenous Peoples: http://issuu.com/karinzylsaw/docs/un_declaration_rights_indigenous_peoples/1?e=1361097/2699565 (accessed 29 May 2015).

Vars, L. (2008) 'Political aspects of the Sámi's right to self-determination', *Galdu Cala – Journal of Indigenous Peoples' Rights* (2), Special Issue: Sámi Self-determination: Scope and Implementation, ed. J. B. Henriksen: 62–79.

Walters, M. D., (2009) 'Promise and paradox: the emergence of indigenous rights law in Canada', in B. Richardson, S. Imai and K. McNeil (eds), *Indigenous Peoples and the Law: Comparative and critical perspectives*, Oxford and Portland, OR: Osgoode Readers, Hart Publishing, pp. 21–50.

Weaver, S. M. (1983a) *Towards a Comparison of National Political Organizations of Indigenous Peoples: Australia, Canada and Norway*, lecture series, Institute of Social Sciences, University of Tromsø, Tromsø, Norway, unpublished manuscript.

—   (1983b) 'Australian Aboriginal policy: Aboriginal pressure groups or government advisory bodies? Part I', *Oceania* 54(I): 1–22; Part II, *Oceania* 54(2): 85–108.

—   (1984) "Struggles of the nation-state to define Aboriginal ethnicity: Canada and Australia', in G. L. Gold (ed.), *Minorities and Mother Country Imagery*, St John's, Newfoundland: Memorial University of Newfoundland, Institute of Social and Economic Research, Social and Economic Papers no 13, pp. 182–210.

—   (1985) 'Political representivity and indigenous minorities in Canada and Australia', in N. Dyck (ed), *Indigenous Peoples and the Nation-State: Fourth world politics in Canada, Australia and Norway*, St. John's, Newfoundland: Memorial University of Newfoundland, Institute of Social and Economic Research, Social and Economic Papers no 14, pp. 113–150.

—   (1990) 'A new paradigm in Canadian Indian policy for the 1990s', *Canadian Ethnic Studies* XXII(3): 8–18.

—   (1992) 'Self-government policy for Indians 1980–1990: political transformation or symbolic gestures?', in J. Burnet, D. Juteau, E. Padolsky, A. Rasporich and A. Sirois (eds), *Migration and the Transformation of Cultures*, Toronto: Multicultural History Society of Ontario, pp. 109–44.

—   (1993) 'Self-determination, national pressure groups and Australian Aborigines: the National Aboriginal Conference 1983–1985', in M. D. Levin (ed.), *Ethnicity and Aboriginality: Case Studies in Ethnonationalism*, Toronto: University of Toronto Press, 53–74.

Wilkins, D. E. and Stark, H. K. (2011) *American Indian Politics and the American Political System*, 3rd edn, Lanham, MD: Rowman & Littlefield Publishers Inc.

Xanthaki, A. and O'Sullivan, D. (2009) 'Indigenous participation in elective bodies: the Māori in New Zealand', *International Journal on Minority and Group Rights* 16(2): 181–207.

Zifcak, S. (2003) *Mr Ruddock Goes to Geneva*, Sydney: University of New South Wales Press.

Chapter Four

Making Space for Indigenous Governments: Comparing Patterns of Institutional Adaptation in Canada and the United States[1]

Martin Papillon

Indigenous peoples around the world are challenging the legitimacy of state authority over their lands and communities. Governments have responded in different ways to indigenous self-determination claims, from active denial and repression to various forms of recognition. In fact, as this volume testifies, both the meaning of self-determination and its translation into institutional terms vary significantly from one place to another. Why is that? This chapter compares responses to indigenous self-determination claims in Canada and the United States, in order to identify some of the factors that explain similarities and variations in institutional models of indigenous autonomy. American Indian tribes in the United States and First Nations in Canada have been at the forefront of the global indigenous self-determination movement.[2] The First Peoples of North America have much in common beyond a shared indigenous identity. They represent less than 4 per cent of the population of the two countries and are, with some exceptions, scattered throughout the continent, making territorial claims more difficult. The two former British colonies have also followed remarkably similar policy trajectories in their relationship with indigenous peoples. The original treaty-based relations were progressively replaced by policies aimed first at displacing indigenous peoples to facilitate settlement and then later at assimilating them into the majority population. Despite differences in their systems of government, Canada and the United States also have in common an important feature for indigenous autonomy claims: both are federal systems, in which sovereignty is already divided along orders of territorially-based governments.

This chapter discusses the relationship between federalism and the development of indigenous autonomy regimes in the former British colonies of North America. It argues that while federalism is creating opportunities

---

1. Sections of this chapter were previously published in Papillon 2012. I would like to thank Oxford University Press and *Publius: The Journal of Federalism* for their permission to use this material here.
2. Indigenous peoples in Canada are collectively defined in the Constitution as Aboriginal peoples, with three distinct groups recognised: First Nations, Inuit and Métis. In the United States, federal policy refers to American Indians and Alaska Natives. The present research focuses specifically on the status and claims of American Indian tribes in the United States and First Nations in Canada.

for indigenous peoples to further establish their self-determination claims in Canada and the United States, it also acts as an institutional lock-in mechanism that considerably limits the range of possibilities for accommodating indigenous autonomy. Federalism, I will argue, is highly resistant to change, leading to a slow, incremental adaptation process rather than a radical shift in the configuration of institutional authority. The outcome is what I define here as multi-level governance (MLG) regimes that are layered over the existing federal system without altering its nature.

While the two federations have adapted in similar ways to indigenous claims, there are also some differences in the resulting governance regimes. In Canada, the federal government has responded to self-determination claims with the recognition of a limited right to self-government, which is implemented through detailed agreements that essentially create new layers of governments, with their own jurisdictional boundaries, within the federal system. In the United States, there are no equivalent institutional processes for the creation of indigenous governments. Tribes are instead recognised as *de facto* self-determining political entities, within the confines of Congressional authority. Tribal governments have utilised this limited jurisdictional space to develop their own models of governance and to establish legislation, policies and programmes that sometimes conflict with the interests and policies of neighbouring states. The core institutional mechanisms for the management of such conflicts are intergovernmental compacts.

These differences have a lot to do with the historical process through which indigenous peoples were incorporated into the two federations. History matters greatly in explaining patterns of incremental institutional change (Pierson 2004) and the response of governments to indigenous self-determination is no exception. In the United States, tribes were initially considered distinct entities existing outside the federal system. In Canada, indigenous peoples were less ambiguously incorporated within the federal regime, as subjects of the Crown with certain rights resulting from treaties and British statutes. These variations in the initial mode of incorporation have created different points of departure for the development of MLG regimes. This chapter explores these legacies and how, faced with different institutional and political circumstances, indigenous leaders in Canada and the United States have used different strategies to establish their self-government rights. Before doing so, I discuss the possibilities and constraints of institutional adaptation under a federal regime.

Indigenous self-determination, federalism and institutional adaptation

Indigenous peoples in Canada and the United States are asserting their right to self-determination. Of course, expectations regarding how this right should or could be exercised vary considerably from one indigenous community to another. While for some indigenous peoples, self-determination is associated with a relatively classic conception of international sovereignty, for others, it is defined in more relational terms as a process of redefinition of the boundaries of state sovereignty, in order to create a space for the self-governing authority of communities. Other indigenous peoples conceive of self-determination in more limited terms, as fair and equal representation and participation in existing state institutions. The common thread here is the opportunity for indigenous peoples to freely redefine historically imposed governance structures in order to establish a fair and lasting relationship with the dominant society (Anaya 2004).

The transformation of governance structures to accommodate such self-determination claims is, of course, a daunting task for small minorities with limited resources and political currency, let alone territorial clout. By their very nature, indigenous claims touch upon the DNA of sovereign states: the substance of citizenship and the territorial reach of state sovereignty are at stake. This challenging task is somewhat compounded in federal contexts, like Canada and the United States.

Federal arrangements are often seen as a possible solution for indigenous minorities seeking simultaneously greater territorial autonomy and better representation in shared institutions, while at the same time maintaining the integrity of national polities. After all, federalism is based on the principle that sovereignty can be shared and territorially diffused across coexisting orders of government, therefore opening the door to a wide diversity of institutional arrangements (Elazar 1987; Watts 2002). Indigenous and non-indigenous political theorists have also argued that North American indigenous political traditions are particularly amenable to various forms of federalism, since unions of self-rule and shared rule existed in North America prior to the arrival of European settlers (Williams 1997). The Haudenosonee (or Iroquois) confederacy is probably the most famous federal-type association between autonomous indigenous nations.

That being said, the constitutional framework of a federation is often the product of complex negotiations between competing interests, whose power and influence are reflected and reproduced in the federal bargain. The balance between forces at the centre and those in the constituent units is progressively institutionalized, creating interlocking vetoes that make changes in the framework of the federation unlikely (Scharpf 1988; Behnke and Benz 2009; Rodden 2006). Once established, it is hard to alter the foundations of federal systems.

Federalism also tends to entrench certain interests that may not be favourable to indigenous rights and political autonomy. In his classic critique of federal systems, William Riker (1964) referred to the 'tyranny of small places' as a fundamental democratic flaw of federations, where too much power is vested in governments controlled by local elites. Indigenous peoples in North America and Australia have often found themselves in unequal battles with local elites who control state or provincial assemblies.[3] In one of its early decisions reaffirming exclusive federal jurisdiction over 'Indian Country', the US Supreme Court referred to American states as 'the deadliest enemies' of American Indian tribes.[4] In Canada too,

---

3.   For a detailed history of state–tribes conflicts in the United States, see Wilkins 1998 and Corntassel 2008. In Canada, see Long and Boldt 1988.

4.   *U.S. v Kagma*, 118 U.S. 375 (1886).

indigenous peoples have historically faced hostile provincial governments with little interest in maintaining their unique status and protected land regimes.

One is therefore left with a certain pessimism regarding the capacity of federations like Canada and the United States to respond to indigenous autonomy claims. Not only were indigenous peoples excluded from the original compact but this initial exclusion tends to be reproduced and reinforced by the specific dynamics of federal governance. Despite this apparent gridlock (Jhappan 1995), I argue in the remainder of this chapter that the Canadian and American federations have adapted to indigenous claims. Change has taken place incrementally, however, through a process of institutional layering rather than through a fundamental alteration of the federal structure of the two countries.

I borrow the concept of institutional layering from the literature on path-dependent change, mostly associated with historical institutionalism (Pierson 2004; Streeck and Thelen 2005; Mahoney and Thelen 2010). Streeck and Thelen, in particular, have developed a useful typology of modes of incremental change. Among other things, they suggest that incremental change can occur in contexts of high institutional rigidity through what they define as *layering*, or the superimposition of new practices and norms over a change-resistant institution. The layering of new rules and practices can explain how otherwise change-resistant governance systems evolve when faced with new challenges, such as indigenous peoples' jurisdictional claims. In both Canada and the United States, indigenous self-determination claims are translated institutionally through a progressive layering of what can be defined as a multi-level governance regime over the existing federal system.

The concept of MLG was developed to make sense of a specific mode of governance resulting from both horizontal and vertical diffusion of the policy process in the European Union (Marks and Hooghe 2003; Piattoni 2009). The policy process in the EU takes place simultaneously at multiple levels, between 'formally independent yet functionally interdependent governing entities', in which formal jurisdictional power is increasingly replaced by negotiated co-ordination mechanisms (Piattoni 2009: 172). While indigenous governance in Canada and the United States is vastly different from European Union governance, I suggest that a similar logic operates here, resulting in the layering of new governance mechanisms that operate in parallel to the federal systems of the United States and Canada. The following sections discuss the specific trajectories of both federations in this respect.

Tribal self-determination in the United States

Indigenous peoples have a somewhat ambiguous status in the American federal system. They are formally mentioned in Article 1, Section 8, of the Constitution, which grants Congress power to regulate commerce 'with foreign nations, ... and with the Indian tribes'. The status of indigenous peoples, or 'Indian tribes', was further clarified in a series of Supreme Court decisions in the 1830s. The Supreme Court under the pen of Chief Justice John Marshall defined the constitutional status of indigenous peoples as 'domestic dependent nations' – distinctive political entities with a limited form of sovereignty over the land. According to Marshall, 'the Indian nations have always been considered as distinct, independent political communities, retaining their natural rights, as undisputed possessors of the soil.'[5] Tribes, pursued Marshall, therefore have a unique trust-based relationship with the federal government and should not be subjected to state jurisdiction.

This status of residual sovereign existing *within* the United States but *outside* its federal system was severely curtailed over time. The trust relationship with the federal government came to be defined as a ward-like status, with Congress firmly established as a guardian, with 'plenary powers' over tribes, their lands and their treaties.[6] Congress can therefore overrule tribal sovereignty at will and it has done so regularly. Throughout the twentieth century, the United States Congress sanctioned the dismantling of traditional systems of tribal governance, the parcelling of tribal lands into individual lots and the 'emancipation' of tribe members to facilitate their assimilation as American citizens (Deloria and Lytle 1984; Wilkins 2007). With the tacit support of Congress, American states also exerted considerable pressure to expand their jurisdictional reach into tribal lands. A succession of court cases sympathetic to states' rights further contributed to the blurring of the legal boundaries between American federalism and tribal sovereignty (Wilkinson 1987). As a result, by the mid twentieth century, tribal sovereignty was more symbolic than real. Key policy directions were, by and large, established in Washington, on behalf of tribes.

It was against this background that tribal self-determination claims emerged to prominence in the American political landscape in the 1960s and 1970s (Deloria and Lytle 1984). In 1969, young indigenous activists occupied the island of Alcatraz, claiming it as 'Indian territory' for the benefit of 'Indians of all tribes' (quoted in Josephy *et al.* 1999: 39). The occupation of Alcatraz marked the beginning of what came to be known as the Red Power movement, a social movement associated with the revival of indigenous political consciousness and cultural identity in the United States. Self-determination, defined broadly as 'Indian control of Indian lives', was a recurring theme of these protests (Deloria and Lyle 1984).

In response to this increased activism, the federal government reoriented federal Indian policy in the 1970s, ushering in a new era in indigenous–state relations. Under the Indian Self-determination and Educational Assistance Act of 1975 and subsequent policies, the government formally repudiated past assimilationist policies and affirmed instead the continuing existence and distinctive status of tribes. It established a framework to facilitate their autonomy within the federal regime, through the contractual delegation of federal authority.

Although often considered a significant moment for indigenous politics in the United States, the shift to a policy grounded on self-determination did not radically alter the institutional foundation of the relationship between tribes and the federal

---

5.   *Worcester v Georgia*, 31 US 515, at 559 (1932).

6.   *Lone Wolf v Hitchcock*, 187 US 553 (1903).

union. Tribal sovereignty is still formally subject to Congressional powers. Significant terms and conditions are also attached to devolved programmes. That being said, devolution provided indigenous governments with a certain space to develop their own policies and expand the scope of their activities. As Cornell and Kalt (2007: 21) argue, 'it opened the door to practical sovereignty' and provided the foundation for a new generation of more assertive tribal leaders to reaffirm the 'dormant' jurisdictional boundaries of their communities.[7]

The policy shift also provided a platform for indigenous tribal leaders to define, in their own terms, what self-determination meant. Self-determination, they increasingly argued, is about the reassertion of tribal sovereignty on traditional tribal lands. The Declaration of Sovereignty issued by the Confederated Tribes of the Warm Spring Reservation in Oregon illustrates this view:

> Our people have exercised inherent sovereignty, as nations, on the Columbia Plateau since time immemorial. This inherent sovereignty was recognized by the United States ... We hereby declare our continuing sovereignty – the absolute right to govern, to determine our destiny, and to control all persons, land, water, resources and activities – throughout our homeland (quoted in Biolsi 2007: 239).

A number of tribal governments were inspired by this definition of self-determination as a continuing right to tribal sovereignty, grounded in the constitutional history of the federation. Many of them unilaterally established new governance structures that directly challenged the division of authority in the American federal system. Conflicts have been especially acute with state legislatures that have seen their authority challenged by newly assertive tribes, notably in areas involving resource-management, such as water policy and hunting and fishing rights, as well as in areas such as criminal justice, taxation and the regulation of high-stakes gambling (Ashley and Hubbard 2004). Many of these conflicts end up in court as tribes seek to assert their sovereignty and limit state influence on their internal affairs.

Court battles over jurisdictions have had mixed results for tribes. In *Oliphant v Suquamish Indian Tribe*, the Supreme Court ruled that tribes do not have criminal jurisdiction over non-Indians on tribal lands, absent delegation of such powers by Congress, whereas a few months later in *United States v Wheeler*, the court recognised tribal sovereignty as a 'third type of sovereignty within the United States'.[8] In the *Cabazon* case, the Supreme Court confirmed that tribes were free to operate gambling facilities since 'tribal sovereignty is dependent on, and subordinate to, only the Federal Government and not the States.'[9]

---

7. The Harvard Project on American Indian Economic Development has documented this process in numerous publications: see, for example, Jorgensen 2007.

8. *Oliphant v Suquamish Indian Tribe*, 435 US 191 (1978); *United States v Wheeler*, 435 US 313 (1978).

9. *California v Cabazon Band of Mission Indians* 480 U.S. 202 (1987).

Faced with the potential costs and uncertainty of lengthy intergovernmental battles and judicial conflicts, the federal government, states and tribes were forced to develop alternative mechanisms to manage their growing interaction. President Reagan was the first to affirm the 'government-to-government' nature of federal–tribe relations.[10] Following in the footsteps of the US Environmental Protection Agency, federal agencies are now expected to develop their own framework in order to act accordingly in consultations with tribal governments.[11] A series of legislative initiatives in the 1980s and 1990s have also contributed to a significant streamlining of fiscal transfers and devolution procedures for federal programmes.

It is, however, at the level of tribal–state relations that the most striking changes have occurred. From informal summit meetings to broad collaborative framework agreements, state–tribe intergovernmental relations have grown exponentially in the past 20 years. A number of states have recognised the need to establish more formal intergovernmental procedures to facilitate co-operation with tribes. For example, under the 1989 Centennial Accord between Washington State and 26 tribes, the signatories recognise each other's sovereignty and establish a series of guiding principles for government-to-government relations.[12] The novelty here is less in the formal structure of tribe–state relations, which remains as uncertain as ever, but more in the layering of governance practices and mechanisms precisely designed to sidestep jurisdictional ambiguities and facilitate conflict-management.

The most significant development in this respect is, arguably, the use of intergovernmental agreements and compacts to clarify state–tribe responsibilities (Steinman 2004). Compacts are legal agreements under which otherwise sovereign parties agree to a set of rules to guide their policies in areas of overlapping or competing jurisdiction (Harvard Law Review 1999: 924). Such agreements are now an integral part of state–tribe relations in a number of policy fields, notably in the area of high-stakes gambling, in which they have emerged as a key mechanism of conflict-regulation and -management. Two hundred and fifty-five such compacts were signed between 1988 and 2000 in the area of gaming regulation (Corntassel and Witmer 2008: 117). They are also common in areas such as the management of water and other resources, child welfare, taxation and the administration of justice and many more (Ashley and Hubbard 2004; Steinman 2004).

---

10. Successive presidents have since reaffirmed this principle: see, for example, President Obama's Memorandum on Tribal Consultation at: http://www.bia.gov/idc/groups/public/documents/text/idc002694.pdf (accessed 23 July 2014).

11. The implementation of such a principle is still inconsistent from one agency to another. For an overview of key consultation policy documents, see http://www.bia.gov/WhoWeAre/AS-IA/Consultation/Templates/index.htm (accessed 23 July 2014).

12. See http://www.goia.wa.gov/Government-to-Government/CentennialAgreement.html (accessed 12 June 2010). See Steinman 2004 and Hicks 2007 for other examples of state-tribes agreements.

The practice of compacting, developed as a response to ongoing litigation, effectively creates a new set of rules and norms that are translating tribal conceptions of self-determination into concrete institutional arrangements. Significantly, compacts do not *create* tribal authority in a given sector, they recognise *existing* tribal jurisdiction, as derived from the tribe's status as residual sovereign under the American constitution.

There are, of course, many limits to the formalisation of tribal self-determination through compacts. First, compacts tend to be sector-specific and therefore limited in scope. Second, while they rest on the principle of tribal sovereignty, they nonetheless force tribes to negotiate the extent of their jurisdiction in a given sector with state governments. In the process, short-term political and economic considerations can play a significant role in determining what exactly tribal self-determination amounts to. The reliance on compacts also effectively provides states with a veto on the exercise of tribal jurisdiction, which is seen by many as a significant limit on self-determination (Corntassel and Witmer 2008).

Compact negotiations are therefore a classic case of multi-level governance. In order to secure a compact, tribes are forced to engage simultaneously in executive-centred intergovernmental relations as well as in local- and state-level legislative politics through lobbying, electoral-campaign contributions, the sponsoring of ballot initiatives and media relations (Light 2008). Dale Mason (1998) documents the case of tribes in New Mexico who engaged extensively in state politics through lobbying activities and campaign contributions in order to secure a gaming compact. Similar cases were documented in Minnesota (Light 2008). In order to protect their interests, tribes are increasingly compelled to lobby at the federal, state and local levels. Some of this occurs through professional and peak organisations, such as the Native American Fish and Wildlife Society or the National Indian Gaming Association (Skopek and Hansen 2006). In the process of negotiating compacts, tribes simultaneously act as governments and as interest groups in a policy process unfolding in the intergovernmental arena and in the various venues of electoral politics (Light 2008: 236). But as is the case with European MLG, it is increasingly difficult for state, tribes and the federal government to operate independently of each other.

The emergence of compacts as a core institutional mechanism for translating tribal self-determination in the American political system is no accident. Compacts are, after all, a well established practice of American federalism. The extension of compacting practices to federal tribes and state–tribe relations is also consistent with the initial status of tribes as 'domestic dependent nations' with an inherent but limited form of sovereignty. Institutional legacies, however, do not tell the whole story. It is the strategic choice of tribal government to define their self-determination claims as jurisdictional claims in court cases that has forced the American federal system to adapt and create this new layer of institutional arrangements. The comparison with the Canadian case is useful to underline the importance of institutional legacies and strategic choices in the process of institutional adaptation of federal systems to indigenous claims.

Indigenous self-determination in Canada

There are many parallels in the history of the two North-American federations, notably as it pertains to their dealings with indigenous peoples. As in the United States, the federal government is the primary interlocutor of First Nations, Inuit and Métis in Canada. Under section 91(24) of the Constitution Act, 1867 'Indians and Lands reserved for Indians' are an object of exclusive federal jurisdiction.[13] A number of principles established under British rule, notably the fiduciary responsibility of the Crown to protect the interests of indigenous peoples, served similar purposes to the trust doctrine in the United States and justified a corresponding federal role in the internal affairs of indigenous nations.

Treaties are also an important structuring element of the relationship between First Nations and the Canadian state. After a 50-year hiatus, the negotiation of treaties to settle disputes over land rights resumed in Canada in 1975, following the recognition by the Supreme Court of Canada that the aboriginal title may continue to exist in common law, in areas where no treaties were previously signed.[14] Comprehensive Land Claims Settlements, or modern treaties, have notably been negotiated in Quebec, British Columbia and in the Northern Territories. These modern treaties, now protected under section 35(2) of the Constitutions Act, 1982, establish extensive rights regimes and create legally enforceable obligations for governments. Indigenous peoples who have signed a treaty, old or new, generally consider the latter as the main constitutional document regulating their relationship with the Canadian federation (Ladner 2005; Macklem 2000).

Despite the treaty-making process, the principle of a residual tribal sovereignty was not and is still not recognised in Canada. The division of powers between the federal Parliament and provincial legislatures is reputed to exhaust all legislative authority within the boundaries of the federation.[15] As a result, unlike tribal governments that exist as pre-constitutional entities in the United States, band councils under the Canadian Indian Act are unambiguously defined as creatures of the federal government, with powers and authorities delegated from the latter. This more limited conception of sovereignty has shaped both indigenous peoples' mobilisation strategies and government responses to the challenges they raise.

The contemporary indigenous-rights movement in Canada also followed in the footsteps of its American counterpart. The Canadian version of the American

---

13. Following the Supreme Court decision in *Reference Re Eskimos* [1939] S.C.R. 104, federal responsibility was extended to Inuit and other indigenous peoples who were not covered by the Indian Act.

14. *Calder v British Columbia (Attorney General)* [1973] S.C.R. 313.

15. According to the doctrine established by the Judicial Committee of the Privy Council, Canada's ultimate appeal court until 1949, 'whatever belongs to self-government in Canada belongs either to the Dominion or to the provinces, within the limits of the British North America Act' (*Attorney-General for Ontario v Attorney-General of Canada* [1912] A.C. 57).

termination policy came in 1969, with a federal policy proposal to do away with the Indian Act and treaties, in order to facilitate the participation of 'Indians' in mainstream society (Canada 1969). The infamous White Paper on Indian Policy had a catalytic effect on First Nations activism. Newly formed pan-Canadian organisations, such as the National Indian Brotherhood (which later became the Assembly of First Nations), rejected the notion that their differentiated status was the source of their disastrous socio-economic conditions. To the contrary, Cree leader Harold Cardinal argued in his famous reply to the White Paper, this status must be recognised to its full extent in order for indigenous peoples to regain their sense of dignity and political agency (Cardinal 1969).

The federal government eventually withdrew the White Paper, creating a policy vacuum that was progressively filled by indigenous political organisations (Steinman 2005). Following the pattern established south of the border, self-determination quickly emerged as a central theme of indigenous discourse in Canada. The Dene Nation of the Northwest Territories probably best articulated the emerging discourse of the time:

> We the Dene of the N.W.T. insist upon the right to be regarded by ourselves and the world as a nation … What we seek then is independence and self-determination within the country of Canada. This is what we mean when we call for a just land settlement for the Dene Nation.[16]

Part of the challenge, of course, was to translate this emerging discourse into concrete actions in a context with limited political or legal opportunities. In the absence of any clear recognition of their pre-existing sovereignty, indigenous peoples in Canada have focused their mobilisation strategies on the constitutional recognition of their status as self-governing nations. The political context of the 1970s was particularly conducive to the articulation of indigenous autonomy claims in constitutional terms. The rise of Quebec nationalism contributed to the destabilisation of the federation and facilitated the inclusion of indigenous demands on the constitutional agenda (Cairns 2000).

The recognition of Aboriginal and Treaty rights in Section 35(1) of the *Constitution Act, 1982* was a major development in this respect. While it did not *per se* alter the status of First Nations band councils and other indigenous governments in the Canadian federation, Section 35 became a significant platform for indigenous peoples to challenge the boundaries of Canadian federalism. Section 35 rights opened new avenues to limit federal and provincial jurisdictions over indigenous lands and traditional activities through litigation.[17] The Supreme Court also established a fairly broad responsibility for governments to consult indigenous communities when natural-resource extraction or other economic activities could

---

16. The *Dene Declaration of 1975* is available at http://www.denenation.com/denedec.html (accessed 1 June 2014).

17. There is a substantial literature on Section 35 jurisprudence: see, for example, Macklem 2000.

affect their unsettled rights.[18] The Court, however, has been reluctant to expand Section 35 rights to a form of residual sovereignty on the land.[19]

The constitutional window did not close in 1982. In fact, Section 35 served as a platform for the Assembly of First Nations and other pan-Canadian organisations to establish themselves as 'constitutional partners' in continuing debates about the future of the federation (Cairns 2000). The AFN and other organisations sought a second constitutional amendment to include an explicit mention of their inherent right to self-government under Section 35. While negotiations ultimately failed to produce concrete change, the inclusion of indigenous peoples in the constitutional conversation remains a significant development. In the process, indigenous organisations gained access to the all-important mechanisms of Canada's executive federalism.

A second indirect outcome of the constitutional rounds of the 1980s was to firmly establish the principle of indigenous self-government in the Canadian political landscape. In 1995, the federal government recognised the principle of an inherent Aboriginal right to self-government and proposed a framework to negotiate bilateral agreements for the transfer of federal jurisdictions to indigenous governments in a number of policy areas (Canada 1995). Unlike compacts in the United States, which operate as a form of mutual recognition of existing jurisdictional authority, the federal self-government policy effectively creates a new type of governmental authority in the federal system. As the 1995 policy clearly establishes, however, 'Aboriginal governments and institutions exercising the inherent right of self-government operate within the framework of the Canadian Constitution ... and should therefore work in harmony with jurisdictions that are exercised by other governments.' (Canada 1995: 2). In the Canadian context, self-government remains firmly anchored in federalism.

The most significant self-government agreements resulting from this federal policy have been negotiated as part of land-claims settlements, or modern treaties. For example, the Nisga'a Final Agreement, or Nisga'a Treaty, signed in 1998, recognises the self-government authority of the Nisga'a over approximately 2,000 km^2 of land in the Nass Valley in British Columbia.[20] The agreement establishes, through enabling federal and provincial legislations, the law-making authority of the Nisga'a Government in a number of areas, including land-management, education and social services, environmental regulation, citizenship and local government. Nisga'a authority is exclusive for matters affecting exclusively Nisga'a citizens but must otherwise be exercised concurrently with federal and

---

18. *Haida Nation v British Columbia (Minister of Forests)*, [2004] 3 S.C.R. 511.

19. See McNeil 2004 for a discussion. In more recent decisions, the Supreme Court has come much closer to the American notion of residual sovereignty. In *Haida Nations*, for example, the Court write about the need to 'reconcile pre-existing Aboriginal sovereignty with assumed Crown sovereignty' (*Haida Nation v British Columbia (Minister of Forests)*, [2004] 3 S.C.R. 511).

20. The agreement is available at: http://www.ainc-inac.gc.ca/al/ldc/ccl/fagr/nsga/nis/nis-eng.asp (accessed 18 June 2014).

provincial legislative and regulatory frameworks. The Nisga'a agreement served as a template for other self-government agreements with First Nations, notably in the Yukon, the Northwest Territories and elsewhere in British Columbia.[21]

Combined with Section 35 jurisprudence and ongoing treaty settlement negotiations, self-government agreements contribute to the redefinition of indigenous peoples' relation with the federal system. As in the United States, indigenous governance in Canada has evolved from a highly centralised, hierarchical and fairly homogenous system concentrated in federal hands to what is now a far more complex multilevel-structure of governance, in which indigenous governments play a growing role.

In Canada, a significant aspect of this change is the participation of indigenous organisations in high-level federal–provincial intergovernmental processes. Building on the precedent of the constitutional negotiation rounds of the 1980s, indigenous organisations have successfully established their status as 'intergovernmental partners' whenever federal–provincial negotiations directly concern their interests. They were most recently integrated into the process leading to the Kelowna Accord, an intergovernmental agreement on a series of social and economic development initiatives for indigenous communities.[22] This unique role for indigenous organisations in Canadian executive federalism has no equivalent in the United States.

Yet this is not the only arena of intergovernmental co-ordination. In fact, as in the United States, much co-ordination work with specific First Nations is achieved through bilateral and trilateral negotiations at the local level, under the Indian Act or a self-government agreement. In a development that parallels the American experience, provinces are playing an increasingly active role in these co-ordination exercises. Most provinces now have policy frameworks to manage their relations with indigenous peoples. British Columbia and Ontario, for example, have recently adopted consultation guidelines under which they recognise the 'government-to-government' nature of their relationship with First Nations.[23] Most provinces also have a dedicated ministry or administrative branch responsible for relations with indigenous peoples.

A rapid survey indicates close to 150 agreements of various types were signed between provinces, territories and First Nations between 2000 and 2010,

---

21. The creation of the Nunavut Territory in 1999 is an example of a different kind of autonomy arrangement resulting from a land-claims settlement. The Nunavut government is a public government controlled by the Inuit majority of the territory. As a territorial government, it exercises broad jurisdictional powers, equivalent to that of provinces, but it remains under the legislative authority of the federal government. For an overview of the various agreements signed or under negotiations, see Morse 2008.

22. See http://www.cbc.ca/news/background/aboriginals/undoing-kelowna.html (accessed 18 June 2014). The intergovernmental initiative was ultimately set aside in 2006 by the newly elected Conservative government of Stephen Harper.

23. For British Columbia, see http://www.newrelationship.gov.bc.ca. For Ontario, see http://www.aboriginalaffairs.gov.on.ca/english/policy/newapproach/newapproach.asp (both accessed 2 October 2011).

more than three times the number for the previous decade.[24] They vary from economic initiatives to policing arrangements and natural resources co-management agreements. These agreements also vary considerably in status, from simple memoranda of understanding to provisions leading to substantial legislative amendments.[25] Agreements between provinces and First Nations do not have the same status as comprehensive self-government agreements with the federal government or compacts in the United States. They are generally limited in time and scope, focused on specific policy issues or funding arrangements and create contractual rather than jurisdictional obligations for the signatories. In this respect, they do not alter the constitutional authority of provinces, let alone the federal government.

This emerging regime of multilevel-governance is thus more squarely located within the existing bounds of the federal system. Despite what indigenous leaders may claim, self-government agreements and other form of governance arrangements are not the expression of an indigenous residual sovereignty in the Canadian context. Indigenous MLG in Canada is also less diffused than in the United States. Unlike their American counterparts, indigenous authorities in Canada rarely have to engage in lobbying campaigns and electoral politics to defend the outcome of land claims and self-government negotiations, or to establish the basis of an intergovernmental agreement with provinces.[26] Negotiations are generally conduced in the strict confines of executive powers. The nature of the Canadian parliamentary system, in which the policy-making role of the legislative branch is limited, obviously facilitates the development of executive-centred relations with indigenous governments, in which relations are primarily 'government to government' rather than through interest representation in the legislatures. This is also partly the result of early strategic choices by the indigenous leadership, who opted to focus on constitutional recognition of their right to self-government, a choice that privileged pan-Canadian intergovernmental venues, which are again government to government structures.

Conclusion

This chapter proposed a theoretical framework to make sense of the process through which indigenous governments are recognised in the Canadian and American federations. Given the strong institutional aversion to jurisdictional

---

24. This number is based on the information publicly available on the website of the 10 provincial and 3 territorial governments as of 12 June 2011.

25. The creation of a pan-provincial First Nation education system in British Columbia is an example of the latter: see http://www2.news.gov.bc.ca/news_releases_2005-2009/2007EDU0161-001500-Attachment1.htm (accessed 10 June 2011).

26. A significant exception to this rule was a province-wide referendum organised by the government of British Columbia following the ratification of the Nisga'a agreement. The backlash against the referendum was significant, however, and the provincial government, which sponsored the popular consultation, ultimately downplayed its significance.

change in federal systems, reforms have largely taken place at the margin, through processes that do not challenge or alter the nature of the two federal systems. Federalism has instead adapted to indigenous autonomy through the development of multi-level governance regimes that are layered over the division of powers and intergovernmental relation systems of the two federations.

Indigenous MLG regimes in Canada and the United States are unique forms of political autonomy. They do not obey a simple vertical decentralisation pattern nor do they establish, or recognise, indigenous governments as truly co-equal, sovereign partners. These MLG regimes are instead characterised by a multiplication of decision-making spaces and processes, under which formal lines of authority, while remaining, are increasingly contested and replaced by negotiated rules. Indigenous MLG regimes are, in this respect, *sui generis*. They exist, as Bruyneel (2007) suggests, 'on the boundaries' of the two federal systems.

While the two models of institutional recognition have much in common, there are differences in their operating logic. In the United States, tribes are only loosely integrated into the federal system. This historical position has led to a different kind of opportunities and constraints for indigenous governments. The very nature of the American federal system, with its diffused model of intergovernmental relations, has also shaped the emerging MLG regime. As extra-constitutional entities with residual sovereignty, tribal governments in the United States assume their jurisdictional authority and, in many cases, compete with states to extend it.

Canadian First Nations, by contrast, have engaged in negotiations to have their jurisdictional rights recognised within the parameters of the Canadian constitution, as an addition to existing authorities. The Canadian context was more conducive to constitutional reforms in the 1980s and 1990s. The outcome is a more formal but, arguably, more limited, regime of self-government grounded in a mixture of constitutional rights and federal legislation. Indigenous governments therefore remain far more tightly integrated into the federal system, as creatures of the federal government, than their American counterparts. Self-government agreements in Canada do, nonetheless, provide greater protection for indigenous authority than American-style compacts. Indigenous multi-level-governance in Canada is also somewhat less diffused than in the United States. Intergovernmental negotiations are still relatively sheltered from external interests and First Nations rarely engage in the same interest-group-type lobbying as their American counterparts.

The comparison confirms that institutional legacies greatly matter in the process of self-determination. In the cases discussed here, different modes of colonial incorporation have led to different MLG regimes. Different federal systems have also led to different configurations in indigenous governance. The comparison also underlines the importance of agency in the institutional adaptation process. Key strategic choices made by indigenous leaders in order to seize opportunities provided by the political and legal landscape they faced have shaped the process of institutional recognition in different ways in Canada and the United States.

Beyond their similarities and differences, what are the consequences of these emerging multi-level governance regimes for indigenous peoples? While they have gained in autonomy and recognition in the process of challenging the institutional power grid of the two federal systems, indigenous governments are also, more than ever, willing participants *in* the very system whose legitimacy they were (and still are) challenging. In this respect, the emerging dynamics of MLG point in a similar direction in both countries. A number of authors see these developments positively. For Getches (1993) and Hicks (2007), the negotiation of compacts in the American context has the potential to reinforce the status of tribes as sovereign entities, with a role equivalent to that of states in the American constitution. In the Canadian context, Abele and Prince (2007) similarly view multi-level governance dynamics as an empowering development for indigenous peoples.

Others are more sceptical regarding the transformative potential of these emerging MLG regimes. In the American context, compacts are a very limited recognition of tribal authority and are still negotiated under the umbrella of the plenary power of Congress over tribal lands. Moreover, as Mason (1998) argues, the politics of compacting has forced tribes to engage more directly in state-level politics, thus shifting their position from one of external sovereigns to that of interest groups seeking political gains in a multi-level political battle. Corntassel and Witmer (2008) similarly conclude that the current model of indigenous multi-level governance increases the vulnerability of tribes to local majorities and contributes to their 'forced incorporation into the existing structure of American federalism' (2008: 5). Ultimately, the very act of engaging in MLG exercises, instead of reinforcing indigenous sovereignty, becomes a form of co-optation. A similar critique of existing models of self-government and treaty-based governance regimes was made in the Canadian context (Alfred 2005). The question, of course, is whether an alternative path actually exists for tribes and First Nations who are seeking to reassert their authority.

References

Abele, F. and Prince, M. (2006) 'Four pathways to aboriginal self-government in Canada', *American Review of Canadian Studies* 36(2): 568–95.

Alfred, T. (2005) *Wasáse: Indigenous pathways of action and freedom*, Peterborough, ON: Broadview Press.

Anaya, J. (2004) *Indigenous Peoples in International Law*, Oxford: Oxford University Press.

Ashley, J. S. and Hubbard, S. (2004) *Negotiated Sovereignty. Working to improve tribal–state relations*, Westport, CT: Praeger.

Behnke, N. and Benz, A. (2009) 'The politics of constitutional change between reform and evolution', *Publius: The Journal of Federalism* 39(2): 213–40.

Belanger, Y. D. and Newhouse, D. (2008) 'Reconciling solitudes: a critical analysis of the self-government ideal', in Y. Belanger (ed.), *Aboriginal Self-government in Canada. Current trends and issues*, 3rd edn, Saskatoon: Purich, pp. 1–19.

Biolsi, T. (2007) *Deadliest Enemies: Law and race relations on and off Rosebud Reservation*, Minneapolis, MN: University of Minnesota Press.

Bruyneel, K. (2007) *The Third Space of Sovereignty: The postcolonial politics of U.S. indigenous relations*, Minneapolis, MN: University of Minnesota Press.

Cairns, A. (2000) *Citizens Plus*, Vancouver: University of British Columbia Press.

Canada, Department of Indian Affairs and Northern Development (1995) *Aboriginal Self-government, Federal Policy Guide*, Ottawa: Public Works and Government Services.

Cornell, S. and Kalt, J. P. (2007) 'Two approaches to the development of Native Nations: one works, the other doesn't', in M. Jorgensen (ed.), *Rebuilding Native Nations. Strategies for governance and development*, Tucson, AZ: University of Arizona Press, pp. 3–41.

Corntassel, J. and Witmer, R. C. (2008) *Forced Federalism: Contemporary challenges to indigenous nationhood*, Oklahoma City, OK: University of Oklahoma Press.

Deloria, V. Jr. and Lytle, C. (1984) *The Nation Within. The past and future of American Indian sovereignty*, New York: Pantheon.

Getches, D. H. (1993) 'Negotiated sovereignty: intergovernmental agreements with American tribes as models for expanding self-government', *Review of Constitutional Studies* 1(1): 121–42.

Harvard Law Review Association (1999) 'Intergovernmental compacts in Native American law: models for expanded usage', *Harvard Law Review* 112(4): 922–39.

Hicks, S. L. (2007) 'Intergovernmental relationships: expressions of tribal sovereignty', in M. Jorgensen (ed.), *Rebuilding Native Nations: Strategies for governance and development*, Tucson, AZ: University of Arizona Press, pp. 246–72.

Jhappan, R. (1995) 'The federal-provincial power-grid and aboriginal self-government', in F. Rocher and M. Smith (eds), *New Trends in Canadian Federalism*, Peterborough, ON: Broadview, pp. 11–36.

Jorgensen, M. (2007) *Rebuilding Native Nations. Strategies for governance and development*, Tucson, AZ: University of Arizona Press.

Ladner, K. L. (2005) 'Up the creek: fishing for a new constitutional order', *Canadian Journal of Political Science*, 38(4): 923–53.

Light, S. A. (2008) 'Indian gaming and intergovernmental relations: state-level constraints on tribal political influence over policy outcomes', *American Review of Public Administration* 38(2): 225–43.

Long, J. A. and Boldt, M. (1988) *Governments in Conflict? Provinces and Indian Nations in Canada*, Toronto: University of Toronto Press.

Macklem, P. (2000) *Indigenous Difference and the Constitution of Canada*, Toronto, ON: University of Toronto Press.

Mahoney, J. and Thelen, K. (2010) 'A theory of gradual institutional change', in J. Mahoney and K. Thelen (eds), *Explaining Institutional Change. Ambiguity, agency, and power*, Cambridge: Cambridge University Press, pp. 1–37.

Marks, G. and Hooghe L. (2003) 'Unravelling the central state, but how? Types of multi-level governance', *American Political Science Review* 97(2): 233–43.

Mason, D. (1998) 'Tribes and states: a new era in intergovernmental affairs', *Publius: The Journal of Federalism*, 28(1): 111–30.

McNeil, K. (2004) *The Inherent Right of Self-government: Emerging directions for legal research*, Ottawa: First Nations Governance Centre.

Morse, B. (2008) 'Regaining recognition of the inherent right of aboriginal governance', in Y. Belanger (ed.), *Aboriginal Self-government in Canada. Current Trends and Issues*, 3rd edn, Saskatoon: Purich, pp. 55–84.

Papillon, M. (2012) 'Adapting federalism: indigenous multilevel governance in Canada and the United States', *Publius: The Journal of Federalism* 42(3): 294–16.

Piattoni, S. (2009) 'Multi-level governance: a historical and conceptual analysis', *Journal of European Integration* 31(2): 163–80.

Pierson, P. (2004) *Politics in Time: History, institutions, and social analysis*, Princeton, NJ: Princeton University Press.

Riker, W. H. (1964) *Federalism: Origin, operation and significance*, Boston, MA: Little, Brown & Company.

Rodden, J. (2006) *Hamilton's Paradox. The promise and peril of fiscal federalism*, Cambridge: Cambridge University Press.

Scharpf, F. W. (1988), 'The joint decision-trap: lessons from German federalism and European integration', *Public Administration* 66(2): 239–78.

Scholtz, C. (2006), 'Negotiating claims: the emergence of indigenous land claim negotiation policies in Australia, Canada, New Zealand, and the United States', New York: Routledge.

Skopek, T. A. and Hansen, K. N. (2006), 'Reservation gaming, tribal sovereignty, and the state of Texas: gaining ground in the political arena?', *Politics & Policy*, 34(1): 110–33.

Steinman, E. (2004) 'American federalism and intergovernmental innovation in state–tribal relations', *Publius: The Journal of Federalism* 34(2): 95–114.

Steinman, E. (2005) 'Indigenous nationhood claims and contemporary federalism in Canada and the United States', *Policy and Society* 24(1): 98–123.

Streeck, W. and Thelen, K. (2005), 'Institutional change in advanced political economies', in W. Streeck and K. Thelen (eds), *Beyond Continuity: Institutional change in advanced political economies*, Oxford: Oxford University Press, 1–19.

Wilkins, D. E. (1998) 'Tribal–state affairs: American Indian States as "disclaiming" sovereigns', *Publius: The Journal of Federalism* 28(4): 55–81

Wilkins, D. E. (2007) *American Indian Politics and the American Political System*, Lanham, MD: Rowman & Littlefield.

Williams, R. A. Jr. (2005) *Like a Loaded Weapon: The Rehnquist court, Indian rights, and the legal history of racism in America*, Minneapolis, MN: University of Minnesota Press.

PART II

INSTITUTIONAL ARRANGEMENTS – COUNTRY STUDIES

Chapter Five

Māori Representation and Participation in National and Local Government Politics

Ann Sullivan

Dedicated Māori seats in parliament have been a unique feature of New Zealand's electoral arrangements since 1867, although they have never been entrenched[1] as have other constitutionally important electoral provisions. The Māori seats were fixed at four, regardless of the size of parliament or the Māori and non-Māori populations, until electoral changes were made in 1993. Since New Zealand changed its electoral system from a simple majority, First-Past-the-Post (FPP) system to Mixed-Member Proportional (MMP) in 1996, the number of Māori Members of Parliament has been proportional to the Māori population.[2] Māori no longer have just a nominal presence in parliament. Under MMP, the substantive parliamentary representation of Māori has included a Māori representative in all major political parties as well as Māori elected by Māori for Māori through the Māori electorates and via an explicitly Māori political party. The proportional electoral system coupled with the dedicated Māori electorates enables the proportional representation of Māori at a national level but this is not mirrored at the sub-national level of governance. Currently, both structural and political barriers prevent equitable Māori representation in local government.[3]

The right of Māori, the indigenous peoples, to be represented by Māori in parliament and sub-nationally on local government councils is considered by Māori to be a fundamental entitlement, guaranteed in 1840 when Māori signed the *te Tiriti o Waitangi*/Treaty of Waitangi. The broad principles of the three Treaty articles were understood to be about partnership, protection and participation (Te Puni Kōkiri 2001: 4). The treaty principles are notable for having been breached rather than honoured by the Crown.[4] Article 1 of the

---

1. The Māori electorates can be amended by a simple voting majority in the House of Representatives, whereas entrenched clauses require a 75 per cent majority of all MPs.

2. The Māori-descent population at the 2006 census was 643,977 or 16 per cent of the total population. The Māori ethnic population was 565,329 or 14 per cent. See Statistics New Zealand 2007b: Quickstats About Māori. http://www.stats.govt.nz/census/2006-census-data/quickstats-about-maori/2006-census-quickstats-about-maori-revised.htm.

3. For the purposes of this chapter, the term local government includes regional councils, the Auckland Council and other territorial authorities that can be either city or district councils. In 2010 there were 78 elected councils (because of the effects of the major earthquake, the 2010 Canterbury Regional Council elections were suspended and its councillors were replaced with commissioners).

4. See http://www.waitangi-tribunal.govt.nz.

Māori language version of *te Tiriti O Waitangi* gave the British Crown the right to govern (*kawanatanga*), which Māori understood to be a partnership between Māori and the Crown. In the English version of the Treaty, the Crown has sovereignty rights but its principle of partnership is still being defined by government, the Courts and a range of government departments (see Te Puni Kokiri 2001).[5] In the second article, the principle of protection was a guarantee by the Crown to protect Māori ownership of their resources and prized possessions. Treaty settlements since the early 1990s are acknowledgements of the Crown's failure to uphold Māori ownership rights to their lands, forests, fisheries, estates and other significant treasures. Māori rights to participate equally with non-Māori are clearly stated in the third article. Current national electoral provisions *are* inclusive of the indigenous peoples (and other minority groups) and enable Māori participation and representation. The reserved Māori seats in the New Zealand Parliament provide symbolic recognition of the unique status of Māori as *tangata whenua*, the indigenous peoples of New Zealand, within New Zealand's constitutional framework, and they are part of the Crown's Treaty obligation to protect Māori interests as Treaty partners. The electoral process ensures that both signatories to the Treaty of Waitangi are represented in the legislature.

This chapter will, first, outline the political environment that divides the two main schools of thought on direct Māori representation. An historical overview of Māori representation will then provide the background and context for the discussion on the type of Māori representation that currently exists in local government and the significance of indigenous political mobilisation, both domestically and internationally, for promoting change to electoral processes that systematically discriminate against indigenous peoples (and minority groups).

Māori representation

Underlying a lack of government support for entrenching dedicated Māori electorates in New Zealand's constitutional arrangements is the long-held, simplistic belief that the existence of formal legal and political equality means that everyone is equal in practice. New Zealand's conservative political parties promote the notion that because Māori have the right to vote there is no need for separate Māori representation through dedicated Māori seats in parliament. That perception has been fostered by the democratic ideals on which British sovereignty in New Zealand was based, with core values of equal rights, equal treatment and equal opportunities. It was an ideal that was articulated and advanced at the signing of *te Tiriti o Waitangi*/the Treaty of Waitangi in 1840 when the British representative, Captain Hobson, made the

---

5. In international law, the principle of *contra proferentem* means that if there is an ambiguous phrase or wording in a document then it will be interpreted against the party responsible for drafting it – in this case, the British Crown. In practice, the English version of the Treaty of Waitangi is recognised by the Crown.

statement '*He iwi tahi tātou*', commonly interpreted, as 'we are all one people'. It encapsulated the generally held belief by the new settlers and the colonial office that Māori would assimilate[6] into a polity based on the British model of representative government. The presumption that 'we are all one nation, all one people and everyone must be treated equally' has been constantly reinforced by government and underpinned government policies of assimilation, integration, devolution and mainstreaming from the 1850s until today (Durie 1998; Fleras and Elliott 1992; Fleras and Spoonley 1999; Sullivan 2003b; Walker 1990; Ward 1974). The New Zealand government continually reminds its citizens that the state is sovereign and its power indivisible and it is concerned with nation-building by constructing and maintaining an imagined community of people with equal rights and a universal citizenship.

Government promotes a strong sense of civic nationalism, which Ignatieff (1993: 7–8) defines 'as a community of equal, rights-bearing citizens, united in patriotic attachment to a shared set of patriotic practices and values'. This construction of a nation strengthens and maintains the state by promoting cohesion among all members of the community, regardless of ethnic, religious, linguistic or community allegiances, ensuring that they adhere to the values and recognise the institutions of the state (Fleras and Spoonley 1999: 288). A universal citizenry based on inclusiveness of social ties fostering a common language, religious freedom and multiculturalism is maintained through a state-led education system, a standard national language and a uniform legal system. It unites the people for political, economic, defence and social purposes. This unity of purpose is used to depoliticise difference, to convince the people that they have a common interest and to engender (and to continually legitimise) support and loyalty of the people to government and for state actions. It is not an identity built on the more exclusive characteristics of *whakapapa*/common descent that bind Māori as a people. It is an identity that seeks to make ethnicity invisible. The rationale for providing and retaining dedicated Māori electorates has shifted from its initial purpose of providing Māori, the indigenous peoples of New Zealand, with a presence in parliament – albeit temporarily because Māori would eventually be assimilated into the universal citizenry on an equal basis (which never happened) – to the symbolic recognition of the position of the Māori as a 'Treaty partner', arising from the status of the Treaty of Waitangi in New Zealand's constitutional framework (Geddis 2006).

A major effect of Māori demands for guaranteed Māori representation nationally and sub-nationally has been to raise the question whether representative democracy should merely treat everyone the same way procedurally or whether everyone should have an equal capacity to participate, even if that means

---

6. According to Ward (1974: 39), the official amalgamation policy of the Colonial Office and the New Zealand settler government aimed to provide Māori with equal standing to the settlers, facilitated by the British-style state institutions. The policy itself was flawed however because of 'European attitudes of racial or cultural superiority, and by pandering to settler prejudices, which denied the Maori real participation in the European order, except at a menial level'.

implementing special measures for some groups (Catt, 1999). Essentially, the two notions of democracy differ over whether it is enough for democracy to recognise just the equal civil and political rights of individuals or whether we must recognise that democracy has the capacity and indeed the responsibility to recognise and respect the *collective* rights of indigenous peoples who have been dispossessed, had lands appropriated and faced cultural genocide and assimilation (Tully 1995; Kymlicka 1995). The simplistic notion of treating everyone the same prevents recognition of the collective (Māori) and does not recognise differences of ethnicity, gender, class or socio-economic circumstances. Equal treatment does not ensure equal outcomes and social, economic and political inequalities can disadvantage or advantage identifiable groups or collectives. In New Zealand, Māori are at the bottom of nearly all social and economic indicators (Ministry of Social Development 2010) and their voter turnout in both national and local government elections is much lower than non-Māori (Sullivan 2010: 543). Turnout is usually related to socio-economic status and, according to Lijphart (1997: 2,7) there is compelling evidence that 'unequal voting participation is associated with policies that favour privileged voters over underprivileged voters', in areas such as taxation and welfare. Plurality electoral systems such as FPP exclude and make invisible minority indigenous groups, allowing governments to pursue '... policies broadly in accordance with the objective economic interests and subjective preferences of their class-defined core political constituencies' (Lijphart 1997: 4). The uncritical, equal-treatment approach gives unequal influence to dominant groups because 'the higher a person's socioeconomic and educational level – especially the latter – the higher his (or her) political interest, participation, and voting turnout' (Berelson, B. and Steiner, A. in Lijphart 1997: 3).

In 1987, the Court of Appeal said that 'the duty of the Crown is not merely passive but extends to active protection of Māori people in the use of their lands and waters to the fullest extent practicable' (New Zealand Court of Appeal 1987: 642). The Crown clearly has an obligation and duty, as directed by the Court, to actively protect Māori interests. Justice McGechan advised the Crown that

> ... there is no doubt Treaty principles impose a positive obligation on the Crown, within constraints of the reasonable, to protect the position of Maori under the Treaty and the expression from time to time of that position ... It is a broad obligation of good faith. Maori representation – Maori seats – have become such an expression. Adding this together, for my own part I consider the Crown was and is under a Treaty obligation to protect and facilitate Māori representation (Anonymous 1994: 69).

The Māori electorates could be abolished by a simple parliamentary majority and political parties are divided in their support for separate Māori representation. The centre-right parties (National, New Zealand First, ACT) argue for abolition of the Māori electorates because 'we are all one people'. However, at the 2011 elections both the National party and the New Zealand First party agreed not to seek to remove the Māori seats without the consent of Māori.[7] That agreement is a political accommodation, however, and leaves the retention of the Māori electorates vulnerable to political whim. The centre-left political parties (Labour, Greens, Māori party, Mana Party[8]) support separate Māori representation. Because the Māori electorates are not constitutionally entrenched and could be abolished by a simple parliamentary majority, Māori are seeking legislative change to guarantee the future of Māori seats in parliament. The Māori seats are an incentive for all political parties to ensure they have Māori candidates elected through their party lists, as has transpired since MMP was introduced in 1996. Prior to MMP, few Māori were elected to parliament outside the (then) four Māori electorates. Post-MMP, Māori on party lists of all the major parties and the Māori electorates have given Māori proportional representation. Māori have mobilised both domestically and internationally to pressure government to secure Māori representation rights permanently.

A history of Māori representation in the national parliament

Hokia nga whakaaro ki onamata, hei whakau onaianei kia anamata.
('Look to the past, so we can understand the present and plan for the future'
Māori proverb)

Following the signing of the Treaty of Waitangi in 1840, the British quickly established parliamentary sovereignty and, in 1852, passed the New Zealand Constitution Act, which provided the framework for responsible government based on the British Westminster system of government. Like other indigenous peoples who signed treaties with colonising powers (see Coates and McHugh 1998; Fleras and Elliott 1992: 31; Havemann 1999) Māori consider the treaty signed by their chiefly ancestors and the British Crown to be a living and binding document. It is a treaty of three Articles; all three Articles have been in dispute since it was signed in 1840 because the Māori version, *te Tiriti o Waitangi*, is incompatible with the English version, the Treaty of Waitangi. In the Māori version, Article 1 provided the British Crown with governing rights but the English version gave the British Crown sovereignty. Article 2 in the Māori version recognised Māori ownership of all resources and treasured possessions[9] while the English version states that Māori were guaranteed 'the full and exclusive and undisturbed possession of their Lands and Estates, Forests, Fisheries and other properties'. Article 3 is the least

---

7. This position did not change following the 2014 elections. See http://www.national.org.nz/ PDF_Government/Maori_Party_agreement-11_Dec.pdf; http://nzfirst.org.nz/sites/nzfirst/files/ manifesto2011-4.pdf; Māori consent presumably refers to Māori voters on the Māori roll but that has not yet been articulated.

8. The Mana Party has a socialist, classed-based ideology. It currently has one seat in parliament and is led by a former member of the Māori party.

9. Treasured possessions refers to both tangible (land) and intangible (language, spiritual) assets.

problematic of the three Articles. It provides rights of equality and, in both the Māori and English versions, Māori are guaranteed reciprocity rights, all rights and privileges of English subjects (Mutu 2003).

The Treaty is more notable for how often it has been breached than for its implied promises and guarantees. The desire of immigrants for Māori land and resources rapidly depleted tribal properties and estates. The 1860s land wars[10] were just the beginning of an insatiable demand for precious Māori possessions. Māori lost much of their economic resource-base through unjust, illegal, excessive or surplus land confiscations (AJHR 1908, 1921, 1928, 1948) and questionable court rulings that said Māori customary rights did not continue once the Crown acquired sovereignty in 1840 (see Brookfield 2005). The combined effects rapidly impoverished most *iwi* (tribe) and *hapu* (subtribe).

Initially, the franchise was granted to all males over the age of 21 years who held title to land. In principle, Māori males were eligible to vote but, in reality, most were disenfranchised as few Māori had individual title to land because Māori land was held communally, in customary title. In 1867, government passed legislation providing four reserved Māori seats in parliament. At that time, parliament had already provided special representation for retired members of the British armed forces, it had enfranchised British subjects who held gold-miner's licenses and, in 1867, a further two parliamentary seats were introduced to accommodate the influx of gold-miners to the South Island (RCER 1986: A16–19). The introduction of Māori seats was initially to be a temporary measure, only deemed necessary until Māori land was converted to individual title. Once Māori had individual title to land, separate representation would no longer be necessary to ensure the Māori equal voting rights guaranteed in Article 3 of *te Tiriti*/the Treaty. In practice, the Māori electorates have been an ongoing component of New Zealand's electoral arrangements.

But other political considerations were taken into account when the Māori electorates were established. Following the land wars of the 1860s, providing Māori seats in parliament was a way for the government to appease those tribes who had resisted government forces as well as rewarding those tribes who supported the government. The seats would not only provide a new leadership structure but also support the assimilation policies of the colonial government, by undermining traditional tribal leadership structures and reducing resistance to land sales. More cynically, the creation of Māori electorates enabled the North Island parliamentarians to retain their numerical parliamentary strength, which would have been lost with the additional seats accommodating the gold-miners of the South Island. The Māori seats also countered the strong criticisms of the lack of Māori participation in New Zealand's electoral processes being voiced by the humanitarian lobby in Britain (see Sorrenson in RCES 1986 B18-21).

---

10. For an overview of the New Zealand land wars, see D. Keenan (2012), 'New Zealand wars', Te Ara – Encyclopedia of New Zealand, updated 9 November 2012: http://www.TeAra.govt.nz/en/new-zealand-wars/sources (accessed 1 April 2015).

The temporary nature of the four reserved Māori electorates was removed in 1876 because the individualisation of Māori land title was taking much longer than initially envisaged and because there were concerns that moving Māori on to the European electoral rolls would jeopardise the *status quo* or allow Māori to exercise undue influence on the European seats.

When the franchise was first introduced, Māori voting was by a show of hands; in 1910, this was changed to Māori voters declaring their choice to a returning officer. Māori voting was a very public act. Māori did not get the secret ballot until 1937 even though it had been employed in the European electorates since 1871. It was not until 1951 that Māori voted on the same day as non-Māori. The Chatham Islands were proclaimed part of New Zealand in 1842 but their inhabitants, predominantly Māori and Moriori, were not enfranchised until 1922. To vote, individuals had to be registered on an electoral roll. It was compulsory for non-Māori to register in 1924 but not considered necessary for Māori until 1956. Blood quantum was removed as the defining characteristic of 'Māori' for electoral purposes in 1975 and the electoral definition of 'Māori' was changed to 'a person of the Māori race of New Zealand and includes any descendant of such a person' (Electoral Act 1993 §3 (1). Currently, anyone of Māori descent has the choice of registering on either the Māori or General[11] electoral roll.

The provision of four reserved Māori electorates did not guarantee Māori equal voting rights. The FPP electoral system and electoral irregularities privileged non-Māori over Māori. A major failing of FPP is its simple majority, winner-takes-all effect. It does not give political parties seats proportional to their voter support. FPP makes it very difficult for any minority group to secure representation commensurate with their electoral support. During the 140 years of parliamentary FPP voting in New Zealand, Māori political parties were unable to register enough support to gain seats in parliament and, as individual members of mainstream parties, only five Māori[12] (outside the Māori electorates) had enough mainstream party support to be elected to parliament via the European/General electorates.

The Māori electorates were fixed at four, regardless of the size of the electoral population: hence, the Māori vote was not equal to that of the European vote since the population quota for the general electorates was not applied to the Māori electorates. The general electoral boundaries are reviewed every five years to reflect changes in the population and to ensure that each electorate has a similar population size. Determining Māori seats on a population basis, just the same as the European/General electorates, did not occur until the Electoral Act 1993 was passed. After each five-yearly census, electoral boundaries are redrawn; at that time, people who indicate on their electoral enrolment form that they are of Māori descent are given the option of registering on either the Māori electoral roll or the General electoral roll.[13] The result of the Māori Electoral Option forms the

---

11. The term 'European' applied to all non-Māori electorates until 1975 when it changed to 'General'.

12. James Carroll, Rex Austin, Ben Couch, Winston Peters, Ian Peters.

13. Māori identity is self-reported for census purposes. However, tribes use *whakapapa*/bloodlines to recognise their own tribal members.

basis for calculating the Māori electoral population, which then determines the number of Māori electorates.[14] The number of Māori electorates can increase or decrease, depending on the number of Māori who choose the Māori electoral roll. The new, more equitable, basis for determining Māori representation resulted in an immediate increase in reserved Māori seats. As Māori realised that the Māori vote finally had the same weight and value as the non-Māori vote, the number of Māori choosing to enrol on the Māori electoral roll resulted in the number of Māori electorates increasing from four in 1993 to seven in 2002. In 2011, nearly 60 per cent of all eligible Māori voters chose to enrol on the Māori electoral roll.[15] Like any other group, Māori vary in their political views and just over two fifths of Māori voters chose to be on the General roll. Their reasons likely range from preferring to be represented by centre-right political parties to believing there is no need for separate Māori electorates. The 1993 electoral changes have removed the structural barriers that had restricted the opportunity for Māori to fully participate as equal citizens. Since the first MMP election in 1993, the number of MPs with Māori ancestry has been proportional to the Māori population. The dedicated Māori seats coupled with the proportional electoral system can be seen as the Crown complying with its Treaty obligation to actively protect Māori interests and its duty to act in good faith towards its Treaty partner.

Māori representation in local government

In New Zealand, local government authorities are responsible for a range of functions that include resource-management and regulation, management of rivers and lakes, coastal marine areas, environmental planning, water supply, sewage treatment, urban transport and community facilities (Department of Internal Affairs 2011). The management of natural and physical resources is integral to every Māori tribe/*iwi* and subtribe/*hapu*, as their culture, traditions and identity come from their relationship with their ancestral lands, sacred sites, waters, mountains, forests and fauna. It has been estimated that the asset base of the Māori economy is more than $36 billion with nearly $11 billion of those assets controlled by tribal entities. Close to 50 per cent of the tribally controlled assets are in agriculture, forestry and fishing (BERL 2010). Māori participation in and contribution to the wider New Zealand economy is growing, with much of their investment channelled through co-operative enterprises based on culturally-based sustainable development principles that emphasise 'the inter-dependence of the spiritual, cultural and physical environments, the individual and the

---

14. See http://www.elections.org.nz/events/māori-electoral-option-2013/about-māori-electoral-option/calculating-future-māori-and-general (accessed 18 December 2014).

15. Following the 2006 census, the 417081 Māori electors were given the option to be enrolled on either the Māori or General electoral rolls. 244,121 (58.5%) are enrolled on the Māori electoral roll. 178,139 are on the General electoral roll. See Statistics New Zealand 2007a. Electoral Populations Calculated: 2006, updated 26 February 2007.

group' (New Zealand Institute of Economic Research and Ministry of Maori Development 2003: 44–5).

Considerable Māori development is taking place at the tribal, regional level and Māori tribal entities are major stakeholders in some regions. Māori engagement with natural resources and with local governments has been ongoing (see Selby *et al.* 2010) and Tawhai (2010) shows that in recent years there has been a growing number of co-management arrangements between tribes and local authorities. However, the political relationship between local Māori and local authorities, Hayward (2011) demonstrates, falls short of the Crown's obligations to actively protect Māori rights of direct representation on local authority councils. To a large extent, local governments shape the direction of local development in their resource-planning and management. Yet even though many tribes heavily invest in their local economies, despite Treaty obligations for councils to consult and encourage Māori participation in local government, and despite the need for elected councils to reflect or mirror the ethnic diversity of their constituents, few Māori manage to get elected to local councils, even though Māori are 15 per cent of the population.

In 1986, a Royal Commission appointed by government to investigate and report on the New Zealand electoral system recommended the New Zealand electoral system change from plurality (FPP) to a proportional system because the plurality system 'fails to reflect the diversity in our society' and was not likely to be integrative (Royal Commission on the Electoral System 1986: 64). The government duly noted the Commission's recommendation and changed to MMP for national elections but it allowed the inequitable FPP system to remain for local elections. However, legislative reform post-2001 to 'address the under-representation of Māori, women and minorities on local councils' resulted in legislation being passed so that now councils have the option to use a proportional electoral system, plus the option to introduce reserved Māori wards (Hayward 2011: 189). These legislative changes appeared to remove historical structural barriers that restricted or inhibited the equitable representation of Māori on local councils. In practice, however, barriers remain.

Local government electoral system: FPP or STV?

Between 1984 and 1990, the New Zealand government carried out a rapid and radical restructuring of its economy and of the state (see Boston 1991; Durie 2005; Kelsey 1995). Electoral change followed and, with triennial reviews of local government, aimed to strengthen public participation in local government politics. Māori had been very active in promoting change that would address Māori concerns (Rikys 2004), including the direct representation of Māori on local councils. Subsequently, the Local Electoral Act 2001 was passed, providing local authorities with the option of retaining the plurality FPP system or changing to STV (Single Transferable Vote). Under STV, voters rank candidates in order of preference and a candidate is elected when they receive a specified number of votes, determined by the size of the electorate and the number of positions to be filled. Any surplus votes are then redistributed to second-preference candidates and so on. Thus, very few votes are wasted, whereas, under FPP, large numbers of votes are wasted. Plurality systems tend to over-represent majority groups and

> ... are grossly unfair to supporters of minor parties ... [They] fail to ensure reasonable recognition and representation for significant minority and other special interest groups. In particular ... plurality denies effective Māori representation (Royal Commission on the Electoral System 1986: 28).

> Majoritarian democracy may provide better government but consensus (proportional) democracy is better at representing (Lijphart 1999: 275).

The New Zealand experience has been that local government councils were disproportionally constituted by wealthy, middle- or upper-class European males, predominantly from professional backgrounds and most likely Eurocentric in outlook and life experiences (Sullivan 2003b: 147). Councils tend to be dominated by people with similar socio-economic standing; local administrations may have been strong and stable but that does not necessarily translate into more representative governance. Voting under STV is more likely to provide a greater diversity of elected candidates that mirrors the characteristics of the community than an FPP-elected council.

In New Zealand, party politics are not a factor in local government elections. Candidates usually stand as independents to emphasise their political independence from national party politics and this has long been a feature of local government politics (Mulgan 2004). According to Summersby (2005: 51–2) the STV option was chosen for local government rather than MMP because it better provides for the local government constituency, where political parties are not a feature of local government elections – in contrast to the national elections. STV is likely to better provide for minority groups because few votes are 'wasted'; instead, votes in excess of the STV quota are redistributed, thereby providing opportunity for selection of a minority candidate (see Dummett 1997).

> Anti-partisan sentiments in New Zealand local body politics run deep. Those political parties that put up candidates in local body elections tend to mask their identity by running as Independents or in ostensibly non-partisan organisations (Miller 2005: 63).

Additionally, Summersby continues, STV was not specifically aimed at improving Māori representation: rather it was intended to give a balance between fairness and effectiveness, so that special-interest groups such as 'islands and remote rural communities' could be given a voice. At the 2010 local authority elections, more than 90 per cent of local councils used FPP rather than STV (only six of the 78 local authorities used STV). According to Hayward (2011) the most influential factor in councils' decisions to retain FPP is the perception that

STV is complex when, in reality, few problems have arisen (it is used for elections to local health boards, for example). Summersby (2005: 77) also suggests that people are resistant to STV because they have a perception that vote-counting under STV takes too long. Additionally, Cheyne and Comrie (2005: 201) argue that STV is resisted because a number of councillors argue (wrongly) that it is more costly to use than FPP. The limited available data indicates that even using STV, Māori are having a difficult time getting elected, although it should be noted that STV is less likely to deliver representatives from populations that are small and four of the STV regions using STV in 2010 had Māori populations of less than 8 per cent.[16]

Reserved Māori wards in local government

It has been already been demonstrated that the combination of both reserved seats and a proportional electoral system provides fair and proportional representation for Māori in New Zealand's national elections but neither of these considerations has led to the mandatory adoption of MMP at local governance levels. In 2001, one local government council (the Bay of Plenty Regional Council) changed its electoral structure to provide three reserved Māori seats on the Council through its own legislative act.[17] It is a region in which Māori comprise some 25 per cent of the total population but, historically, few Māori have been elected to the Council and none have been re-elected for a second term (Trapski 1998). As with national elections, Māori Councillors are elected by Māori registered on the Māori Electoral Roll, according to where they reside. The number of Māori wards depends on the size of the Māori population. The reserved Māori wards are widely supported in the Bay of Plenty region. They have enabled the Council to be inclusive of Māori communities and the Māori stakeholders that they represent and to be better-informed on local Māori perspectives; Māori Councillors can engage with their local Māori communities. Even Councillors who initially opposed the idea of dedicated Māori wards have publicly supported the positive contribution of Māori Councillors to decision-making (Human Rights Commission 2010).

Since 2002, all other local government councils have had the option to provide better for their Māori constituents by establishing reserved Māori wards without the need for special legislation like that of the Bay of Plenty Council. Up to 2013, no council chose to do so. The Waikato regional council and the New Plymouth regional councils intend to have two Māori wards in the 2016 local government elections but Māori are still severely under-represented on the policy- and decision-making bodies that directly affect Māori resources, lands, forests, fisheries, water and sacred sites. The official data[18] suggests that around 9 per cent of all

---

16. Local councils have on average about 12–14 members and Māori populations are dispersed throughout the region so they are unable to vote as a block for a candidate.

17. Bay of Plenty Regional Council (Māori Constituency Empowering) Act 2001.

18. Department of Internal Affairs 2011, 'Local Authority Election Statistics 2010', Wellington, NZ: Department of Internal Affairs: 146.

elected local government councillors in 2010 were of Māori descent; however, the substantive representation of Māori, Sullivan (2011: 63) argues, is likely to be less than 2 per cent. Official data on descent does not reliably indicate whether a person identifies as Māori: it only provides descriptive data that identifies a person as having some Māori ancestry. Being able to claim Māori ancestry does not mean that person understands and reflects the ideals and aspirations of Māori electoral roll voters; nor do claims to Māori ancestry reflect an individual's active connection to Māori culture and values. Sullivan's (2011) research shows that few of the elected councillors who claim Māori descent are enrolled on the Māori electoral roll; they do not claim to represent Māori nor do they promote specific Māori interests, which means most of the councillors who have Māori ancestry are unlikely to identify with the Māori roll constituency.

The experience of the one local council with dedicated Māori wards has been extremely positive. Research by the Human Rights Commission demonstrates the existence of Māori wards in the Bay of Plenty is a beneficial arrangement for Council and councillors, the community and local Māori. They also help the council meet its legal Māori participation obligations.

> They have proven their worth to Māori and non-Māori. They appear [to] have given Māori a sense of participation and a sense belonging in the democratic process that they did not appear to have before. The Bay of Plenty Regional Council is a richer democracy for their participation (Human Rights Commission 2010: 7).

Māori representation and the Auckland Council

In 2010, the New Zealand government refused to adopt the recommendation of the government-appointed Royal Commission on Auckland Governance (Salmon *et al.* 2009: 487)[19] that there be mandatory Māori representation on the new unitary Auckland Council,[20] which was to replace the existing eight local authorities in Auckland. The rationale for the Royal Commission's recommendation was the special status of Māori as partners under the Treaty of Waitangi. The Commission argued that a mandatory requirement for dedicated Māori seats would give effect to Treaty of Waitangi obligations and ensure that Māori had an opportunity to contribute to decision-making. The Commission also recognised 'that the under-representation of Māori was not a result of Māori failing to stand for election but was instead attributed

---

19. The Royal Commission on Auckland Governance was appointed by government in 2007, to identify and make appropriate recommendations for the long-term governance arrangements for Auckland.

20. On 1 November 2010, the Auckland Council replaced the Auckland Regional Council, Auckland City Council, Manukau City Council, North Shore City Council, Papakura District Council, Rodney District Council, Waitakere City Council and Franklin District Council as the unitary authority for the Auckland District.

to the inability of many Māori candidates (particularly if they were perceived to have an overtly Māori agenda) to secure election by a non-Māori majority' (Royal Commission on Auckland Governance, 2009: 486). Additionally, the Commission (2009: 487) argued that the special status of Māori in the Auckland region being *mana whenua*/'people of the land' and their status as partners under the Treaty of Waitangi made it important to safeguard Māori wards and, even more importantly, should Māori as a proportion of the population decline over time then their interests needed continuing protection.

The argument made to Cabinet by the Minister of Local Government against supporting dedicated Māori seats on the Auckland Council was that the current legislation, the Local Electoral Act 2001, provided an appropriate mechanism to enable communities themselves to decide whether they wanted separate Māori representation in local government; as such, this provided for community engagement and fulfilled Treaty obligations. The opposing argument, made by the Minister of Māori Affairs, was that while provisions already existed for establishing Māori representation in local governance, which did signal Crown support of direct Māori representation, the provisions of the Local Electoral Act 2001 were flawed and had never been invoked; moreover, provision for Māori representation had only ever been made via the establishment of special legislation. The current legislation, the Minister of Māori Affairs argued, in fact left it to the decision of the general populace whether Māori should have direct representation, whereas this question should be determined by Māori themselves (CAB Min 2009: 8–9). The government supported the Minister of Local Government and chose not to legislate for separate Māori seats on the Auckland Council.

Several thousand Māori and large numbers of non-Māori protested the government's decision not to accept the Royal Commission's recommendation for dedicated Māori seats on the Auckland Council. Local Māori mobilised and led a march along the main street of Auckland to demonstrate their disappointment with government for failing to recognise that an inclusive partnership with Māori not only recognised the contribution Māori made to the region but also made good business sense. In Auckland, there is considerable tribal wealth. One local *iwi*, Ngati Whatua o Orakei,[21] had assets valued at $422 million in 2012 and another tribal provider, Te Whanau o Waipareira Trust[22] had assets valued at $24 million and also generated more than $14 million of social services and was a major employer and Māori service-provider. Sullivan (2010: 542) documents how the active engagement of local councils with local *iwi*/tribes has resulted in proactive sustainable developments.[23] For example, Māori were instrumental in forcing

---

21. See Ngati Whatua Orakei 2012, Annual Report 2011–2012: http://www.ngatiwhatuaorakei.com/images/stories/downloads/wha_annual_report_final_071112.pd4.

22. See Te Whanau o Waipareira Trust 2012, Annual Report July 2011–2012: http://www.waipareira.com/literatureretrieve.aspx?id=112869 (accessed 28 May 2015).

23. 'Report of the Royal Commission on the Electoral System', M. J. H. Wallace (ed.), Wellington: Government Printer, 1986); 'Report of the Royal Commission on Auckland Governance', (Auckland, 2009).

petrochemical plants in Taranaki to clean up their waste before it was discharged into the sea. In Auckland, the magnificent Takaparawha Point (Bastion Point) is the jewel in Auckland's Crown, only because local Māori tribes prevented the prime real estate from going into private ownership.

In the 2010 elections to Auckland Council, none of the 21 elected councillors identified as Māori. Three councillors acknowledged having some Māori ancestry but none were on the Māori electoral roll and none identified themselves as being part of the local Māori community or tribe.

Substitute model of Māori representation

Instead of accepting the advice of its Royal Commission to include dedicated Māori wards on the new Auckland council, Government chose to set up an Independent Māori Statutory Board (IMSB) to represent Māori interests in Auckland. The purpose of the IMSB is to monitor both the Auckland Council's performance relating to its Treaty of Waitangi responsibilities and its response to 'issues of significance' for Māori. The Board is an independent statutory board funded by the Council and it has nine Māori members appointed by a Iwi Selection Body that is made up of mandated representatives nominated from the local tribes in the Auckland region. Seven are from local sub-tribes (*mana whenua*) and two represent urban Māori who have migrated to the Auckland region (*matāwaka*). The makeup of the Board reflects the importance Māori place on *mana whenua* – the people on whose land the city of Auckland has prospered. The composition of the IMSB recognises traditional Māori structures of *iwi*/tribe and *hapu*/subtribe. The appointment process both recognises both ancestral occupancy and acknowledges the need for representation of Māori who have migrated to the Auckland region. The structure of the Board provides accountability to local Māori because the Board members are appointed from the local, sub-tribal Māori communities and have reporting responsibilities back to their sub-tribe. Because they are funded by the Council they are accountable to it for expenditure but they are otherwise independent. Members are politically accountable to their people (their term of office is a three-year appointment that may be renewable) for promoting cultural, economic, environmental and social issues that are significant to Māori in the Auckland region to the Council.

The Board does not have voting rights on the Auckland Council; rather, its members attend and participate in Council sub-committee meetings. In other words, Māori can make representations to the Council but they are not part of the governing, decision-making body. The IMSB is an advisory body with formal processes of engagement clearly defined. ISMB members convey Māori views to Council committees, which can then be taken into account by the Auckland Council. The IMSB was first established in July 2010. The IMSB members 'sit as members' of council committees that deal with the management and stewardship of natural and physical resources. They are able to participate in committee deliberations and have voting rights on those sub-council committees. There has been some debate over the IMSB members being able to vote on council committees because they are not 'elected' members. However, they are 'not observers or advisors but members', with voting rights as determined in the Local Government Act 2002 (§7). There has also been criticism of the funding required to make the IMSB functional, operational, effective and efficient. It requires premises, a secretariat and operating expenses. In 2011, the IMSB threatened to take the Auckland Council to court when it initially refused to fund reasonable operational costs; the issue was finally settled outside of court. Following the public debate about these two issues, some of the IMSB's critics have suggested 'that dedicated Māori wards are a more acceptable option for Māori representation than an appointed Independent Māori Statutory Board' (Sullivan 2011: 70). It is too soon to assess the effectiveness or otherwise of the ISMB but it seems reasonable to expect it will help inform elected council members of Māori perspectives when Council makes its deliberations. Council has an obligation to consider Māori advice but it is not obliged to act on that advice. The IMSB is a means of representing Māori interests to Council; however, that representation is only partial. The IMSB has participatory rights on council committees but those rights are denied at the decision-making table and the Māori struggle for equality continues.

Conclusion

Because the government is unwilling to mandate direct Māori representation in local government, Māori organisations have mobilised to heighten and highlight their grievances beyond the borders of New Zealand. The government of New Zealand endorsed the UN Declaration on the Rights of Indigenous Peoples in April 2010. That endorsement recognises the collective right of Māori to fully participate in the governance of New Zealand. Article 18 of the Declaration declares that indigenous peoples have 'the right to participate in decision-making in matters which would affect their rights'. Dedicated Māori wards would realise the fundamental right to participate and comply with the intent of the Declaration. The Declaration is an international instrument that could be used to bring international attention to grievances that Māori consider have been unfairly dealt with by government. In 2011, the United Nations Special Rapporteur on the Rights of Indigenous Peoples recommended the government 'consider reversing its decision to reject the findings of the Royal Commission on Auckland Governance and guarantee Māori seats on the Auckland Council (Anaya 2011). The Special Rapporteur has also recommended that the government entrench the Treaty of Waitangi in constitutional law.

Two Royal Commissions have recommended that seats be reserved for Māori in government and on local government councils. Royal Commissions of Inquiry are appointed by the Governor-General in the name of the Crown and are set up by government when a matter of public importance needs to be considered objectively and in depth. They advise government on policy and possible courses of action. They are not part of the legislature, the executive or the judiciary. Traditionally, Royal Commissions deliberate on matters of great national importance (Ringer 1991: 231). Māori consider reserved Māori seats to be of great importance and the United Nations Special Rapporteur agrees, as do the independent, objective members of the two Royal Commissions. The Courts have determined that the Crown has Treaty obligations to provide reserved Māori seats. Government recognises that obligation at the national level by retaining reserved Māori electorates. That recognition has yet to filter down to local government and is, instead, subject to 'the political whim of local electorates. The creation of the Independent Māori Statutory Board provides limited Māori representation. It gives Māori some, but not full, participation rights. While local government councillors have the option of changing their electoral system to a system that better provides for minority representation and the option to provide reserved Māori wards, there are few incentives for councillors to support electoral change. Councillors generally fail to recognise that the economic development and the social wellbeing of their communities requires both engagement with Māori and the participation of Māori.

The signatories to the Treaty of Waitangi were the Māori and the Crown. The Courts have determined that the Crown has obligations to Māori as the Treaty partner to actively protect Māori interests. The Māori electorates are an expression of that good-faith requirement. Local government elected councils are not Treaty partners; their powers are derived from the Crown. Local government legislation clearly states it is '… the Crown's responsibility to take appropriate account of the principles of the Treaty of Waitangi' and it is the Crown's responsibility to provide opportunities for Māori to participate in its decision-making processes (Part 1, §4 Local Government Act 2002). The mechanisms that would provide for better Māori representation in local government are not mandatory; rather, local councils can choose to have separate Māori wards or not. They generally choose not to have Māori wards. Local councils can choose to use a proportional electoral system but less than 5 per cent have chosen to use STV. Despite being urged to recognise its Treaty obligations and make it mandatory to have Māori representation on local government councils, the government is not yet willing to do so. The effect is that, as a minority, Māori interests are not represented and Māori are unable to effect policy change. Having a Māori organisation sit alongside Council gives Māori the opportunity to contribute to decision-making processes but Maori are not part of the decision-making process. Local authorities are currently absolved from the Crown's duty to actively protect Māori participation rights and, unless government is willing to make legislative changes, the active participation of Māori at the sub-national level of governance will continue to be limited.

References

(1987) 'New Zealand Maori Council v Attorney-General', New Zealand Law Review 641 (64, 641: Court of Appeal).

(1994) 'Taiaroa and Others v Attorney-General', unreported (29 Aug, CP No 99/94 (HC)).

AJHR (1908) 'Appendices to the Journals of the House of Representatives G-1e', Wellington, NZ: Parliament.

— (1921) 'Appendices to the Journals of the House of Representatives G-5, 1928 G-8', Wellington, NZ: Parliament.

— (1928) 'Appendices to the Journals of the House of Representatives. Report of the Royal Commission to inquire into confiscation of native lands and other grievances alleged by natives G-7', Wellington, NZ: Parliament.

— (1948) 'Appendices to the Journals of the House of Representatives. Report of the Royal Commission to inquire into and report on claims preferred by members of the Maori race touching certain lands known as surplus lands of the Crown E13', Wellington, NZ: Parliament.

Anaya, S. J. (2011) United Nations Report of the Special Rapporteur on the Rights of Indigenous Peoples, A/HRC/18/XX/Add.Y, 17 February.

Berelson, B. and Gray, A. (1964) Human Behaviour: An inventory of scientific findings, New York: Harcourt, Brace.

BERL Economics and Māori Economic Taskforce (2010) The Asset Base, Income, Expenditure and GDP of the 2010 Māori Economy, Wellington, NZ: Te Puni Kokiri and BERL Economics: http://www.tpk.govt.nz/_ documents/taskforce/met-rep-assetbaseincexpend-2011.pdf (accessed 2 March 2015).

Boston, J., Martin, J., Pallot, J. and Walsh, P. (1991) Reshaping the State, Auckland, NZ: Oxford University Press.

Brookfield, F. M. (2005) 'Maori claims and the special juridical nature of the foreshore and seabed', New Zealand Journal of Public and International Law 2: 179–188.

CAB MIN (2009) Local Government (Auckland Council) Bill: Options for Maori Representation and Participation. in Office of the Minister of Local Government and Office of the Minister of Maori Affairs, (CAB Min (09) 30).

Catt, H. (1999) Democracy in Practice, London: Routledge.

Cheyne, C. and Comrie, M. (2005) 'Empowerment or encumbrance? Exercising the STV option for local authority elections in New Zealand', Local Government Studies 31(2) 185–204.

Coates, K. and McHugh, P. G. (1998) Living Relationships – Kokiri Ngatahi: The Treaty of Waitangi in the new millennium, Wellington, NZ: Victoria University Press.

Department of Internal Affairs (2011) Local Authority Election Statistics 2010, Wellington, NZ: Department of Internal Affairs.

Dummett, M. (1997) Principles of Electoral Reform, New York: Oxford University Press.

Durie, M. (1998) Te Mana Te Kawanatanga. The politics of Maori self-determination, Auckland and New York: Oxford University Press).

— (2005) Nga Tai Matatu: Tides of Maori endurance, Melbourne: Oxford University Press.

Fleras, A. and Elliott, J. (1992) *The 'Nations Within': Aboriginal–state relations in Canada, the United States, and New Zealand*, Toronto: Oxford University Press).

Fleras, A. and Spoonley, P. (1999) *Recalling Aotearoa: Indigenous politics and ethnic relations in New Zealand*, Auckland and New York: Oxford University Press).

Geddis, A. (2006) 'A dual track democracy? The symbolic role of the Māori seats in New Zealand's electoral system', *Election Law Journal* 5(4): 347–71.

Havemann, P. (ed.) (1999) *Indigenous Peoples' Rights*, Auckland, NZ: Oxford University Press.

Hayward, J. (2011) 'Mandatory Māori wards in local government: active Crown protection of Māori Treaty rights', *Political Science* 63(2): 186–204.

Human Rights Commission (2010) *Maori Representation in Local Government. The continuing challenge*, Auckland, NZ: Human Rights Commission.

Ignatieff, M. (1993) *Blood and Belonging: Journeys into the new nationalism*, New York: Farrar, Strauss and Giroux.

Keenan, D. (2012, ed.) 'New Zealand Wars', *Te Ara – The Encyclopedia of New Zealand*: http://www.TeAra.govt.nz/en/new-zealand-wars/sources) (updated 9 Nov 2012): http://www.TeAra.govt.nz/en/new-zealand-wars/sources (accessed 22 Dec 2014).

Kelsey, J. (1995) *The New Zealand Experiment*, Auckland, NZ: Bridget Williams Books.

Kymlicka, W. (1995) *Multicultural Citizenship: A liberal theory of minority rights*, New York and Oxford: Clarendon Press.

Lijphart, A. (1997) 'Unequal participation: democracy's unresolved dilemma', *American Political Science Review* 91: 1–14.

— (1999) *Patterns of Democracy. Government forms and performance in thirty-six countries*, New Haven, CT: Yale University Press.

Miller, R. (2005) *Party Politics in New Zealand*, Melbourne: Oxford University Press.

Ministry of Social Development (2010) *The Social Report/ Te Pūrongo Oranga Tangata*, Wellington, NZ: Ministry of Social Development.

Mulgan, R. (2004) *Politics in New Zealand*, Auckland, NZ: Auckland University Press.

Mutu, M. (2003) 'Constitutional intentions: the Treaty of Waitangi texts', in M. Mulholland and V. Tawhai (eds) *Weeping Waters – The Treaty of Waitangi and constitutional change*, Wellington, NZ: Huia, 13–40.

New Zealand Institute of Economic Research. and Ministry of Maori Development (2003) *Māori Economic Development – Te Ohanga Whanaketanga Māori*, Wellington, NZ: Ministry of Māori Development/Te Puni Kōkiri.

Ngati Whatua Orakei (2012) *Annual Report 2011–2012*: http://www.ngatiwhatuaorakei.com/images/stories/downloads/wha_annual_report_final_071112.pd4 (accessed 22 December 2014).

Rikys, P. (2004) *Local Government Reform and Māori, 1988 to 2001*, Waiheke Island, NZ: Te Ngutu O Te Ika Publications.

Ringer, J. B. (1991) *An Introduction to New Zealand Government*, Christchurch, NZ: Hazard Press.

Salmon, P., Bazley, M. C. and Shand, D. (2009) *Report of the Royal Commission on Auckland Governance*, Auckland, NZ: Royal Commission on Auckland Governance.

Royal Commission on the Electoral System (1986) *Report of the Royal Commission on the Electoral System*, ed. M. J. H. Wallace, Wellington, NZ: Government Printer: http://www.elections.org.nz/voting-system/mmp-voting-system/report-royal-commission-electoral-system-1986.

Selby, R., Moore, P., and Mulholland, M. (2010, eds) *Maori and the Environment: Kaitiaki*, Wellington, NZ: Huia.

Statistics New Zealand (2007a) *Electoral Populations Calculated: 2006* (updated 26 February 2007).

Statistics New Zealand (2007b) *Quickstats About Māori*: http://www.stats.govt.nz/census/2006-census-data/quickstats-about-maori/2006-census-quickstats-about-maori-revised.htm: Statistics New Zealand (accessed 22 Dec 2014).

Sullivan, Ann (2003a) 'Māori affairs and public policy', in R. Miller (ed.) *New Zealand Government and Politics*, 3rd edn, Auckland, NZ: Oxford University Press, pp. 503–13.

Sullivan, A. (2003b) 'Māori representation in local government', in Hayward, J. (ed.) *Local Government and the Treaty of Waitangi*, Sydney: Oxford University Press) 135–56.

—   (2010) 'Māori participation', in Raymond Miller (ed.) *New Zealand Government and Politics*, 5th edn, Melbourne: Oxford University Press, 537–47.

—   (2011) 'Māori representation, local government and the Auckland Council', in J. Drage, J. McNeill and C. Cheyne (eds) *Along A Fault-Line. New Zealand's changing local government landscape*, Wellington, NZ: Dunmore Publishing Ltd), pp. 59–74.

Summersby, K. (2005) *STV, and Māori Wards and Constituencies: Local government reform and its effects on Māori representation*, unpublished MA Thesis, University of Auckland.

Tawhai, V. (2010) 'Rāwaho: in and out of the environmental engagement loop', in R. Selby, P. Moore and M. Mulholland (eds) *Māori and the Environment: Kaitiaki*, Wellington, NZ: Huia, pp. 77–94.

Te Puni Kōkiri (2001) *He Tirohanga o Kawa ki te Tiriti o Waitangi. A Guide to the Principles of the Treaty of Waitangi as expressed by the Courts and the Waitangi Tribunal*, Wellington, NZ: Te Puni Kōkiri/Ministry of Maori Development.

Te Whanau O Waipareira Trust (2012) *Annual Report July 2011–2012*: http://www.waipareira.com/LiteratureRetrieve.aspx?ID=112869 (accessed 22 December 2014).

Trapski, P. (1998) *The Proposal to Establish a Maori Constituency for Environment B.O.P. (The Bay of Plenty Regional Council) Report of the Hearings Commissioner*, The Bay of Plenty Regional Council: http://www. envbop.govt.nz/Reports/Maori-980829-EstMaoriConstituencyReport. pdf (accessed 14 October 2013).

Tully, J. (1995) *Strange Multiplicity: Constitutionalism in an age of diversity*, Cambridge: Cambridge University Press.

Walker, R. (1990) *Ka Whawhai Tonu Matou. Struggle Without End*, Auckland, NZ: Penguin).

Ward, A. (1974) *A Show of Justice: Racial 'amalgamation' in nineteenth century New Zealand*, Canberra: Australian National University Press.

Chapter Six

Action, Organisation and Confrontation: Strategies of the Sámi Movement in Sweden during the Twentieth Century[1]

Patrik Lantto and Ulf Mörkenstam

In the last two decades, we have witnessed a growing global acknowledgement of indigenous rights, manifested in the 2007 UN Declaration on the Rights of Indigenous Peoples (UNDRIP). With the adoption of the Declaration, the questions that had dominated the debate in international law for a long time – on what conventions or treatises were applicable to indigenous peoples – got an unequivocal answer: indigenous rights are human rights and indigenous peoples are equal to other peoples within international law (see, for example, Burger 2011; Henriksen, Scheinin and Åhrén 2007; Xanthaki 2007). This recognition of indigenous rights, including the right to self-determination and rights to land, territories and resources, is in many ways a result of the international indigenous mobilisation during the last decades (Anaya 2009; Brysk 2000; Minnerup and Solberg 2011a). In the Nordic countries, the ethno-political mobilisation of the Sámi people was inspired by this global mobilisation in the 1960s and 70s and the Sámi had an active role in its development (Minde 2003: 108–23). However, conflicts on a local or national level, such as the legal process in the Taxed Mountain Case in Sweden or the political protests during the Alta dam project in Norway, were mainly responsible for causing a broader Sámi ethno-political mobilisation in the late 1970s.

This intensification in the mobilisation of the Sámi did not occur in a vacuum. In Sweden, for instance, a more organised ethno-political mobilisation among the Sámi had started around the year 1900, with protests against the prevailing Reindeer Grazing Act. From the nineteenth century, the Sámi had become increasingly enclosed in separate national arenas. These arenas, with diverse local, regional and national contexts, and thus opportunities and obstacles, created differing preconditions for the Sámi movement in each country. These preconditions, in combination with different strategies chosen by the Sámi leaders, created unique circumstances for the movement in each state and, consequently, for contemporary politics and the standing of the Sámi in the different countries they inhabit. The aim

1. The article is written under the auspices of two projects: Indigenous peoples' rights to self-determination: The Institutional Design and Policy Process of the Swedish Sámi Parliament (funded by the Swedish Riksbankens Jubileumsfond) and The Sámi Parliaments as Representative Bodies: A Comparative Study of the Elections in Sweden and Norway 2013 (funded by the Swedish Forskningsrådet för miljö, areella näringar och samhällsbyggande, FORMAS).

of this chapter is to schematically delineate the historical development of the Sámi movement in Sweden and its more-than-a century-long struggle to strengthen the position of the Sámi and preserve their land rights. The structure and reality of the Sámi movement today is very different from what the leading Sámi activists faced at the beginning of the 1900s but it was their work that laid the foundation for the current position of the Sámi movement. How has the Sámi movement developed during the twentieth century? What strategies have been used and in what arenas? What impact has the Sámi movement had?

Some remarks on theory: The Sámi movement and social-movement theory

In our attempt to answer the research questions formulated above, we will analyse the Sámi movement and its historical development in terms of three analytical dimensions often used in social-movement theory (see, for example, Melucci 1991: 41–5). The first is *solidarity*, which refers to a mutual recognition of a common 'we' by individuals within a movement. The second is *conflict*, as the social movement is deeply engaged in a conflict with an adversary making claims on the same goods or values. The third dimension is a breaking of the social system's limits of compatibility, that is, a *challenge* to dominant social ideas, beliefs and practices. A social movement, then, is dependent on the construction of a collective identity to mobilise action based on solidarity, that is, a common 'we', and it is very much this collective identity, intertwined with personal identity, which is at stake in contemporary societal conflicts (Melucci 1980: 218). The collective identity

> brings with it a sense of common purpose and shared commitment to a cause, which enables single activists and/or organisations to regard themselves as inextricably linked to other actors, not necessarily identical but surely compatible, in a broader collective mobilization (della Porta and Diani 2006: 21).

In this perspective, social movements will be seen as the outcomes of historical-political processes in which a collective identity is constructed – through action, conflict and organisation – and as such, not to be taken for granted as empirical artefacts. Furthermore, social movements are not unitary and homogeneous; just as the collective identity is the outcome of a process, so is the (eventual) unity of a movement (see, for example, Melucci 1991: 33–6, 49–51). This means, for instance, that the question of the success or failure of an entire social movement most often lacks an unambiguous and uncontroversial answer. This is due to the fact that social movements, to use the words of Marco Guigni (1999: xx), 'are complex sets of groups, organisations and actions that may have different goals as well as different strategies for reaching their aims. Hence, a given change is not necessarily perceived as a success [or failure] by all sectors of a movement'.

In more concrete terms, we will make use of the analytical dimensions of solidarity, conflict and challenge in our study. Solidarity will be used as an analytical dimension by asking who is the 'we' of the Sámi movement during different time periods. How is the Sámi 'we' formulated? Conflict, in turn, will be used to study the direction, or main target, of the Sámi movement's actions. Who or what is the main adversary? In analysing the systemic challenge of the Sámi movement, finally, we will pose the question of what ideas and practices of the dominant society the movement has tried either to break with or transcend.

The institutionalisation of a modern Swedish Sámi policy

Towards the end of the nineteenth century, the Sámi were not recognised as an indigenous people with the right to self-determination, although they were recognised as the original inhabitants of northern Sweden. They were not, however, perceived as owners of the land (Lantto 2012: 14–15). During previous centuries, their rights had been considered equal to those of farmers but, during the nineteenth century, a new view became dominant (Lundmark 2006: 20–118). The nomadic Sámi had only *used* the land for themselves and their reindeer but this usage did not exclude the development of true ownership of the land by other parties, mostly the state, in a modern society. This was well in accordance with the dominant theories of property of the day and time, which focused on agricultural rights. In a historical perspective (at least since the days of John Locke) nomadic customary land use has not been considered to be 'a legitimate type of property' (Tully 1993: 139; see also Korpijaakko-Labba 1994: 20–43).

During the last decades of the nineteenth century, Swedish Sámi policy became more structured. The policy was based on a view of cultural hierarchies, in which a nomadic people such as the Sámi were considered to be inferior to Swedish agricultural and industrial society (Mörkenstam 2014). The policy was centreed on a view of the Sámi as reindeer-herders, endowed with a physique uniquely adapted to the reindeer industry and to this specific animal, as Bishop Olof Bergqvist argued in a well known statement: 'the reindeer is created for the Lapp and the Lapp for the reindeer' (Mot. AK 1908: 41).[2]

The focus on the Sámi as reindeer-herders in Swedish politics meant that other aspects of Sámi culture and Sámi with other livelihoods were marginalised and, in the end, excluded; the group was considered to be homogenous and only nomadic Sámi herders were considered to be 'genuine'. The use of certain objects and aspects of Sámi reindeer husbandry – a nomadic lifestyle, the Sámi cot, the *gákti* (traditional clothing) – in the creation of an idealised and romanticised Swedish image of Sámi culture also constructed a specific Sámi identity that

---

2.   Mot. AK is an abbreviation of Motioner i Andra Kammaren, Private Motion in the Second Chamber. Up until the 1960s, the Sámi in Sweden were officially referred to as Lapps, an originally Finnish term that they themselves perceived as derogatory; this has been changed to the endonym Sámi. The term Sámi will be used consistently throughout the article, except for some quotations and expressions in which the old term Lapp occurs.

had political ramifications. Instead of being internal markers of Sámi identity, these symbols became externally imposed necessary preconditions for being considered a 'genuine' Sámi; they became producers of an ethnic identity (Ruong 1981a: 15; Ruong 1981b: 20–4; *Samefolket* [henceforth *Sf*] 1980: 3, 15; Thuen 1995: 82–98).

According to this so-called 'Lapp-shall-remain-Lapp' view, the Sámi should be preserved as reindeer-herders, as their physical and psychological adaptation to the nomadic life of reindeer-herding meant that they were unable to support themselves through other professions (see, for example, Riksdagens debatt, AK 1913: 52).[3] But the industry and the Sámi were viewed as threatened, the expansion of agriculture limited grazing areas and led to conflict, and increasing contact with Swedish culture led to a (perceived) demoralisation of the Sámi, which undermined their nomadic character and thus threatened their future. If the Sámi abandoned reindeer husbandry it would mean the beginning of the end of them as a people, a development Sámi policy was aimed at preventing. The goal of Sámi policy was to segregate the Sámi from the detrimental influences of Swedish society and thus preserve reindeer husbandry (Lantto 2000: 39–42). The 'Lapp-shall-remain-Lapp' view created a dualistic Swedish Sámi policy. The reindeer-herders were included in the official definition of the Sámi, they were considered to be 'genuine' Sámi and, through segregation, they were to be protected from the threat of modern society and the more developed Swedish culture. Sámi who stood outside reindeer-herding, however, were excluded from the Sámi context and the general view was that they soon would become assimilated into the Swedish population (Mörkenstam 1999: 232–43).

The two most important means for preserving the Sámi were the Reindeer Grazing Acts and the Lapp Administration. To protect the grazing land of the Sámi from further encroachment, and thus to protect and preserve the Sámi, the first Reindeer Grazing Act was enacted in 1886 (SFS 1886: 38).[4] At the same time, however, the Act also guaranteed the spread and development of agriculture in the north of Sweden, by spatially separating reindeer-herding and farming (Lantto and Mörkenstam 2008: 29). The new legislation was meant to regulate the relationship between reindeer husbandry and agriculture but it soon became an important instrument of control. Complete segregation of the Sámi was not possible; but the idea was that, through close control of their actions and their reindeer husbandry, the Sámi could safely be led past the threats that loomed around them. Two new Reindeer Grazing Acts were enacted in 1898 and 1928 respectively, which strengthened the control aspects of the legislation (SFS 1898: 66; SFS 1928: 309).

This legislation created the framework for achieving control but was not thought to be enough in itself. Knowledge of the Sámi was limited within the regional authorities, the County Administrative Boards, and, for this reason, it was

---

3. Riksdagens debatt, AK, is an abbreviation of Parliamentary debate in the Second Chamber.
4. SFS is an abbreviation of Svensk Författningssamling, the Swedish Code of Statutes.

considered necessary to create a new governmental body that could focus solely on the Sámi: the Lapp Administration. The work of the Lapp Administration was led by Lapp Bailiffs and, even though the first position created in Jämtland in 1885 was meant as a temporary measure for managing conflict between reindeer husbandry and agriculture, the authority grew; in the following decades, the positions of Lapp Bailiffs in Norrbotten and Västerbotten were created, as well as other levels of civil servants. The Lapp Administration was created as a part of Swedish Sámi policy but would thereafter also have a major influence on the development of this policy (Lantto 2012).

The dominant conception of the Sámi as reindeer-herders in Swedish Sámi policy not only determined which solutions were possible within the policy field; it also placed limitations on the actions the Sámi movement could take. The early Sámi leaders and later Sámi organisations had to respond to the politically defined identity of the Sámi: they could accept it and adjust their actions and demands in accordance with it or they could challenge it and present an alternative identity. How did the Sámi movement respond to the dominant conception of the Sámi as reindeer-herders? What strategies did they use to challenge Swedish Sámi policy?

Two Sámi leaders, two strategies: Moderate action *v* disruptive tactics

The institutionalisation of a coherent Swedish Sámi policy in legislation was soon followed by a more organised ethno-political mobilisation among the Sámi. The year 1900 can be said to mark the start of a period of strong political activism. Initially, there were protests against the 1898 Reindeer Grazing Act and Swedish Sámi policy. Protest action then focused on developing a vision of an alternative political solution to the Sámi situation and demands for Sámi ownership of the reindeer-grazing lands. This vision was based on a view of the Sámi as a people, not just as reindeer-herders. Elsa Laula came to symbolise the movement during these years (see, for example, Kungl. Jordbruksdepartementet 1905, 1907; Lantto 2000: 57–61).[5]

In 1904, the activity developed into a more structured form with the establishment of the first Sámi organisations in Sweden, a national organisation and five local Sámi societies. A Sámi newspaper was also launched (*Lapparnes Egen Tidning*, *LET*). However, the establishment of national and local organisations and the newspaper marked the peak of the mobilisation. *LET* ceased operating in 1905; the national organisation, together with four of the five local Sámi societies, became inactive. This was due to economic difficulties, internal conflicts and strong external criticism of the movement, not least from the Lapp Administration and the County Administrative

---

5. Many Sámi leaders were active during the first half of the twentieth century: besides Elsa Laula, we can, for instance, mention Andreas Wilks, Hans-Magnus Nilsson, Karin Stenberg, Lars Rensund and Jonas Åhrén. However, two names came to dominate the Sámi movement during this period: Torkel Tomasson and Gustav Park. We will analyse their aims and political strategies below.

Board in Västerbotten, which did not accept the alternative view of the Sámi presented by the movement: the Sámi as a people with property rights (Laula 1904; *LET* 1904:1–1905: 4; Lantto 2000: 61–9; Lantto 2002: 9).

Torkel Tomasson, the editor in chief of *LET*, was the chief architect behind the resurgence of the Sámi movement during the second half of the 1910s. He helped organise the first national meeting of the Sámi in Östersund, Sweden in 1918, at which issues concerning the Reindeer Grazing Act, reindeer husbandry, Sámi policy and education, as well as Sámi organisation and plans to launch a new Sámi newspaper were discussed (Svenska lapparnas landsmöte 1918). The meeting had great significance for the Sámi movement; it put the movement and Sámi issues under a national spotlight. One of the decisions of the meeting was to form a new national Sámi organisation and, later that year, Tomasson launched the *Samefolkets Egen Tidning*, or 'Sámi Peoples' Own Newspaper' (*SET*). However, as with the forming of organisations in 1904, little substance followed from the national meeting. The national organisation was unable to raise the necessary funds to maintain a stable economic base and the work was discontinued in 1923, a fate shared by many of the local Sámi societies that had been established in the period around the national meeting. Only a few of them survived, as did *SET* (Lantto 2000: 79–85, 98–111).

In his leading role within the Sámi movement, Tomasson sought to organise the Sámi and to establish a newspaper in which they could discuss both important and more mundane matters. These two aims were defining aspects of his leadership. He was convinced that the Sámi needed to change how they worked politically. He considered it necessary to establish organisations similar in form to those already existing within Swedish society, if the Sámi movement was to be taken seriously. It was thus a conscious decision of the early Sámi movement to try to organise as a special-interest organisation within the dominant Swedish society, like the trade unions or the temperance movement. This may have affected the decision of the Sámi in 1918 not to work within or participate in the traditional Swedish party system, in contrast to the Sámi movement in Norway. Moreover, the Sámi movement had its main strength in the region with the harshest conflicts between the Sámi and the Swedish majority; it was therefore harder to build any alliances with local parties (see, for example, Minde 1980, 1995).

In Tomasson's vision, the Sámi movement would be a grassroots movement, in which the Sámi were active and formed local Sámi societies around the Sámi area, societies that could form the basis of a national Sámi organisation. The problem with this vision was that there were never more than ten or so local Sámi societies during the 1920s and 30s and, in large areas, mainly in northern Norrbotten, the Sámi were not organising and had yet to take an interest in the Sámi movement. The Sámi societies were too few and too weak, not least economically, to build a united national organisation. Furthermore, Tomasson focused on achieving change through dialogue. He believed that working towards long-term goals was necessary to effect change and that ongoing dialogue, patience and moderate actions were the key to success. Tomasson had obviously learned from the failure of the movement at the beginning of the century, as he now placed great emphasis on reindeer husbandry (see, for example, Lappdeputationen 1933; *SET* 1930: 4: 29, 1932: 1: 2, 1932: 3: 18, 1932: 4: 32–3, 1933: 1: 2). He was, however, criticised by regional authorities who questioned his right to speak on behalf of the Sámi. They portrayed him as someone far removed from reindeer husbandry and claimed he had no legitimacy as a representative of Sámi interests (Lantto 2012: 245).

The man who succeeded Tomasson as the leader of the Sámi movement, Gustav Park, had a quite different and more conflict-oriented approach to leading the Sámi movement. Park became heavily involved in the Sámi movement during the 1920s, when a series of problems within reindeer-herding emerged in his home parish, Arjeplog.[6] In 1931, after several years of conflict and with increasing reindeer herds, the County Administrative Board decided to order a forced slaughter of more than 11,000 reindeer. Park, together with a number of the affected herders, protested strongly against both the decision and the methods used by the Lapp Administration to carry out the slaughter; this forced the operation to be halted before the full implementation of the policy. The forced slaughter became the starting point for a long period of intense conflict, in which Park aggressively attacked the regional authorities through the media and strongly questioned their competence (Lantto 2000: 174–81; Lantto 2012: 235–40). He was also the architect of a report to the Parliamentary Ombudsmen (*Riksdagens Ombudsmän*), in which he demanded that the County Administrative Board be held responsible for neglect in its handling of the forced slaughter. In the report, he pointed out the absurdity that Swedish civil servants, 'with their superficial experience and lacking knowledge in the field of reindeer herding', were supposed to regulate an industry they only could observe a few times each year (Park 1933: 76). The response from the County Administrative Board and Lapp Administration was to charge a number of the herders with wilfully giving false information concerning the number of their reindeer and Park was accused of having instigated this deception by the herders (Lantto 2000: 185–8).

In 1933, supported by the Sámi in Jämtland, Västerbotten and southern Norrbotten, Park led the so called Lapp Deputation to Stockholm to represent Sámi issues to the government. Those issues had earlier been identified in *SET* by Tomasson, who sought to create a united Sámi view that would influence government policy and the Lapp Administration (see, for example, Lappdeputationen 1933; Lappdeputationen 1934; *SET* 1932: 1: 2; 1932: 3: 19–20; 1933: 1: 5; 1933: 2: 14; 1933: 3: 20–1; 1933: 4: 31–5). Park was also the driving force behind the arrangement of a second national Sámi meeting in Arvidsjaur,

---

6. The source of the conflicts in Arjeplog was the new Reindeer Grazing Convention between Sweden and Norway in 1919, as the Convention limited the grazing land available for Sámi from Sweden. As a consequence of the agreement, forced relocations of herders were executed and Arjeplog received a large number of these herders during the following years. This caused problems and conflicts within the industry and increased tensions between the Sámi and the regional authorities in Norrbotten. The main reason for the problems was a clash between different herding methods (Lantto 2000: 134; Lantto 2010: 544–50).

Norrbotten, in 1937. In 1945, he led a new deputation (the Sámi Deputation) to Stockholm, which, among other things, demanded changes in the rules concerning the taxation of reindeer-herders (Lantto 2000: 210–12, 233–57). Like Tomasson before him, Park placed the interests of reindeer husbandry at the centre of the Sami movement's concerns.

Park had quite a different agenda from Tomasson. He did not, for example, see any potential or immediate need for a national Sámi organisation based on local Sámi societies (Park 1943). He preferred direct action – rallying support, locally, regionally or on a larger scale if necessary, and then bringing demands forward – in order to gain influence and tackle Sámi problems. He believed this would prove to be a more realistic and effective method of improving the situation of the Sámi than trying to duplicate Swedish organisations. When Park saw a need for change or reform, he wanted to act and see results quickly and he therefore used more disruptive tactics than Tomasson. With Park in a leading role, the rhetoric of the Sámi movement changed radically. He often created conflictual situations and even seemed to thrive on the encounters between him and the County Administrative Boards and Lapp Administration (see, for example, Lantto 1998 169–70; Lantto 2000 221–5, 250–6). Park's strong language and sharp criticism made him an obvious target for reprimands and attacks from the regional authorities. They questioned his right to represent the Sámi, due to the many years he had been working in Swedish society and his attitude towards the authorities. These attacks could not stop him, however, and, even if some Sámi disagreed with Park's tactics, his disrespectful manner towards the regional authorities helped to break down the subservient attitude many Sámi had towards the authorities and gradually freed them from the domination and control of the Lapp Administration.

During this phase of mobilisation, it was very difficult for the Sámi leaders to create a movement based on solidarity and a firm identification with a common 'we'. To create a common Sámi identity was likely the main objective for both Tomasson and Park, albeit from different perspectives. The former identified a national organisation as the way to create solidarity in accordance with a moderate strategy that worked with the current administrative structures; the latter sought to mobilise the Sámi in direct action and civil disobedience. Attempts to mobilise the Sámi at a national level were, however, futile, as we have seen; at the local and regional levels, though, the mobilisation was more successful. That may be explained by looking into the major conflicts during this period, in which the most frequent adversaries were the Country Administrative Boards and/or the Lapp Administration. Although the national legislation, that is, the Reindeer Grazing Acts, was severely criticised, the Swedish state was not the main adversary of either Tomasson or Park.

The challenge to dominant social ideas, beliefs and practices manifested in Laula's view of the Sámi as a people, and not as nomadic reindeer-herders, and the claim that the Sámi had ownership rights to the reindeer-grazing lands, was not to be developed further during the first half of the twentieth century. On the contrary, as we have seen, both Tomasson and Park based their demands on the needs of reindeer husbandry and land rights were not an important part of their political agenda. In order to understand their strategy, the social, political and economic subordination of the Sámi has to be kept in mind. As Linda Tuhiwai Smith (1999: 68–72) has shown, similar patterns are evident in the history of indigenous peoples elsewhere. She argues that the knowledge and opinions of indigenous peoples have, historically, been marginalised; they were considered to lack value in a political context that was created by the dominant majority society. The legitimacy of leaders of indigenous peoples was often challenged by authorities in an effort to marginalise them. Neither Tomasson nor Park conformed to how the dominant society perceived the Sámi and the prevailing idea of how a genuine Sámi should act, that is, to the 'criteria of authenticity'. If the two dominant leaders of the Sámi movement were to be accepted by the Swedish state as legitimate representatives of the Sámi, then it would be difficult for them to challenge the justificatory foundations of government policy.

The birth of a national organisation: Land rights and legal processes

In 1950, the Sámi finally succeeded in establishing a national organisation, the National Union of the Swedish Sámi (*Svenska Samernas Riksförbund*, SSR), and, ironically, it was the sceptical Park who made it happen. The background was the hastily gathered third national Sámi meeting in Arvidsjaur in 1948, which was called to discuss a report of a government committee concerning the slaughter of reindeer (1946 års köttbesiktningskommitté 1947). The question of a national Sámi organisation was also raised at the meeting and a working group, with Park as one of the members, was appointed to work towards this goal (Protokoll m.m. 1948). Although, only a few years earlier, he had advocated patience concerning Sámi organisations – arguing that increased education was necessary to develop the Sámi consciousness necessary for a national organisation to succeed (Park 1943) – he now believed that a national organisation was necessary. It was, in his opinion, not viable to call a national Sámi meeting every time issues of importance arose and needed to be addressed. A national organisation was needed to represent Sámi interests, negotiate with the authorities and make Sámi views public (*SET* 1949: 1: 10; 1949: 2: 13).

In spite of the somewhat lukewarm reception given to the plans by the Sámi, a new national meeting was called in October 1950, this time in Jokkmokk in Norrbotten. At the meeting SSR was founded and, as a tribute to his work and a signal of his very strong position in the Sámi movement, Park was elected the first chairman of the organisation, a position he would hold for a decade. To give the organisation greater stability, Park had decided to base it on both the local Sámi societies and the reindeer-herding districts (*Samebyar*). These were administrative units created as a part of the regulation of the industry through the first Reindeer Grazing Act in 1886 but they were permanent and stable, with a relatively strong economic base (in contrast to the Sámi societies) and they existed throughout the Sámi areas. If they could be secured as members, the new national organisation would have a stable foundation (Svenska Samernas Riksförbund 1950). To reach the reindeer-herding districts, to have them join as members of SSR, was a central goal of the organisation. Without them, SSR would both lack stability and have difficulty in credibly claiming to represent the Sámi. Initially, however, the interest in the national organisation seems to have been limited among the herders; eleven years would pass before all the villages joined (Lantto 2003: 96–113, 137–57).

Nationally, SSR quickly became established as an actor in the policy field and was given a role as a consultative body by the Swedish government, indicating that the organisation was regarded as representative of Sámi opinion by the central authorities. This, however, did not necessarily mean that SSR was successful in achieving results based on its demands. The positive results of the early work of the organisation were few and small but the fact that SSR was consulted and provided policy advice meant that the authorities were being exposed to Sámi perspectives that could influence the policy direction (Lantto 2000 264–6; Lantto 2003: 50–6, 201, 219–24).

With the strengthened position of SSR at the beginning of the 1960s, and a change in leadership (Park was replaced by Israel Ruong), the strategy of SSR changed. The organisation challenged established Sámi policy and its ideological foundation in two different ways. Firstly, SSR put forward a more inclusive view of Sámihood and thus slowly changed the Sámi collective identity. Ruong wanted to accentuate the situation of the non-reindeer-herding Sámi and involve them more in the work of the organisation (Svenska Samernas Riksförbund 1962: 7–8, 48, Appendix 9a–9b; *Sf* 1961: 1 10–14, 1962: 4–5: 43–4). He argued that the Reindeer Grazing Act had 'become a sharp knife', which 'cuts through Sámi groups, and separates those who belong together and should form a social unity', weakening the Sámi people in the process (*Sf* 1961: 1: 13). In his opinion, Sámi rights should be expanded to include other natural resources in the Sámi area, not just reindeer pasture. Language as well as occupation should be used to decide who should be allowed to exercise Sámi rights. Thus, culture and not occupation should be the determining factor for entitlement to the rights of the Sámi. Such a definition would enlarge the Sámi community and facilitate unity within the group, as well as increasing the possibility of a more positive development for the Sámi as a people (*Spörsmål av samiskt intresse*: 31–3, 105–6; *SET* 1959: 5: 35–6, *Sf*, 1961: 1: 13—4). The ambition of SSR was to represent all Sámi and this view was explicitly stated in the organisation's Sámi Political Programme from 1968: 'The national meeting asserts that, the national meeting, chosen representatives for the Sámi people, speaks on behalf of the Sámi and expresses the will of the Sámi' (Svenska Samernas Riksförbund 1969, Appendix 2, p. 7). It is important to note, however, that reindeer-herding still maintained its central position within the organisation; according to Ruong (cited in Sjölin 2002: 304) the 'Sámi idea' was the basis but 'helping the core group', the reindeer-herders, was prioritised.

Another important development in the formation of a collective Sámi identity was increased cross-border co-operation after WWII, through the establishment of a Nordic Sámi Council (today the Sámi Council) – the first conferences were held in 1953 and 1956 – which emphasised that the Sámi are a single people divided by the borders of four nation-states. This mobilisation at the Nordic level also led to increased international engagement, in which the collective Sámi identity was compared to indigenous peoples in other parts of the world: 'The Sámi are Sweden's Indians', as it was expressed in the headline of an article in *Samefolket* 1963 (*Sf* 1963:11–12: 190). In 1975, the Sámi Council actively participated in the establishment of the World Council of Indigenous Peoples and they have participated in international debate and in organisations like the International Work Group for Indigenous Affairs (see, for example, Heininen 2002: 226–9; Robbins 2011: 59). Although the collective Sámi identity as an indigenous people is well established in contemporary debate, Henry Minde (2003: 100–6) describes this process of identity-construction as much-disputed, versatile and fluid, and very much an outcome of the ongoing political struggles of the day.

The second strategy for challenging the Swedish state concerned reindeer-herding based on Sámi rights to land and water. This challenge escalated – both rhetorically and in practice through legal proceedings – in the early 1960s, when SSR received state funding for the creation of a position of Sámi Ombudsman (SO), a person who would act as a legal representative of the Sámi. The new SO position increased the ability of the organisation to challenge the Swedish state from a juridical standpoint; and the first SO, Tomas Cramér, contributed to a more militant rhetoric within the organisation (Lantto 2012: 336–50; Svensson 1973: 77–80; Svensson 1997: 161–170). The changed attitude of SSR became especially evident in two legal proceedings: Altevatn and the Taxed Mountain Case. The former process, in which two Swedish reindeer-herding districts, Saarivouma and Talma, won a legal action against the Norwegian Water Resources and Energy Directorate, was very important, as it proved the ability of the Sámi to challenge the Nordic states in Courts (Cramér 1970: 99–107; Svensson 1973: 97–105).

The Taxed Mountain Case was initiated by SSR in 1966, when the reindeer-herding districts in Jämtland, and some individual Sámi, sued the Swedish state and claimed ownership of the reindeer-grazing areas in the county, the so-called taxed mountains (*Skattefjällen*).[7] This was a challenge to the established view of the Swedish state concerning the land rights of the Sámi as a privilege granted by the state. The Sámi claimed 'full ownership rights to the property in dispute ... located in taxed mountains' while the Swedish state 'maintained that the State is the owner of the properties in dispute, and that only the special rights stated in the Reindeer Farming Act now belong to the Sámi and the Sámi villages [reindeer-herding districts]' (Supreme Court Decision No. DT2. Case No. 324/76: 148–51). Fifteen years passed before the case was finally settled by the 1981 Supreme Court decision against the Sámi. The Supreme Court ruled that the state was the rightful owner of the taxed mountain areas. At the same time, however, the court's ruling was interpreted

---

7. 'Taxed mountains' is an administrative term for certain geographical areas in the county of Jämtland.

in terms of a strengthened legal position of the reindeer-herders, since it states that the Sámi have 'a firmly protected usufructuary right of a particular kind, based upon use and prescription from time immemorial' (SOU 1989: 41: 257).[8] Furthermore, through the case, the Sámi 'established a legally defined basis' from which they could act in political confrontations in the future (Svensson 1997: 171). However, the ruling of the Supreme Court in the Taxed Mountain Case was a hard blow for SSR and, for a period, the organisation suffered from the effects. One result was that the strategy of the SSR changed; legal challenge was replaced by dialogue and participation in the political process (see, for example, Wasara-Hammare 2003: 340–3).

It was during this period, and with SSR as its prime mover, that the mobilisation of the Sámi gained momentum. The ambition of the organisation to represent all Sámi created solidarity with the Sámi movement on a national level, an identity that was further strengthened by the parallel organisation at both the Nordic and international levels, where the struggle of the Sámi was gradually interpreted in terms of being part of a worldwide struggle for the rights of indigenous peoples. Together, this multi-level mobilisation created a strong collective identity: 'we' the Sámi people. The broad mobilisations of the 1960s and 70s made the heterogeneity within the Sámi movement more evident, however, especially the divide between reindeer-herders and non-reindeer-herders that was created by government policy and institutionalised in the Reindeer Grazing Acts. Both the early leaders of the Sámi movement and, later on, SSR, considered that achieving both internal and external legitimacy, being accepted as representatives of the Sámi by the group and by the Swedish state, was vital. Only then could they put forward their demands with authority. With the choice to base the organisation primarily on the reindeer-herding districts, SSR made reindeer husbandry central; and the organisation focused most of its attention on issues concerning the reindeer-herders. This obviously made it difficult for the organisation to fulfil its aim of representing all Sámi in Sweden (Lantto 2003: 91–162, 205–15). What initially began as discontent with the organisation's strong focus on the interests of reindeer husbandry among non-reindeer-herding Sámi soon developed into an opposition movement, which not only protested against Swedish Sámi policy but also actively opposed SSR as the representative of the Sámi people. Several new organisations were formed during the later 1960s representing these groups and, in 1980, they formed a national organisation of their own, the Swedish Sámi National Union (Landsförbundet Svenska Samer, or LSS) (Lantto 2003: 187 –203, 215–18). The strong collective identity was thus no longer expressed as solidarity with one organisation, SSR, but with the Sámi people.

Of great importance in the construction of a collective Sámi identity was the more confrontational strategy of SSR, in which the Swedish state was the main

---

8. SOU is an abbreviation of Statens Offentliga Utredningar, Swedish Government Official Reports.

adversary. The ongoing local and regional conflicts that were the focus during the first half of the twentieth century were given new meaning when they were situated in the context of an indigenous people's struggle against a colonising state. Nordic co-operation and international engagement gave the Sámi a new position, no longer 'from below', which made it easier to challenge the state and to put forward demands and rights claims.

By this development, the Sámi movement broke with the social system's limits of compatibility in a new fashion. This is most obvious in legal actions in which they challenged the dominant ideas about and practices of ownership rights; but also in the way they situated Sámi rights in the international debate: Sámi rights are the rights of an indigenous people. However, this collective 'we' was, as a rule, used to mobilise the Sámi on a national level. This is, of course, an effect of the historically imposed partition of the Sámi between four nation-states. According to Johan Eriksson, however, it is also due to a tendency among the Sámi themselves to keep a nation-state-centred view and 'to make a distinction between "domestic" and "international" issues ... despite their common identity, the Saami follow the state practice of distinguishing between what happens within each separate state and what goes beyond the limits of a single state' (Eriksson 2002: 24; see also Eriksson 1997: 127–32). Thus, the focus of the Sámi movement was still on day-to-day politics in Sweden.

The actions of the Sámi movement had a major impact on the development of Swedish Sámi policy, both in practice and on a symbolic level. In 1971, for instance, the Reindeer Grazing Act of 1928 was replaced by the (still in effect) Reindeer Farming Act (SFS 1971: 437). Although this legislation was heavily criticised by the Sámi movement, one important change was the dismantling of the paternalistic Lapp Administration, which was replaced by a more modern and, at least on the surface, less repressive and controlling organisation, in which reindeer-herding districts were granted a larger degree of self-determination (Lantto 2012: 279–83, 299–305). In 1977, the Sámi were recognised as an indigenous people and a minority in their own country by a Swedish government for the first time (Prop. 1976/77: 80: 107).[9] Perhaps the most important result of this ethno-political mobilisation, however, was the appointment of the Sámi Rights Commission shortly after the ruling of the Supreme Court in the Taxed Mountain case, something that SSR demanded as part of their new and less conflict-oriented strategy (Svenska Samernas Riksförbund 1982, Resolution A). As the ruling was interpreted as a strengthening of reindeer-herding rights, it was considered necessary to investigate how these rights could be implemented in legislation. According to the government remit to the commission, the commission was also to consider the need for a new representative body of the Sámi people and to discuss efforts to protect and develop the Sámi languages (Dir. 1982.71, in SOU 1989: 41).[10]

---

9. Prop. is an abbreviation of *Proposition*, i.e. a government bill.

10. Dir. is an abbreviation of *Direktiv*, a government remit to the Commission.

Self-determination as a people and the establishment of a Sámi Parliament

Much of the Sámi movement's activities during the 1980s were focused on influencing the work of the Sámi Rights Commission, both as participants in the Commission and by lobbying. The major tangible outcome of the work of the Commission was the proposal to establish a Sámi Parliament (see, for example, SOU 1986: 36; SOU 1989: 41; SOU 1990: 91). Inaugurated in 1993, the new parliament was, however, given status as a government agency under the Swedish government. This construction was explained and justified as a way to guarantee the Sámi people's cultural autonomy, while making it clear that the parliament was not 'a body for self-government, [acting] in place of the parliament or municipal councils or in competition with those bodies' (Prop. 1992/93: 32: 35). In accordance with this view, the parliament was assigned two functions: to act as an administrative authority *and* as a popularly elected assembly representing the Sámi people.

With the status of government agency, the parliament was not granted a right of participation in decision-making, veto-rights concerning administrative decisions or independent sources of income (like taxation rights); and as an administrative authority it had to 'observe objectivity' (SOU 1989: 41: 151–9, 305–11; Prop. 1992/93: 32: 35). The limited mandate of the Sámi Parliament, its institutional design and organisational structure had already been heavily criticised in the comments on the initial proposal from the Sámi Rights Commission. SSR, for instance, was supportive of the idea of establishing a Sámi Parliament in Sweden as a representative of the Sámi people but considered the proposed structure and role of the parliament a disappointment, as the new political body would lack any real authority and influence (Ds 1989: 72: 126–7; Svenska Samernas Riksförbund 1988: 231).[11] SSR also indicated that its own national meetings had filled much of the same purpose and role as the new parliament would (Ds 1989: 72: 126).

Criticism of the Sámi Parliament continues and focuses mainly on its institutional design. There is a perceived clash of interests between the role of the parliament as an administrative authority and its role as a popularly elected representative body (see, for example, Lawrence and Mörkenstam 2012). This was, for instance, distinctly expressed in a written compilation by the Sámi Parliament to the UN Special Rapporteur in 2010:

> It is not completely without problems that the Sámi Parliament, in its capacity as a State agency, shall carry out the politics and decisions that are made by Riksdag and government, since the Sámi Parliament's elected members have been elected through party programs and election promises that are often directly contrary to the politics expressed by the government and Riksdag. ... The Sámi Parliament in Sweden is for now not a body for Sámi self-determination (Sametinget 2010).

---

11. Ds is an abbreviation of *Departementsserien*, i.e., ministerial reports.

In spite of this critique, however, the parliament has been an important forum wherein previously neglected and marginalised Sámi groups have been given an opportunity to be represented at a national level. The heterogeneous Sámi movement is reflected in the number of political parties represented in the parliament, which has ranged between six and eleven during the five lengths of office since the first election. In the scramble to establish parties for the historic first election to the Sámi Parliament, both existing Sámi organisations and new political parties registered; some in the latter category represented oppositional voices to SSR. Existing Sámi organisations chose somewhat different strategies. SSR and LSS both fielded candidates in the election without clearly separating party from organisation, while persons who had been active in Sáminuorra – a youth section of SSR – formed the party Min Geaidnu, which was described as having its ideological roots in Sáminuorra but being organisationally separate. Both SSR and LSS have since followed similar paths, separating the parties from the organisations, delineating their different functions (*Sf* 1993: 3: 15; 1993: 4: 8–25; 1993: 6–7: 64–73; 1997: 4: 6–23; 1997: 5: 32; 1997: 6–7: 3–21; 2001: 4: 12–25; 2001: 6–7: 14–20; Svenska Samernas Riksförbund 1993: 7; Svenska Samernas Riksförbund 1996: 14–15, 41–2). The representation of a more heterogeneous Sámi movement has, however, also contributed to a divided and sometimes fragmented parliament (see, for example, *Sf* 2012: 4: 21–34; Wasara-Hammare 2003: 359–60).

The establishment of the Sámi Parliament has changed the position and status of the Sámi movement, as the Sámi are now empowered on an institutional level.[12] The institutional status of the Sámi Parliament as a government agency makes the parliament vulnerable to criticisms of being an extended arm of the Swedish state, however, rather than a body for Sámi self-determination (see, for example, Lawrence and Mörkenstam 2012: 226–7). According to SSR, for instance, it has 'gradually become a straitjacket for Sámi autonomy' (Svenska Samernas Riksförbund 2012a: 2). This potential crisis of legitimacy can be seen as a constant risk in a state like Sweden, which is traditionally imbued by 'corporatism', in which the implementation of government policy is to be exercised by representatives from those very groups that are directly affected. If members of the group consider their representative body as too closely allied with the state, it will be difficult for the body to maintain legitimacy (see, for example, Rothstein 1992: 59–61). The Sámi Parliament's institutional design implies that it could run the risk of being 'co-opted' by the state, because

---

12. The Sámi Parliament is, for instance, to allocate funding to cultural activities and Sámi organisations, appoint the Board of Directors of the Sámi School, guide and direct the work on the Sámi languages, and look after matters of special importance to the Sámi people (SFS 1992: 1433: Ch. 2, Art. 1). Moreover, the Sámi Parliament must keep track of, evaluate and keep the government informed on the development of the politics on national minorities and minority languages concerning the Sámi people and languages (SFS 2009: 1395: Art. 2). The parliament is, since 2007, also responsible for a number of administrative tasks regarding the reindeer industry regulated in the Reindeer Farming Act (SFS 1971: 437).

it both participates in making and takes responsibility for implementing government policy.

The institutional design of the Sámi Parliament thus makes a strategy of dialogue and participation in relation to the Swedish state necessary; but the parliament can also challenge government policy in its capacity as a government agency. This has basically been done in three different ways. Firstly, through administrative decisions, as government agencies in Sweden enjoy relative independence from the government and ministries. This administrative challenge can be illustrated by the political developments following the decision of the Sámi Parliament in 2009 only to allocate 71 per cent of the eligible predator compensation instead of 100 per cent to the reindeer-herding communities, due to lack of funds. When the Sámi communities appealed the decision of the Sámi Parliament to the District Court in Norrbotten, the court ruled in their favour, stating that they had the right to full compensation (Länsrätten i Norrbottens Län 2009). The matter was brought up in the Plenary of the Sámi Parliament, after which the Board of the Parliament decided not to appeal the ruling. The decision not to appeal was severely criticised by the Ministry of Agriculture, the ministry in charge of Sámi affairs, which claimed that the decision was a politicisation of a government agency matter, since a government agency ought to appeal such Court decisions. Thus, the Sámi Parliament had not fulfilled its tasks as a responsible government agency, according to the Ministry (Lawrence and Mörkenstam 2012: 222–3). In its capacity as a representative body of the Sámi people, however, the decision not to appeal the ruling of the District Court must be seen as rational and in the interest of the Sámi people.

Secondly, the Sámi Parliament challenges traditional government policy through its own policy-making or public investigations, something that has been accentuated following developments in international law on the rights of indigenous peoples. Almost all claims made by the Sámi Parliament take as their starting-point the assumption that the parliament is the representative body of an indigenous people with rights recognised both at a national and international level. The policy determinations of the Sámi Parliament on, for instance, minerals and mining, language, industry, and on self-determination are often formulated in opposition to the traditional or conventional politics of the Swedish Government (see, for example, Sametinget 2004ab, 2006a, 2014; SáOU 2009: 3).

Thirdly, this critical stance is also put forward in statements of opinion on government policy proposals or official reports. In 2008, for instance, when a proposal for a new Instrument of Government (*Regeringsform*) was presented, the Sámi were defined as an indigenous people, giving them a special position compared to other national minorities (SOU 2008: 125, Part 1: 454–8). In the proposal for the text of the new Instrument of Government, however, neither the terms 'indigenous' nor 'Sámi people' were included. This was strongly criticised by the Sámi Parliament, which said it showed that the Swedish government lacked an indigenous policy (Sametinget 2008; Sametinget 2009). The Sámi protests had some effect, because the final text of the Instrument of Government (effective from 1 January 2011) stated that the 'opportunities of the Sámi people and ethnic, linguistic and religious minorities to preserve and develop a cultural and social life of their own shall be promoted' (SFS 2010: 1408: Ch. 1, §2). This new wording clearly distinguished the Sámi and placed them in a separate category; however, there was still no explicit recognition of them as an indigenous people.

Although much of the recent collective action of the Sámi movement has its origins in the Sámi Parliament, this does not mean that other forms of political action have been abandoned (as seen above in the work of SSR). Direct action in different forms has been used to challenge government policy. For example, there were protests against the Swedish Government's small-game-hunting policy in the early 1990s (see, for example, Beach 1995; Eriksson 1997: 141–4; Wasara Hammare 2002: 351–7). The protests highlighted the land-rights conflict between the Sámi people and the Swedish state. That conflict arose because of a decision to open the exclusive hunting and fishing rights of the members of the reindeer-herding districts to any hunter, provided they had a license granted by the County Administrative Board. The reindeer-herding districts had previously controlled who would be allowed to hunt and fish in the year-round reindeer-breeding areas historically considered as 'reserved for the Lapps' (Prop. 1928: 43: 48). The Swedish state was claiming hunting and fishing rights parallel to the rights of the Sámi, and thus the right to grant this right to others. Protest actions included hunger strikes, road blocks, protest marches and rallies, because, it was argued, the small-game policy was an abusive, denigrating and humiliating way to handle Sámi rights (*Sf* 1992: 11: 13; 1993: 9: 4–22; 1994: 9: 4–8). In 2009, SSR launched a legal challenge against the state on behalf of Girjas reindeer-herding district, in which it was claimed that the Sámi have exclusive rights to hunting and fishing (see, for example, Svenska Samernas Riksförbund 2012b). The case is still – in April 2015 – in a preliminary phase.

The heterogeneity of the contemporary Sámi movement can be further illustrated by the continued work of the first national organisation of the Sámi, SSR. Together with the Sámi Parliament, SSR is still a powerful and important actor within the Sámi movement because it directly represents the reindeer-herding districts in Sweden. The activities of SSR show that a heterogeneous Sámi movement can neither be expected nor requested to speak with a single voice. On certain issues, such as the discussion on predator-compensation, SSR challenges the decision-making power of the Sámi Parliament. Predator-compensation is not, SSR claims, an issue of interest to all Sámi; rather, it is a local issue concerning the right of private reindeer-herders to be compensated the full amount for lost property, that is, reindeer. Thus, predator-compensation is an issue where the interests of a particular group are better represented by an organisation like SSR, rather than the Sámi Parliament (Svenska Samernas Riksförbund 2011: 45–61). The ensuing discontent with the parliament's handling of reindeer-herding led SSR to put forward a proposal to establish a new government agency, a Reindeer Husbandry Agency, separated from the Sámi Parliament, in 2012 (Svenska Samernas Riksförbund 2012a).

Another important form of Sámi mobilisation has been demands for Sweden to ratify or adopt international conventions and declarations on indigenous rights. The Sámi movement has, for instance, been working for Swedish ratification of the 1989 ILO Convention No. 169 on Indigenous and Tribal Peoples in Independent Countries. In 1999, the Sámi Parliament emphasised the importance of ratification, as it would strengthen the current weak legal protection of Sámi land rights, which are still defined in the Reindeer Farming Act of 1971 (Sametinget 1999: 2; Brännström 2009: 201–2).[13] Ratification would also 'create huge possibilities for the advent of a new Swedish indigenous and Sámi policy ...' (Sametinget 1999: 2). In line with this view, the UN Special Rapporteur on the situation of indigenous peoples stated in a 2011 report that Sweden should consider ratifying the Convention. The importance of land rights for indigenous peoples was emphasised and Sweden was directly criticised for its handling of this issue: the Swedish juridical system places the Sámi at a disadvantage in legal processes because of the high burden of proof concerning traditional Sámi rights required and Sweden has not demarcated traditional Sámi land areas (UN 2011: Art. 72, 78, 81–2). Although there is a consensus on the need of ratification within the Sámi movement, the necessary preconditions for such a step are contested. Some political parties in the parliament claim, for instance, that ratification must be preceded by a confirmation by the Swedish state that all Sámi have rights in accordance with the Convention, not only reindeer-herders (see, for example, Albmut 2009; Jakt- och fiskesamerna 2009; Landspartiet Svenska Samer 2009). This, in turn, challenges the Swedish state's historical stereotype of Sámi as reindeer-herders, which is still its main justificatory argument for Sámi rights.

More important in this context, perhaps, is the continued and expanded co-operation at the Nordic level, where the starting point is a collective Sámi identity as, for instance, expressed at the nineteenth Sámi Conference in Rovaniemi in 2008: 'the Saami constitute one people', the 'national borders shall not infringe on our national unity, and 'as a people the Saami have the right to self-determination' (Sámi Conference 2008). This transnational political work has also been strengthened with the establishment of a Sámi Parliamentarian Council in 2000, with the Sámi Parliaments in Finland, Norway and Sweden as members, and Russian Sámi as observers (see, for example, Heininen 2002: 227). The clearest manifestation of the work of the Sámi movement at the Nordic level has been its participation in the development of a common Nordic Sámi Convention. The Convention has been described as 'a modern treaty between the Finnish, Norwegian and Swedish state-forming people, on one hand, and the

---

13. This is also evident in the many legal actions the Sámi have lost since the Taxed Mountain Case in legal proceedings on the right to use land and water for the maintenance of Sámi reindeer on private property. In 2011, however, the Swedish Supreme Court ruled in favour of the Sámi for the first time in the case of Nordmaling (HD 2011).

Saami people, indigenous to the three countries, on the other' (Åhrén 2007: 12). The Draft Convention takes the development in international law as its starting-point. Like the UN Declaration, for instance, the Sámi Convention's third article concerns the right to self-determination:

> As a people, the Sámi have the right to self-determination in accordance with the rules and provisions of international law .... [T]he Sámi people has the right to determine its own economic, social and cultural development and to dispose, to their own benefit, over its natural resources' (Draft Nordic Sámi Convention 2005).

The Plenary of the Swedish Sámi Parliament decided to propose an adoption of the Convention in 2006 and was willing to accept the wordings of all articles in it (Sametinget 2006b: 1). However, after the Draft Convention was presented in 2005, the negotiating process between the Nordic countries and the Sámi did not begin again until 2011, and still in 2015 the outcome of these negotiations is most uncertain.

It is obvious that the solidarity of the Sámi movement and the collective identity of 'we' the Sámi people, established during the 1960s and 70s, is still a firm basis from which to mobilise resources for collective action. In recent years, this collective Sámi identity has been more firmly articulated across the borders of the four states partitioning the Sámi; it has been increasingly institutionalised in and through the 'symbolic construction of a Sami nation, Sápmi, with its own flag, National Day, and national anthem' (Pietikäinen 2003: 582). With the Sámi Parliament, the movement has a popularly elected body with the capacity to represent heterogeneous interests, although it is severely restricted in its actions by its status and function as a government agency. Trust in the parliament among the Sámi constituency seems, however, to be low. The first election study in connection with elections to the Sámi Parliament, in 2013, showed that the Sámi constituency had lower trust in the Sámi Parliament than in other well established political institutions in Sweden, such as the national parliament (*Riksdag*) and the government. Only 16 per cent of the respondents stated that they had high or very high trust in the parliament, and around 50 per cent reported that they were not satisfied with the work of the parliament. At the same time, however, the study clearly showed that the Sámi constituency wanted the parliament to have greater influence and autonomy on issues of importance in the Sámi society (Dahlberg and Mörkenstam 2014a). This duality is also discernible in the pattern for registration to the Sámi electoral roll and in the electoral turnout.[14] While turnout has declined from 72 per cent in the first

---

14. All Sámi above the age of 18 can register as voters, if they fulfil two criteria. First, there is a question of self-declared identity: those who register must declare that they regard themselves as Sámi. Second, there is an objective, language-based criterion: (i) the voter himself/herself or (ii) one of his/her parents or grandparents, must have used Sámi as a home language, or (iii) one of the parents must be (or have been) registered on the electoral roll.

election in 1993 to 54 per cent in the election in 2013, the number of persons registered on the electoral roll has increased during the same period of time: from 5,390 to 8,322. In spite of the decline in turnout measured in per cent, the actual number of voters has continued to increase, as new persons have registered on the electoral roll (Dahlberg and Mörkenstam 2014b).[15] The decline in trust and the falling electoral turnout should therefore not be interpreted as signs of a lack of solidarity within the Sámi movement, although they might indicate a lack of solidarity and identification with the Sámi Parliament. Rather, it seems as if it is the collective Sámi identity in itself that mobilises resources for collective action and creates solidarity within the Sámi movement today, not an organisation or a specific institution.

In addition to already existing strategies of the Sámi movement such as moderate action through dialogue and participation, legal proceedings or more disruptive strategies of direct action – the establishment of a Sámi Parliament has made new strategies possible because it serves as an institutional basis for collective action. This institutional base is also something the Sámi movement has used, through its role as a government agency and through the political activities of the popularly elected representative body. The main adversary of the Sámi movement is still government policy and thus, ultimately, the Swedish state. The Sámi–state conflict has been intensified as a direct result of the Sámi movement's conscious strategy to situate their struggle firmly within international law and as part of the international indigenous movement. The Nordic governments are very sensitive 'to their global reputation as upholders of international law and conventions' (Minnerup and Solberg 2011b: 14; see also Semb 2001). Hence, the rights of the Sámi as an indigenous people are the starting-points of the Sámi movement today, both in their rights claims and in their relationship to the Swedish state, as stated by the Sámi Parliament in a 2004 report: 'Sweden is a country founded on the territory of two peoples', which implies that 'these peoples have to exercise their right to self-determination side by side' and that 'neither of the two people's right to self-determination has priority over that of the other people (Sametinget 2004a: Ch.7.1).

The recognition of the Sámi as an indigenous people challenges the justificatory foundations of Swedish government policy. Firstly, it challenges the stereotype of Sámi as reindeer-herders rather than as a people. Secondly, it challenges the traditional nation-state-centred understanding of political rights and democracy. If two peoples with a right to self-determination share a territory, this must set limits to 'the rights of existing nation-states' and set 'these into more co-operatively regulated relationships' (Young 2005: 52). From a Sámi perspective, the right to self-determination implies a 'right for the Saami to control their economic, social, political and cultural development,

---

15. For a similar development in Norway, see Pettersen (2011: 75–9) and Bergh and Saglie (2011: 87–8).

including the right to dispose of land, water and natural resources in the Saami areas' (Henriksen, Scheinin and Åhrén 2007: 81). Primarily at stake here is thus the unchallenged convention that nation-states have far-reaching discretion in interpreting and institutionalising political rights. The Sámi have argued that the right to self-determination should be discussed in terms of a 'sliding scale, which essentially awards the Saami people a varying degree of influence over the decision-making process depending on how important the question at hand is to the Saami people' (Åhrén 2007: 16).

Thirdly, the Sámi movement continues to challenge traditional theories of property rights. No doubt land and resource rights have been among the most contentious issues in Swedish Sámi politics, as the reluctance to ratify ILO Convention 169 clearly shows. In the contemporary debate, this challenge to the Swedish state comes from two different directions. One is the challenge of individual reindeer-herders and the reindeer-herding districts – something that started with the legal processes initiated by SSR in the 1960s – taking as their starting point the right to private property or that the Sámi rights are based on use and prescription from time immemorial and, as such, constitutionally protected in the same way as ownership rights. Another challenge follows from the recognition of the Sámi as an indigenous people, whereby rights claims to land and natural resources find support within international law, most explicitly in ILO Convention 169.

As indigenous peoples cultures and communities are closely linked to their traditional land and water areas as well as natural resources [...i]t does not make sense to talk of a right to self-determination for indigenous peoples without including a resource dimension' (Henriksen, Scheinin and Åhrén 2007: 89).

Hence, property rights must be seen in a wider context, in which control of the use of land and natural resources presupposes some kind of political autonomy in relation to the dominant majority society (see, for example, Buchanan 2004: 418; Weigård 2008: 187–9).

Concluding remarks: Some reflections on the contemporary situation

The contemporary challenge has come full circle, back to the demands made by the Sámi movement a century ago, when Laula's rights claims were explained and justified by a conception of the Sámi as a people with ownership rights over the reindeer-grazing lands. The most important effect of the collective action of the Sámi movement in the last century may thus be the Swedish government's recognition of the Sámi as a people with a right to self-determination, something stated for the first time in a Government Bill in 2006: 'The Sámi people is ... a "people" in the international legal sense, that has rights, including the right to self-determination' (Prop. 2005/06:86: 38). Thus today two peoples are recognised in Sweden: the Swedish people and the Sámi people. The Swedish

Instrument of Government states that '[a]ll public power in Sweden proceeds from the people' (SFS 1974: 152: Ch. 1, §1), but what happens when there are two peoples?

So far, this fundamental challenge has not had any major effects on Swedish government policy. This can be illustrated by Sweden's statement in conjunction with the signing of the UNDRIP in 2007. The statement emphasised that the right to self-determination could be granted to indigenous peoples through their participation in the democratic system as a whole (as in Sweden), and through consultations with indigenous peoples' representative institutions (like the Sámi Parliament). Furthermore, it points out that individual rights had precedence over collective rights in Sweden and that the right to self-determination did not involve any veto-right for the Sámi people. Finally, concerning Sámi land rights, the Swedish representative stated that 'the Swedish government must maintain a balance between competing interests of different groups living in the same areas of the north of the country' and that the Swedish Government interprets 'references in the Declaration to ownership and control of land to apply to the traditional rights of the Sámi people ... called reindeer herding rights' (UN 2007). It thus seems as if, despite adopting the Declaration, the Swedish government expects to go on with business as usual.

If we conclude by returning to the early activists of the Sámi movement, facing a Swedish society in which an indigenous nomadic people like the Sámi were considered to be inferior in comparison to the 'civilised' and 'modern' Swedish people, the contemporary Sámi movement both explains and justifies their action, conflict and organisation by reference to their status as an indigenous people and to contemporary international law. With the 2007 UNDRIP, for instance, the Sámi (and indigenous peoples in general) have an international platform from which to leverage their rights claims. In addition, the Declaration can also be used as a yardstick in evaluations of government policy, by the Sámi movement or by external observers. International law thus guarantees the Sámi international exposure when it challenges the Swedish state and its policy but, in practical matters, it is not of much help. The meaning of indigenous self-determination seems to be 'notoriously difficult to pin down' in international law and, to use the words of Helen Quane (2011: 269), 'there is little if any guidance as to what [...it] means in actual practice'. The meaning of the right to self-determination is thus still very much under negotiation.

If recognition of indigenous rights internationally has been the result of indigenous mobilisation both at an international and a national level, our historical analysis shows that almost all major changes in Swedish Sámi policy have been the result of collective actions by the Sámi movement at both national and local levels. The Sámi movement is thus of utmost importance in the ongoing struggle for the recognition of indigenous rights.

References

Unpublished sources

National Archives Sweden

Ecklesiastikdepartementets arkiv
Park, Gustav (1943). Brev till Biskop Bengt Jonzon, 23 februari 1943. Konseljakter 21 april1943, nr 75.
Jordbruksdepartementets arkiv
Lappdeputationen (1933). Skrivelse till regeringen, 7 november 1933. Konseljakter 28 januari 1944, nr 65.
Lappdeputationen (1934). Påminnelseskrift till regeringen, 28 april 1934. Konseljakter 28 januari 1944, nr 65.
Justitieombudsmannens arkiv
Park, Per Larsson *et al.* (1933). Skrivelse till justitieombudsmannen, 15 juni 1933 [The document written by Gustav Park]. F I. Akter i avgjorda mål, mapp II.

Folkrörelsearkivet i Umeå (FRAU)

Sven Hallströms arkivsamling (SHA)
1946 års köttbesiktningskommitté (1947). Betänkande med förslag till reformering av renslakten m.m. Rättegångshandlingar, akt A 9345.

Published sources

Åhrén, M. (2007) 'The Nordic Saami Convention', *GÁLDU CÁLA Journal of Indigenous Peoples Rights* 3: http://www.galdu.org/govat/doc/samekoneng_nett.pdf (accessed 8 April 2015).
Albmut (2009) *Albmut, Almasj, Almetjh, Folket. Visioner 2009*: http://www.samiskafolket.se/visioner.pdf (accessed 31 August 2012).
Anaya, S. J. (2009) 'Why there should not have to be a declaration on the rights of indigenous peoples', in S. James Anaya (ed.) *International Human Rights and Indigenous Peoples*, Chicago: Wolters Kluwer Law & Business.
Beach, H. (1995) 'The new Swedish Sámi policy – a dismal failure: concerning the Swedish Government's proposition 1992/93:32, *Samerna och samisk kultur m.m.* (Bill)', in E. Gayim and K. Myntti (eds) *Indigenous and Tribal Peoples' Rights – 1993 and After*, Rovaniemi: University of Lapland's Printing Service.
Bergh, J. and Saglie, J. (2011) 'Valgdeltakelsen ved sametingsvalg: Hvor viktig er tilgjenglighet?', in E. Josefsen and J. Saglie (eds) *Sametingsvalg. Velgere, partier, medier*, Oslo: Abstrakt Forlag AS.
Buchanan, A. (2004) *Justice, Legitimacy, and Self-determination: Moral foundations for international law*, Oxford: Oxford University Press.

Brysk, A. (2000) *From Tribal Village to Global Village: Indian Rights and International Relations in Latin America*, Stanford: Stanford University Press.

Brännström, M. (2009) 'Samerna och naturresurserna', in L. Elenius and L. Ericsson (eds) *Är vi inte alla Minoriteter i Världen? Rättigheter för urfolk, nationella minoriteter och invandrare*, Stockholm: Ordfront.

Burger, J. (2011) 'The UN Declaration on the Rights of Indigenous Peoples: from advocacy to implementation', in S. Allen and A. Xanthaki (eds)) *Reflections on the UN Declaration on the Rights of Indigenous Peoples*, Oxford: Hart Publishing.

Cramér, T. (1970) 'Om de svenska samernas rätt till renbete i Norge och dess bakgrund', in T. Cramér and G. Prawitz, *Studier i Renbeteslagstiftning*, Stockholm: PA Norstedt & Söners Förlag.

Dahlberg, S. and U. Mörkenstam (2014a) 'Preliminär rapport från Valundersökning Sametinget 2013', unpublished paper presented at the project conference The Sámi Parliaments as Representative Bodies: a Comparative Study of the Elections in Sweden and Norway 2013, Oslo, Norway, 13–14 January 2014.

Dahlberg, S. and U. Mörkenstam (2014b) 'Valdeltagande vid val till Sametinget', unpublished paper presented at University of Bergen, Norway, 27 November 2014.

della Porta, D. and M. Diani (2006) *Social Movements: An introduction*, 2nd edn, Oxford: Blackwell Publishing.

Draft Nordic Sámi Convention (2005): http://www.regjeringen.no/ Vedlegg_5_d.pdf (accessed 11 May 2013).

Ds 1989:72. Remissyttranden över samerättsutredningens betänkanden (SOU 1986: 36) Samernas folkrättsliga ställning och (SOU 1989: 41) Samerätt och sameting.

Eriksson, J. (1997) *Partition and Redemption: A Machiavellian analysis of Sami and Basque patriotism*, Umeå: Umeå Universitet.

—— (2002) 'The construction of Sápmi: towards a transnational polity?', in K. Karppi and J. Eriksson (eds) *Conflict and Cooperation in the North*, Umeå: Norrlands Universitetsförlag.

Guigni, M. (1999) 'Introduction. How social movements matter: past research, present problems, future developments', in M. Guigni, D. McAdam and C. Tilly (eds) *How Social Movements Matter*, Minneapolis, MN: University of Minnesota Press.

Heininen, L. (2002) 'The Saami as a pan-national actor', in K. Karppi and J. Eriksson (eds) *Conflict and Cooperation in the North*, Umeå: Norrlands Universitetsförlag.

Henriksen, J. B., Scheinin, M. and Åhrén, M. (2007) 'The Saami people's right to self-determination', *Gáldu Cála – Journal of Indigenous Peoples Rights* 3: 52–97.

HD (Högsta Domstolen [Swedish Supreme Court]) 2011. Mål nr T 4028-07, Sedvanerätt till vinterrenskötsel [Nordmalingsmålet]: http://www.hogstadomstolen.se/Pages/33434/2011-04-27%20T%204028-07%20 Dom.pdf (accessed 10 November 2011).

Jakt- och fiskesamerna (2009) *Jakt- och fiskesamernas partiprogram*: http://www.jaktochfiskesamerna.se/default.asp?path=18335%2C18338&page id=8820 (accessed 31 August 2012).

Josefsen, E., Mörkenstam, U. and Saglie, J. (2015) 'Different institutions in similar states: the Norwegian and Swedish *Sámediggis*', *Ethnopolitics* 14(1): 32–51, publication online July 10, 2014. DOI:10.1080/17449057.2014. 926611.

Korpijaakko-Labba, K. (1994) *Om samernas rättsliga ställning i Sverige-Finland: en rättshistorisk utredning av markanvändingsförhållanden och – rättigheter i Västerbottens lappmark före mitten av 1700-talet*, Helsingfors: Juristförbundets Förl.

Kungl. Jordbruksdepartementet (1905) *Handlingar angående ifrågasatta åtgärder till förbättrade af lapparnes existensvillkor i Västerbottens län*, Stockholm.

— (1907) *Handlingar angående ifrågasatta åtgärder till förbättrade af lapparnas existensvillkor i Västerbottens län, Ny följd*, Stockholm.

Landspartiet Svenska Samer (2009) *Valplattform*: http://www.landspartietsvenskasamer.com/dokument/LSS_VALPLATTFORM_081105.pdf (accessed 31 August 2012).

Lantto, P. (1998) 'Språkrör, budbärare, väktare, förkunnare och upplysare. En analys av Samefolkets Egen Tidning/Samefolket och dess roll för de svenska samernas etnopolitiska mobilisering 1918–1962', in P. Sköld and K. Kram (eds) *Kulturkonfrontation i Lappmarken. Sex essäer om mötet mellan samer och svenskar*, Umeå: Kulturgräns Norr, pp. 137–88.

— (2000) *Tiden Börjar På Nytt. En analys av samernas etnopolitiska mobilisering i Sverige 1900–1950*, Umeå: Kulturgräns norr.

— (2002) ' "För att med sin fackla få sprida ljus, där mörker varit rådande". Samefolkets Egen Tidning – Torkel Tomassons livsskapelse och samernas språkrör. *Oknytt* 23(1–2): 8–26.

— (2003) *Att Göra Sin Stämma Hörd: Svenska Samernas Riksförbund, samerörelsen och svensk samepolitik 1950–1962*, Umeå: Kulturgräns norr.

— (2010) 'Borders, citizenship and change: the case of the Sámi people, 1751–2008', *Citizenship Studies* 14(5): 543–56.

— (2012) *Lappväsendet: Tillämpningen av svensk samepolitik 1885–1971*, Umeå: Centre for Sami Research.

Lantto, P. and Mörkenstam, U. (2008) 'Sámi rights and Sámi challenges: the modernization process and the Swedish Sámi movement, 1886–2006', *Scandinavian Journal of History* 33(1): 26–51.

Lapparnes Egen Tidning (LET) 1904–1905.

Laula, E. (1904) *Inför lif eller död? Sanningsord i de lappska förhållandena*, Stockholm.

Lawrence, R. and Mörkenstam, U. (2012) 'Självbestämmande genom myndighetsutövning? Sametingets dubbla roller', *Statsvetenskaplig Tidskrift*, 115(2): 207–39.

Lundmark, L. (2006) *Samernas Skatteland i Norr-och Västerbotten under 300 år*, Stockholm: Institutet för Rättshistorisk Forskning.

Länsrätten i Norrbottens Län (2009) DOM 2009-09-09 Meddelad i Luleå, Mål nr 1565-09, Rotel 6.

Melucci, A. (1980) 'The new social movements: a theoretical approach', *Social Sciences Information* 19(2): 199–226.

— (1991) *Nomader i nuet. Sociala rörelser och individuella behov i dagens samhälle*, Göteborg: Daidalos.

Minde, H. (1980): 'Samebevegelsen, Det norske arbeiderparti og samiske rettigheter', in T. Thuen (ed.) *Samene – Urbefolkning og minoritet*, Tromsø: Universitetetsforlaget.

— (1995) 'The international movement of indigenous peoples: an historical perspective', in T. Brantenberg, J. Hansen and H. Minde (eds) *Becoming Visible – Indigenous politics and self-government*, Tromsö: Centre for Sámi Studies.

— (2003) 'Urfolksoffensiv, folkerettsfokus og styringskrise: kampen for en ny samepolitik 1960–1990', in B. Bjerkli and P. Selle (eds) *Samer, Makt Og Demokrat. Sametinget og den nye samiske offentligheten*, Oslo: Gyldendal Norsk Forlag.

Minnerup, G. and Solberg, P. (eds) (2011a) *First World, First Nations: Internal Colonialism and Indigenous Self-Determination in Northern Europe and Australia*, Brighton: Sussex Academic Press.

— (2011b) 'Introduction', in G. Minnerup and P. Solberg (eds) *First World, First Nations. Internal Colonialism and Indigenous Self-Determination in Northern Europe and Australia*, Brighton: Sussex Academic Press.

Motioner i Andra Kammaren, 1908:163, av herr G.A.E. Kronlund m. fl. om skrifvelse till Kungl. Maj:ts angående den nomadiserande lappbefolkningens vidmakthållande m.m.

Mörkenstam, U. (1999) *Om 'Lapparnes privilegier': Föreställningar om samiskhet i svensk samepolitik 1883–1997*, Stockholm: Stockholm Studies in Politics 67.

— (2014) 'The constitution of the Swedish Sámi people: Swedish Sámi policy and the justification of the inner colonisation of Sweden', in J. Tripathy and S. Padmanabhan (eds) *Becoming Minority: How discourses and policies produce minorities in Europe and India*, London: SAGE, pp. 88–110.

Pettersen, T. (2011) 'Valgmanntall og valgdeltakelse 1989–2009: grunnlag, utvikling og hovedtendenser', in E. Josefsen and J. Saglie (eds) *Sametingsvalg: Velgere, partier, medier*, Oslo: Abstrakt Forlag.

Pietikäinen, S. (2003) 'Indigenous identity in print. Representations of the Sami in news discourse', *Discourse & Society* 14(5): 581–601.

Proposition 1928:43. Kungl. Maj:ts proposition till riksdagen med förslag till lag om de svenska lapparnas rätt till renbete i Sverige m.m.
— 1976/77:80. Om insatser för samerna.
— 1992/93:32. Om samerna och samisk kultur.
— 2005/06:86. Ett ökat samiskt inflytande.
— 2009/10:1. Förslag till statsbudget för 2010, finansplan och skattefrågor m.m.

Protokoll m.m. från samelandsmötet i Arvidsjaur den 26-27 februari 1948. Uppsala, 1948.

Quane, H. (2011) 'New directions for self-determination and participatory rights?', in S. Allen and A. Xanthaki (eds) *Reflections on the UN Declaration on the Rights of Indigenous Peoples*, Oxford: Hart Publishing.

Riksdagens debatt, Andra Kammaren 1913: 31.

Robbins, J. (2011) 'Indigenous representative bodies in Northern Europe and Australia', in G. Minnerup and P. Solberg (eds) *First World, First Nations. Internal colonialism and indigenous self-determination in Northern Europe and Australia*, Brighton: Sussex Academic Press.

Rothstein, B. (1992) *Den Korporativa Staten: Intresseorganisationer och statsförvaltning i svensk politik*, Stockholm: Norstedts.

Ruong, I. (1981a) *Om en helhetssyn på samernas verklighet*, Stockholm: Nordiska Museet.
— (1981b) 'Samerna: entitet och identitetskriterier', *Nord-nytt* 11: 17–32.

Samefolkets Egen Tidning/Samefolket (SET/Sf) 1930, 1932–1933, 1949, 1959, 1961–1963, 1980, 1992–1994, 1997, 2001, 2012.

Sametinget (1999) *Yttrande. Samerna – ett ursprungsfolk i Sverige, betänkandet av Utredningen om ILO:s konvention 169 (SOU 1999:125)*: http://www.sametinget.se/1635 (accessed 8 June 2012).
— (2004a) Betänkande av det svenska Sametingets kommitté med uppgift att ta fram ett förslag till strategi för en implementering av det Sámiska folkets rätt till självbestämmande på den svenska sidan av Sápmi: http://www.sametinget.se/1328 (accessed 12 August 2012).
— (2004b) Start för en offensiv samisk språkpolitik: http://www.sametinget.se/1511 (accessed 12 August 2012).
— (2006a) Näringspolitisk strategi för Sametinget: http://www.sametinget.se/1143 (accessed 21 August 2012).
— (2006b) Yttrande. Nordisk samekonvention. Jo 3006/632: http://www.sametinget.se/1517 (accessed 5 September 2012).
— (2008) 'Samerna erkänns som urfolk i ny grundlag?': http://www.sametinget.se/6352 (accessed 12 February 2009).
— (2009) 'Sverige saknar en urfolkspolitik': http://www.sametinget.se/6698 (accessed 12 February 2009).

– (2010) Extract from the written compilation made for the conference in Rovaniemi 15–16 April: http://www.galdu.org/govat/doc/self_ determination_samiparliament_sweden.pdf (accessed 29 August 2012).

– (2014) Sametingets syn på mineraler och gruvor i Sápmi: http://www. sametinget.se/gruvpolicy (accessed 11 December 2014).

Sámi Conference (2008) The Rovaniemi Declaration: http://www.saamicouncil. net/includes/file_download.asp?deptid=2161&fileid=2940&file=Rovani emi_DeclarationFINAL.pdf&pdf=1 (accessed 29 May 2012).

SáOU 2009:3, Sveriges grundlagsanpassning till gällande folkrätt. Betänkande från självbestämmandeutredningen lesjmierredimjuogos.

Semb, A. J. (2001) 'How norms affect policy – the case of Sami policy in Norway', *International Journal of Minority and Group Rights* 8(2): 177–222.

SFS 1886:38. Lag, angående de svenska Lapparnes rätt till renbete i Sverige.

– 1898:66. Lag om de svenska lapparnas rätt till renbete i Sverige.

– 1928:309. Lag om de svenska lapparnas rätt till renbete i Sverige.

– 1971:437. Rennäringslag.

– 1974:152. Kungörelse om beslutad ny regeringsform.

– 1992:1433. Sametingslag.

– 2009:1395. Förordning med instruktion för Sametinget.

– 2010:1408. Lag om ändring i regeringsformen.

Sjölin, R. (2002) *En studie i ickemakt: Samer och samefrågor i Svensk politik*, Kautokeino.

Smith, L. T. (1999) *Decolonizing Methodologies: Research and indigenous peoples*, London: Zed Books.

SOU 1986:36. Samernas folkrättsliga ställning. Delbetänkande av samerättsutredningen.

– 1989:41. Samerätt och sameting. Huvudbetänkande av samerättsutredningen.

– 1990:91. Samerätt och samiskt språk. Slutbetänkande av samerättsutredningen.

– 2008:125. En reformerad grundlag. Del 1.

Spörsmål av samiskt intresse vid Nordiska rådets 7:e session 1959: Samernas rättigheter och samverkan på renskötselns område. Stockholm, 1960.

Supreme Court Decision No. DT2. Case No. 324/76, in B. Jahreskog (ed.) *The Sami National Minority in Sweden*, Stockholm: Almqvist & Wiksell International.

Svenska lapparnas landsmöte i Östersund den 5-9 februari 1918. Uppsala: Almqvist & Wiksell, 1918.

Svenska Samernas Riksförbund (1950) *Protokoll från Svenska Samernas Riksförbunds landsmöte 1950*. Umeå: Svenska Samernas Riksförbund.

– (1962) Protokoll från Svenska Samernas Riksförbunds landsmöte 1962. Umeå: Svenska Samernas Riksförbund.

– (1969) Protokoll från Svenska Samernas Riksförbunds Urtima landsmöte i Östersund den 3–5 oktober 1968 jämte samernas samepolitiska program. Umeå: Svenska Samernas Riksförbund.

— (1982) Protokoll från Svenska Samernas Riksförbund. Landsmötet i Umeå den 10–12 juni 1981. Umeå: Svenska Samernas Riksförbund.

— (1988) Protokoll från Svenska Samernas Riksförbund (SSR) Landsmötet i Kiruna 10-12 juni 1987. Umeå: Svenska Samernas Riksförbund.

— (1993) Protokoll Svenska Samernas Riksförbund (SSR) Landsmötet i Luleå 22–23 oktober 1992. Umeå: Svenska Samernas Riksförbund.

— (1996) Protokoll Svenska Samernas Riksförbund (SSR) Landsmötet i Åre 13– 15 juni 1995. Umeå: Svenska Samernas Riksförbund.

— (2011) *Protokoll samernas landsmöte Jokkmokk 2011*. Umeå: Svenska Samernas Riksförbund.

— (2012a) Förändring av Sametingets funktion och organisation: http://www. sapmi.se/resolution_ny_rennaringsmyndighet.pdf (accessed 4 September 2012)

— (2012b) Sameby har rätt att få domstolsprövning av rätten till jakten och fisket i fjällvärlden: http://www.sapmi.se/jaktfiske20121.pdf (accessed 10 September 2012).

Svensson, T. G. (1973) *Samernas politiska organisation*, Stockholm: Rotobeckman.

— (1997) *The Sámi and their land: The Sámi vs the Swedish Crown. A study of the legal struggle for improved land rights: the Taxed Mountain Case*, Oslo: Novus Forlag.

Thuen, T. (1995) *Quest for Equity: Norway and the Saami challenge*, St John's: Institute of Social and Economic Research, Memorial University of Newfoundland.

Tully, J. (1993) *An Approach to Political Philosophy: Locke in Contexts*, Cambridge: Cambridge University Press.

UN (2007) General Assembly. GA/10612, 13 September, 'General Assembly adopts declaration on rights of indigenous peoples': http://www.un.org/ News/Press/docs/2007/ga10612.doc.htm (accessed 28 August 2011).

— (2011) A/HRC/18/XX/Add.Y, 12 January 2011, *Report of the Special Rapporteur on the Situation of Human Rights and Fundamental Freedoms of Indigenous People*, James Anaya: http://www.regjeringen.no/upload/ FAD/Vedlegg/SAMI/Anaya_rapport.pdf (accessed 8 June 2012).

Wasara-Hammare, N. (2002) 'Sametinget i Sverige – parlament eller myndighet?', *Statsvetenskaplig tidskrift*, 105(2): 158–65.

— (2003) 'Makt och demokrati i svensk samepolitik', in B. Bjerkli and P. Selle (eds) *Samer, makt og demokrati: Sametinget og den nye samiske offentligheten*, Oslo: Gyldendal Norsk Forlag.

Xanthaki, A. (2007) *Indigenous Rights and United Nations Standards. Self-determination, culture and land*, Cambridge: Cambridge University Press.

Weigård, J. (2008) 'Is there a special justification for indigenous rights?', in H. Minde (ed.) *Indigenous Peoples: Self-determination, knowledge and indigeneity*, Delft: Eburon Academic Publishers, pp. 177–92.

Young, I. M. (2005) *Global Challenges: War, self-determination and responsibility for justice*, Cambridge: Polity Press.

Chapter Seven

The Sámediggi Electoral Roll in Norway: Framework, Growth and Geographical Shifts, 1989-2009

Torunn Pettersen

Introduction

In recent decades, indigenous peoples all over the world have mobilised to improve their social conditions and their cultural and political rights. This is also the case for the Sámi, whose traditional settlement area, often referred to as Sápmi, covers the middle and northern parts of Norway, Sweden and Finland, and the Kola Peninsula in north-west Russia. As a result of Sámi political mobilisation, among other things, a separate Sámi popularly elected body – *Sámediggi* in Northern Sámi, *Sameting* in the Scandinavian languages – has been established in Norway, Sweden and Finland respectively. Each Sámediggi is a complement to the political system of the state and the Sámi can still participate in all other elections. Due to significant variations in Sámi history and present situation within the respective states, the three Sámediggi differ with respect to voting requirements, scope of authority, available resources and organisational structures (Smith 2005; Henriksen 2008; Lantto 2010). Also, although the Sámi consider themselves one people, there is no pan-Sámi definition of who 'is' Sámi (Smith 2005). Hence, despite the identical designation, analysis and description of a given Sámediggi must always take as a starting point the circumstances of the state in question.

This chapter deals with the Sámediggi in Norway. Here, the decision to establish a Sámediggi was made in 1987, when the Norwegian Parliament, the Storting, passed a separate Sámi act: *Act concerning the Sameting (the Sámi parliament) and other Sámi legal matters*. Based on preparatory work between 1980 and 1984 by the government-appointed Sámi Rights Commission, the act stated that the Sámi in Norway should have a national assembly – a Sámediggi – whose main purpose was to be a forum for Sámi deliberation and formulation of Sámi policy in matters concerning the Sámi as a people (NOU 1984: 18; Ot.prp. nr 33 (1986–87)).

Sámi ethnicity is not registered in Norway's national censuses. Therefore, the establishment of the Sámediggi introduced a need for some kind of definition: who is entitled to vote and who is not? This chapter thus expands on the theme discussed in de Costa's contribution to this volume – the definition of indigenous peoples – in the context of elections to the Norwegian Sámediggi. In this case, the definition was drawn up in a process that included both state representatives and the Sámi themselves. The outcome of this process was that to be eligible and entitled to vote in the Sámediggi elections, a person must a) satisfy certain legally specified Sámi ethnicity criteria and b) choose to join a particular electoral roll established for the purpose of these elections. Other main elements of the election system are that 39 representatives should be directly elected from a given number of constituencies – originally 13, reduced to seven for the 2009 election and after. The Sámediggi elections would be held every four years, simultaneously with elections to the Storting.

The purpose of this chapter is to describe the framework for the Sámediggi electoral roll in Norway and to provide an overview of how this electoral roll developed, from the first Sámediggi election in 1989 up to and including the sixth election in 2009. The main aim is to present the roll's development at various geographical levels over these 20 years. Some explanatory factors for the outcomes are also suggested. The chapter starts with a review of the ideas behind having a separate Sámediggi electoral roll and a description of the roll's main features. It continues with an outline of the roll's overall development, followed by more detailed presentations of distributions of electors at the constituency and municipality level respectively. The subsequent section provides a summary discussion of the two main tendencies observed in the material, namely, overall growth and geographical shifts. The chapter concludes with a commentary on representativeness and the need for further research.

A separate electoral roll – purpose and framework

The idea of having a central assembly for the Sámi in Norway was not new, nor was it in itself controversial. Established in 1964, the Norwegian Sámi Council had already, in varying forms, functioned as an advisory body for regional and national authorities in matters of special concern for and to the Sámi population. The council members were appointed by the government on the basis of proposals from selected organisations. Gradually, however, Sámi stakeholders started to question the mode of appointment of members and, hence, the representativeness of the council as a Sámi body. Consequently, when the issue of the establishment of a central Sámi assembly was included in the mandate given to the Sámi Rights Commission in 1980, the main controversy turned out to be not the need for a Sámi body but how the selection of its members should be organised to achieve a composition that could best represent Sámi views on Sámi matters (NOU 1984: 18).

The Sámi Rights Commission comprised both Norwegian and Sámi experts and interest-group representatives. In its preparatory work, the Commission described the purpose of a Sámi representative body as providing a forum for discussion of Sámi matters and for formulation of Sámi policy in fields in which the Sámi collective wished to make its voice heard. It was emphasised that in '… a sufficiently representative Sámi Assembly, contentious issues can be voted over, and thereby achieve an outcome which is in conformity with generally accepted democratic principles …' which in turn could lead to '… a more legitimate and often more rapid solution to some Sámi matters' (NOU 1984: 18: 497). In retrospect, the ethno-political mobilisation that preceded the establishment of the Sámediggi has been especially linked to the struggle for a right to Sámi internal disagreement and individual differences. That is, the mobilisation surrounding Sámi policy concerned the right to diverge as Sámi and the right to be diverse as Sámi. The establishment of a Sámediggi represented an institutionalisation of this political right (Oskal 2003). Nevertheless, the main justification for the Sámediggi is that it is an assembly elected by and for the Sámi people; as a popularly elected Sámi body, the Sámi population in Norway constitutes its source of political legitimacy (Broderstad 1999).

Controversies and complications

Members of the Sámi Rights Commission, as well as the stakeholders whose views were sought during the consultation round in 1984–6, were strongly divided with regard to the establishment of a separate electoral roll (NOU 1984: 18; Ot.prp. nr 33 (1986–87)). The *supporters* argued that the use of such a register is the common practice when holding direct elections and is intended to produce the best representativeness. Additionally, a separate electoral roll was also perceived as a potential means for Sámi cultural mobilisation: an opportunity to register on Sámi electoral roll could induce individuals to (re)assess their ethnic affiliation and the existence of such a roll could thereby generate stronger Sámi awareness and self-confidence and enhance the status of the Sámi as a distinct people. The *opponents* of a separate electoral roll argued that matters of ethnic identity and ethnic boundaries were emotionally too heavily laden and that a separate roll could potentially cause harmful antagonism in local communities as well as personal distress for individuals. In fact, it was claimed that '… in reality, the ethnic boundaries are so fluid that any attempt to establish fair and applicable criteria for the enfranchisement is doomed to fail from the start' (Ot.prp. nr 33 (1986–87): 505).

The controversies and complications regarding the Sámediggi electoral roll can be linked to two issues that are partly interrelated. The first issue is the one of assimilation policy. At the time when the Sámi Rights Commission started its work in 1980, a systematic policy of assimilation had been in effect in Norway for more than a century, involving the use of governmental instruments to persuade the Sámi to give up the Sámi language, change the basic values of their culture and relinquish their ethnic identity (Minde 2003). This so-called 'Norwegianisation' policy was, by and large, successful – especially in coastal areas – and, gradually, many who could have identified themselves as Sámi and/or as Sámi-speakers, no longer wished to or chose to do so (see, for example, Hirsti 1967; Homme 1969; Eidheim 1971; Nielsen 1986; Minde 2005).

The second issue concerning the separate Sámediggi electoral roll is the absence of an up-to-date nationwide demographic register of the Sámi population. While information on Sámi affiliation in various ways was included in most Norwegian censuses up till 1930, this practice was abandoned after World War

II (Lie 2002) and replaced with a normative census policy of not collecting data on citizens' ethnicity, whether Sámi or other. In this matter, Norway is not among those countries in which recording of ethnicity data is a conventional part of the census (Morning 2008). Rather, Norway holds the widespread European position: collection of such data is not merely contested but rejected (Simon 2011).[1]

One minor exception to the Norwegian post-war census practice has occurred, however. This was in 1970, when the census included four questions about whether the respondent and his/her parents and grandparents used Sámi as their home language; and whether the respondent self-identified as Sámi (Aubert 1978). The background for this exception was that even though the Sámi data in the pre-World War II censuses were characterised by a number of inconsistencies, due to varying criteria used for ethnic categorisations (Evjen and Hansen 2009), the total absence of up-to-date Sámi demographic data had given rise to new challenges. In 1959, a resolution by the Third Nordic Sámi Conference stated that Sámi organisations as well as Norwegian authorities needed '... better statistical information on the size and distribution of the Sámi population and data on its living conditions' (Aubert 1978: 16). In the subsequent years, the data issue was repeatedly put on the agenda by Sámi stakeholders (NOU 1984: 18, Ch. 10.2.2), resulting in this inclusion of four questions about Sámi affiliation in the 1970 census. But though Sámi stakeholders had argued that the 'Sámi questions' should be treated as standard census questions, the questions were instead printed on a separate questionnaire for use in a number of preselected census tracts in Norway's three northernmost counties. The argument was that inclusion of the four Sámi questions on the regular census form would be too expensive (Thorsen 1972). As the tracts where at least one Sámi census form was completed corresponded to 2.9 per cent of the country's population, the result was, of course, that the Sámi 1970 census data had little potential to reveal the geographical and demographic distribution of Norway's Sámi population at the time.

The exact outcomes of the Sámi questions were that 9,175 persons identified themselves as Sámi, another 10,535 reported Sámi as their first language, while 16,808 and 19,635 respondents reported to have at least one parent or grandparent respectively whose first language was Sámi. However, at the time of the 1970 census (the effects of) the assimilation policy were still in operation. This not only means that many people were hesitant to acknowledge Sámi affiliation (Eidheim 1971); some may have been even more reluctant to have their ethnic affiliation recorded in a public register (Aubert 1978). In addition, the atrocities committed against ethnic community members during World War II were still fresh in memory and it is highly probable that many Sámi would have been unwilling to record themselves as having an identity considered 'the Other' (Seltzner and Anderson 2001; Søby 2001).[2] Furthermore, overall

---

1. Neither the complex and contentious issue of the recording of ethnicity data for administrative purposes nor the ethnicity concept itself is further elaborated in this chapter.

2. The title of Statistics Norway's 1930 census publication containing the Sámi data was *Sámi and Kven. – Other countries' citizens, blinds, deaf mutes, retards and lunatics* (Statistics Norway 1933).

opposition to official recording of information about ethnicity (Kertzner and Arel 2002), might be found among all citizens, including Sámi. The outcomes of the Sámi questions in the 1970 census must thus be interpreted with all these reservations in mind. Sociologist Vilhelm Aubert, who had a central role in the census planning, suggested in his analysis of the census data that – when all known restrictions and possible unintended sources of error in the material were taken into account – '[t]here are in Norway probably some 40 000 persons whose life is in one way or another affected by their Sámi [Lappish] ancestry' (Aubert 1978: 118f).

To sum up: as only historical demographic data were available about the Sámi population in Norway, the development of an electoral system for a representative Sámi assembly was carried out against a backdrop of an assimilation policy combined with the absence of census data on ethnic affiliation. Consequently, the Sámi Rights Commission had a fragile basis for predicting the number of persons who could be qualified to enrol on a future Sámediggi electoral roll – in total and particularly per proposed constituency.

Change of term – from Sámi Census to Sámediggi Electoral Roll

The Sámi Act did originally refer to the Sámediggi electoral roll as the Sámi census; *samemanntallet* in Norwegian. The use of the word census did probably stem from a blending of two issues; claims about the need for a Sámi demographic register and the discussions about having a separate Sámi electoral register for use in elections to a Sámi assembly. However, it turned out that the term Sámi census gave rise to confusion. Indeed, quite often, the electoral register was perceived as a register of the total Sámi population, instead of what it was explicitly stated to be, an electoral roll for use for Sámediggi elections. To clarify this, the term was in 2007 changed to the Sámediggi electoral roll; *Sametingets valgmanntall* in Norwegian (Sametinget 2007).

Inclusion criteria

The right to enrol on the Sámediggi electoral roll is set out in Section 2, subsection 6 of the Sámi Act:

> All persons who make a declaration to the effect that they consider themselves to be Sámi, and who either a) have Sámi as their domestic language, or b) have or have had a parent, grandparent or great-grandparent with Sámi as his or her domestic language, or c) are the child of a person who is or has been registered on the Sámediggi electoral roll may demand to be included on a separate register of Sámi electors in their municipality of residence.

Persons who want to join the roll must also comply with the general criteria for the right to vote in local elections in Norway, including age (18 years or older in the election year) and place of residence. Those who have joined the Sámediggi electoral roll can later request to be deleted. Declaring oneself as Sámi is often referred to as the *subjective* criterion of enrolment; the other conditions are referred to as *objective* criteria. As the Sámi Act states that persons *may* demand to be included in the electoral roll, this emphasises that enrolment is voluntary; a voluntariness which was repeatedly stressed in the preparatory work of the act (NOU 1984: 18; Ot.prp. nr 33 (1986–87)).

Basically, to enrol on the Sámediggi electoral roll requires compliance with two legally defined criteria while, at the same time, those who fulfil the criteria must decide for themselves whether they want to join or not. In Figure 7.1 this situation is captured by the schematic populations P0–P3.

P0 represents a population of persons who, *de facto*, fulfil at least one of the objective criteria for enrolment. Those persons within P0, who are familiar with and acknowledge this, constitute the population P1. The population P2 comprises those persons within P1 who self-identify as Sámi, be that as mainly Sámi,

Figure 7.1: Schematic populations related to inclusion criteria for enrolment on Sámediggi electoral roll

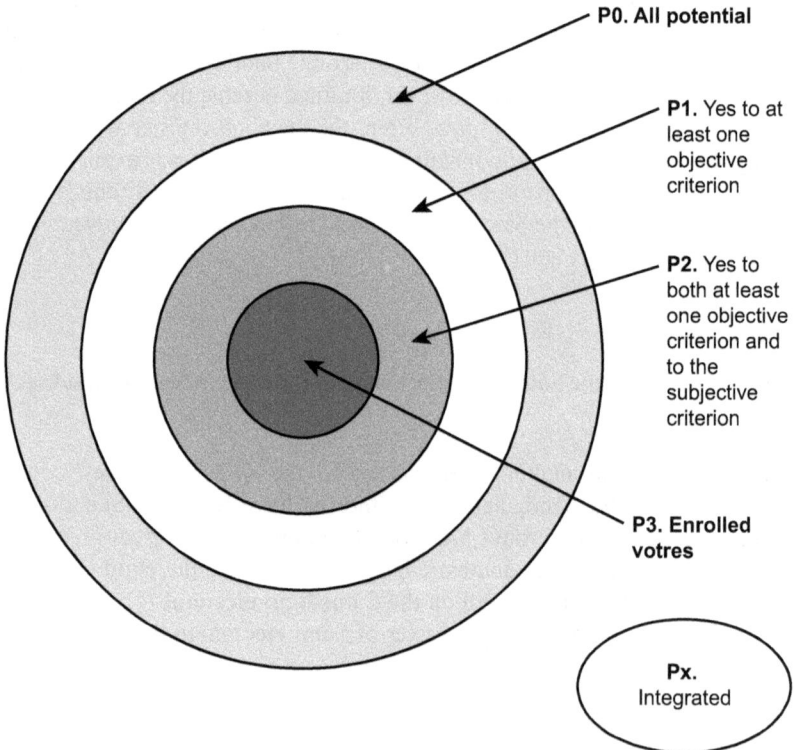

mostly Sámi, sufficiently Sámi and/or Sámi in combination with another ethnic identity. Finally, P3 comprises those persons within P2 who actually choose to enrol on the Sámediggi electoral roll.

Figure 7.1 also comprises a population Px, placed outside the figure's main structure. Px has been added to illustrate that ever since the initial work on establishing a Sámi assembly, there have been discussions on whether the Sámediggi electoral roll should be open to non-Sámi persons who are married to Sámi and/or are integrated into a Sámi environment by place of residence (NOU 1984: 18; Sametinget 2007). The population Px thereby represents persons who are considered – by themselves and/or others – to be affiliated with a Sámi family or community but who do not comply with the current criteria for joining the Sámediggi electoral roll. Proposals to expand the inclusion criteria to encompass one or more groups within Px have so far been rejected. The fact that this has been a recurring issue for more than three decades indicates that the enrolment criteria are not regarded as written in stone. Actually, the criteria have been slightly adjusted once since their adoption in 1987. This happened when the language criterion prior to the 1997 elections was extended from just the grandparents to include the great-grandparents.

Requests for inclusion on the Sámediggi electoral roll can be made at any time. An enrolment is valid as long as no active request for deletion is made. The electoral roll is made available for public inspection prior to each election. Use of the roll for other purposes than election-related ones requires special permission from the Sámediggi.

Data challenges

While the registration procedure until 2004 was undertaken in each municipality, the responsibility for record-keeping was transferred to the Sámediggi administration in 2005. In retrospect, the methods and principles of registration have varied considerably between municipalities and over time, leading to partly incomplete and partly uncertain data about the four first Sámediggi elections (Sametinget 2007). For example, when a name disappeared from the electoral roll of a given municipality, it was not clear whether this was due to deletion, relocation or death. Nor are complete figures available for the roll's age and gender distribution. From 2001, however, the Sámediggi electoral roll has been directly linked to the Norwegian National Population Register, making the procedures for inclusions and deletions more straightforward and secure.

Following each of the first four elections, the Sámediggi published a booklet containing election statistics for all constituencies and some selected municipalities (Hætta 1992, 1994, 1998, 2002). The figures had not been subject to systematic quality-control, however, and these statistics must therefore be used with some reservations. In 2005, some Sámediggi electoral statistics were included in Statistics Norway's regular portfolio of election statistics at http://www.ssb.no/valg. This information is, however, provided only at the constituency level. To obtain the number of enrolments per municipality for the 2005 and 2009 elections, it was necessary to consult the Sámediggi website at http://www.sametinget.no/valg.

In total, this rather complex data situation implies that a number of sources might have to be be utilised to fulfil even modest data requirements. It also implies that some reservations are in order with respect to the data quality. The following analyses are thus preliminary observations using the available data.

Development and status: Main features of the Sámediggi electoral roll

During the first 20 years of its existence, the Sámediggi electoral roll increased by 152.3 per cent: from 5,505 enrolled voters in 1989 to 13,890 in 2009 (Table 7.1).

The largest relative growth took place between the first and the second election (31.4 per cent) and the smallest between the elections in 2005 and 2009 (10.8 per cent). The largest nominal increase is the one prior to the elections in 2005, when more than 2,600 new voters were registered: approximately twice as many as during the preceding and the subsequent elections. The 2005 election was, however, a special case because it involved an additional four compensatory seats on top of the 39 ordinary Sámediggi seats, to be distributed among the four constituencies with the highest numbers of registered voters. The new seats were introduced as part of a process aimed at counteracting the gradually decreasing proportion of female Sámediggi representatives. However, the four compensatory seats also became an incentive for voter-enrolment, as they introduced an element of competition for seats between the constituencies (Pettersen 2005, 2010).

Majority of males, but increased proportion of women among the young[3]

No reliable figures are available about the electoral roll's age and gender distribution at the first four Sámediggi elections. At the 2005 and 2009 elections, the proportion of women voters was 46.1 and 46.9 per cent respectively. The proportion of voters under 25 years was 11.0 and 8.4 per cent, respectively. With respect to age distribution, the proportion of first-time voters – those aged 18 to 21 – decreased from 5 to 3 per cent between 2005 and 2009; the proportion of those aged 60 and above, however, increased from 21 to 24 per cent. There was thus a minor shift in the electoral roll's age profile in favour of the oldest group. At the 2009 election, persons younger than 30 years accounted for 15 per cent of the electoral roll. Women were in the majority in this group (55 per cent). Women made up 48 per cent of the 30–49 age group, while the proportion of women

---

3.   The estimations of the gender and age distributions were undertaken by Yngve Johansen at Sámi University College on behalf of The Analysis Group for Sámi Statistics (*Faglig analysegruppe for samisk statisikk*). These issues are further elaborated in Pettersen 2010.

Table 7.1: Sámediggi electoral roll 1989–2009, number of enrolments per election and nominal and relative change from one election to the next

Election year	Number of enrolments	Nominal change from former election (n)	Relative change from former election (%)
1989	5,505	–	–
1993	7,236	1,731	31.4
1997	8,665	1,429	19.7
2001	9,921	1,256	14.5
2005	12,538	2,617	26.4
2009	13,890	1,352	10.8

Source: http://www.samediggi.no

among voters aged 50 and above was 43 per cent. These figures indicate that a generational replacement may lead to a future higher proportion of women on the Sámediggi electoral roll.

Few active deletions

A person on the Sámediggi electoral roll can request to be deleted from it at any time. Statements from those who form an intention to resign in order to demonstrate disagreement with the Sámediggi's doings and/or specific decisions are, from time to time, publicly set forward. However, since the available data between 2004 and the summer of 2010 show a total of 65 deletions, this can hardly be regarded as a noteworthy defection rate when related to the roll's growth over these years. There is nothing to indicate any geographical concentration of deletions and they have a close-to-even gender distribution and no clustering with respect to age. Some minor concentrations of deletions during the election years 2005 and 2009, comprising 17 and 19 persons respectively, are probably due to the greater attention given to the electoral roll during election years.

Electoral participation

Participation in the Sámediggi elections is not a topic of this chapter. But as the explicit purpose of the Sámediggi electoral roll is to be a tool for elections, it is suitable to briefly mention how electoral participation has developed. While the overall trend has been a steady increase in the number of persons entitled to vote, there has been a gradually decline in the relative voter turnout per election; from 77.8 per cent in 1989 to 69.3 in 2009 (Pettersen 2010). However, as Figure 7.2 illustrates, the noticeable growth in enrolments implies that the

Figure 7.2: Sámediggi elections 1989–2009, number of enrolments and number of votes cast* per election

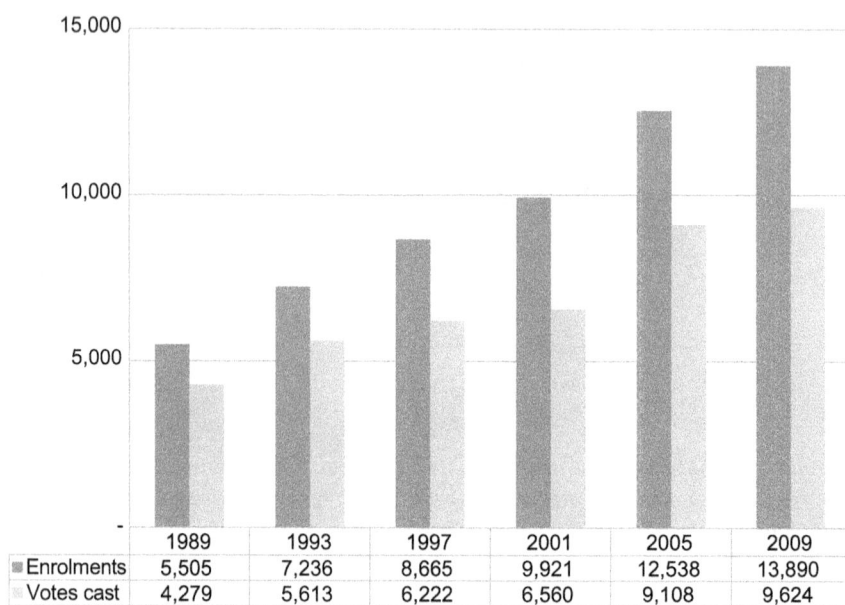

	1989	1993	1997	2001	2005	2009
▪Enrolments	5,505	7,236	8,665	9,921	12,538	13,890
Votes cast	4,279	5,613	6,222	6,560	9,108	9,624

Sources: Hætta 1992, 1994, 2002, Statistics Norway 2006, 2010
* As the available sources lack information on votes cast in 1997 and 2001, these are the valid votes.

number of votes cast at the 2009 election had more than doubled since the first Sámediggi election in 1989. Hence, measured as a percentage of the 'true', but unknown, Sámi population, the turnout has increased.

Geographical distributions

Geographical representativeness can be built into election systems by the distribution of seats among a number of constituencies. The Sámediggi election system follows this model. Technically, the Sámediggi constituencies are composed of a number of municipalities, which also perform the practical tasks of holding an election. This relationship calls for attention to how the Sámediggi electoral roll develops at both levels.

In a European comparison, Norway is an stretched-out country (1,800 km from north to south), with low population density (5 million inhabitants in 2013; 15 per km^2). These characteristics may explain why the overall level of attention given towards settlement patterns, regional conditions and centre–periphery cleavages is higher in Norway than in most other European countries

(Sørlie 2010); and also why geographical distribution has been a recurring theme in discussions about the Storting electoral system and its revisions (Aardal 2011). This tradition of emphasising the geographical dimension was also present when the Norwegian Sámediggi's constituencies were constructed. The issue emerged, first and foremost, because the Norwegian part of Sápmi traditionally included various Sámi lingustic groups – Northern, Eastern, Lule, Pite and Southern – each associated with a geographical core area with more or less different climatic, cultural and economic characteristics. While the Northern Sámi have, for a long time, been the dominant group in both the numerical and institutional sense, the Eastern Sámi in Norway have always been few in number (NOU 1984: 18, Ch. 3.2.1) and the Pite Sámi were, until recently, widely considered to be more or less assimilated (St.meld. nr. 28 (2007-2008). The main geographical concern was thus to ensure the representation of the Lule and Southern Sámi populations (Ot.prp.nr 33 (1986–87), Ch. 5.4.4). A second 'geographical' aspect was if, and how, the interests of an assumed rather substantial number of Sámi settled south of the traditional Sápmi area should be weighted. Thirdly, the Sámediggi electoral system was also expected to take into account that because the pressure to assimilate had varied across the Sápmi area, this had likely given rise to geographical differences in individual inclinations to join a Sámediggi electoral roll (NOU 1984: 18). Proposals to include a separate constituency for Sámi reindeer husbandry representatives were also set forth but were rejected.[4]

Changing constituencies

The Sámi Rights Commission's proposal on the Sámediggi constituencies was based on a combination of concerns with respect to Sámi-internal geographical representativeness and rather fragile knowledge about contemporary Sámi settlement in Norway (NOU 1984: 18, Ch. 11.11). When the Sámi Act was adopted in 1987, the election system was designed to have 13 constituencies, each returning three seats. The constituencies differed widely in terms of geographical area: *cf.* Map 7.1 for their locations and names (in Norwegian only). At the extremes were two constituencies (3 and 4) consisting of one single municipality, whereas the southernmost constituency (13) covered all the municipalities located to the south of the Sápmi area.

It was commonly expected that, at the first Sámediggi election in 1989, the number of enrolled Sámi would vary among the constituencies. And this proved to be the case: the lowest number of enrolments was 80 and the highest was 1,152. A more even population distribution was expected to emerge over time but never did. On the contrary, by the fifth Sámediggi election in 2005, it seemed

---

4. In Norway, Sámi reindeer husbandry is a (nomadic) primary industry legally restricted to individuals of Sámi descent.

Map 7.1: Original Sámediggi constituencies in 1989

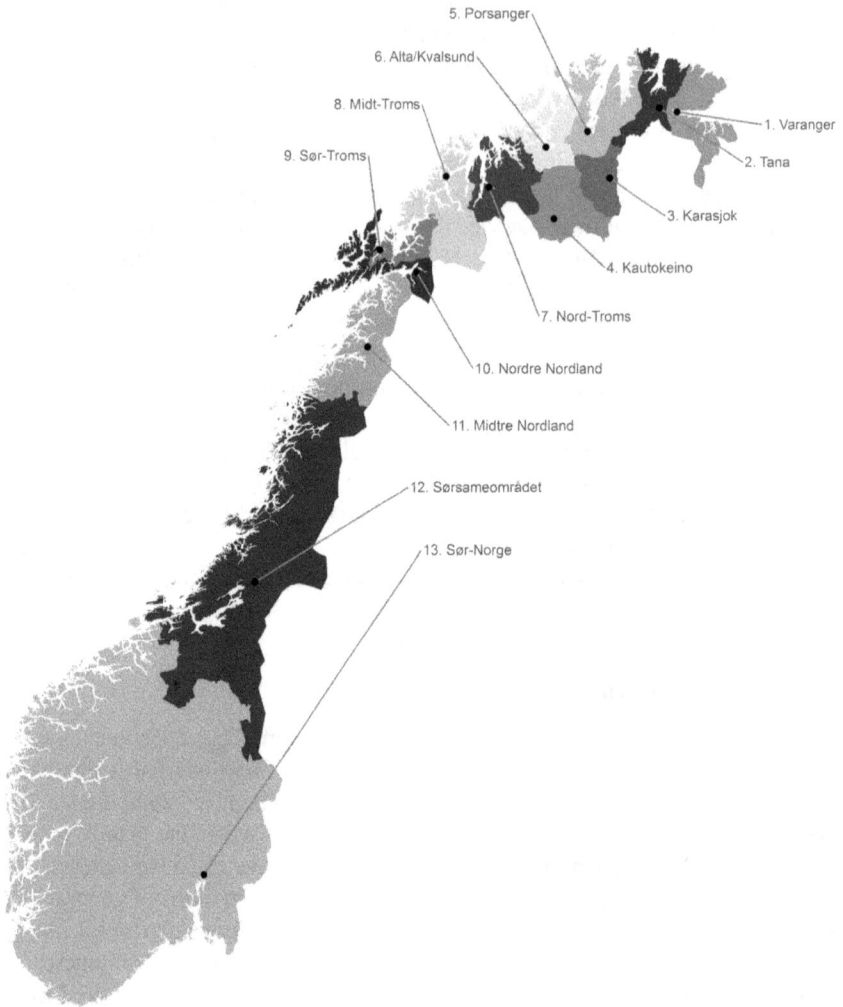

5. Porsanger

6. Alta/Kvalsund

8. Midt-Troms

1. Varanger

9. Sør-Troms

2. Tana

3. Karasjok

4. Kautokeino

7. Nord-Troms

10. Nordre Nordland

11. Midtre Nordland

12. Sørsameområdet

13. Sør-Norge

Source: The Sámediggi

obvious that the number of enrolled per constituency was unlikely to converge. At this election, the number of enrolled varied between 203 and 1,536 and even though the relative difference between the smallest and the largest constituency had decreased since 1989, the differences remained glaring, as can be seen in Figure 7.3.

The imbalance between the fixed number of three seats per constituency and the significant and enduring differences in the number of enrolled per constituency

Figure 7.3: Sámediggi electoral roll in 1989 and 2005, number of enrolments per constituency, by enrolments in 2005

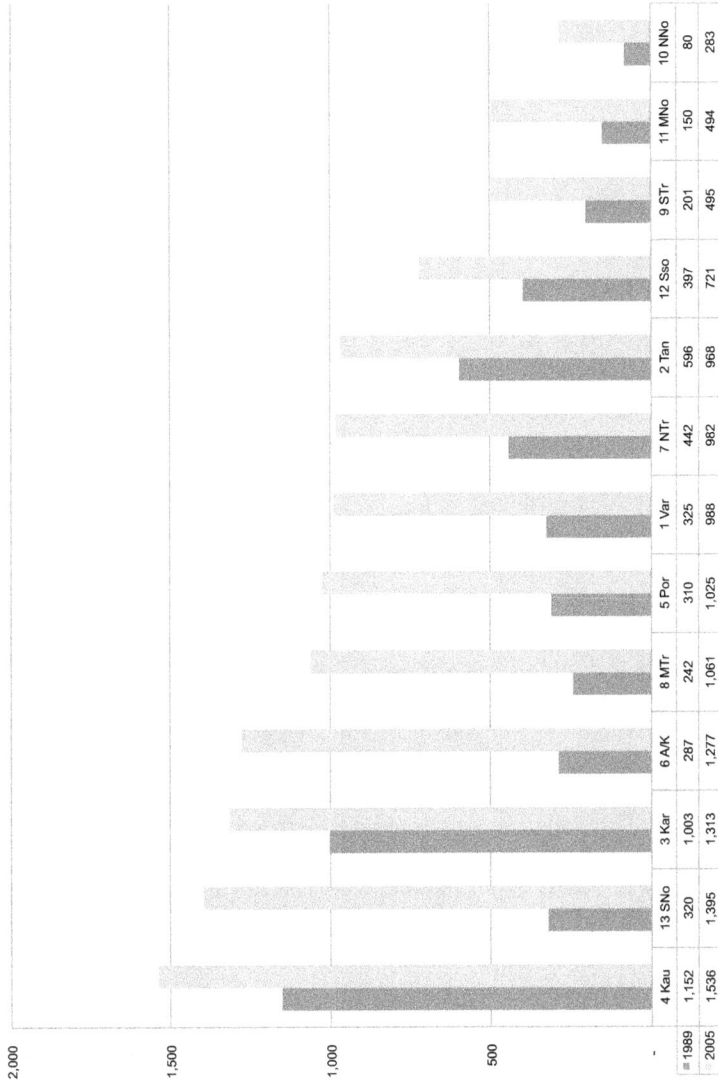

	4 Kau	13 SNo	3 Kar	6 A/K	8 MTr	5 Por	1 Var	7 NTr	2 Tan	12 Sso	9 STr	11 MNo	10 NNo
1989	1,152	320	1,003	287	242	310	325	442	596	397	201	150	80
2005	1,536	1,395	1,313	1,277	1,061	1,025	988	982	968	721	495	494	283

Source: Sametinget 2007

invoked more and more negative attention. Hence, after the 2005 election, the Sámediggi initiated a process to amend the electoral system (Sametinget 2007). This resulted, among other things, in the number of constituencies changing from 13 to seven at the 2009 election. Also, the fixed number of three seats per constituency was replaced by a system in which the number of seats allocated to each constituency is revised between each election, on the basis of the number of enrolled voters. Geographically, the two southernmost of the seven new constituencies stayed practically identical to the original ones. The other five comprised new compositions of the municipalities which previously made up the eleven northern constituencies, *cf.* Map 7.2.

Noticeable differences at the municipal level

While the constituencies represent the main framework for the Sámediggi elections, the municipality-level characteristics of the electoral roll provide opportunities for more detailed analyses of how the Sámediggi electoral roll has developed. The reason for this is the possibility of relating the municipal figures to characteristics of the respective local communities, including (former) assimilation experiences and (more recent) Sámi mobilisation. An informative starting point in this matter is a map provided by Statistics Norway, which – based on figures released by the Sámediggi – gives a snapshot of how the Sámediggi's electoral roll was distributed at the municipality level in 2009, *cf.* Map 7.3.

The map clearly demonstrates that enrolled Sámi were found across the entire country and in a majority of the municipalities. But it is also obvious that most of the municipalities with high numbers on the electoral roll were concentrated in the north. An examination of the corresponding figures (http://www.sametinget.no/valg) reveals that 109 of Norway's 430 municipalities were without enrolments on the Sámediggi electoral roll in 2009; another 148 had either one, two or three persons enrolled. In the remaining 173 municipalities, the number of enrolments were at least four; 26 municipalities had more than 100 enrolments. While the latter 26 made up 6 per cent of all Norway's municipalities, they accounted for 78 per cent of all voters on the Sámediggi electoral roll in 2009. Geographically, 24 of the 26 are located in one of Norway's three northernmost counties: 11 in Finnmark, 9 in Troms and 4 in Nordland. The two municipalities further south are Trondheim, the largest city in the Southern Sámi area, and Norway's capital, Oslo, located south of Sápmi. Nine of the northern municipalities had, by 2009, either awarded or self-declared city status.

Table 7.2 provides an overview of these 26 municipalities, sorted by their numerical share of the Sámediggi electoral roll. The relative increase per municipality from 1989 to 2009 is also presented. Additionally, the last column in Table 7.2 introduces a calculated value referred to as a municipality's *Sámi political density.* This value corresponds to a municipality's number of enrolled voters on the Sámediggi electoral roll, as a percentage of enrolled voters on the Storting electoral roll. The idea behind this concept is that, in the absence of Sámi demographic data, it might serve as a proxy measure indicating where (enrolled)

Map 7.2: Sámediggi constituencies at the 2009 election

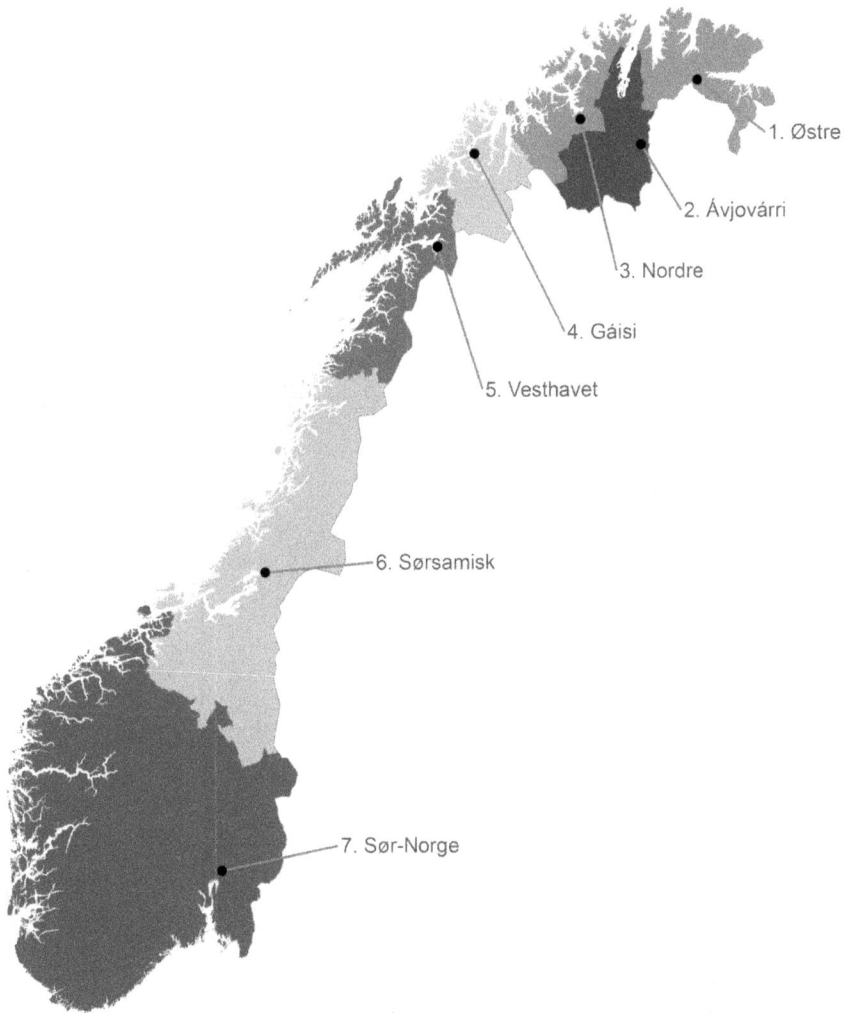

1. Østre
2. Ávjovárri
3. Nordre
4. Gáisi
5. Vesthavet
6. Sørsamisk
7. Sør-Norge

Source: The Sámediggi

Sámi in Norway cluster in a relative sense. For instance, while the numbers of voters enrolled on the Sámediggi electoral roll were practically the same in the municipalities of Nesseby (377) and Sør-Varanger (374), the Sámi political density in the former was ten times larger than in the latter: 53.9 versus 5.3.[5]

5.　In 2009, the number entitled to vote in the Storting election was 3,531,000 (http://www.ssb.no/en/valg/). This implies a Sámi political density of 0.4 in Norway as a whole.

Map 7.3: Persons on Sámediggi electoral roll 2009, by municipality

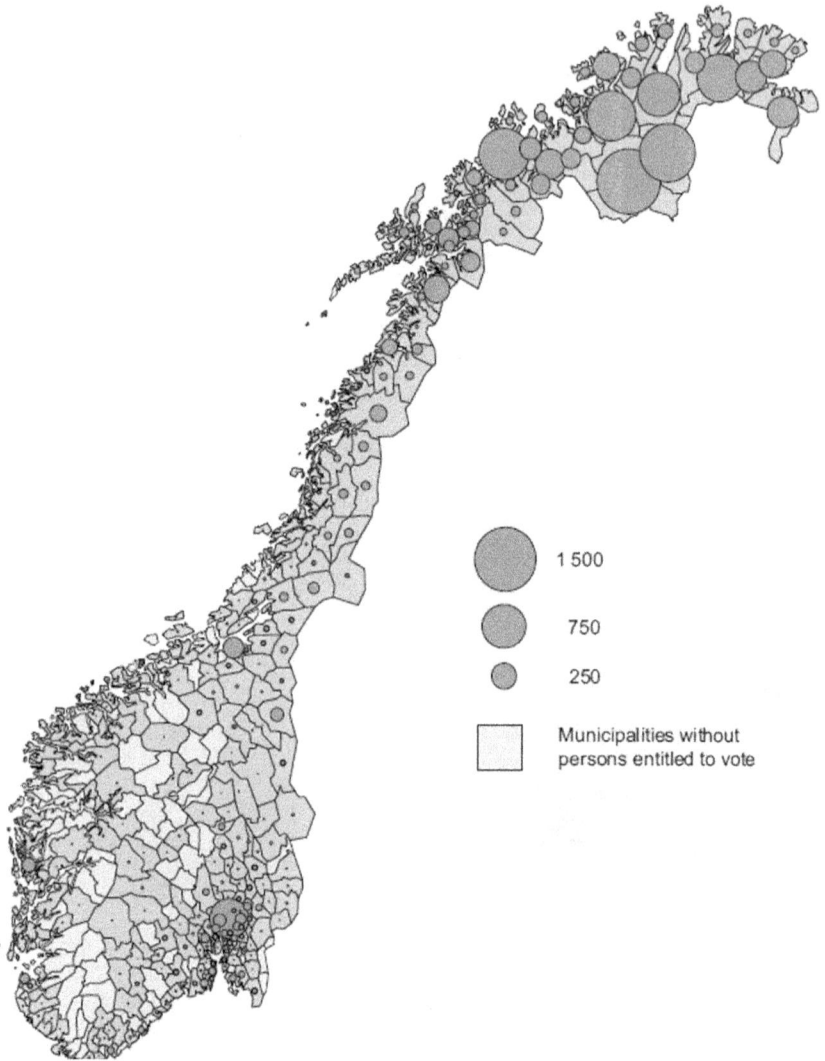

⬤	1 500
⬤	750
●	250
☐	Municipalities without persons entitled to vote

Source: Statistics Norway 2010: 32

Main tendencies: overall growth – geographical shifts

In 1989, the Sámediggi electoral roll in Norway consisted of 5,505 persons aged 18 or older. By the 2009 election, this number had increased to 13,890. Thus, the population P3 in Figure 7.1 grew by 152 per cent over the Sámediggi's first 20 years. The overall growth did, however, have an unequal geographic distribution, as can be seen in Figure 7.3 and Table 7.2.

Table 7.2: Sámediggi electoral roll 2009 (municipalities with more than 100 enrolments)

Constituency (cf. Map 7.2)	Municipality (Norwegian name)	Number of enrolled 2009	Percentage increase between 1989 and 2009	Sámi political density 2009 #
2	Kautokeino	1,557	35	70.4
2	Karasjok	1,276	27	63.8
4	Tromsø *	994	481	2.1
3	Alta (*)	943	461	7.3
1	Tana	859	48	39.2
2	Porsanger	727	285	23.7
7	Oslo *	623	299	0.1
1	Nesseby	377	130	53.9
1	Sør-Varanger (*)	374	368	5.3
4	Kåfjord	347	41	20.0
3	Hammerfest *	295	502	4.3
1	Vadsø *	288	343	6.7
5	Tysfjord	272	263	17.1
4	Lyngen	186	417	7.8
3	Lebesby	175	187	17.9
5	Skånland	175	146	7.7
6	Trondheim *	167	318	0.1
3	Kvalsund	159	279	19.2
3	Nordreisa	151	372	4.2
4	Storfjord	148	97	10.6
5	Narvik *	147	444	1.1
3	Kvænangen	123	156	11.9
6	Rana (*)	114	322	0.6
5	Bodø *	113	352	0.3
5	Harstad *	105	556	0.6
5	Lavangen	102	20	11.0

Sources: Sametinget 2001, http://www.samediggi.no, http://www.ssb.no
*Municipalities with city status awarded by the authorities
(*)Self-declared city status after 1996
#Sámediggi electoral roll as a percentage of the Storting electoral roll in 2009

Firstly, several municipalities with a high Sámi political density in 2009 experienced less increase in their Sámediggi electoral roll, measured in per cent, than many of the others. Secondly, the two municipalities with the largest Sámediggi electoral roll and the highest density of Sámi voters in 2009 had their combined proportion of the total Sámediggi electoral roll halved from 1989 to 2009: from 40 to 20 per cent. Thirdly, among municipalities with a high number of enrolled voters, the growth has been especially pronounced in some of those with city status. For example, the two city municipalities with the largest Sámediggi electoral roll in 2009 accounted for 14 per cent of total voters, compared to 6 per cent in 1989. And finally, the proportion of voters registered in the southernmost constituency increased to 13 per cent in 2009, up from 6 per cent in 1989. The main tendencies in the Sámediggi electoral roll between 1989 and 2009 can thus be summarised as overall growth and geographical shifts. The chapter's subsequent sections provide a summary discussion of these two tendencies.

Despite the Sámi movement's achievements during the last decades in getting rid of the (local) social stigma assossiated with being Sámi (Eidheim 1971; Stordal 1997), earlier generations' rather widespread denials of having Sámi affiliation may have caused many descendants to be unaware of their Sámi ancestry (Nielsen 1986; Hegg 2000; Olsen 2010). While some of those in this position – included in P0 in Figure 7.1 – might be interested in obtaining information about the past but are without access to relevant sources, others may regard a quest for Sámi presence in their family history as irrelevant to their current life situation. And while some people who are familiar with their Sámi family background might still be reluctant to acknowledge and/or announce it to others, a substantial number would probably currently consider this unproblematic in most, if not all, contexts. In Figure 7.1, the latter group corresponds to the schematic population P1.

But to consider Sámi descent as a straightforward matter does not automatically lead to perceiving Sámi descent as relevant for ethnic (self-)identification today. In fact, dealing with the subjective criterion for enrolment on the Sámediggi electoral roll – a premise for becoming a part of population P2 in Figure 7.1 – appears to be even more challenging than dealing with the objective criterion. At stake here is what it means to consider oneself to be Sámi; on what grounds and under what conditions do people self-identify as Sámi today? Or – as is commonly known in many local communities – why do people with 'objectively' comparable Sámi backgrounds regard the question of Sámi self-identification differently? These types of questions are neither new nor unique to the Sámi. Rather, they represent typical ambiguities and controversies with respect to ethnic (self-) identification for indigenous individuals around the world (for selected examples, see Weaver 2001; Snipp 2002; Paradies 2006; Tsosie 2006; Pratt 2007; Friedman 2008; Callister, Didham and Kivi 2009; Rowse 2009; Gover 2010; Kukutai 2010; Gorringe, Ross and Fforde 2011).

In Norway, issues of Sámi affiliation and Sámi (self)-identification have been discussed over several decades: in everyday settings; in media; in fiction and in scholarly texts (selected examples are Hirsti 1967; Jernsletten 1969; Høgmo 1986; Nielsen 1986; Stordahl 1996; Kramvig 1999; Paine 2003; Thuen 2003; Dankertsen 2006; Gaski 2008). A recurring theme is how to relate to Sámi ancestry, often combined with more or less critical explorations of the (consequences of) stereotypical images of a 'real' Sámi. The main stereotypical elements are: to be involved in reindeer husbandry; to be able to speak the Sámi language and/or to possess other 'typical' Sámi cultural skills; to wear the traditional Sámi costume; and, last but not least, to be resident in one of the local communities traditionally known to be Sámi (Andersen 2003; Andresen 2008). Another issue is whether a person can self-identify as Sámi if/when not recognised as Sámi by others, whether Sámi or non-Sámi. Besides, some persons' life-histories might have resulted in a self-understanding of having left the Sámi identity behind; they used to be Sámi but have ceased to be (Agenda Utredning and Utvikling 2002). At the same time, an unknown number of persons in Norway have, over time, possessed a confident and undisputed Sámi identity – as primarily Sámi, a little Sámi, sufficiently Sámi and/or Sámi in combination with one or more other ethnic identity/-ies. Also, as more inclusive notions of what it means to be Sámi in contemporary Norway seems to be gradually developing (St.meld. nr. 28 (2007–2008)), this might motivate even more people of Sámi ancestry to self-identify as Sámi over time.

Together, all persons who self-identify as Sámi account for population P2 in Figure 7.1. However, self-identification as Sámi does not equal joining the Sámediggi electoral roll and hence becoming a part of population P3. No wide-ranging systematic studies have so far been undertaken to investigate personal choices in this respect but there is a widespread notion that a substantial number of persons who fulfil the subjective inclusion criteria choose not to enrol (Sametinget 2007, Ch. 2.9). One reason for this might be a lack of interest in politics in general or Sámi politics in particular. Some may regard the Sámediggi as an appropriate institution for others but irrelevant to their own life situation. Others might object strongly to the very existence of the Sámediggi as a separate Sámi political body. And finally, the same kind of arguments that made people refrain from answering the 1970 census questions about Sámi affiliation may also cause reluctance to join the Sámediggi electoral roll today, namely, opposition to the idea of recording ethnicity information in a public register and/or hesitation in publicly announcing one's own Sámi self-identification. Nevertheless, the notable growth in the Sámediggi electoral roll might be taken to be a result of increased recognition of the Sámediggi as a democratic idea and as an appropriate institution for the formulation of Sámi policy. Also, the growth might indicate that the initial resistance to a separate Sámediggi electoral roll is waning.

Based on the review above, the reasons for the growth of the Sámediggi electoral roll might be described as threefold: knowledge about factual existence of Sámi language speaker(s) in families; the issue of self-identification as Sámi; and individual decisions about whether to register on the electoral roll. At the same time, these three elements may be influenced by a number of factors at different levels. Among such factors are global ethno-political discourses and national legislation at the macro level; historical and contemporary general and Sámi-related circumstances at the meso level; and general and Sámi-associated personal life experiences at the micro level. Thus, in order to understand how the electoral roll developed over time, it is essential to take into consideration the whole range of these interrelated conditions.

With respect to the roll's geographical shifts, the meso level is of particular interest. On the one hand, if significant changes take place in a local community's Sámi cultural and political 'climate', this may influence and/or alter an individual's decision to enroll on the Sámediggi electoral roll or not. For instance, an obvious hypothesis is that Sámi revitalisation in formerly heavily assimilated areas might explain most/much of the roll's growth in these municipalities. On the other hand, while an investigation of such issues is beyond the scope of this chapter, it may well be that some of the observed geographical shifts in the Sámediggi electoral roll are due to changes not *in*, but *of* local communities – understood as migration.

Over the last decades, a major demographic trend in Norway has been migration from north to south and from rural to urban areas (Høydahl and Rustad 2009; Sørlie 2010). Firstly, this migration has probably had an effect on where Sámi today are resident and thus in which municipalities Sámi are recorded on the electoral roll. Secondly, when people migrate from one local community to another, this might trigger a desire to 'formalise' and 'display' a Sámi affiliation that otherwise may have been either taken for granted or perceived as less relevant in everyday life. Hence, if an increasing proportion of Sámi voters enrol with the primary intention of demonstrating Sámi affiliation, not influencing Sámi politics, this could also explain some of the decreasing relative participation in Sámediggi elections. A related but unexplored question is whether some persons may join the electoral roll primarily to acknowledge, reveal and pay respect to the fact that they have Sámi ancestry, without having further interest in being a part of the current Sámi political collective. If the latter kind of rationale for enrolment should turn out to be 'trendy', it would imply that the Sámediggi electoral roll, to some degree, does serve *also* as a kind of Sámi census – just as the supporters of a separate Sámediggi electoral roll once anticipated.

How, then, should the 150 per cent increase in the Sámediggi electoral roll over the first 20 years be assessed? On the one hand, in percentage terms, this growth might be regarded as considerable . On the other hand, based on what is known about the legacy of the prolonged Norwegian assimilation policy towards the Sámi, it might well be that if all persons with known or unknown Sami ancestry (P0 and P1 in Figure 7.1) had self-identified as Sámi (P2) and also decided to join the electoral roll, the growth of the Sámediggi electoral roll (P3) would have been even larger. But as long as the numerical sizes of Figure 7.1's P0, P1 and P2 are unknown, it remains practically impossible to determine the potential size of population P3 and hence the maximum possible growth of the formally recorded Sámi electorate between 1989 and 2009.

One of the conclusions in the analysis of the 1970 census was that

[r]egardless of how the concept of 'Sámi' ['Lapp'] is defined, it covers a peripherally located segment of the population, not only on a national scale, but also on the municipal and local level' (Aubert 1978: 118).

Whatever the reasons for the geographical shifts within the Sámediggi electoral roll are, this study demonstrates that if the roll's geographical distribution is interpreted as an indicator of how Sámi settlement-patterns have developed, the perceptions of the Sámi as a primarily northern and rural population need to be somewhat modified (*cf.* also Sørlie and Broderstad 2011). The political impact of these geographical shifts remains to be seen but a growing awareness of them has been observed in both the political and the general discourse (*cf.*, for example, St. meld. nr. 28 (2007–2008).

Conclusion

Like many other indigenous peoples, the Sámi have experienced a prolonged assimilation policy and the corresponding cultural and social marginalisation. Over recent decades, the establishment of the Sámediggi as a nationwide representative Sámi political body has, together with other Sámi achievements, improved the conditions of Sámi in Norway (Stordahl 1997). Establishing the Sámediggi also entailed a structural change to the Norwegian political system, because it expanded the concept of democracy and political governance in Norway (Broderstad 1999). The separate Sámediggi electoral roll was designed to ensure that the Sámediggi should be a representative assembly of the entire Sámi population in Norway. Whether individuals self-identify as Sámi, and hence fulfil the subjective criterion to enrol on the Sámediggi electoral roll, is closely related to the Sámediggi's ability to claim that it represents all Sámi (Bjerkli and Selle 2003). Thus, Sámi identity issues have a direct impact on the legitimacy of the Sámediggi, given that this legitimacy depends on support from a sufficient proportion of the Sámi population.

The starting point of this chapter was the absence of an up-to-data Sámi demographic register combined with historically conditioned ambiguities on whether to self-identify as Sámi. As shown above, these factors make it impossible to determine to what degree those who actually have joined the Sámediggi electoral roll coincide with those who fulfil the criteria to enrol. Nevertheless, the Sámediggi might still be regarded as a representative Sámi body in the sense that it is elected by and among voters who fulfil Sámi inclusion criteria.

But the representativeness of the Sámediggi and its electoral roll also relates to internal Sámi affairs, such as the representation of Sámi geographical and/ or cultural minorities and representation in terms of gender, age and socio-economic characteristics. While there has been some interest in the gender distribution (Bjerkli and Selle 2003; Stordahl 2003) and the presence of young Sámi (Sametinget 2007), little scholarly attention has so far been devoted to the overall composition of the (potential) Sámi electorate. This may be due to a general lack of interest in contemporary Sámi demographics, perhaps combined with the limited amount of data available for such studies (Pettersen 2011) and also with formal restrictions on using the electoral roll for other purposes than electoral matters. Nevertheless, stakeholders have stressed a need to expand the repertoire of analyses and descriptions of contemporary Sámi political, social and cultural affairs. One contribution in this direction could be to strengthen knowledge about the Sámi electorate as it appears in the shape of the Sámediggi electoral roll.

References

Aardal, B. (2011) 'The Norwegian electoral system and its political consequences', *World Political Science Review* 7(1): 1–32.

Agenda Utredning & Utvikling (2002) *De nye samene: Kvalitative intervjuer i to målgrupper,* Sandvika: Agenda Utvikling.

Andersen, S. (2003) 'Samisk tilhørighet i kyst- og fjordområder', in B. Bjerkli and P. Selle (eds) *Samer, Makt og Demokrati: Sametinget og den nye samiske offentligheten,* Oslo: Gyldendal Akademisk, pp. 246–64.

Andresen, A. (2008) 'Health citizenship and/as Sámi citizenship: Norway 1985–2007', in A. Andresen, T. Grønlie, W. Hubbard, T. Ryymin and S. A. Skålevåg (eds) *Citizens, Courtrooms, Crossings. Conference proceedings*, Bergen: Stein Rokkan Centre for Social Studies, pp. 71–83: http://rokkan.uni.no/rPub/files/237_Report_10-2008.pdf (accessed 1 February 2010).

Aubert, V. (1978) *Den samiske befolkning i Nord-Norge,* Oslo: Statistisk Sentralbyrå.

Bjerkli, B. and Selle, P. (2003) 'Sametinget – kjerneistitusjonen innenfor den nye samiske offentligheten', *Samer, Makt og Demokrati: Sametinget og den nye samiske offentligheten,* Oslo: Gyldendal Akademisk, pp. 48–86.

Broderstad, E. G. (1999) 'Samepolitikk: selvbestemmelse og medbestemmelse', in E. G. Broderstad, A. Schanche and V. Stordahl (eds) *Makt, Demokrati og Politikk: Bilder fra den samiske erfaringen,* Oslo: Makt-og Demokratiutredningen 1998–2003, pp. 1–26.

Callister, P., Didham, R. and Kivi, A. (2009) *Who Are We? The conceptualisation and expression of ethnicity*, Wellington, NZ: Statistics New Zealand / Tatauranga Aotearoa: http://www3.stats.govt.nz/statisphere/official_ statistics_research_series/who_are_we_the_conceptualisation_and_ expression_of_ethnicity.pdf (accessed 1 November 2013).

Dankertsen, A. (2006) *'Men du kan jo snakke frognersamisk!' Tradisjon og kulturell innovasjon blant samer i Oslo,* unpublished Masters thesis, University of Oslo.

Eidheim, H. (1971) *Aspects of the Lappish Minority Situation*, Oslo: Universitetsforlaget.

Evjen, B. and Hansen, L. I. (2009) 'One people – many names: on different designations for the Sami population in the Norwegian county of Nordland through the centuries', *Continuity and Change* 24(2): 211–43.

Friedman, J. (2008) 'Indigeneity: anthropological notes on a historical variable', in H. Minde, H. Gaski, S. Jentoft and G. Midré (eds), *Indigenous Peoples: Self-determination. Knowledge. Indigeneity*, Delft: Eburon, pp. 29–48.

Gaski, L. (2008) 'Sami identity as a discursive formation: essentialism and ambivalence', in H. Minde, H. Gaski, S. Jentoft and G. Midré (eds) *Indigenous Peoples: Self-determination. Knowledge. Indigeneity*, Delft: Eburon, pp. 219–36.

Gorringe, S., Ross, J. and Fforde, C. (2011). '"Will the real Aborigine please stand up?": strategies for breaking the stereotypes and changing the conversation', AIATSIS Research Discussion Paper, Canberra: Australian Institute of Aboriginal and Torres Strait Islander Studies (IATSIS).

Gover, K. (2010) 'Comparative tribal constitutionalism: membership governance in Australia, Canada, New Zealand, and the United States', *Law & Social Inquiry* 35(3): 689–762.

Hegg, L. (2000) *Norsk eller samisk? I spenningsfeltet mellom eksistens og vitenskap*, unpublished Masters thesis, University of Tromsø.

Henriksen, J. B. (2008) 'The continuous process of recognition and implementation of the Sami people's right to self-determination', *Cambridge Review of International Affairs* 21(1): 27–40.

Hirsti, R. (1967) *En Samisk Utfordring*, Oslo: Pax.

Homme, L. R. (ed.) (1969) *Nordisk Nykolonialisme. Samiske problem i dag*, Oslo: Samlaget.

Hætta, O. M. (1992) *Sametinget i navn og tall: høsten 1989 – høsten 1993*, Karasjok: Sametinget.

— (1994) *Sametinget i navn og tall: høsten 1993 – høsten 1997*, Karasjok: Sametinget.

— (1998) *Sametinget i navn og tall: høsten 1997 – høsten 2001*, Karasjok: Sametinget.

— (2002) *Sametinget i navn og tall: høsten 2001 – høsten 2005*, Karasjok: Sametinget.

Høgmo, A. (1986) 'Det tredje alternativ: barns læring av identitetsforvaltning i samisk-norske samfunn preget av identitetsskifte', *Tidsskrift for Samfunnsforskning* 27(5): 395–416.

Høydahl, E. and Rustad, Ø. (2009) 'Befolkningsvekst – men ikke overalt', *Samfunnsspeilet* 23(5/6): 13–28.

Jernsletten, N. (1969) 'Kvifor vere same?', in L. R. Homme (ed.) *Nordisk Nykolonialisme. Samiske problem i dag*, Oslo: Samlaget, pp. 70–98.

Kramvig, B. (1999) 'I kategorienes vold', in H. Eidheim (ed.) *Samer og Nordmenn. Temaer i jus, historie og sosialantropologi*, Oslo: Cappelen, pp. 117–40.

Kukutai, T. (2011) 'Building ethnic boundaries in New Zealand: representations of Maori identity in the census', in P. Axelsson and P. Sköld (eds) *Indigenous Peoples and Demography: The complex relation between identity and statistics*, Oxford: Berghahn, pp. 33–54.

Lantto, P. (2010) 'Borders, citizenship and change: the case of the Sami people, 1751–2008', *Citizenship Studies* 14(5): 543–56.

Lie, E. (2002) 'Numbering the nationalities: ethnic minorities in Norwegian population censuses 1845–1930', *Ethnic and Racial Studies* 25(5): 802–22.

Minde, H. (2003) 'The challenge of indigenism: the struggle for Sami land rights and self-government in Norway 1960–1990', in S. Jentoft, H. Minde and R. Nilsen (eds) *Indigenous Peoples: Resource management and global rights*, Delft: Eburon, pp. 75–106.

— (2005) *Assimilation of the Sami: Implementation and consequences*, Kautokeino: Galdu Resource Centre for the Rights of Indigenous Peoples.

Morning, A. (2008) 'Ethnic classification in global perspective: a cross-national survey of the 2000 census round', *Population Research and Policy Review* 27(2): 239–72.

Nielsen, R. (1986) *Folk Uten Fortid*, Oslo: Gyldendal.

NOU 1984: 18 *Om Samenes Rettsstilling*, Oslo: Justisdepartementet.

Olsen, K. (2010) *Identities, Ethnicities and Borderzones: Examples from Finnmark, Northern Norway*, Stamsund: Orkana Akademisk.

Oskal, N. (2003) 'Samisk offentlighet og demokrati på norsk', in B. Bjerkli and P. Selle (eds) *Samer, Makt og Demokrati: Sametinget og den nye samiske offentligheten*, Oslo: Gyldendal Akademisk, pp. 318–37.

Ot.prp. nr. 33 (1986-87) *Om lov om Sametinget og andre samiske rettsforhold (sameloven)*, Oslo: Justis-og politidepartementet.

Paine, R. (2003) 'Identititetsfloke same-same: om komplekse identitetsprosesser i samiske samfunn', in B. Bjerkli and P. Selle (eds) *Samer, Makt og Demokrati: Sametinget og den nye samiske offentligheten*, Oslo: Gyldendal Akademisk, pp. 291–317.

Paradies, Y. C. (2006) 'Beyond black and white. Essentialism, hybridity and indigeneity', *Journal of Sociology* 42(4): 355–67.

Pettersen, T. (2005) 'Hvorfor er kvinneandelen på Sametinget i Norge blitt så liten?', in P. Axelsson and P. Sköld (eds) *Ett folk, ett land – Sápmi i historia och nutid*, Umeå: Centrum för samisk forskning, Umeå Universitet, pp. 257–71.

— (2010) 'Valgmanntall og valgdeltakelse ved sametingsvalgene i Norge 1989–2009 / Jienastuslohku ja válgaoassálastin Norgga sámediggeválggain 1989–2009', in Faglig Analysegruppe for Samisk Statistikk (ed.) *Samiske Tall Forteller 3. Kommentert samisk statistikk 2010 / Sámi logut muitalit 3. Cielggaduvvon sámi statistihkka 2010*, Guovdageaidnu: Sámi Allaskuvla / Samisk Høgskole, pp. 46–101.

—   (2011) 'Out of the backwater? Prospects for contemporary Sámi demography in Norway', in P. Axelsson and P. Sköld (eds) *Indigenous Peoples and Demography: The complex relation between identity and statistics*, Oxford: Berghahn, pp. 185–96.

Pratt, M. L. (2007) 'Afterword: indigeneity today', in M. D. L. Cadena and O. Starn (eds) *Indigenous Experience Today*, Oxford: Berg, pp. 397–404.

Rowse, T. (2009) 'Official statistics and the contemporary politics of indigeneity', *Australian Journal of Political Science* 44(2): 193–211.

Sametinget (2001) *Sametingets Valgregelutvalg. Rapport av 30.09.01*, Karasjok.

—   (2007) *Ny Valgordning til Sametinget. Fagutvalgets rapport 4. april 2007*, Karasjok: http://folk.uio.no/berasch/NyValgordningSametinget. pdf (accessed 1 November 2013).

Sámi Act (1987) *Act of 12 June 1987 No. 56 Concerning the Sameting (the Sami Parliament) and other Sami Legal Matters (the Sami Act)*, trans.: http:// www.regjeringen.no/en/doc/laws/Acts/the-sami-act-.html?id=449701 (accessed 12 December 2014).

Seltzer, W. and Anderson, M. (2001) 'The dark side of numbers: the role of population data systems in human rights abuses', *Social Research* 68(2): 481–513.

Simon, P. (2012) 'Collecting ethnic statistics in Europe: a review', *Ethnic and Racial Studies* 35(8): 1366–91.

Smith, C. (2005) (ed.) *Nordisk Samekonvensjon: Utkast fra finsk-norsk-svensk-samisk ekspertgruppe: oppnevnt 13. november 2002, avgitt 26. oktober 2005*, Oslo: Ekspertgruppen.

Snipp, M. C. (2002) 'American Indians: clues to the future of other racial groups', in J. Perlmann and M. C. Waters (eds) *The New Race Question: How the census counts multiracial individuals*, New York: Russel Sage Foundation, pp. 189–214.

St.meld. nr. 28 (2007–2008) *Samepolitikken,* Oslo: Arbeids-og Inkluderingsdepartementet.

Statistics Norway (2010) *Sami Statistics 2010*, Oslo: Statistics Norway.

Statistisk Sentralbyrå (2006) *Samisk Statistikk / Sámi Statistihkka 2006*, Oslo: Statistisk sentralbyrå.

Stordahl, V. (1996) *Same i den Moderne Verden. Endring og kontinuitet i et samisk lokalsamfunn*, Karasjok: Davvi Girji.

—   (1997) 'Samene: Fra "lavtstaaende race" til "urbefolkning"', in T. H. Eriksen (ed.) *Flerkulturell Forståelse*, Oslo: Tano Aschehoug, pp. 139–52.

—   (2003) 'Sametinget, kvinner begrenset adgang? Refleksjoner over debatten om kvinnerepresentasjonen på Sametinget', in B. Bjerkli and P. Selle (eds) *Samer, Makt og Demokrati: Sametinget og den nye samiske offentligheten*, Oslo: Gyldendal Akademisk, pp. 219–45.

Søbye, E. (1998) 'Jødeforfølgelsene under den annen verdenskrig – et mørkt kapittel i statistikkens historie?', *Samfunnsspeilet*, 12(4): 2–17.

Sørlie, K. (2010) 'Bosetting, flytting og regional utvikling', in I. Frønes and L. Kjølsrød (eds) *Det Norske Samfunn*, Oslo: Gyldendal Akademisk, pp. 457–78.

Sørlie, K. and Broderstad, A. R. (2011) *Flytting til Byer fra Distriktsområder med Samisk Besetting*, Oslo: Norsk Institutt for by- og Regionforskning. http://munin.uit.no/bitstream/handle/10037/3722/report.pdf?sequence=3 (accessed 1 November 2012).

Thorsen, H. C. (1972) *Registreringen av den samiske befolkning i Nord-Norge fra 1845 til 1970*, Oslo: Institutt for Samfunnsforskning.

Thuen, T. (2003) 'Lokale diskurser om det samiske', in B. Bjerkli and P. Selle (eds) *Samer, Makt og Demokrati: Sametinget og den nye samiske offentligheten*, Oslo: Gyldendal Akademisk, pp. 265–90.

Tsosie, R. A. (2006) 'What does it mean to "build a nation"? Re-imagining indigenous political identity in an era of self-determination', *Asian-Pacific Law & Policy Journal* 7(1): 38–64.

Weaver, H. N. (2001) 'Indigenous identity: what is it and who really has it?', *American Indian Quarterly* 25(2): 240–55.

Chapter Eight

Self-Determination as a Political Cleavage: The Norwegian Sámediggi Election of 2009

Johannes Bergh and Jo Saglie[1]

Introduction

The Norwegian Sámediggi (Sámi Parliament) was established in 1989 as a democratically elected institution, elected by and designed to represent the Norwegian Sámi population. Similar institutions exist in Finland and Sweden. An elected Sámi parliament can be said to represent a balance between unity and diversity. On the one hand, the Norwegian Sámi need to speak with one voice when dealing with the Norwegian authorities – which, in turn, need a unitary counterpart representing Sámi interests. On the other hand, of course, there is disagreement among the Sámi on a number of issues. The Sámediggi is an institutionalisation of such disagreement: it is an arena in which the Sámi publicly can articulate different political views and where these differences can be channelled into political processes.

However, observers of Norwegian Sámediggi election campaigns are often struck by the degree to which there is agreement on most political issues. Apparently, the ideological differences that are on display in national Norwegian elections are a less prominent feature of Sámediggi elections. What, then, explains voting in these elections? Are there 'unspoken' political cleavages that materialise at the ballot box, without being an explicit part of election campaigns? Are Sámediggi elections a reflection of the national Norwegian political landscape? Or are Sámediggi elections fundamentally apolitical – in which case, is voting determined by habit, attachment to individual candidates or perhaps some minor non-ideological issues?

In her contribution to this volume, Pettersen discusses the basis for Norwegian Sámediggi elections: the electoral roll. In this chapter, the focus is on political cleavages *within* the registered Sámi electorate. We aim to explore cleavage structures and explain voting in Norwegian Sámediggi elections, based on data from the 2009 election. Sámediggi elections have not previously been subjected to electoral research. The 2009 election survey – which is analysed in this chapter – is the first of its kind.

1.   We would like to thank the Sámediggi for granting us permission to draw a sample from the Sámediggi electoral roll for the purpose of conducting an election survey. We also thank the Research Council of Norway for funding of the Norwegian Sámi Election Study.

We first discuss the relevance of nation-building and political cleavages for Norwegian Sámediggi elections and then continue with some background information about the Sámediggi and its party system. We then look at the 2009 election results. After a brief description of the Sámediggi election survey of 2009, we look for evidence of political cleavages and their possible effects on voting in the 2009 elections. We finish with a discussion of our findings and their relevance for what we hope will be continued research on Norwegian Sámediggi elections.

Nation-building and political cleavages: Relevant for Sámediggi elections?

The idea that political cleavages are formed as a result of nation-building is central to Lipset and Rokkan's (1967) influential theory of cleavage structures in Western Europe. Lipset and Rokkan underlined the importance of history in today's politics. Contemporary party systems are deeply rooted in choices made and alliances formed in the past. A central cleavage in all West European countries is social class. This is not only a conflict between classes but also an ideological division that remains in today's distinction between left and right. Other cleavages, such as church *v* state or agriculture *v* industry, were salient in many countries. They may also be significant in a Sámi context; but conflicts resulting from the process of nation-building – between the nation-building elite and a country's periphery – are particularly relevant.

Lipset and Rokkan (1967: 14) described political cleavages in Western Europe partly as a result of a 'national revolution', involving processes of 'centralizing, standardizing, and mobilizing' towards a nation-state. According to them (1967: 41),

> Nation-building invariably generates territorial resistances and cultural strains. .... Territorial-cultural conflicts do not just find political expressions in secessionist and irredentist movements, however; they feed into the overall cleavage structure in the national community and help to condition the development not only of each nationwide party organization but even more of the entire system of party oppositions and alignments.

Today's Norwegian Sámi politics can be described as an intersection of two processes of nation-building: the older Norwegian and the newer Sámi. On the one hand, the Norwegian Sámi were subject to the assimilation policy of the Norwegian state throughout most of the twentieth century. Even though official Norwegian policy has changed, and the Sámi are now accepted as an indigenous people, this historical experience is hardly forgotten.

On the other hand, a separate Sámi political system – with political institutions and a nation-building elite of its own – has been established since the 1980s. It is, in many ways, parallel to the political system of a nation-state; but it also has important differences. The Sámediggi has very limited powers compared to a national parliament. It is an attempt to establish a limited degree of self-determination for the Norwegian Sámi people, within the Norwegian state.

Secession is thus not on the political agenda: the unsettled issue is the extent of Sámi self-determination within the Norwegian state. There is an inherent ambiguity in the Sámediggi itself, which is both an advisory body for the Norwegian government and a representative of the Sámi people. The political role of the Sámediggi is contested – in public debate and in negotiations between the Sámediggi and the Norwegian state. There are those who favour a strengthening of the independence of the Sámediggi *vis-à-vis* the Norwegian government, while others prefer the *status quo* or believe that the Sámediggi has too much power and independence as it is. The degree of Sámi self-determination may form the basis of a political cleavage and shape the pattern of political competition – within the Sámi polity as well as in Norwegian politics in the Sámi settlement areas. If Sámi voters differ in their view on self-determination, this issue may constitute the basis of party-formation – or existing parties may choose to compete on the basis of self-determination policy.

Self-determination is not a precise concept. In the Norwegian debate on Sámi self-determination, political actors often give different meanings to this word. This broad concept may nevertheless be useful to sum up a number of different concrete policy measures and proposals that concern Sámi rights and Sámi political influence. Questions on such policy proposals were included in our survey.

The Norwegian Sámi Parliament

The Norwegian Sámediggi was established mainly as an advisory body to the Norwegian government. However, the relationship between the Norwegian authorities and the Sámediggi is a dynamic process in which the Sámediggi has gradually gained a stronger and more independent position (Josefsen 2011; Josefsen *et al.* 2015). The Sámediggi's standing has been strengthened by Norway's ratification of the ILO Convention on Indigenous and Tribal Peoples and by the development of a system of consultation between the Sámediggi and the Norwegian authorities. Such consultation played an important role in the adoption of the Finnmark Act in 2005. This act transferred ownership and management of most of the land in a core Sámi settlement area – Norway's northernmost county, Finnmark – from the state to a separate body: the Finnmark Estate. Half of the executive board members of the Finnmark Estate are appointed by the Sámediggi; the other half by the county council of Finnmark. In addition to its political role, the Sámediggi is also an administrative body that manages various tasks delegated by the Norwegian government, for example, concerning Sámi education, cultural heritage and the distribution of a variety of subsidies.

An electoral roll has been established for Sámediggi elections. All Norwegian Sámi over the age of 18 may register as voters, if they fulfil two criteria. First, there is a question of self-declared identity: you must declare that you regard yourself as Sámi. Second, there is an objective, language-based criterion: you or one of your parents, grandparents or great-grandparents must have used Sámi as your home language. Alternatively, one of your parents must be (or have been) registered on the electoral roll. The number of voters who have joined the Sámi electoral roll has increased from 5,505 in 1989 to 15,005 in 2013 (see Pettersen, Chapter 7 in this volume).

The Sámediggi elections are held every fourth year, concurrently with the Norwegian parliamentary elections. The Sámediggi is elected by proportional representation (see Josefsen and Aardal 2011). Thirty-nine seats are elected from seven multi-member constituencies, covering all of Norway. The number of seats ranges from three in the smallest constituency to nine in the largest.[2] The Sámediggi has a system of parliamentary government: a president is elected by the plenary assembly. He or she appoints an executive council from the plenary assembly. The executive council, which serves as a cabinet, consists of the president and four other members.

The Sámediggi party system

The party system in the Norwegian Sámediggi differs from its counterparts in Sweden and Finland (see Josefsen 2007; Josefsen *et al.* 2015; Robbins, Chapter 3 in this volume). Elections to the Finnish Sámi Parliament are mainly choices between individual candidates. Swedish Sámi Parliament elections bring out a number of Sámi parties or lists but the mainstream Swedish parties do not participate.

In contrast, Norwegian Sámi politics comprises a 'double party system'. All parties represented in the Norwegian parliament present lists at Sámediggi elections. There are also several Sámi lists or parties. Some are national Sámi organisations, fielding candidates in all or most of the constituencies. Others are local lists, running for election in a single constituency. Some of these local lists represent minorities within the Sámi society, such as the Southern Sámi community, others represent some local interests (for example, the reindeer-herders) and some lists are formed around an individual candidate.

The presence of national Norwegian parties might reflect the fact that the Norwegian Sámi are generally well integrated in Norwegian politics (Selle and Strømsnes 2010; Semb 2010). Moreover, the divide between reindeer-herders and other Sámi that characterises Swedish Sámi politics (see Lantto and Mörkenstam, Chapter 6 in this volume) is less prominent in Norway. This may provide space for Norwegian political cleavages in Norwegian Sámi politics.

Even though there are many parties and lists, most of them receive only a small share of the votes – as shown in Table 8.1, in which the results from the 2005, 2009 and 2013 elections are presented. Two parties have been dominant in Norwegian Sámi politics since the Sámediggi was established (Pettersen 2011). One is a Norwegian party – the Labour Party – and the other a Sámi organisation – the Norwegian Sámi Association (Norgga Sámiid Riikkasearvi, NSR).

---

2.   The constituencies were changed before the 2009 election. There were 13 constituencies, each with 3 seats, from 1989 to 2005. The number of seats in each constituency is now revised before each election, to adjust for changes in the number of registered voters.

Table 8.1: Norwegian Sámediggi elections, 2005, 2009 and 2013, percentage votes and number of seats, by party/list

	Votes %			Seats		
	2005	2009	2013	2005	2009	2013
Norwegian political parties						
Labour Party – Bargiidbellodat	31.8	26.8	21.1	18	14	10
Progress Party – Ovddádusbellodat	2.3	7.8	9.0	–	3	2
Centre Party – Guovddášbellodat	6.7	4.9	4.7	1	–	–
Conservative Party – Olgešbellodat	2.5	4.6	7.0	–	1	2
Other Norwegian parties	4.4	1.7	1.0	–	–	–
National Sámi organisations						
Norwegian Sámi Association – Norgga Sámiid Riikkasearvi (NSR)	26.3	21.0	24.2	16	11	11
Árja	–	10.0	11.5	–	3	4
Joint list NSR and Sámi People's Party	5.7	3.9	4.7	2	2	2
Sámi People's Party – Sámeálbmot bellodat	3.9	2.3	1.9	1	–	–
Other national Sámi organisations	5.0	3.1	–	–	–	–
Local Sámi lists						
Reindeer Herders' List – Johttisápmelaččaid listu	2.8	4.4	3.3	1	2	1
Sámi in Southern Norway – Sámit Lulde	1.8	2.0	1.2	1	1	1
The Northern Cap People – Nordkalottfolket*	1.8	1.9	4.3	1	1	3
Southern Sámi Voices – Åarjel-Saemiej Gïelh	–	1.5	2.1	–	1	2
Non-Reindeer Herders' List – Dáloniid listu	1.8	1.3	2.7	1	–	1
Southern List – Åarjel læstoe	1.6	–	–	1	–	–
Other local Sámi lists	1.6	2.5	1.3	–	–	–
Turnout	**72.6**	**69.3**	**66.9**			
Total number of seats				**43**	**39**	**39**

*Called the Finnmark List in 2005
Source: Statistics Norway (2005, 2009, 2013)

The NSR had a majority of the seats in the Sámediggi during the first two (four-year) parliamentary terms (1989–97); neither party has had a parliamentary majority since. The two main competitors thus need to seek support from minor parties and lists to get their presidential candidate elected and control the executive council.

The NSR held power from 1989 until 2007; halfway through the 2005–9 parliamentary term. At that point, the co-operation between NSR and a minor group broke down and a Labour Party president was elected. Labour continued in office after the 2009 election, this time in a coalition with the newly formed Sámi organisation Árja and three local lists. NSR returned to office after the 2013 election.

As Gaski (2008: 4) points out, the two main Sámediggi competitors started out with very different histories. Like other Norwegian parties, the Labour Party was an established political actor in the traditional Sámi settlement area long before the Sámediggi was founded. In 1906, the first Sámi was elected to the Norwegian parliament, representing the Labour Party. Several Sámi have represented Labour in national and local politics since then. This did not, however, prevent the Labour Party – as a governing party in Norway in most of the post-war era – from implementing an assimilation policy towards the Sámi. This was also the case locally. According to Minde (2003: 96), support for assimilation was especially predominant in the Labour Party's Finnmark County Branch during the 1960s and 1970s.

The NSR was also an established organisation before the Sámediggi was founded. It was – and still is – a cultural organisation, as well as a political movement. The NSR worked for Sámi rights and for the revitalising of a Sámi identity during the 1970s and 1980s – often with the Labour Party as its main opponent, for instance, during the controversial damming of the Alta river.[3] The NSR stood as an all-embracing Sámi movement struggling against Norwegianisation, bringing together Sámi activists with otherwise diverging political views. In Gaski's (2008: 11) words, the NSR started out as a 'catch-all party'.

According to Gaski (2008), NSR's and Labour's 2005 election campaigns lacked explicit ideological positions: 'throughout the campaign it was difficult to distinguish between the two parties' agendas' (Gaski 2008: 2). However, her discourse analysis also calls attention to the role of national identity in the two main opponents' self-presentation. Being an independent Sámi organisation, the NSR can easily depict Labour's Sámi politicians as subservient to the Norwegian Labour Party headquarters in Oslo. As a division of a Norwegian party, Sámi Labour cannot be a true spokesman for Sámi interests – according to the NSR.

---

3. The building of the Alta river dam and hydroelectric plant around 1980 was opposed by Sámi political activists and others. The dam was built in a traditionally Sámi area and flooded parts of what was seen as Sámi-owned land. The protests in connection with the Alta river dam project led to an awakening of Sámi political consciousness, as well as increased attention to Sámi interests in national Norwegian politics.

Nevertheless, Labour's Sámediggi politicians have, in recent years, increasingly spoken in favour of Sámi self-determination. The actual policy differences between Sámi Labour and the NSR appear to have become less prominent, also regarding Sámi self-determination. This does leave room for conflict between Sámi Labour and the main Labour Party organisation – especially in northern Norway, where scepticism towards Sámi rights and self-determination is widespread among non-Sámi (Norwegian and Kven[4]) voters. Since elections for the Norwegian Parliament and the Sámediggi are held on the same day, this creates some strategic dilemmas for the Labour Party. Prior to the 2009 election campaign, for example, the leader of Labour's Finnmark County branch said: 'I was appalled when I saw [Labour's] Sámediggi election manifesto' (NRK Sápmi 2009). When Labour candidates for the Sámediggi speak for more Sámi self-determination while the same party's candidates for the general election speak against, the NSR can score some easy points. A solution to Labour's dilemma has been to emphasise the mutual interests of the people in the north. According to Gaski (2008: 14–15), the Sámi Labour Party prefers to address 'ordinary people' rather than 'Sámi people'.

Both the main opponents lost ground in the 2009 Sámediggi elections, although they remained the largest parties by far (*see* Table 8.1). A newly formed Sámi party, Árja (the Northern Sámi word for 'commitment') broke through as the third largest party, with 10 per cent of the votes and three seats. In its campaign, Árja spoke for the rural and coastal Sámi population outside of reindeer-herding, and emphasised the important role of the elderly and of traditional knowledge. After the election, Árja entered a coalition with Labour and some minor lists; Árja's leader was elected vice-president of the Sámediggi.

A Norwegian political party – the right-wing populist Progress Party – also had a breakthrough in Sámi politics in 2009. The party had fielded candidates before but without gaining seats. In 2009, however, the party emerged as the fourth largest in terms of votes, winning three seats. The Progress Party's Sámi policy differs radically from all its competitors: its position is that the Sámediggi should be abolished. According to the Progress Party, the Sámediggi is a case of ethnic discrimination. The party's argument is that the Sámi and other nationalities have lived side-by-side in the north for centuries and that none of these groups should be given special privileges (that is, a separate elected assembly). Unlike the case of the Labour Party, campaigning for two simultaneous elections does not seem to create any difficulties for the Progress Party. The party's criticism of so-called Sámi privileges is supported by many non-Sámi living in the traditional Sámi settlement area. However, the Progress Party also finds support within the Sámi community – even among those who have signed up to the political system that encompasses the Sámediggi by joining the electoral roll.

---

4.   Descendants of Finnish immigrants who settled in northern Norway during the eighteenth and nineteenth centuries.

So far, we have looked into the policies and arguments of the political actors. Gaski's analysis of the 2005 election concluded that although the political actors have argued on the basis of self-determination,

> we still do not know anything about the attitudinal bases for cleavage formation in the Sámi society; if the framing of the opposition lines which are initiated by the political actors reflects attitudes in the electorate or has any resonance with the voters. But the results indicate that the nature of social and ideological divisions which structure the Sámi party competition do not necessarily follow the patterns for cleavages in the old democracies in the West. Rather one can expect cleavage formation along other lines, reflecting the historical legacy of the Sámi society (Gaski 2008: 17–18).

In the following analyses, we will look into the question raised by Gaski: what can survey data from the Sámi Election Study tell us about political cleavages in Norwegian Sámi politics?

Data: The 2009 Sámediggi election survey

The 2009 Norwegian Sámi election survey was carried out in September–October 2009, starting immediately after the 2009 Sámediggi election. The survey sample was drawn from the Sámi electoral roll. The data was collected by means of telephone interviews, in which the respondents could choose to be interviewed in either the Norwegian or Northern Sámi languages. The fieldwork was carried out by TNS Gallup. In total, 973 respondents participated in the survey, of whom 731 said that they had voted in the election and responded to the question asking for whom they had voted. This gives us a sufficient number of respondents to analyse support for each of the four largest parties – Labour, NSR, Árja and the Progress Party.[5]

Attitudes and political differences among Sámediggi voters

The Sámediggi election survey of 2009 contains a limited number of attitudinal questions. We therefore have to bear in mind the possibility that significant attitudinal or ideological differences not covered by this survey are present in Sámi society. There are, however, a number of policy questions in the survey

---

5. The interviewers attempted to phone 6487 individuals. However, this apparently high level of non-response includes both those who declined to be interviewed and those the interviewers could not reach (no answer; only answering machines, etc.). The percentages of men and women are approximately the same in the sample and the electoral roll but our sample is geographically skewed: the constituency of Ávjovárri is underrepresented (15.4% of the sample against 25.6% of the electoral roll), while the constituencies of Southern Norway and Gáisi are somewhat overrepresented. Labour and NSR voters are overrepresented in the sample, whereas Árja and the Progress Party are somewhat underrepresented.

pertaining to issues that have been debated in the Sámediggi or in public debates in Sámi society at large. One example is the question of ownership of natural resources in the traditionally Sámi areas of northern Norway. There is a growing mining industry in the area; some feel Sámi society should be financially compensated for mining activities because they see the Sámi people as the original owners of the land and its resources. Another issue dealt with in the survey is the education of Sámi children. Schools that have Sámi pupils and teach the Sámi language are also part of the Norwegian education system. The survey looks at people's views about the extent to which the Sámediggi should be able to control the curriculum and mode of education at these schools. There are also questions about trust in and satisfaction with the Sámediggi. The Progress Party policy to abolish the Sámediggi is covered in another survey question and there is one question about the power of the Sámediggi *vis-à-vis* the national Norwegian Parliament.

The Sámediggi election survey furthermore includes a political left–right self-placement scale, in which voters categorise their political views on a scale from 0 (far left) to 10 (far right). As a proxy for political preferences in national Norwegian politics, we have created a dummy of voting in the concurrent national parliamentary election. Left-of-centre voting[6] is coded as 1, all others are 0. Table 8.2 displays a rotated factor analysis of these attitudinal variables in the Sámediggi election survey.

While the survey questions seem to cover a range of political issues, the factor analysis in Table 8.2 reveals only two attitude dimensions in this set of questions.[7] Factor 1 appears to be complex, since it covers several policy issues. The factor analysis indicates that they are derived from some other underlying ideological or value dimension. What, then, do these questions have in common, which would induce voters to answer them in a congruent manner? While they deal with policy issues that are not directly linked, they could also be interpreted as dealing with the role of the Sámediggi and of Sámi society more generally. On the one hand, there appears to be a group of people who favour a strengthening of the Sámediggi, of other Sámi institutions and of Sámi society in general. They are inclined to say that the Sámediggi should have increased power over any policy-area; to believe that the mining industry should compensate Sámi society; and to express trust and satisfaction with the Sámediggi.

---

6. This category includes three political parties: the Labour Party, the Socialist Left Party and the Red Party.

7. The survey included four other questions on political attitudes, concerning a) gender equality; b) the use of cross-country motor vehicles; c) the political influence of inner Finnmark (the core Sámi settlement area) in the Sámediggi; and d) whether Norwegian parties should participate in Sámediggi elections. These questions did not load clearly on any substantial factor (Bergh and Saglie 2011: 145) and preliminary analyses showed that they were not strongly linked to party choice. These four questions are therefore not included in the analyses reported here.

Table 8.2: Factor analysis of attitudinal data in Sámi election study 2009, varimax rotated factors

	Factor 1	Factor 2
The Sámediggi should have substantial influence over the education of Sámi children*	-0.59	-0.12
The Sámediggi should have increased influence over fisheries in Sápmi*	-0.80	-0.08
The Norwegian Parliament should have the power to overturn decisions made by the Sámediggi*	0.69	0.04
The mining industry in Sápmi should financially compensate Sámi society*	-0.69	-0.03
The Sámediggi should be closed down*	0.77	0.23
The Sámediggi should have less influence over natural resources in Sápmi*	0.73	0.08
Political trust towards the Sámediggi (0 = no trust; 10 = very high trust).	0.79	0.10
How satisfied are you with the job the Sámediggi has done since its formation? (1 = very satisfied; 4 = not satisfied)	-0.74	-0.15
Left–right self-placement scale (0 = far left; 10= far right)	-0.16	-0.85
Voted for a left-of-centre party in the Norwegian parliamentary election (1 = yes; 0 = no)	0.07	0.88

*1 = strongly agree; 5 = strongly disagree

One the other hand, there appears to be a group of voters who are sceptical of the Sámediggi and believe that Sámi society has already gone too far in the direction of nation-building. This group expresses low levels of trust and does not favour giving increased powers to the Sámediggi. They are also sceptical of Sámi claims of ownership of natural resources.

We create an index of the eight questions that load strongly on Factor 1. We believe this index taps into peoples' beliefs about Sámi self-determination, so we dub it the 'Sámi self-determination index'. If there is a political cleavage within Sámi society related to the issue of nation-building, we expect this index to have an effect on voting in the 2009 Sámediggi election.

Factor 2 reveals a left–right ideological divide that is central to Norwegian politics, which also appears to be present among Sámi voters. We therefore expect left–right ideological placement to have an effect on voting in Sámediggi elections. We use the left–right self-placement scale to measure those political differences. We do not include a measure of voting in the national parliamentary elections as an independent variable when explaining voting in the Sámediggi election, as the two variables are strongly linked.

Explaining voting in the 2009 Sámediggi election

Since the Sámediggi election survey of 2009 is the first of its kind, our analyses of voting in the election start from scratch when it comes to identifying relevant independent variables. Our main goal is to test the effect of the two ideological dimensions: Sámi self-determination and left–right ideology. However, we also look for other relevant explanatory variables.

There is one feature of Sámediggi elections that especially make them distinct from most other elections: the ethnically based electoral roll. The number of enrolled voters has grown steadily since the formation of the Sámediggi in 1989. While those who enrolled in 1989 tended to reside in the core Sámi areas, the growth that has occurred since then comes mostly from other areas of Norway (see Pettersen, Chapter 7). We expect that those who registered at the time of the formation of the Sámediggi in 1989 will have a stronger identity as Sámi political activists than those who enrolled more recently. The creation of the Sámediggi was the culmination of a long political struggle for Sámi rights. Those who registered at a later stage may not have the same attachment to that struggle. Generally speaking, the time of registration on the electoral roll is a variable that could influence voting. As a point of departure in our exploration of voting in the 2009 Sámediggi election, we look at differences in voting by time of enrolment.

Figure 8.1 reveals a number of notable differences in voting between those who registered as a voter in 1989 compared to those who signed up at a later point. These differences reflect changes in the fortunes of the parties through the history of the Sámediggi. The NSR was the dominant party at the time of the formation of the Norwegian Sámi Parliament. While the Labour Party started out as a smaller party, it had in 2009 outgrown the NSR in terms of vote-share and representation in the Sámediggi (Pettersen 2011). The NSR clearly has its strongest supporters among those who registered in 1989; while those who enrolled at a later stage tend to favour the Labour Party and also, to some extent, other national Norwegian political parties.[8] It seems critical for the future fortunes of the NSR that the party finds a way to attract new voters.

The overall trend as shown in Figure 8.1 is strong support for national Norwegian political parties among newly enrolled voters, while Sámi lists, including the NSR, are favoured by those who enrolled in 1989. This indicates that time of enrolment in the electoral roll is a useful independent variable when studying voting. Still, the differences in Figure 8.1 could be explained by a number of factors that are not just about the time of enrolment.

First, a number of social background variables that are related to time of enrolment could also be related to voting. Age is an obvious example. You cannot sign on to the electoral roll until the age of 18, so recently enrolled voters are, on average, quite a bit younger than those who registered in

---

8. Due to a small N, we had to merge all these parties into a single category.

Figure 8.1: Voting in Sámediggi election 2009, by time of enrolment on electoral roll, percentages

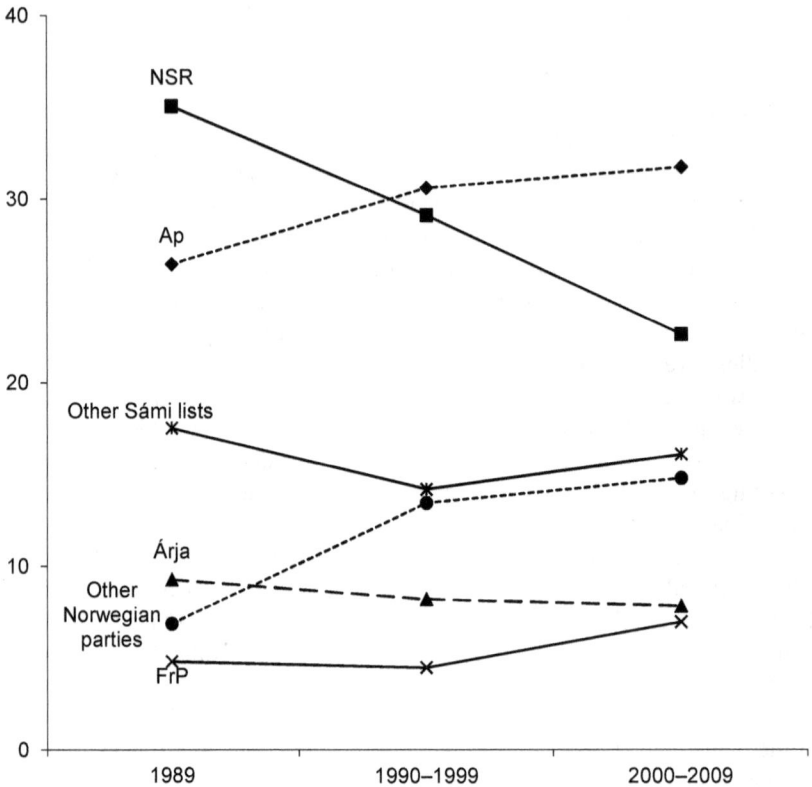

1989. Differences in voting by age are interesting by themselves. We will further include gender, since there have been historic variations in the gender composition of the Sámi electorate and because we are interested in revealing any gender differences in voting.

The survey includes a question of whether the respondents' first language is Sámi. After decades of assimilation policy, the first language of many Sámi is Norwegian. Language may signify identity, which, in turn, may affect party preferences. Parts of the Sámi political debate takes place in Sámi and this may cause differences between Sámi-speakers and others. This may potentially affect voting as well. We therefore want to explore the effect of language on party choice.

The success of two new political parties in 2009 gives us reason to believe that a lack of satisfaction with 'business as usual' in the Sámediggi was widespread among some groups of voters (see Balto 2011). The Sámi self-determination index includes measures of political trust and satisfaction with the Sámediggi. What is not covered in that index is satisfaction with the two main political parties and the job that they have done in the last 20 years. We include two independent variables in the analyses that measure the voters' rating of the NSR and of the Labour Party on a 0 to 10 scale.

Furthermore, we make use of a question that asks the voters to pick one factor, of the following three, that especially influenced their choice of party in the election: 1) political issues; 2) individual candidates on the list; and 3) general trust in the party/list. We expect Árja voters to pick alternative 1, 'political issues', to a larger extent than the other voters. As a newly formed party, Árja could not rely on established party loyalties or trust in experienced politicians (although some Árja candidates had experience from other parties). We use a dummy variable in the analysis to identify those who chose 'political issues' as a reason for their vote choice.

Another possible reason for discontent with the work of the Sámediggi and of the two main political parties could be the issues that have been prioritised over the years. A group of survey questions asks about the Sámediggi's priorities in previous years. The respondents are asked if the Sámediggi has focused 'too little', 'too much' or 'just right' on each specific issue. Among those issues are four that have been central to the work of the Sámediggi since its founding: education, language, culture, and reindeer-herding. Responses to the first three (education, language and culture) are correlated[9] and load on a single factor in a factor analysis, so we have merged those into a single index. We include the final issue-rating with respect to reindeer-herding as a separate independent variable in our analyses.

Multivariate analyses of voting in the 2009 Sámediggi election

An analysis of voting in the Sámediggi election survey is limited by the number of respondents in the survey: 731 respondents answered the question about voting in the election, of whom a little over 200 voted for Labour and a similar number for NSR. The third and fourth largest parties, Árja and the Progress Party, received 62 and 48 votes respectively.

We analyse support for each of these four parties in the 2009 election by use of logistic regression analysis. Logistic regression is preferable to ordinary least squares (OLS) regression in this case, given that we use dichotomous, and in some cases highly skewed, dependent variables.

The first model in each regression contains four social background variables: gender; age; time of enrolment on the electoral roll; and first

---

9. The correlations (Pearson's r) are: (education and language) .28; (education and culture) .21; and (language and culture) .33.

language. The second model introduces the variables related to issues and issue priorities. Third, we include our two measures of political cleavages: the Sámi self-determination index and the left–right self-placement index. Finally, we control for rating of the NSR and the Labour Party. When analysing voting for the Labour Party or the NSR, we exclude the rating of the same party as an independent variable; it is too highly correlated with voting and therefore obscures our other findings.[10]

Table 8.3: Modelled support for Labour Party in Sámediggi election 2009, logistic regression coefficients

	Model 1	Model 2	Model 3	Model 4
Gender (male = 1)	-0.09	-0.08	-0.01	-0.05
Age (years)	0.01	0.01	0.01	0.01
Enrolled in the electoral roll in 1989? (1 = yes; 0 = later)	-0.18	-0.22	-0.17	-0.12
First language (Sámi = 1; Other = 0)	-0.88**	-0.85**	-0.72**	-0.86**
Reason for vote choice: political issues (= 1)		-0.37*	-0.34	-0.46*
The Sámediggi has emphasised the issues of *education, language and culture* too much (= -1); just right (0); too little (= 1).		0.30	0.30	0.33
The Sámediggi has emphasised the issue of *reindeer herding* too much (= -1); just right (0); too little (= 1).		-0.10	-0.05	0.01
Sámi self-determination index (0 to 10)			-0.10*	0.07
Left (0) to right (10) self-placement index			-0.17**	-0.19**
Rating of the NSR (0 = strongly disapprove; 10 = strongly approve)				-0.25**
Constant	-1.12**	-1.08**	0.35	0.63
Cox & Snell R^2	0.03	0.04	0.08	0.13
Nagelkerke R^2	0.05	0.06	0.11	0.18

Source: The Sámediggi Election Study of 2009
*Significant at the 5% level, **Significant at the 1% level.
N = 720

10. The reason for including rating of Labour and the NSR is to explore its effect on support for other parties than the one that is being rated. This is especially interesting with regard to Árja and Progress Party voters.

Table 8.3 displays the analysis of voting for the Labour Party in the 2009 Sámediggi election. Of the social background variables, first language is the only significant predictor of Labour Party support. People whose first language is Sámi tend not to vote for the Labour Party. Our second model indicates that, in accordance with our expectations, Labour Party voters tend not to state that political issues are the reason for their vote choice. Rather, these voters are motivated by trust in the party and individual candidates on the list.

Model 3 shows, unsurprisingly, that the left–right self-placement index has a significant effect on voting for the Labour Party. The Labour Party is a left-of-centre party, which is also reflected in the ideological orientation of its voters. The Sámi self-determination index has a weak negative effect on support for the Labour Party. These voters probably favour the *status quo*; they are not looking for changes in the direction of Sámi nation-building. Finally, rating of the NSR has a significant negative effect on Labour Party support. Those who favour the Labour Party tend, in other words, to be critical of the NSR. This is no surprise but confirms that the two parties are seen as opposites. We expect to find a similar effect *vis-à-vis* the Labour Party among NSR voters.

The analysis of voting for the NSR in the 2009 Sámediggi election is found in Table 8.4. The first model reveals that time of enrolment has a strong effect on voting for the NSR. As seen in Figure 8.1, those who signed on to the roll in 1989 are strong supporters of the NSR. NSR voters are not distinguishable by first language: they are a cross-section of the Sámi electorate in that respect. In contrast, age has a statistically significant effect. NSR voters are somewhat younger than the average person who took part in the Sámediggi election but this effect is only statistically significant after controlling for time of enrolment in the electoral roll. Model 2 shows that NSR voters perceive political issues as less important for their party-choice than the average voter. Like Labour Party voters, they are influenced by trust in the party and support for candidates on the list. NSR voters also tend to believe that the Sámediggi has put too little emphasis on the issue of reindeer-herding, which suggests that the NSR gets support from people who are associated with that industry.

The Sámi self-determination index in Model 3 shows a strong positive effect. It is not surprising that NSR voters favour strengthening the Sámediggi and other Sámi institutions. The steep rise in the pseudo-R^2s is nevertheless noteworthy, as it indicates that this is a salient cleavage for NSR supporters.

NSR voters hold an average position on the left–right self-placement scale, although the effect of that index becomes statistically significant after the control for Labour Party rating in Model 4. The negative effect of the voters' rating of the Labour Party on NSR-votes confirms the impression that the two parties are opposites. Those who favour one party tend to have a low rating of the other.

What then of the newcomers to Sámi politics in 2009: Árja and the Progress Party? Do supporters of these parties reject both the major political parties in the Sámediggi? The analysis of voting for Árja is presented in Table 8.5.

Table 8.4: Modelled support for NSR in Sámediggi election 2009, logistic regression coefficients

	Model 1	Model 2	Model 3	Model 4
Gender (male = 1)	-0.28	-0.30	-0.17	-0.26
Age (years)	-0.01*	-0.01*	-0.01	-0.01
Enrolled in the electoral roll in 1989? (1 = yes; 0 = later)	0.68**	0.56**	0.25	0.19
First language (Sámi = 1; Other = 0)	0.09	0. 06	-0.21	-0.27
Reason for vote choice: political issues (= 1)		-0.44*	-0.40*	-0.52*
The Sámediggi has emphasised the issues of *education, language and culture* too much (= -1); just right (0); too little (= 1).		0.35	-0.04	-0.07
The Sámediggi has emphasised the issue of *reindeer-herding* too much (= -1); just right (0); too little (= 1).		0.54**	0.33*	0.35*
Sámi self-determination index (0 to 10)			0.48**	0.49**
Left (0) to right (10) self-placement index			-0.05	-0.12*
Rating of the Labour Party (0 = strongly disapprove; 10 = strongly approve)				-0.32**
Constant	-0.41	-0.21	-3.55**	-1.36*
Cox & Snell R2	0.03	0.07	0.18	0.25
Nagelkerke R2	0.04	0.10	0.26	0.36

Source: The Sámediggi Election Study of 2009
*Significant at the 5% level, **Significant at the 1% level.
N = 720

Árja voters are clearly distinguished by having Sámi as their first language. This is probably an effect of the geographical distribution of Árja votes. Árja's electoral stronghold is the constituency of Ávjovárri – a core Sámi settlement area, where the Sámi language has a strong position. Age is close to statistical significance in Model 1 and reaches significance after the controls for other variables in Models 2 and 3. Even though Árja emphasised the role of the elderly in its campaign, its voters are, on average, a little younger than other voters in the 2009 election.

Model 2 in Table 8.5 reveals some distinctly different effects from those in our analysis of NSR. Árja voters tend to respond that political issues are the reason for their vote-choice. They are not motivated by trust in the party or support for candidates on the list, which were more common responses among Labour and

Table 8.5: Modelled support for Árja in Sámediggi election 2009, logistic regression coefficients

	Model 1	Model 2	Model 3	Model 4
Gender (male = 1)	0.39	0.32	0.32	0.26
Age (years)	-0.02	-0.02*	-0.02*	-0.02
Enrolled in the electoral roll in 1989? (1 = yes; 0 = later)	0.02	0.26	0.22	0.22
First language (Sámi = 1; Other = 0)	1.20**	1.28**	1.19**	1.14**
Reason for vote-choice: political issues (= 1)		1.04**	1.03**	0.98**
The Sámediggi has emphasised the issues of *education, language and culture* too much (= -1); just right (0); too little (= 1).		-0.45	-0.52	-0.49
The Sámediggi has emphasised the issue of *reindeer-herding* too much (= -1); just right (0); too little (= 1).		-0.90**	-0.98**	-0.97**
Sámi self-determination index (0 to 10)			0.08	0.16
Left (0) to right (10) self-placement index			0.06	0.05
Rating of the NSR (0 = strongly disapprove; 10 = strongly approve)				-0.09
Rating of the Labour Party (0 = strongly disapprove; 10 = strongly approve)				-0.09
Constant	-2.07**	-2.78**	-3.62**	-3.09**
Cox & Snell R2	0.03	0.08	0.09	0.09
Nagelkerke R2	0.07	0.19	0.20	0.21

Source: The Sámediggi Election Study of 2009
*Significant at the 5% level, **Significant at the 1% level.
N=720

NSR voters. Furthermore, supporters of Árja believe that the Sámediggi has put too much emphasis on the issue of reindeer-herding. This is an issue on which Árja campaigned, so the effect is not surprising.

There is no significant effect of the Sámi self-determination index or the left–right self-placement index on support for Árja. We are also surprised to find that Árja voters do not give a particularly negative rating to the NSR or the Labour Party. All in all, our model does not predict Árja votes very well.

Is that also the case with the other new political party in the 2009 Sámediggi election? Progress Party voting is analysed in Table 8.6. The effects of the social background variables indicate that Progress Party voters are, on average, older

Table 8.6: Modelled support for Progress Party in Sámediggi election 2009, logistic regression coefficients

	Model 1	Model 2	Model 3	Model 4
Gender (male = 1)	0.45	0.51	0.12	-0.04
Age (years)	0.04**	0.04**	0.05**	0.06**
Enrolled in the electoral roll in 1989? (1 = yes; 0 = later)	-0.79*	-0.67	-0.49	-0.86
First language (Sámi = 1; Other = 0)	-0.10	-0.06	0.51	0.43
Reason for vote choice: political issues (= 1)		0.63	0.53	0.75
The Sámediggi has emphasised the issues of *education, language and culture* too much (= -1); just right (0); too little (= 1).		-1.50**	0.05	-0.03
The Sámediggi has emphasised the issue of *reindeer herding* too much (= -1); just right (0); too little (= 1).		-0.60*	-0.14	-0.24
Sámi self-determination index (0 to 10)			-0.66**	-0.73**
Left (0) to right (10) self-placement index			0.45**	0.42**
Rating of the NSR (0 = strongly disapprove; 10 = strongly approve)				0.14
Rating of the Labour Party (0 = strongly disapprove; 10 = strongly approve)				-0.31**
Constant	-4.62**	-5.10**	-5.62**	-4.99**
Cox & Snell R2	0.02	0.07	0.22	0.23
Nagelkerke R2	0.06	0.18	0.56	0.61

Source: The Sámediggi Election Study of 2009
*Significant at the 5% level, **Significant at the 1% level.
N = 720

than other voters in the election.[11] Also, these voters tend to have enrolled in the electoral roll after 1989.

Model 2 finds that supporters of the Progress Party believe the Sámediggi has put too much emphasis on all of the traditional issues that have been central to the work of the Sámi Parliament since its founding: education, language, culture and reindeer-herding. This suggests an amount of dissatisfaction with the Sámediggi

---

11. This is also true in a bivariate analysis in which we do not control for time of enrolment in the electoral roll.

Figure 8.2: Modelled effect of Sámi self-determination index on support for four political parties in the 2009 Sámediggi election

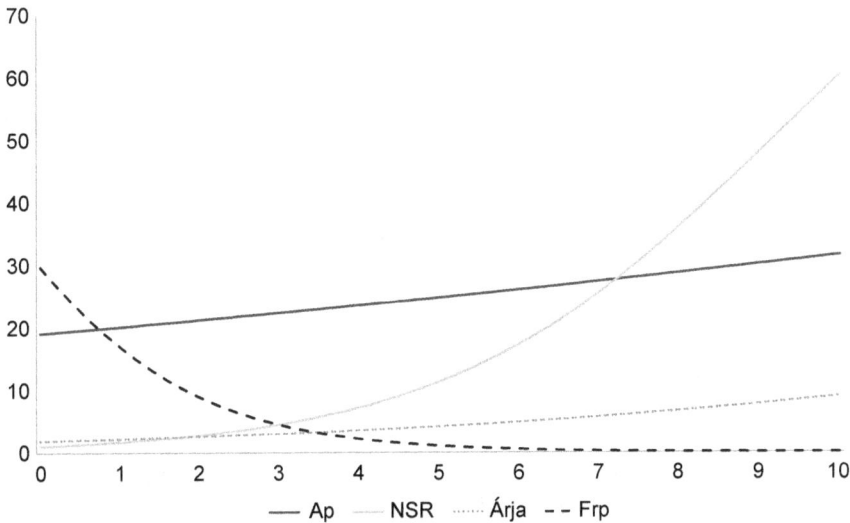

itself, which is further confirmed in Model 3 by the strong negative effect of the Sámi self-determination index. Progress Party voters are clearly opposed to Sámi nation-building and the voters are thus in line with their party. As such, self-determination seems to be a salient cleavage for Progress Party voters, which places these voters as ideological opposites to NSR voters.

The Progress Party is a right-wing populist party, so it is not surprising that the party's voters place themselves to the right of most voters on the left-right scale. Finally, disapproval of the Labour Party seems to attract voters to the Progress Party. There is no similar effect of NSR-rating; that effect is controlled for by the inclusion of the Sámi self-determination index. All in all, our model shows a fairly good fit when explaining Progress Party support. The two cleavage indices are strong predictors of votes for the Progress Party in the 2009 Sámediggi election.

Summing up: Party voters and self-determination

What, then, is the overall effect of the Sámi self-determination index on voting in Sámediggi elections? Figure 8.2 displays modelled support for each of the four political parties in our analysis, dependent on the Sámi self-determination index. The analysis is based on Model 4 in Tables 8.3 through 8.6, in which we vary the value of the index and keep all other variables at their mean value.

Two political parties are diametrical opposites in terms of the question of Sámi self-determination, as the figure shows. Support for the NSR rises steeply when moving towards the high end of the Sámi self-determination index. Voters who are favourable to nation-building are most likely to vote for the NSR. Those same voters are predicted to have close to zero probability of voting for the Progress Party. A voter who is placed at the other end of the scale – opposing the Sámediggi and any attempt at nation-building – is likely to vote for the Progress Party. Both the NSR and the Progress Party should be seen as mobilising voters based on this political cleavage.

Support for the other two parties, Árja and the Labour party, is less related to this dimension. Labour Party voters are on the left of the national Norwegian political spectrum and more often have Norwegian as their first language. Árja voters are often native Sámi speakers and appear to be discontented with the issue priorities of the Sámediggi in previous years.

Concluding remarks: Self-determination as a political cleavage

The concept of nation-building is central to Lipset and Rokkan's (1967) theory of the development of political cleavage structures in Western Europe. Their idea was that the process of nation-building led to conflicts between different groups in society that found themselves to be a part of the same nation. Our study suggests that although this perspective comes from the context of Western political development, it can be also be helpful in understanding conflict structures related to Sámediggi elections in Norway. We assumed that the issue of self-determination might form the basis of a political cleavage, as the extent of self-determination has not been settled. 'Self-determination', in our analysis, refers to a preference for increasing the power and independence of the Sámediggi. Nation-building or the idea of self-determination itself can mobilise voters with different views and, accordingly, structure party competition. The issue of self-determination is, of course, important for indigenous peoples around the world. Whether the concept of nation-building might also be helpful for understanding the internal politics of other indigenous peoples remains to be seen.

There are different views within Norwegian Sámi society on the role of the Sámediggi *vis-à-vis* Norwegian governing institutions. Our findings indicate that people's beliefs about Sámi self-determination structure their political preferences and influence attitudes toward specific policy questions.

Does this mean that the idea of self-determination should be seen as a political cleavage within Norwegian Sámi society? In Lipset and Rokkan's (1967) perspective, political parties play an important role as 'agents of conflict', translating social conflicts into the political system. In this regard, however, the two opposites in Figure 8.2 seem to differ. On the one hand, the Progress Party's rejection of Sámi self-determination is radically different from all other parties – and the party's voters stand out in a similar way. On the other hand, the case of the NSR seems less clear-cut. It could be argued that the actual policy differences on self-determination between Sámi Labour and the NSR are less conspicuous. Furthermore, these two main competitors in Sámi politics have, at times, stood together in a united front when dealing with the Norwegian government. This was evident in the consultations between the Sámediggi and the Norwegian Parliament on the Finnmark Act (Josefsen 2011: 39–40).

Why, then, do Labour and NSR voters take different positions on our self-determination index – perhaps more different than we would expect from current party policies? First, the two parties' rhetorical strategies have been different – as discussed by Gaski (2008). Second, as Lipset and Rokkan (1967: 2) state: 'parties do not simply present themselves *de novo* to the citizen at each election; they each have a history'. The two competitors have obviously very different historical records when it comes to Sámi self-determination and nation-building. Past conflicts are not easily forgotten. Third, Sámi Labour is attached to the Norwegian Labour Party, which is much less supportive of Sámi self-determination. This presumably makes Labour's self-determination policy more muddled, in the eyes of the voters.

Even though self-determination may be seen as an important political cleavage in Sámi politics, other ideological dimensions and issue priorities also influence voting. The political landscape with respect to Sámediggi elections in Norway is multidimensional, just like the national Norwegian political landscape. The issues of indigenous rights and Sámi self-determination is, however, almost absent from election campaigns at the national level in Norway. This gives Sámi politics in Norway a distinctive stamp of its own, compared to Norwegian national politics. The Norwegian national party system has not been able to absorb indigenous rights movements and their demands. Consequently, the party system in the Norwegian Sámediggi differs from the Norwegian party system, as it comprises both Norwegian and Sámi parties.

How, then, will the balance between 'Norwegian' and 'Sámi' elements in Norwegian Sámi politics develop in the future? Elections to the Sámi and the Norwegian Parliaments are held on the same day, and the Norwegian national media pay little attention to Sámi politics (see, for example, Josefsen and Skogerbø 2013). Moreover, the increase in the Sámi electoral roll – which has been strongest outside of the traditional Sámi settlement area – has brought in a new group of voters. Such factors might lead to a 'Norwegianisation' of Norwegian Sámi politics. However, there has been no clear development in that direction so far. The influence of the Sámediggi and the extent of Sámi self-determination is still contested and that may preserve the distinctive character of Norwegian Sámi politics.

References

Balto, Á. M. V. (2011) 'Sametingets tillit blant egne velgere: holdninger til et demokrati i støpeskjeen', in E. Josefsen and J. Saglie (eds) *Sametingsvalg: Velgere, partier, medier*, Oslo: Abstrakt.

Bergh, J. and Saglie, J. (2011) 'Stemmegivning ved sametingsvalg: selvbestemmelse som skillelinje', in E. Josefsen and J. Saglie (eds) *Sametingsvalg: Velgere, partier, medier*, Oslo: Abstrakt.

Gaski, L. (2008) 'Contesting the Sami polity: discursive representations in the Sami electoral campaign in 2005', *Acta Borealia* 25: 1–21.

Josefsen, E. (2007) 'The Saami and the national parliaments – channels for political influence', *Gáldu Čála – Journal of Indigenous Peoples Rights* 2/2007, Guovdageaidnu: Gáldu.

— (2011) 'The Norwegian Sámi Parliament and Sámi political empowerment', in G. Minnerup and P. Solberg (eds) *First World, First Nations. Internal colonialism and indigenous self-determination in Northern Europe and Australia*, Brighton: Sussex Academic Press.

Josefsen, E. and B. Aardal (2011) 'Valgordningen ved sametingsvalg – en viktig rammebetingelse', in E. Josefsen and J. Saglie (eds) *Sametingsvalg: Velgere, partier, medier*, Oslo: Abstrakt.

Josefsen, E, Mörkenstam, U. and Saglie, J. (2015): 'Different institutions within similar states: the Norwegian and Swedish *Sámediggis*', *Ethnopolitics* 14(1): 32–51.

Josefsen, E. and Skogerbø, E. (2013) 'An indigenous public sphere? The media and the 2009 Sámediggi election campaign', *Arctic Review on Law and Politics* 4(1): 62–89.

Lipset, S. M. and Rokkan, S. (1967) 'Cleavage structure, party systems, and voter alignments: an introduction', in S. M. Lipset and S. Rokkan (eds) *Party Systems and Voter Alignments*, New York: Free Press.

Minde, H. (2003) 'Urfolksoffensiv, folkerettsfokus og styringskrise: kampen for en ny samepolitikk 1960–1990', in B. Bjerkli and P. Selle (eds) *Samer, Makt og Demokrati*, Oslo: Gyldendal Akademisk.

NRK Sápmi (2009) 'Selvstyre-krav kan føre til bråk': http://www.nrk.no/kanal/nrk_sapmi/valg_2009_sami_radio/1.6503692 (accessed 14 March 2011).

Pettersen, T. (2011) 'Fem valg i tretten kretser. Det sametingspolitiske landskapet i Norge 1985–2005', in E. Josefsen and J. Saglie (eds) *Sametingsvalg: Velgere, partier, medier*, Oslo: Abstrakt.

Selle, P. and K. Strømsnes (2010) 'Sámi citizenship: marginalization or integration?', *Acta Borealia* 27(1): 66–90.

Semb, A. J. (2010) 'At the edge of the Norwegian state? Territorial and descent-based political membership among Norwegian Sami', in B. Bengtsson, P. Strömblad and A.-H. Bay (eds) *Diversity, Inclusion and Citizenship in Scandinavia*, Newcastle-upon-Tyne: Cambridge Scholars.

Statistics Norway (2005) 'Sami Election, 2005: female majority in Sametinget': http://www.ssb.no/en/valg/statistikker/sametingsvalg/hvert-4-aar/2005-12-19 (accessed 21 January 2014).

— (2009) 'Sami Election, 2009: lower electoral turnout': http://www.ssb.no/en/valg/statistikker/sametingsvalg/hvert-4-aar/2009-10-28 (accessed 21 January 2014).

— (2013) 'Sami Election, 2013: even lower electoral turnout': http://www.ssb.no/en/valg/statistikker/sametingsvalg (accessed 21 January 2014).

Chapter Nine

Who Shall Represent the Sámi? Indigenous Governance in Murmansk Region and the Nordic Sámi Parliament Model

Mikkel Berg-Nordlie[1]

The Sámi are the indigenous people of northern and central Norway and Sweden, northern Finland, and Russia's north-western Murmansk Region. While this volume's other chapters on the Sámi deal with the representative institutions of the Swedish and Norwegian Sámi, the chapter at hand will focus on Russian Sámi politics.

The Russian Sámi are a minority within the border-transcending Sámi nation, since most Sámi live in the Nordic countries (Berg-Nordlie 2013: 389), as well as a minority in their corner of Russia, and one of the more small-numbered among Russia's indigenous minorities (*korennye maločislennye narody*, 'native, small-numbered-peoples').[2] In Norway, Sweden and Finland, the Sámi have long been able to participate in border-transcending activities through international networks that involve both civil society and state-based actors. The Russian Sámi were, until the late 1980s, isolated from these processes of increased international integration that took place on the Nordic side of the border. Even today, the Russian Sámi are less than fully included in pan-Sámi structures (Berg-Nordlie 2011: 27–9, 2013: 370–1, 374). The roots of the organisations and institutions of the Russian Sámi are also to be found in the late 1980s. This ethno-political landscape has come to be markedly different from that of the Nordic Sámi (Berg-Nordlie 2015a).

This chapter explores how modes of indigenous governance changed in Murmansk Region during the period from the fall of the USSR to the time of writing (1992–2014)[3] and whether the Russian Sámi can be said to have

---

1. This chapter is partly based on 'Striving to unite. The Russian Sámi and the Nordic Sámi Parliament model' (*Arctic Review on Law and Politics* 2011, 2.1:52–76) by the same author. The data from that article has been updated and subjected to new analysis. The former article was written as part of the research project 'Russia in Pan-Sámi Politics', financed by the Norwegian Research Council's Programme for Sámi Research. The chapter at hand has also been finished partly through support from that research programme.

2. While the largest group (Nenec) is 44,640 people, only 1,771 Russians consider themselves Sámi (2010 Census). Note that census data is not exact since people can only write one ethnicity and people with multiple ethnic identities may hence choose to write something other than Sámi (Stepanov 2012). Note also that there are many more people in Russia that are of Sámi heritage. Due to assimilation, the numbers of the Russian Sámi have remained relatively constant since the 1800s (Alymov 2006; Overland and Berg-Nordlie 2012: 113–15).

3. The chapter was written before November 2014 and its content does not reflect subsequent changes in Russian Sámi politics.

gained better political representation during this period. Representation is here defined as becoming 'better' if more mechanisms are established to include representatives of the group in policy-making and policy-implementation; and if representatives are, to an increasing extent, formally dependent on support from the group they claim to represent in order to continue their political activity. The chapter also accounts for how inspiration from the Nordic model for indigenous governance, the *Sámedikkit* or Sámi Parliaments, has coloured local Russian Sámi politics.

The chapter begins with a presentation of key theoretical concepts. Following this, it accounts for how the idea of a Russian Sámi Parliament emerged and introduces the major actors in Russian Sámi civil society. This is followed by an overview of mechanisms to include Sámi representation in Murmansk Region indigenous politics in the periods 1991–2003, 2004–8, and 2009–14. Methods utilised have been document studies, non-participating observation at political meetings, and semi-structured interviews. Interviews have been performed individually and in groups, with both civil-society- and state-based political actors. Interviewees have always been informed about the research project and its expected output. Documents studied include Russian and Nordic media, project/ programme documents, meeting reports, official declarations and websites. All studied documents are either openly accessible to the general public or have been supplied freely by the documents' owners. Interviews have taken place in eight localities in Norway and Russia, as well as over the internet, during the period 2009–2014.

A list of abbreviations and shorthand names for NGOs, committees and other relevant actors can be found at the back of the article.

Network governance: Influence and representativeness

Modes of governance

During the last decades, new arrangements to include indigenous people in policy-making and policy-execution have been created across the world. Such arrangements can be examined with the analytical concept of *network governance* in mind. One may subdivide modes of governance into three ideal types or 'modes': *hierarchical*, *market* and *network* governance. The *hierarchical mode* is when the policy field in question is considered the exclusive domain of state structures and input from non-state actors is absent or extremely limited. In a *market mode*, the state has left market-based actors to regulate the field through free interaction and competition. Finally, *network governance* is when actors from civil society and/or business participate in policy-formation or -implementation through *ad hoc* or more institutionalised inclusion structures – governance networks. These are ideal types and, in the real world, mixtures of the three will often be observed (Winsvold *et al.* 2009: 408–21). In the Russian context, we must also be aware of a fourth 'mode of governance', what Ledeneva (2013: 4, 11, 13–17, 19–26, 32, 247–55) refers to as *Sistema*, 'the System', an all-pervasive culture of informal networking based on mutual support, hidden hierarchies and (often illegal) forms of utility exchange. This political culture operates in addition to openly declared, legal governance mechanisms, as actors based in the official state hierarchy make use of informal networking to govern. Informal networks may utilise the institutions of the other, legal governance modes to enforce their will – for example, through selective law enforcement; private firms engaging in politically motivated behaviour; formal governance networks being staffed with selected individuals in order to 'whitewash' pre-existing informal networks; and so on (Bækken 2009: 22–9, 32–8). In this chapter, when 'governance networks' are referred to, this means *formal, legal* governance networks – not informal networks.

Potential for political influence through participation in networks

When governance approaches the network mode, non-state actors gain opportunities to influence policy-making in formally regulated, legal and open ways. Inclusion structures such as councils, boards, hearings and round tables give non-state actors the opportunity to advise the state structures. In some cases, the included actors also achieve *de facto* or formalised negotiation-partner status *vis-à-vis* state structures. Under network governance, non-state actors (or the inclusion structures in which they participate) may even be delegated the authority to make political decisions and take part in implementation. Ideally, network governance gives marginalised groups and user-groups influence over decision-making processes that concern them. In practice, state-based or economically powerful actors, or constellations of these, may prevail anyway – for example, by deciding on matters in informal networks 'on the side', networks in which representatives of marginalised groups are not included.

The state structures may also control governance networks through formal, legal mechanisms for 'network management'. The latter is often referred to as *metagovernance*. Different types of metagovernance can, for example, be issue-framing (authorities define the scope of non-state actors' activities in the governance network); economic framing (authorities regulate the economic means available); participant-selection (authorities choose who participates in the governance network); and direct participation by authorities in the governance network (*cf.* Davies 2011: 62–4; Røiseland and Vabo 2012: 62–3, 80; Sørensen and Torfing 2009: 246–7, 251). Metagovernance is usually discussed as a way of safeguarding the power of representative democracy, a set of tools to prevent non-elected actors from taking over politics completely. However, this presupposes a functioning representative democracy, which is not always the case (*cf.* Tarasenko *et al.* 2011: 11–16) and certainly not the case when it comes to Russia. When representative democracy has failed, or is not fully developed, the involvement of civil society in governance networks may be a rare opportunity to achieve real grassroots input into political decision-making. Furthermore, also in states where representative democracy functions well, the inclusion of subaltern groups in decision-making processes to make sure they are heard can still be considered a democratising element, particularly when the subaltern groups are particularly affected by the decisions to be made. Hence, metagovernance can also be a *counterweight* to democracy – working against the democratisation implied by the inclusion of marginalised groups through network governance.

In addition to metagovernance, there are less refined and less legal ways for dominant groups to control non-dominant groups' representatives in network governance – such as bribes, blackmail, threats or softer forms of 'hinting' about what the included should or should not say and do. This is hardly an unknown phenomenon in Russia, where the use of illegal means of exerting power – such as, for example, the production of *kompromat* (compromising material, falsified or real) or the harassment of family and friends (Lebedeva 2013: 36) – is, unfortunately, widespread.

Finally, unless veto-rights or decision-making powers have been formally granted to non-state actors or the governance network in which they participate, the authorities may simply choose to ignore entirely all signals given.

The power granted to marginalised groups through network governance clearly has its limits but, within these limits, network governance arrangements may result in a wide array of outcomes – on a sliding scale from manipulative or symbolic-only inclusion (the status of the included is heightened but they are still not being heard); through effective consultancy (actors' advice is taken into account in policy-making to a lesser or greater extent, so the included leave a detectable 'footprint' on policy); via *de facto* or formalised negotiating position; to the bestowment of limited decision-making authority on the included actors or the governance network of which they form part (*cf.* Arnstein 1969; Schmidt *et al.* 2011: 51).

When actors representing the groups that would be most affected by the decisions taken are given delegated authority or involved as negotiation partner, we can talk about a measure of *self-determination* for the included group – at least in the sense that 'self-determination' is most often used in the context of indigenous politics, that is, not full sovereignty but, rather, co-determination under the ultimate control of the state (*cf.* Robbins' chapter in this book). Indigenous groups are in a special position since conventions, declarations and laws give them the right to certain levels of self-determination. The Russian Federation has, however, not ratified ILO 169 and abstained from voting on the UN Declaration on the Rights of Indigenous Peoples.

Representativeness and the proxy demos

All talk about 'self-determination' is empty rhetoric if the actors included to speak for the affected group are not ultimately dependent on the group's approval. In order to ensure genuine representativeness, certain demands can be made of representatives in governance networks: for example that they are identified by the groups in question as part of their collective 'Us'; that they do not participate as individuals but as envoys from organisations; that the represented groups are able to critically evaluate their representatives' activities; or that representatives are 'sensitive to criticism from the represented' (Røiseland and Vabo 2012: 63–4; Sørensen and Torfing 2009: 244–5; Torfing, Sørensen and Fotel 2009: 6–7). The chapter at hand applies the following criteria to determine if there is any detectable 'chain of popular sovereignty' (Törnquist 2009: 6–8) from the 'mass' of Russian Sámi to their representatives:

1. Are the representatives elected by and do they depend on the continued support of an organised body of people identified with the mass whose interests are said to be represented?
2. Can this organised body be convincingly stated to constitute an adequate 'proxy' for the mass whose interests are said to be represented?

A social group is, in itself, just a mass of individuals who share some objective traits or have a common identity. An unorganised mass in itself is not capable of choosing representatives. It cannot even reach a democratic decision on what its political goals should be, much less who should work for those goals. In order for democratic decision-making to take place, an organised group is needed to act on behalf of the mass. To apply a neologism, we can call this a 'proxy demos' – an approximation of the mass discursively constructed as represented (*cf.* Berg-Nordlie 2015a).

In representative democracies, the approximation of the 'nation' claimed to rule itself through its elected representatives is the registry of inhabitants with voting rights. Inclusion in the electoral register is granted or denied based on objective criteria such as citizenship, age, or the number of years a person has been settled in the country. In more restrictive cases, we find criteria based on gender, income level, property, conviction of criminal offence and so on. Electoral registries never include the entire population of a country, or the entire populace that considers itself part of the 'nation' in question. They are approximations. It is difficult to set an exact threshold for when a proxy demos should be considered an adequate approximation of the mass that is claimed to be represented. Ideally, such a proxy should be defined liberally enough that all members of the group to be represented are allowed entry – and yet restrictively enough to prevent the inclusion of group-external individuals. One could argue that it is impossible to find criteria that create a perfect equilibrium between restrictiveness and liberality – not least because there might not be any broad agreement on who should be considered a member of the group that is to be represented, and who should not.

The question of how to define the proxy demos for the Sámi causes much debate in the Nordic countries. Sámi electoral registries function as proxies for the population that self-identifies as Sámi (*cf.* Pettersen's chapter in this book) but the three states have ended up applying different criteria for who shall be allowed to enter the Sámi proxy demos (Berg-Nordlie 2015; Nyyssönen 2015). In Russia there is no Sámi electoral registry. Instead, regimes for political representation rely on civil-society formations that claim to act on behalf of the indigenous group. The proxy demos of the Russian Sámi is, hence, constituted by the members of the organisations from which 'Sámi representatives' are drawn into political processes. When determining if these approximations are adequate, the relevant questions are whether or not the organisations in question are open to all individuals self-defining as Sámi or if a significant number of Sámi are barred from participating in them.

Indigenous governance in Sápmi

Sápmi is the area traditionally inhabited by the Sámi. Four states have absorbed parts of this territory: Finland, Norway, Russia and Sweden. These states have different approaches to indigenous governance but there are structural similarities between the Nordic countries: they all have Sámi Parliaments (North Sámi *Sámedikkit,* sing. *Sámediggi*), advisory and participatory institutions that are based around assemblies of elected Sámi and have their own employed staff. The institutions are established by the states and financially dependent on them but their legitimacy as indigenous representatives rest on democratic elections within a proxy demos for the country's Sámi population. Hence, while the *Sámedikkit* are state-organised bodies, they simultaneously represent a non-state interest, that of an indigenous minority (Berg-Nordlie 2015a; Falch and Selle 2015).

The Sámi Parliaments have the right to give advice and speak on behalf of the Sámi of their states and are consulted or even negotiated with (*cf.* Josefsen 2008: 102, 107, 115). They are also given some decision-making authority, for example, through managing funds and/or specific policy sectors seen as highly relevant to the Sámi, or through inclusion into governance networks (boards, councils, committees and so on) that have been given decision-making authority. An example of the latter is the Board of the Finnmark Estate, an institution that governs natural resources in Norway's northernmost county. Representatives of state structures do not participate directly in the Sámi Parliaments' internal decision-making processes and the *Sámedikkit* enjoy (although to different degrees) great autonomy to set their own agenda and act politically. Nevertheless, they are subject to some metagovernance measures: though liberally defined, the Sámi Parliaments' freedom of action is still ultimately framed by state laws and regulations. Furthermore, they are financially dependent on the states and there is also a high degree of earmarking of the funds shared out to Sámi civil society through the *Sámedikkit*. Also, much of the Sámi Parliaments' potential for influence lies in their participation in governance networks in which the state *does* participate directly (Anaya 2011: 8; Berg-Nordlie 2015a; Broderstad *et al* 2015; Falch and Selle 2015; Josefsen, Mörkenstam and Saglie 2015: 37–39; Semb 2015; Selle 2011: 14–15).

Ideally, a Sámi Parliament will serve as a unifying political organ for all the Sámi of a country. Sámi civil society will need to relate to the institution, since it serves as the central political link between authority and minority and thus can voice indigenous civil society's concerns *vis-à-vis* the state. Another factor that 'pulls' Sámi civil society towards the Sámediggi is its role as 'ambassador', that is, the institution that makes contact with foreign actors (such as the Sámi institutions of other countries) on behalf of the state's Sámi population. Furthermore, the

Sámediggi may receive devolved powers that make it necessary for NGOs to relate to it, such as the power to channel funding (Bjerkli and Selle 2003: 83–5; Berg-Nordlie 2013: 374–86; Broderstad 2003: 164–74; Selle & Strømsnes 2015; SPR 2008: 2,8). Apart from these more practical-political concerns, a Sámediggi is also unifying for a country's Sámi population at the symbolic level – a common parliament is a symbol of, and evidence of, the existence of the nation. In order to be perceived by the Sámi populace as a unifying entity, it is important that the Sámi Parliament is generally regarded as representative. The *Sámedikkit* attempt to achieve representativeness by giving voting rights to individuals self-enrolled on the Sámi electoral registers. Through contested, democratic elections, enrolled Sámi voters elect representatives every four years, ideally ensuring that the politics of the assembly's majority are in line with popular opinion and that various internal groups are represented (Berg-Nordlie 2015a; Bjerkli and Selle 2003: 49, 81–3; Bergh and Saglie 2015).

In Russia, contrariwise, there is no officially established central organ that speaks for the indigenous peoples. Russia has the non-governmental umbrella organisation RAIPON – the Association of Native, Small-Numbered Peoples of the North, Siberia and Far East of the Russian Federation. It has been suggested, at times with explicit reference to the Sámi Parliament model, that RAIPON could be legally defined as the 'authorised representative' of the Russian indigenous peoples (Mikkelsen 2010: 43; Wessendorf 2005: 24–5, 64–7). So far, this has not happened but RAIPON has, over time, come to work closely with the authorities at the federal level. As the name implies, RAIPON does not speak for *all* indigenous people in Russia. There is a geographical specification, albeit one that includes most of Russia's vast territory, and a population limitation that excludes major groups. Russia has many peoples that would be considered indigenous by other states, such as the Komi or Sakha, but federal indigenous legislation, and RAIPON, has a narrower focus on 'native, small-numbered peoples' – groups that (among other things) number less than 50,000 individuals (*cf.* de Costa, in this volume). RAIPON also limits itself to including one NGO per people: an understandable practical limitation but one that obviously reduces RAIPON's overall representativeness since there are competing NGOs among some indigenous groups. The Russian Sámi are represented through the organisation AKS (Association of the Kola Sámi). RAIPON has an accountability system through its leadership being elected at a congress of member organisations every four years. However, the last chair election (2013) ended with the incumbent pulling out of the race, allowing a candidate affiliated with the party in power (United Russia) and the conference-hosting province (Jamalo-Nenec Autonomous Area) to take over. This happened after RAIPON had gone through a prolonged struggle to ensure its survival against threats of closure from the federal Ministry of Justice. Some consider the election to have signalled the informal subjugation of the organisation to state structures (BarentsObserver.com A, B). It remains to be seen how RAIPON will function in the future.

In any case, RAIPON's focus is on the federal level, whereas, at the provincial level, indigenous governance structures are different from place to place. When we go deeper into Russian indigenous politics, we find various kinds of civil-society formations (RAIPON-affiliated or not), state-based institutions and organs of the executive power, which are engaged in different constellations of conflict and co-operation. This chapter takes us to Murmansk Region, which is isomorphic with the Kola Peninsula, the home of the Russian Sámi. The Russian Sámi have the distinction of being the only Sámi community without a Sámi Parliament. Some local indigenous activists have long worked to get one; others are lukewarm to the idea or opposed to it. The authorities of Murmansk Region, for their part, have built on other models than *Sámedikkit* when establishing structures for Sámi representation.

The idea of a Sámi Parliament in Russia

The Sámi Parliament (*Sámediggi*) model for indigenous inclusion and empowerment grew during the period 1971–1996 as a result of indigenous demands for improved representation and influence, the states' needs for ordered and controlled forms of dialogue with Sámi representatives and inter-Nordic learning (Berg-Nordlie 2013: 442; Falch and Selle 2015).[4] In this section we will study how the Sámi Parliament model as an ideal for indigenous governance spread in Murmansk Region following the collapse of the USSR.

The beginning of the Russian Sámi Parliament movement

In 1992, the Soviet Union had given way to the Russian Federation and for the first time a Russian Sámi NGO – AKS – participated in an international Sámi Conference. The fifteenth Sámi Conference, in Helsinki, was an historic pan-Sámi event in many ways. Most significantly, it accepted AKS as a member organisation of the Nordic Sámi Council. This international NGO network was now for the first time truly pan-Sámi, since it included NGOs from all the four countries that had divided Sápmi. It now dropped the word 'Nordic' from its name (Berg-Nordlie 2013: 370–3).[5] The 1992 Sámi Conference also established an international Sámi People's Day (6 February, commemorating the first international Sámi conference, in 1917) and agreed on a common national anthem (Rantala 2004: 10–11; SR 1994: 85–94).[6]

---

4. Milestone years: 1971, the establishment of the Sámi Delegation in Finland; 1989, Sámi Parliament of Norway; 1992, Sámi Parliament of Sweden; 1996, Sámi Delegation reorganised to Sámi Parliament of Finland.

5. The Sámi Council is an international NGO network that unites Sámi NGOs. The Sámi Conferences serve as the basis for the Council's internal democracy. The first NGO to become truly pan-Sámi was not the Sámi Council, but the Sámi women's group *Sáhráhkka*, in 1991 (Hætta 2003: 49). The importance of international womens' networking in post-Soviet Russian Sámi politics could be an interesting study in itself. Sámi politics in Russia have been characterised by female dominance and several central Russian Sámi activists have been active in the international Sámi women's networks *Sáhráhkká* and *Sámi Nissonforum* (Lindi 2005; Overland and Berg-Nordlie 2012).

6. To be precise, it was the melody that was agreed upon. The 1986 Conference had already agreed that Isak Saba's poem *Song of the Sámi People* should serve as the lyrics. The 1986 conference had also agreed on a common Sámi flag (SR 1987: 99–100, 133–40).

It was thus in keeping with the spirit of the conference that the Russian delegation concluded that the Sámi are 'one people and ought to attempt having the same systems', and embarked upon a course towards a Russian Sámi Parliament (Interviews A and B). AKS held discussions on the matter and presented it for a broader audience in a 1995 letter to the newspaper *Poljarnaja Pravda* (Kal'te 1995).[7] The 1996 international Sámi Conference was held in Russia and its resulting 'Murmansk Declaration' underscored the need to consider a 'popularly elected Sámi organ on the Russian side [of the border]'. In her closing speech, AKS leader Nina Afanas'jeva stated that the Russian Sámi would work towards this goal but 'may have to wait long for results to manifest' (SR 1997: 84, 87, *cf.* Šaršina and Jakovleva 2010; OOSMO Y.N.G). These words proved prophetic.

Pro-Parliament activists encountered resistance to their idea from regional officials, including accusations that the Sámi ultimately wanted a state of their own (Interview C).[8] Then Governor of Murmansk Region, Jevgenij Komarov (1991–1996), also opposed the idea of a Russian Sámi Parliament (IWGIA 1996: 37). In addition, there was little active support at the grassroots level among the Russian Sámi.

…people just weren't ready. They didn't understand what a Sámi Parliament was, they didn't get enough information about what functions it would have. So it ended up as just an internal discussion in AKS (Interview D).

Nevertheless, the idea had taken root. Since the early 1990s, the notion that indigenous governance in Murmansk Region should be modelled after that of the Nordic countries has re-surfaced several times.

The Sámi Parliament as pan-Sámi ideology and practice

Modern Sámi politics has long been characterised by a discourse of 'pan-Sámism', which frames as natural the existence of common national symbols, border-transcending co-operation and equal rights for Sámi of different countries (Berg-Nordlie 2011: 20–1; 2013: 437). This discourse of pan-Sámi unity can be summed up in an oft-quoted 'political creed': '*We Sámi are one people, and state borders shall not divide us*'. A good example of such discourse articulation is the Sámi Political Program of 1980, a joint statement from Nordic Sámi activists that called for states to implement similar Sámi political reforms. Among these, that 'in each state a representative Sámi assembly or other representative Sámi

---

7. The letter was written by Zinaida Kal'te, who headed AKS' working group for a Russian Sámi Parliament and was also a member of the Sámi Council legal committee during the early 1990s. The latter committee debated an envisioned pan-Sámi rights convention (SR 1997: 78), which evolved into the Nordic Sámi Convention project (Berg-Nordlie 2013: 377–8). Kal'te later wrote a dissertation on Russian Sámi politics (Ka'lte 2003).

8. False accusations of separatism against the Russian Sámi are nothing new. Such allegations were also made during the Stalinist purges (Larsson-Kalvemo 1995: 32–4).

organ shall be recognised by law' (SR 1980: 11), a demand eventually answered by the creation of the *Sámedikkit*. Another example is the 2005 Draft Nordic Sámi Convention, which aimed to standardise Sámi rights – including the right to representation through *Sámedikkit* (FNSSE 2005: Art. 15). Although the Sámi Parliaments are organs under the states and predominantly focused on domestic matters, they have a pan-Sámi symbolic aspect in that their existence constitutes a border-transcending similarity between different states' Sámi communities and an international standardisation of Sámi politics. They are also active in practical pan-Sámi politics: The Sámi Parliamentary Council (est. 2000) constitutes, together with the Sámi Council, the symbolic 'heart' of institutionalised pan-Sámism (Berg-Nordlie 2013: 369, 374–86).

Both the symbolic and practical pan-Sámi aspects of the Sámi Parliament model increase its attractiveness. The absence of a *Sámediggi* in Russia symbolically underscores the group's deviation from the majority, and constitutes a practical problem for participation in pan-Sámi politics. While the Russian Sámi are represented fully in the NGO-based Sámi Council through the organisations AKS and OOSMO, the group only has participating observer status in the *Sámediggi*-based Sámi Parliamentary Council (Berg-Nordlie 2013: 443). In the words of AKS ex-leader Nina Afanas'jeva:

> We have no parliament, no president.[9] Of course this [the creation of the Sámi Parliamentary Council] meant that a Sámi Parliament of our own became even more important (Interview B).

However, no local interviewees other than the above emphasised the pan-Sámi aspect of having a Russian Sámi Parliament as being particularly important. Interviewees talked more about what a Russian Sámi Parliament could do locally. The central pro-Parliament activist, Valentina Sovkina, even explicitly downplayed the importance of the pan-Sámi function.

> We mainly want Russia to notice us, not the West. We need our own Sámi laws and help from our own government. That's why we want a Sámi Parliament (Interview E).

The Sámi Parliament as an answer to local needs

When asked to define a Sámi Parliament, interviewees tended to highlight its role as an organ connecting 'the authorities and the Sámi leaders' (Interview F), and carrying a level of political influence that would enable it to address major issues such as language revival and protection of the resource base for traditional economic activities. Both pro-Parliament interviewees and sceptics referred to perceptions among the Russian Sámi that the *Sámedikkit* had been successful in this regard.

---

9. The heads of the *Sámedikkit* are called presidents.

We consider the Sámi Parliaments to be organisations that radically changed the life of the Sámi. Like the Norwegian example (Interview G).

I think this idea of a Russian Sámi Parliament originated abroad. In any case, the roots of the idea lie in the West. People go there and see how good everything is, and ask how this has happened, and they are told 'we have a Sámi Parliament' (Interview H).

Another local problem that the Sámi Parliament model was seen as capable of addressing was the lack of a universally acknowledged common political organ for the Russian Sámi. As we will return to below, Russian Sámi politics fragmented in 1998 and several interviewees expressed hope that an elected organ could unite them.

[a Sámi Parliament] can unite us, all the organisations, the entire people ... Now there are all these councils and all these [NGOs] ... There's too little unity among us (Interview I).

Rooting the Sámi Parliament discursively in local soil

Finally, new discourses on local history have also, to an extent, fuelled desires for a Russian Sámi Parliament. At the 2002 conference 'People and Land,' Sámi-Norwegian researcher Johan A. Kalstad held a lecture called 'The *Sijt*[10] and the Sámi Parliament in old Russia' (Bol'šakova 2005: 226; Interviews D and J). The 'Sámi Parliament' in question was the *Koladak Sobbar* of the late 1800s, an institution that, according to Kalstad, met annually in Kola town[11] on February 6, which Kalstad notes was later (for unrelated reasons) made the Sámi national day. Kalstad furthermore describes the Sobbar as an 'independent' organ that united Sámi representatives and Russian bureaucrats to debate and decide on issues of importance to the Sámi (Kalstad 2009: 20–8). This presentation of the *Koladak Sobbar* is discussed critically in Berg-Nordlie 2015b. Although Tanner (1929: 332–8) had discussed memories of the Sobbar seventy years earlier, it was not generally remembered among today's Russian Sámi. This take on Russian Sámi history inspired some of the local activists; it 'rooted' the Sámi Parliament model in local governance traditions and it added an element of 'returning to a better past' to the pro-Parliament activism.

That Kalstad found this out clearly had an influence on us. I know it had on me. We didn't know that there had been such an assembly earlier. Sometimes history is silent about the good things ... So we ask ourselves, why shouldn't we return to that which we had before? (Interview E).

---

10. *Sijt* – traditional Sámi social unit – a collective that jointly owned and used specific resources.

11. South of modern-day Murmansk City.

Russian Sámi civil society: An overview

Before investigating how Russian Sámi civil society is included – or not included – in indigenous governance, we need to have a reasonable overview over what that civil society is. This section briefly introduces some key actors and organisation types.

AKS (1989–present) and OOSMO (1998–present)

Russian Sámi civil society has its roots in the 1980s, when an intelligentsia began working to revitalise Sámi culture and language and connect with Nordic kin (Kalstad 2009: 51–2; Overland and Berg-Nordlie 2012; Utvik 1985: 15). This pre-organisational phase culminated and ended in 1989, with the formation of the Association of the Kola Sámi (*Associjacija kol'skikh saamov*). AKS dominated Russian Sámi politics until 1998. This was a 'unipolar' phase of Russian Sámi organisational history, characterised by a unitary and region-wide NGO with local chapters and a democratic structure. AKS proclaimed itself 'the unitary organ of Soviet Sámi society' and set out to connect with both the Murmansk Region authorities and the Nordic Sámi (LP 1989). During the early *Perestrojka* period, activists on both sides of the Iron Curtain had already managed to establish some border-transcending ties (Berg-Nordlie 2013: 370–1) and several AKS activists now had contacts in Western Sápmi. AKS were to have less success with the regional authorities.

A political schism within AKS led to the founding of OOSMO (*Obščestvennaja organizacija saamov Murmanskoj oblasti*, the Civil Society Organisation of the Murmansk Region Sámi) in 1998. OOSMO was centred on Lovozero, the major settlement area of the Russian Sámi, instead of Murmansk City (Overland and Berg-Nordlie 2012: 101).[12] AKS now lost its position as the only catch-all Russian Sámi organisation. OOSMO also began representing the Russian Sámi abroad, becoming Sámi Council members in 2000 (Rantala 2004: 12). A 'multipolar' phase of Russian Sámi organisational history began. Yet more Sámi organisations were created, none of which were catch-all oriented like AKS and OOSMO – rather, they were geographically or sectorally specific. It became increasingly obvious that a central point of orientation for Russian Sámi civil society was lacking; the question of who could legitimately parlay with the authorities on behalf of the Sámi became increasingly difficult to answer.

The Obščiny (2002–present)

The *Obščiny* (Russian, sing. *obščina*, 'community' or 'commune') are non-commercial kin- or community-based membership organisations aimed at the 'defence of ancient habitats, traditional ways of life, rights and legal interests' of indigenous groups (Obščina Law: Introduction, Arts. 1 and 5). In 2000 a federal

---

12. AKS had considered basing their organisation in Lovozero but, in the end, chose Murmansk City, because the offices of the regional authorities were there (Overland and Berg-Nordlie 2012: 101).

law to regulate the establishment of such organisations was enacted. They have, according to Stammler (2005: 111), become 'the leading institutional structure employed in the post-Soviet reorganisation of indigenous tundra and taiga dwellers'. Their effectiveness varies from place to place and case to case. *Obščina*-activist (and from 2010, AKS leader) Jelena Jakovleva stated in 2003 that although AKS had done much, that NGO consisted of 'people with higher educations and stable incomes'. She argued that most Russian Sámi were not part of this social class and would benefit from a return to traditional activities – like kin-based reindeer-herding – which *obščiny* could provide (Kalstad 2009: 56, 64–6).

Murmansk Region *obščiny* have, as a rule, only been registered in 'places of traditional inhabitance and traditional economic activities' (*mesta tradicionnogo proživanija i tradicionnoj khozjajstvennoj dejatel'nosti*). This is not a demand in the *Obščina* Law but a practice that has developed in Murmansk Region.[13] The 'traditional places' are designated on a federal list from 2009 (Krjažkov 2012: 29–31; Federal list of Traditional Places). While the entire Kola Peninsula is traditional Sámi land, the federal list only contains the districts Lovozero, Ter, Kola and Kovdor – that is, most of Murmansk Region's territory but excluding municipalities with larger, urban settlements. Urban Sámi therefore have no opportunity to form *obščiny*. Exceptions were 'Kil'din', the first Murmansk Region *obščina*, which was based in Murmansk City (founded in 2002, now closed), and 'Jokan'ga' in Ostrovnoj. The Indigenous Centre (*see below*) is trying to include Ostrovnoj on the federal list but has so far not succeeded, likely because Ostrovnoj is a closed military city. As will be explained below, the limitations on *obščina*-formation has become a democratic problem in Murmansk Region's contemporary indigenous governance system.

During the early new millennium, several Sámi *obščiny* were founded. Today there are 23 but many have an uncertain future (http://gov.murman.ru A). Creating and running an *obščina* is hard work, due both to the nature of the traditional activities and the bureaucracy (Interviews J and K). Furthermore, in order to practise reindeer-herding, *obščiny* need land, which, in practice, they often have to lease from the authorities (Interviews K and L; Stammler 2005: 116–17). Currently, four *obščiny* have been granted land-leases by the regional authorities: *Puaz* in Kola district; *Voavskhèss*, *Sám' syjt* and *Šèntèmbal'* in Lovozero district (http://gov.murman.ru A).

The NCAs: National Cultural Autonomies (2007–present)

The National Cultural Autonomies are inspired by Austro-Marxist ideas from around the turn of the century 1800/1900. The end of the Soviet era saw renewed interest in and discussion of the concept of non-geographical autonomy. A federal

---

13. These should not be confused with 'Territories of Traditional Nature-Use' (*territorii tradicionnogo prirodopol'zovanija*), designated areas preserved for traditional indigenous nature usage. Sámi activists have worked to get such territories on the Kola Peninsula but this has encountered problems all over Russia (Interview U; Krjažkov 2010: 243–59 and 2012: 28–9, 31).

law on the formation of such entities came in 1996 (Osipov 2010: 33–5). The 'autonomies' are not state structures and do not have formal powers over territory (NCA Law: Arts 1, 4). They are civil-society organisations meant to enable ethnic minorities to 'decide on issues linked to the conservation of their heritage, language development, education and national culture'. NCAs can, ostensibly, still play the role of political representative of their constituencies but are generally more involved with the promotion of minority culture. NCAs are not limited to indigenous peoples and, in fact, are more often associated with diaspora groups, such as Armenians and Azerbaijanis. Yet, in Murmansk Region, the Sámi have also created NCAs, a phenomenon that originated in a pro-Parliament project.

After OOSMO was formed, it launched the project 'White Reindeer' to 'create structures for self-government and coordination', in co-operation with the Jona village AKS chapter and the Danish indigenous-oriented aid organisation Infonor (Interviews M and C). The project hired a law firm to investigate the legal possibilities for a Russian Sámi Parliament. The firm concluded that 'it will not be possible to copy the Sámi Parliament completely under Russian conditions. It is, however, fully realistic to form an analogous structure, taking into account Russian specifics.' They pointed to NCAs as a realistic alternative (Infonor Y.N.G.). White Reindeer decided on this option. Since 2007, Sámi NCAs have been established in the urban districts Mončegorsk and Apatity and the rural district Lovozero (Infonor 2008). The NCAs have also united in a regional autonomy.

Hypothetically, the regional NCA could serve as a unifying representative structure for the Russian Sámi. The NCAs have democratic structures and bridge organisational gaps. The Lovozero newspaper *Lovozerskaja Pravda* expressly introduced the NCAs to the public as intended to 'protect the interests and rights of all Sámi: be they members of AKS or OOSMO' (*LP* 2007). A challenge to the NCAs' potential to unify all the Sámi is that, like a mirror image of the rural-exclusive *obščiny*, the NCAs are based in urban areas. NCA activists themselves described their activity as an urban form of indigenous organisation:

> ..it works well here, where there are few Sámi, but in Lovozero there are organisations, *sovkhozes*,[14] they are living compactly … Here we are spread among many others. This is our way of uniting (Interview N).

The NCAs could thus encounter difficulties achieving legitimacy among the rural majority of the Sámi if they tried to position themselves as *the* Sámi representative structures of Murmansk Region. But they do not. They mostly restrict their activities to the preservation of identity and culture in urban contexts and do not claim to represent the entire Russian Sámi community.

Having introduced the main actors in Russian Sámi civil society, we will now turn our attention to how Murmansk Region has included that civil society in indigenous governance since the fall of the USSR.

---

14. *Sovkhoz*: state farm. The large Kola reindeer-herding companies are still often referred to as such, despite post-Soviet restructuring.

1992–2004: Rapid reorganisation and haphazard inclusion

The Indigenous Issues Committee (1992–7)

In 1992 the regional government established a Committee on the Issues of Native, Small-Numbered Peoples of the North (*Komitet po voprosam korennykh maločislenykh narodov Severa*, henceforth 'the Indigenous Issues Committee') (http://docs.pravo.ru A; Kal'te 2004: 103–4; http://murmansk.news-city.info A and B; http://www.regnum.ru). According to Gutsol and Riabova (2002: 329) the Indigenous Issues Committee dealt mainly with requests for financial support from NGOs, individuals and local self-government organs. It was headed by the Sámi Sergej Semjaškin. Also taking part in the committee was non-Sámi Nikolaj Bogdanov, who was to become a prominent figure in Russian Sámi politics through his constant involvement in the official structures and his frequent writing on the subject.

It was AKS that, in 1991, had asked the Government to establish the Indigenous Issues Committee (Kal'te 2003: 103). According to the head of AKS at the time, they had even been invited by the authorities to suggest committee staff members, and Semjaškin had been one of their suggestions (Interview B). Furthermore, Indigenous Issues Committee statutes from 1994, and other formal documents, specified that the committee should work with AKS. The committee was also charged to work with a number of other organisations, national and international, including 'organisations (movements) of the Nordic Sámi' (http://murmansk. news-city.info B and C). For AKS, being specifically named as a partner of the committee promised well. By proclaiming themselves to be 'the unitary organ of Soviet Sámi society' and claiming a right to work with the authorities on issues affecting their people (*LP* 1989), they had positioned themselves as a potential partner in governance arrangements with the state structures. The latter now seemed to reply positively.

The promise of what AKS could be likely contributed to the above mentioned lack of grassroots' enthusiasm for the idea of a Russian Sámi Parliament: AKS already aimed to fulfil some core functions of a *Sámediggi*: unifying the Sámi around a common structure, working for them on the pan-Sámi arena and representing them in domestic politics. But being a civil-society formation and not a body set up by the state, AKS' chances of being given delegated decision-making authority were meagre, to say the least. The regional government did, indeed, reserve all decision-making power for itself, committing only to including AKS in policy deliberation. Furthermore, the inclusion of AKS in decision-making processes was never strongly institutionalised. There were meetings, there was dialogue, but there was no formalised system for representation. Still, the committee was formally obliged to work with AKS, a proxy demos the statutes of which made membership obtainable for all the Sámi of Murmansk region (*LP* 1989). However, during the 1990s, many Sámi activists began to question whether or not AKS' internal democracy was functioning adequately and major internal conflicts erupted, conflicts that further muddled the internal democratic processes of AKS. The chain of representation broke and the members of AKS lost the power to control who represented them (Overland and Berg-Nordlie 2012: 94–102).

Returning to the Indigenous Issues Committee, its number of employees and working capacity was progressively reduced. Listed as having five employees at first, in 1993 it already had just three and, by the end of its existence, only had two (http://docs.pravo.ru A and B; Gutsol and Riabova 2002: 329; http://www.regnum ru). In 1997, the Indigenous Issues Committee was reorganised into the Sector for Northern Native Peoples' Affairs (*Otdel po delam korennykh narodov Severa*, 'Indigenous Sector') under the Committee on Governance of the Agricultural-Industrial Complex, Trade, Connections at the Inter-Provincial Level and with Former Soviet States (*Komitet po upravleniju agropromyšlennym kompleksom, togorvle, svjazjam na mežregional'nom urovne i so stranami SNG*) (http://murmansk.news-city.info D). Judging by the name, Sámi issues were not highly placed on the agenda of that committee. Furthermore, when Semjaškin left his post he was not replaced so that, until 2001, the Indigenous Sector only employed one person, who was not ethnically Sámi (Nikolaj Bogdanov).

In sum, the Sámi were given the possibility of cultivating dialogue with the authorities, but in a weakly institutionalised way and through an NGO whose representativeness increasingly suffered under its own internal conflicts. Furthermore, the branch of the government designated to indigenous politics was given low priority and did not pack much of a political punch.

The Indigenous Advisor (1997–2009)

In the same year in which the Indigenous Issues Committee was downgraded, the leader of AKS was given the position of Advisor (*sovetnik*) to the Governor on indigenous issues (Gutsol and Riabova 2002: 329). While placed close to the top of the formal hierarchy, this was still only an advisory position, carrying no decision-making power or veto rights. As for representativeness, the position was a personal one, bestowed by Governor Jurij Jevdokimov (1996–2009). The Advisor was not dependent on approval from her organisation, or any other Sámi proxy demos. In any case, AKS was at this point undergoing a crisis and, in 1998, split in two. The section of Russian Sámi civil society that supported the new organisation OOSMO had no organisational connection whatsoever to the Advisor. The Advisor would, in a later interview (2009) argue that the AKS/OOSMO schism was caused by people in the regional administration fomenting discord as part of a divide-and-rule strategy against the Sámi, and with the specific target of undermining the Advisor's attempts to have the Governor disband the Indigenous Sector. Nevertheless, a main cause of the schism appears to have been AKS' poorly functioning internal democracy which led many members to feel it was impossible to change the leadership of AKS through democratic means. This discontent was fertile ground for the idea of founding a new Sámi civil-society organisation.

The position of Advisor apparently remained in existence until in 2009. The degree to which it was based on personal connections is evidenced by the fact that it was discontinued when a new Governor took over Murmansk Region (Dmitrij Dmitrijenko, 2009–12). Since then, there has been no Advisor to the governor on indigenous issues.

The Indigenous Problems' Committee and Sector (2000–4)

In 2000, indigenous governance was reorganised again. The Indigenous Sector was renamed the Committee for Native Small-Numbered Peoples' Problems (*Komitet po problemam korennykh maločislennykh narodov Severa*; 'Indigenous Problems Committee') and hence placed higher up in the hierarchy as it was now a committee in its own right. Like its predecessor, the Indigenous Problems Committee was also charged with working with Sámi civil society – both Russian and Nordic. Its reinstatement as a higher-level structure did not, however, result in more human resources: there were still only two employees: a Sámi leader, Anna Prakhova, and a non-Sámi consultant, Nikolaj Bogdanov (http://2004.murman.ru; http://docs. pravo.ru C; Interview O; http://murmansk.news-city.info E, F, G and H).

In 2002 there was yet another reorganisation. The Indigenous Problems Committee was now combined with two other down-graded committees into the Committee for Issues of Local Self-Government, Problems of Military Garrisons and the Affairs of Native, Small-Numbered Peoples (*Komitet po voprosam mestnogo samoupravlenija, problemam vojennykh garnizonov i delam korennykh maločislennykh narodov*). The administrative employees working with indigenous affairs once more constituted just a sector within a committee that had responsibilities for a broad range of topics. This committee was again nested under the Department for Legal Projects and Local Self-Government (*Departament zakonprojektnoj dejatel'nosti i mestnogo samoupravlenija*). The authorities' dialogue with activists from the (now increasingly complex and many-faceted) Russian Sámi civil society continued, but fixed, formal structures for dialogue were not established.

Murmansk indigenous governance 1992–2004 was characterised by being given generally low priority by the Murmansk regional government, and by being subject to frequent reorganising. Indeed, even people who participated in indigenous politics at the time have, in hindsight, during interviews, had difficulty reconstructing all the reorganisations that took place. Nevertheless, despite the profoundly unstable administrative situation, continuity was rather high in terms of which individuals were involved – both as employees in the committees/sectors and as representatives of the indigenous organisations. The personal networks were more stable than the formal ones. Another characteristic is the lack of formalised, permanent structures for indigenous grassroots representation in politics. Leader figures appear to have been contacted by the authorities on an *ad hoc* basis. Furthermore, taking into consideration that the internal democracy of the proxy demos was weakened during the 1990s, it becomes difficult to conclude that the Sámi were adequately represented in indigenous governance during this period.

2004–8: The Centre, the Council and the Congress

In 2004, there was a general reform of Murmansk Region's administrative structures (Vinogradova 2005: 3). There was now no separate committee or sector for indigenous governance. Instead, the regional government established a new type of co-ordination organ for indigenous governance, at a lower level in the administrative hierarchy. In the years that followed, the regional authorities also created the Kola Peninsula's first formalised governance network, which included representatives of several Sámi civil-society organisations.

The Indigenous Centre (2004–present)

The regional authorities' new co-ordination organ for indigenous policy was called the State Regional Budgetary Institution 'Centre for Native, Small-Numbered Peoples of the North' (*Gosudarstvennoje oblastnoje bjudžetnoe učreždenie 'Centr korennykh maločislennykh narodov Severa'*, 'Indigenous Centre'). At first, the Indigenous Centre was nested under the Department for Legal Projects and Reforms of Local Self-Government, which, again later, became a committee under the Justice Department of Murmansk Region (Interview P; http://gov.murman.ru B; http://murman.city-news.info I). In 2009, the Indigenous Centre was transferred to the Committee for Contacts with Civil Society Organisations and Youth Affairs (*Komitet po vzaimodeystviju s obščestvennym organizacijam i delam molodjoži*, 'Civil Society Committee'). The Indigenous Centre's low placement in the hierarchy when compared to a committee or sector has led several Sámi activists to see its creation as a further marginalisation of the indigenous policy field. Nevertheless, in contrast to some of its predecessors, this organ works solely with indigenous affairs and has also proved to be more stable, having now existed for a decade.

According to its charter, the Centre is charged with representing Sámi interests at all levels of society, preparing and realising projects and programmes aimed at improving the group's social situation, defending their rights to 'historical and cultural, social and economic development' and their 'ancient area of habitat, traditional life and economy' (Indigenous Centre 2011). The Centre's charter opens for co-operation with foreign organisations – but in practice AKS and OOSMO have largely remained the 'ambassadors' of the Russian Sámi in pan-Sámi affairs (Berg-Nordlie 2013: 383–5; Indigenous Centre Charter, Art. 3.2).[15] The Indigenous Centre's stated mission of voicing Sámi interests and its intended role in Sámi policy-creation and -execution would make it a natural point of orientation for Russian Sámi civil society. The institution did not, however, have any set mechanism that enabled the Sámi to give input. Its leader, Andrej Agejev, and some staff were Sámi, but the institution's legitimacy as an advocate of Sámi interests was not backed up by any form of democratic representation.

The Indigenous Co-ordination Council (2006–8)

The first real move towards a network governance model in Murmansk Region's indigenous politics came in 2006. That year, the Indigenous Centre established the Indigenous Co-ordination Council (*Koordinacionnyj sovet pri gosudarstvennom*

---

15. The Indigenous Centre did have one co-operative venture, with the Finnish Sámi Education Institute (Interview H).

oblastnom učreždenii 'Murmanskij oblastnoj centr korennykh maločislennykh narodov Severa'). This council included representatives from all (at the time 18) Russian Sámi civil-society formations – ordinary NGOs, NCAs, and *obščiny* (Indigenous Centre 2006). The Co-ordination Council has been referred to as 'the first common organ of the Sámi organisations [in Russia] – a bridge between the Sámi people and the official powers' (Šaršina and Jakovleva 2010).

If we go back to the criteria for representativeness established above, we find the following. Concerning criterion (1), the statutes of the Co-ordination Council specified that the civil-society representatives had to be leaders or vice-leaders of Sámi civil society formations (http://gov.murman.ru C). The members of these organisations were formally able to elect new leaders if they were dissatisfied with their activities; hence, the representatives were dependent on the support of organised Sámi bodies. Of course, formalities aside, the practical possibility of members to evaluate and replace their leaders varied between organisations. Nevertheless, the system aimed to include Sámi individuals that were chosen by Sámi organisations. Concerning (2), the large number of participating organisations must be said to have laid the foundation for a rather decent proxy demos for the Sámi living in Murmansk Region. Most individuals considering themselves as Sámi would have at least one organisation on the list which they would be able to join in order to influence who was sent to the Co-ordination Council. A proxy demos constituted by members of civil-society organisations does favour the segment of the population that is already most politically/culturally active – but so does any proxy demos based on active self-enrolment, the Nordic Sámi electoral registers included.

Regarding practical influence over Sámi policy, the Co-ordination Council was placed very low in the hierarchy. The state structures had here 'outsourced' carefully framed political tasks to a self-managed but state-based structure (the Indigenous Centre), which again took on a group of NGO representatives to advise them. There was also a strong element of direct participation by the authorities in that advisory group: the Indigenous Centre's leader co-ordinated their activities and took part in meetings (Indigenous Centre 2006). Nevertheless, the Indigenous Centre has some influence, and if the Sámi included in the Co-ordination Council had managed to get any decisive influence over that institution's activity this would have given Russian Sámi civil society more political clout than it had had before. To what extent did the representatives perceive that this governance network gave them genuine influence? During fieldwork it became clear that many of them thought the network functioned poorly as a vehicle for Sámi influence. There were two discourses on why the representation structure had gone wrong – and they were polar opposites.

On the one hand, there were those who portrayed the basic problem as one of internal friction – particularly between AKS and OOSMO on the one hand, and certain *obščiny* on the other. Some *obščina* activists displayed a highly sceptical attitude towards AKS and OOSMO. One former *obščina* representative in the Co-ordination Council felt that the NGOs' conduct caused 'fighting and disorder [in the council], we just lost interest in going there' (Interview Q) while another referred to the council as full of ... the kind of Sámi that form the basis for the non-governmental organisations. They aren't interested in us and what we do, the traditional way of life. Fishing, reindeer, hunting, land. Those people who go over to you [Nordic Sámi] and say 'we are the Sámi' – they don't represent us. (Interview R)

The anti-AKS/OOSMO discourse articulated here seems related to a phenomenon noted by both Overland (1999) and Vladimirova (2006: 29–35): some Sámi perceive NGOs as self-enrichment tools for activists belonging to the urban and/or educated class. Vladimirova discusses such accusations of 'egoism' towards the *obščiny* from the general Sámi public; but it seems that similar attitudes are also found within some of the *obščiny*, directed towards the larger NGOs. Such attitudes to civil society are not unique to the Russian Sámi but rather generally prevalent in the Russian public (Overland and Berg-Nordlie 2012: 104–5). The interviewees who focused on internal frictions argued that the council could not 'solve problems constructively' (Interview H) because of them. Later on, the council experienced problems reaching a quorum, as certain *obščiny* representatives ceased to attend.

In the other discourse, the main problem was the council's low degree of influence. Interviewees focusing on this aspect argued both that the council was too far removed from those who would, in the end, make the decisions, and that there was a lack of will from the state structures to take council opinions into account:

Many decisions that the council made were not listened to by the regional authorities, important questions were not solved. As we know, the interests of the Sámi and the authorities do not always coincide (Sovkina 2008).

Interviewees belonging to this 'camp' tended to describe the organ as a purely symbolic or even manipulative form of indigenous representation.

One of the major issues that caused friction was that some members of the Co-ordination Council demanded a representation structure more like the *Sámedikkit*. In 2007, AKS and OOSMO signed a written agreement that they would work together for a Russian Sámi Parliament and, in March 2008, they institutionalised that co-operation through a joint Initiative Group (Interviews C and S).[16] The existing governance structures fell short of the standards some activists expected, having long held the *Sámedikkit* as the model for Sámi representation.

The Co-ordination Council should have decided matters and [the Indigenous Centre] executed its decisions. That would have been a Sámi Parliament. Except that in the Council there were only the leaders of the organisations, not elected people (Interview S).

---

16. The Initiative Group had four members from AKS and four members from OOSMO. One of these also represented the Monchegorsk NCA and another headed an *obščina*, though was not listed as such. Six of the eight members were listed as members of the pan-Sámi women's network *Sámi Nissonforum* (Sovkina 2008).

The *Sámedikkit* were considered, by most interviewees, to have made practical improvements for the Nordic Sámi, and were seen as institutions capable of addressing major issues such as language revival and protection of natural resources for traditional usage. Nevertheless, some Sámi felt that the model could not be imported to Russia. Some of these held that the large number of indigenous peoples in Russia made individual ethnic parliaments for indigenous groups undesirable; others that the demographic specifics of the Russian Sámi (their small numbers) and Russian authorities' scepticism towards Western models made the idea unrealistic; and others again that RAIPON already served the function of 'a Sámi Parliament for all the native, small-numbered peoples of Russia' (Interview H). An interesting aspect of the Sámi Parliament debate was that many interviewees from different 'camps', presented the existing Sámi Parliaments as having more authority than what is actually the case, for example, referring to them as 'legislative organs' or having general 'veto-rights' over Sámi policy. Many were also of the opinion that Sámi Parliaments are 'independent from the state'. However, none of the actually-existing Sámi Parliaments have legislative powers or general veto-rights over Sámi policy and when the *Sámedikkit* are described as fully 'independent' this indicates little understanding of their legal position and the metagovernance to which they are subject (*cf.* Berg-Nordlie 2015a; Falch and Selle 2015; Josefsen *et al.* 2015). Rantala (2009) argues that such impressions of the *Sámedikkit* may stem, in part, from the term 'parliament', as this is 'perceived much more literally [in Russia] than in the Nordic states,' carrying strong connotations of a high level of authority that, for example, the Norwegian/Swedish term *Sameting* in Rantala's analysis does not. One interviewee similarly commented that 'the word "parliament" scares the bureaucrats. ... We need another kind of organ here. Another name, but working closely with the Murmansk government' (Interview Q).

The First Congress of the Murmansk Region Sámi (2008)

When the Initiative Group for a Sámi Parliament met with the counter-argument that all of Russia's indigenous groups could not each have their own parliament, they first discussed whether the arrangement could be offered only to *border-transcending* indigenous peoples like the Sámi. In the end, they suggested that the structure should not be on the federal level, but rather be an indigenous-elected second chamber of the regional parliament. They pointed to the Federal law on Guarantees for the Rights of Indigenous Peoples that gave provinces the right to establish such entities (Sovkina 2008).[17] When this position did not meet with support, they again reduced their ambitions, instead proposing a separate council of elected Sámi representatives, funded by the regional authorities, that would represent the group internationally and at the regional level (Initiative Group

---

17. KMNS Law, Art. 6.8, states that in order to defend traditional indigenous economic activities, ways of life and industries, provinces (regions, autonomous areas and so on) may create official councils of indigenous representatives.

2008; Interview E; Sovkina 2008). The authorities suggested a different model: a council of representatives, the members of which would first be suggested by a 'Sámi Congress' and subsequently approved by the governor (Interview H; http:// www.nrk.no A; Šaršina and Jakovleva 2010).

It was proposed that in December 2008 a 'First Congress of the Murmansk Region Sámi' should gather to debate indigenous issues, including the Sámi Parliament issue, and give officials advice on Sámi policy (First Congress Document: Art. 1.1., 2.1., 3.3., 9.1). In April 2008 those present at a Co-ordination Council meeting gave their approval to the Initiative Group for a Russian Sámi Parliament and declared that the Co-ordination Council now constituted the 'highest political authority' of the Russian Sámi, until the First Congress (Sovkina 2008). Shortly after this, the Co-ordination Council was disbanded. The Indigenous Centre turned its attentions towards arranging the First Congress. Meanwhile, the Initiative Group also continued its work, hoping to have the First Congress decide on the necessity of a Russian Sámi Parliament. The scene now seemed set for a decisive meeting about the Sámi Parliament issue.

At the First Congress, the relationship between an indigenous assembly and the regional authorities was discussed. One of the Initiative Group faction's main concerns was that the government should not be able to silence the assembly or to remove people from it. According to Initiative Group leader Valentina Sovkina, they wanted 'a unitary, elected organ, and not just a new civil society organisation', independent, but 'not in the sense of a separate private institution' (Interview E). Interviews indicate that there was some conceptual confusion about what 'independence' actually meant in practice, as well as disagreement about how much 'independence' could realistically be achieved while still retaining real political influence (cf. Robbins Chapter 3 in this book). The word 'parliament' did not help to clarify matters.

> We do live in Russia, and we, the Russian citizens, already have a parliament. There can't be two independent parliaments in one country. ... an independent parliament means separation from the authorities. ... I understand this as an [NGO], of which we have a few already.

The opposition to the Initiative Group was centred on activists from a number of *obščiny* and the Lovozero NCA. This camp supported the authorities' suggested model of a Council that was not to be structurally independent, and subject to approval by the Governor.

The Congress majority eventually voted in favour of the Initiative Group's model. It also elected a group of individuals – the Council of Authorised Representatives of the Sámi (*Sovet upolnomočjonnykh predstavitelej saamov Murmanskoj Oblasti*, henceforth referred to by its Russian acronym 'SUPS') – which was to represent the Sámi until the holding of an envisioned Second Congress, which, it was hoped, could establish an officially recognised representative organ (SUPS 2008). The SUPS members were elected not as representatives of organisations or institutions but on an individual basis. Still, one can sum them up as people with backgrounds from AKS, OOSMO, one *obščina*, the Mončegorsk NCA and an individual who, at the time, worked for the Indigenous Centre. Valentina Sovkina was elected as their leader.

The regional authorities reacted negatively. Speaker Jevgenij Nikora of the regional parliament stated that 'ethnic parliaments are not possible in Russia. You can call it a parliament, but it will not have any real power,' (http://www.finnmarken no) and Nikolay Šuškin of the Legal Projects' Committee told journalists that:

> violations of procedure – participation in the voting by citizens of Sámi ethnicity who were not original delegates [to the Congress], has forced the organs of the executive power to consider this Congress rather [just] a gathering of citizens … we will work with them [SUPS] as we would with yet another civil society formation (*LP* 2008).

The First Congress had made its choice but the conflict was far from over.

The period 2004–8 begins with a 'downgrading' of the Sámi policy field: responsibility is delegated to a lower level of the Murmansk Region's state structures. We might have expected this to result in less attention to Sámi affairs but, instead, 2004–8 saw an increase in Sámi political activity. Under the Indigenous Centre, the Russian Sámi received their most genuinely representative advisory organ to date: through the Co-ordination Council, representatives of Sámi civil society organisations were included in a common, institutionalised governance network for the first time. The Co-ordination Council had little political influence but apparently functioned as a catalyst for non-governmental action: it brought representatives of different Sámi civil society formations together in a common forum, kick-starting the first genuinely large-scale campaign for a Russian Sámi Parliament. This common forum also brought to the fore internal antagonisms, and it caused increased friction between the authorities and the emergent pro-Parliament movement. In the end, the Centre/Council network could not carry the conflicts, and this system for including Sámi representatives was discontinued by the authorities.

2009–2014: The Sobbar and the Sovet

As 2008 came to a close, the Indigenous Centre no longer had a civil-society-based Co-ordination Council but a large gathering of Sámi had recently elected a group of people to represent them. This group, SUPS, consisted of activists who wanted a Russian Sámi Parliament, an idea to which the Murmansk Region authorities had expressed open antipathy.

The Indigenous Council (2009–present)

In February 2009, the regional government established an official advisory and participatory body of Sámi representatives: the Council of Representatives of Native, Small-Numbered Peoples of the North under the Government of

Murmansk Region (*Sovet predstaviteley korennykh maločislennykh narodov Severa pri pravitelstve Murmanskoy Oblasti*, 'Council of Representatives') aimed at the 'defence of rights and legal interests' of the Sámi. The *obščiny* were given the right to suggest members of the Council of Representatives and the regional government subsequently chose representatives from among the nominated. Each Council of Representatives works for a two-year period. Those who support this system for Sámi civil society inclusion hold the Council of Representatives to be a natural reply to the request of the First Congress for a Sámi representative council (Jakovleva 2013). Those who do not support it are of the opinion that the authorities should rather have accepted as Sámi representatives those individuals elected by the First Congress – that is, the SUPS.

Let us analyse the Council of Representatives, applying the criteria for representativeness presented earlier in this chapter. Regarding (1), the representatives are indeed anchored in Sámi civil society organisations, since members must be nominated by *obščiny*. However, the *obščiny* do not actually decide who shall represent them. This power lies with the regional government. There are currently 23 *obščiny* so there can, potentially, be a very large number of candidates to choose from, when the government chooses the nine council members. Governmental power is limited only by whom the *obščiny* choose to nominate. If an *obščina* is dissatisfied with its representative, it is free not to re-nominate this person; and if you are not nominated you cannot be chosen. The actual capacity of the Sámi *obščiny* to evaluate and remove representatives will vary from case to case. Many of them are too small to have a functioning organisational democracy, in practice consisting only of a few individuals.

Regarding (2), the *obščiny* cannot be said to constitute an adequate proxy demos for the mass of people that the Council of Representatives, according to its own statutes, is set to represent – the Sámi of Murmansk Region (http://gov.murman.ru D: Art. 1, 3.3, 4.1, 4.2, 4.5). The *obščiny* (a) are only of interest to Sámi who want to practise traditional economic activities; (b) take a lot of work to register and maintain; and (c) are, in practice, subject to a geographic limitation that excludes urban Sámi (*cf.* Berg-Nordlie 2015a). Most ethnic Sámi in Murmansk Region cannot and do not participate in the *obščina* sector of civil society. In sum, the Council of Representatives fulfils criterion (1) poorly and criterion (2) not at all.

However, this is not the entire 'recipe' for the Council of Representatives' formation: there is a tenth member: an ethnic Sámi from the Regional Public Chamber (*Obščestvennaja palata Murmanskoj oblasti*) (http://gov.murman.ru D: Art 1, 3.3, 4.1, 4.2, 4.5), which is another official structure for including civil society representatives in governance. The Public Chamber is constituted by 15 citizens selected by the governor; 15 representatives of regional civil-society formations, who are chosen on an individual basis by the regional parliament; and 15 representatives of local civil society formations who are selected by the 30 others (http://uma.murman.ru; Stuvøy 2013). The statutes of the Public Chamber do not, in fact, guarantee that there *are* any ethnic Sámi in this institution but in practice there have always been some – earlier three, presently two (Interviews

L and U). The presence of a Public Chamber-based Sámi increases the possibility for non-*obščina* Sámi to be represented. The first Sámi civil society representative chosen by the Public Chamber to the Council of Representatives (2009–11) was Julija Čuprova, associated with the Lovozero NCA that supported the authorities' model at the First Congress. The current (2011–present) is Andrej Jakovlev, who is associated with the *obščina* 'Puaz'. Jakovlev is currently the leader of the Council of Representatives.

The Council of Representatives' quarterly meetings are, in principle, open to the public. Making use of this opportunity, civil society activists from AKS and OOSMO have been present at many meetings. They are allowed to speak and to send in suggestions for items to be put on the meeting's agenda (Interviews K, V and W). The openness of the governance network is not limited to people who toe the line politically – for example, OOSMO's position is that the Council of Representatives should be expanded to include non-*obščina* representatives and that the representatives should be elected rather than selected, but they are allowed to participate nevertheless (Interview W). Even central pro-Parliament activists have been allowed to attend the council meetings. Furthermore, the council's working groups on fisheries (*rabočaja gruppa po rybolovstvu*) and on language revitalisation (*rabočaja gruppa po sokhraneniju saamskogo jazyka*) include members external to the *obščina* sector, among them pro-Parliament activists.

All these mechanisms that bring in non-*obščina* participants improve the representativeness of the council somewhat, but voting rights are still only given to the council's full members. Recommendations and initiatives from the council are formally decided on solely by these full council members, and it is also these who, together with the Indigenous Centre, decide who participate in the working groups (Interview U).

The regional authorities exert a high degree of metagovernance over the council. They determine the council's composition and, through its statutes, frame its tasks. The Indigenous Centre is tasked with 'organisational and technical' management of the council, which includes preparing the meeting agendas. The authorities furthermore participate directly in the council, as a regional government representative is to be present at their meetings (http://gov.murman. ru D). In practice, a vice-governor has filled this role. In addition, representatives of various government committees can be and are invited to council meetings as speaking guests, for example, the Civil Society Committee and the Fisheries' Committee (http://nord-news.ru). Participants in network governance elsewhere in Russia have underscored the importance of involving high-ranking politicians directly, in order for a governance network to obtain actual political influence (Tarasenko *et al.* 2011: 31–2). The direct participation of authorities can hence be a two-edged sword: it deprives the indigenous representatives of the opportunity to discuss matters and decide on issues alone, but it may also reduce the chances of being ignored by decision-makers (*cf.* Robbins, in this volume).

The Council of Representatives is, formally, only an advisory organ. Among issues that it has worked with are strengthening of the *obščiny* through subsidies from the region, and challenges regarding mechanisms for distributing indigenous fishing quotas to the Sámi. Much of their activity is oriented towards the funding programme 'Economic and Social Development of the Native, Small-Numbered Peoples of the North in Murmansk Region', which also funds the activities of the council (Jakovleva 2013). The council is entitled to advise the executive powers about who shall receive subsidies from this programme (Interviews L, U, V, W and X). As for the degree to which the council's advice is listened to, different interviewees give different replies. Some of those critical of the council dismiss it as purely symbolic/manipulative. Others, not least those who participate in the council, claim that it does wield actual influence, albeit over limited matters. Several interviewees suggest that the council and the Centre indeed have a decisive influence over who gets subsidies from the funding programme. On the whole, it seems unfair to say that the Council of Representatives is an entirely symbolic/manipulative structure, but nor can its advisory-participatory influence be called 'indigenous self-determination'. The Council of Representatives fulfils neither the 'determination' aspect (too little power) nor the 'self' aspect (not representative enough). The council is not actually *intended* to be an institution for self-determination – it is framed only as an advisory body, representing the interests of the Sámi community in political affairs – but it cannot be said to realise that ambition either, since it is not very representative.

The Sám' Sobbar (2010–present)

SUPS, the council elected at the First Congress, did not give up when the Council of Representatives was created. Immediately after the congress, its members began to seek recognition as the legitimate representatives of the Russian Sámi, both in Russia and in western Sápmi. They had some success in the West. In Nordic Sámi media, SUPS members made use of existing personal contacts to link up with pan-Sámi political networks and SUPS was from day one presented as an entity on its way to becoming a Russian Sámi Parliament. The Council of Representatives, on the other hand, initiated no cross-border co-operation with Nordic indigenous governance structures and received next to no Nordic media coverage. In Russia, SUPS was supported by RAIPON, who published an article after the First Congress that congratulated it for having 'founded a national representative organ – the Sámi Parliament, officially called the Council of Authorised Representatives' (Berg-Nordlie 2011: 27–8, 33–4 and 2014: 376, 383–5; http://www.raipon.info). In its relations with the regional authorities, SUPS fared much worse.

During the two years following the First Congress, SUPS did not succeed in convincing the regional government of the necessity of a Russian Sámi Parliament. When the time came for the Second Congress, the authorities did not organise any such event. In December 2010, SUPS instead organised their own 'Second Congress' in Murmansk City. Being organised by non-state actors, this congress could not establish any official representative body. Still, the participants elected what they would refer to in Russian as a *Saamskij parlament*, a Sámi Parliament. The term *Sámediggi* was not used for this assembly since that word is from North Sámi, a language not native to the Kola Peninsula. A Kildin Sámi (*cf.* Scheller

2011: 84, 86–8) name was instead chosen: *Kuèllnègknjoark Sám' Sobbar*, which refers back to the Imperial-era '*Koladak Sobbar*' discussed above. This assembly of Sámi was intended to be active for four years and work towards recognition by the authorities (SUPS 2010). Continuity from SUPS may be observed in the Sobbar through the presence of activists associated with AKS, OOSMO and the Mončegorsk NCA. Three of the SUPS members continued, in leading roles: Nina Afanas'jeva, Andrej Danilov and Valentina Sovkina (leader). The *Sobbar* furthermore included people active in the Russian branch of the international Sámi Womens' Forum, the youth organisation Sám' Nuraš, the Lovozero-based '*sovkhoz*' 'Tundra' and the *obščina* 'Jona'. While SUPS included one member who worked in the Indigenous Centre and one who was simultaneously a full member of the Council of Representatives, there were no such overlaps in the case of the Sobbar.

If we are to speak about the representativeness of the Sobbar, the body has its democratic 'anchor' not in civil-society organisations but in the congress that elected it. The next opportunity for voters to replace it would be a 'Third Congress' that the Sobbar aimed to hold by the end of 2014 (Interview X). If we return to our criteria for representativeness, we observe that (1) the Sobbar was indeed elected by a body claiming to represent the Russian Sámi, but (2) the degree to which the 'Second Congress' was valid as a proxy demos is disputed. On the one hand, most Russian Sámi did not have the opportunity to participate in it. On the other hand, several AKS and OOSMO members describe the 'Second Congress' as involving a large number of Sámi activists from various organisations and, hence, that it at least reflected Sámi civil society well. Nevertheless, the current leader of AKS (Jelena Jakovleva) has expressed doubts about the extent to which this congress was representative of the Russian Sámi (http://www.nrk.no B and C). The Sobbar's legitimacy as a representative of the Sámi may be said to have received a 'boost' during the Twentieth International Sámi Conference (Murmansk City, 2013) when the Russian delegation to the conference unanimously voted for the Kuellnegk Neark Declaration, which included a statement of support for the Sobbar. The Declaration did not ask the authorities to recognise the Sobbar as a 'Sámi Parliament', or as the sole representative organ of the Russian Sámi, but it did request them to treat the entity as a relevant civil society actor.[18] This was also backed by the AKS members of the Russian delegation, which included activists who were normally critical of the Sobbar, such as the AKS leader and the leader of the Council of Representatives.

In the period up to the fall of 2014 the Sobbar was not granted any formal political recognition. In fact, formally the Sobbar does not exist: there is no registered entity called *Kuellnegknjoark Sám' Sobbar*. Its members have not registered it as an NGO, partly because they wish for it to be accepted as an official body but also as a tactic to avoid harassment from authorities looking for 'foreign agents'

---

18. 'The Saami Conference supports the Kuellnegk Neark Sam Sobbar's efforts to build partnership with the regional government for sustainable cooperation between the Saami and the majority population in the Saami territory on Kola. The Saami Conference calls on the Governor of the Murmansk region to support the activity of Kuellnegk Neark Sam Sobbar' (SR 2013).

among critical NGOs. The Sobbar has established a legal leg to stand - the Fund for Sámi Heritage and Development (*Fond saamskogo nasledija i razvitija*), chaired by Sobbar member Andrej Danilov. This enables them to receive financial support and be formally involved in Sámi-oriented projects (Interview X). Apart from the fund, the Sobbar is an informal network of activists headed by Sovkina, Afanas'jeva and Danilov that works in opposition to the established system of indigenous governance in Murmansk Region. They criticise the indigenous politics of the region and the regional authorities treat them with relative disregard. There have been a few notable exceptions, for example, in August 2012, when a regional government media spokesperson accused the Sobbar of being foreign agents, financed and co-ordinated by the Norwegian Sámi Parliament (http://www.7x7-journal.ru). Sovkina, Afanas'jeva, Danilov and a fourth Sobbar member were explicitly named as facilitating conflict between the Sámi and the Russian state. These accusations fall in line with a general tendency in Russia for critical civil-society activists with ties to the West to be accused foreign agency (Aasland *et al.* 2013). In the Sobbar case there was no subsequent legal action, such as in the comparable Mosejev case in nearby Arkhangelsk Region (Barentsobserver.com C).

Despite this apparent rift between pro-Parliament activists and the authorities, when we apply a network governance perspective to the issue we observe that the wall between them is not entirely solid. Sobbar activists, either individually or representing the fund, attend the Council of Representatives' meetings as participating observers, just like AKS and OOSMO. While they cannot vote, this at least gives them the opportunity to speak in the governance network (Interviews V and X). According to Sovkina, representatives of the Civil Society Committee were invited to a conference arranged by Sobbar activists in Lovozero, and did indeed attend – even if this was right after the allegations of foreign agency (Interview X). Furthermore, Sobbar activists at times participate in arranging cultural events together with the Indigenous Centre and other state institutions. Most notable is still that Afanas'jeva and Danilov, who were accused of foreign agency by the Government's media spokesperson in 2012, were made respectively leader and secretary of the Council of Representatives' Working group on language preservation in 2013 (http://www.lovozerocentre.ru; http://www.mvestnik.ru). Naturally, since the Sobbar does not formally exist, this is all officially just the activities of two or three committed individuals. The Sobbar activists themselves, however, construct their political participation discursively as activities of the Sobbar.

In sum, despite there being some bursts of outright hostility in the relationship between the Sobbar and the different bodies under the region, the Sobbar activists are allowed to participate in policy-discussing and event-organising networks together with representatives of the state structures. It is difficult to call this 'manipulative inclusion', since the Sobbar activists appear entirely aware that the authorities do not take their opinions into account. Nor can it be called 'symbolic inclusion', since the authorities do not discuss the matter as 'including the Sobbar': quite the contrary, interviewees affiliated with the state structures underscore that, from their point of view, these are just individual Sámi activists and not representatives of any 'Sámi Parliament'. Perhaps it would be better to say that it is the Sobbar activists who are performing a sort of 'symbolic participation' – they utilise the symbolic value of participating in a governance network together with the authorities, as part of their campaign to demonstrate that they exist and are ready to assume the role of representatives of the Sámi.

Conclusion: Sámi representation in Murmansk Region

This chapter has attempted to answer the questions of how indigenous governance has developed in Murmansk Region 1992–2014; how inspiration from the Nordic indigenous governance model has impacted the region's indigenous politics; and if indigenous representation has improved.

The evolution of indigenous governance in Murmansk Region can be described as having undergone three distinct phases since the collapse of the USSR.

The first period (1992–2003) was characterised by indigenous governance structures that were unstable and understaffed and inclusion mechanisms for Sámi civil society that offered only poor representativeness. This was partly due to the authorities' failure to develop a system for representation more sophisticated than simply inviting individual leader figures to participate – but also because internal problems within Sámi civil society made it difficult for the Sámi population to evaluate and recall their representatives. For most of this period, AKS served as the proxy demos for the Sámi population. AKS was open to all Sámi citizens of Murmansk Region to become active members and, as such, could have made a decent proxy demos, but its internal democracy did not function well enough to ensure that Sámi representatives were truly dependent on support from below. By the end of the period, Russian Sámi civil society had fragmented so much that AKS alone could not be considered as an adequate approximation of Murmansk Region's Sámi population.

The second period (2004–8) saw the establishment of a new central institution for indigenous governance – placed at a lower level in the hierarchy but more stable in the sense that it was subject to less rapid reorganisation. This institution, the Indigenous Centre, created a system for indigenous inclusion that was fairly representative: it gathered the leaders of all Sámi civil-society formations in Murmansk Region into a Co-ordination Council. The combined memberships of all these organisations made for a rather broad and inclusive proxy demos, although the state of the internal democracy of each of the 18 participating organisations varied. While inclusive, the Coordination Council was not very politically influential. During this period, the future of Sámi governance in Russia came under explicit discussion, culminating in 2008 with a gathering called the First Congress of the Russian Sámi. That congress failed in the sense that no common solution was found between the authorities and the participants. The authorities also failed to perform effective metagovernance: they lost control over the proceedings at the congress, and the gathered non-state participants ended up demanding something that the authorities were not ready to give – a body of officially authorised Sámi representatives elected by Sámi citizens of Murmansk Region or, in other words, a Sámi Parliament for Murmansk Region.

The third period (2009–present) saw the establishment of a relatively stable indigenous inclusion structure that has more political influence than its predecessor but is weak in terms of representativeness. The Council of Representatives is chosen by the authorities and the only organisations allowed to nominate candidates are the *obščiny* – a far too narrow base to be considered an adequate proxy demos. Further arrangements allow other Sámi organisations the possibility of sending individuals to participate in the Sámi governance network but these are not given full rights.

Throughout all the three periods, a constant element of Murmansk Region's indigenous governance is active metagovernance from the side of the authorities. The authorities have always retained their freedom to select whom they should include in governance networks, except for 2004–8, when they bound themselves to include leaders or deputy leaders of Sámi civil society formations in the Co-ordination Council. Still, in both the Co-ordination Council and in today's Council of Representatives, the authorities framed the activities of the representation structures by controlling the means available to the councils, deciding their areas of activity, preserving their own power to set meeting agendas and participating directly.

Hence, while we observe a shift towards more of a network governance mode starting in 2004, the authorities still deal with included civil-society actors in a highly 'hands-on' manner. Therefore, while post-Soviet Sámi politics is elsewhere discussed in terms of 'AKS-unipolarity' (1989–98) and subsequent 'multipolarity' (1998–onwards) (Overland and Berg-Nordlie 2012: 102), we must recognise that this historical periodisation refers to conditions within Sámi *civil society*. In terms of official Sámi governance, the tendency has remained very 'unipolar' indeed, as the authorities hold the reins firmly. Nevertheless, we must conclude that the involvement of indigenous civil society that we see in 2014 is decidedly more broad and complex than what we observed at the outset of the period under analysis, when the mode of governance was even more strictly hierarchal and civil society inclusion rather weakly systemised.

Another constant element in Russian Sámi politics is the influence of the Sámi Parliament model. One notable consequence of the pro-Parliament activism is the creation of National Cultural Autonomies, cultural NGOs for urban Sámi, which evolved from a project aimed at founding a Russian Sámi Parliament. The Sámi Parliament model has also had a decisive impact on local conflict dynamics: Many Russian Sámi are inspired by the model and create political pressure from below to introduce it locally. This causes disagreements between Sámi activists – some of whom are more pragmatic and focused on 'Russian realities' in their discourse and outlook, whereas others have a more pronounced pan-Sámi and indigenous-rights-based ideological orientation. The disagreements are even more substantial between the latter activists and Murmansk Region's authorities, who have been very sceptical towards the Sámi Parliament model.

We observe an element of change in the degree of grassroots pressure for a Russian Sámi Parliament over time. While the idea had been present since the early 1990s, pressure from below peaked in 2008–10. Following this, a self-declared

'Sámi Parliament' has been operating without the authorities' approval. The intensified pro-Sámi-Parliament activism seems, at least partially, to be a result of the Murmansk authorities' establishment of the Co-ordination Council (2006–8). While this structure brought some internal disagreements to the fore, it also contributed to increased co-ordination between some civil society groups, particularly AKS and OOSMO, which facilitated the movement for a Russian Sámi Parliament. Despite the observed intensification of pro-Parliament activism, we must – if defining a Sámi Parliament as an official representative organ which is controlled by an assembly of Sámi who are elected by an adequate proxy demos – conclude that there still is no institution in Russia that could be considered a Sámi Parliament. If we look at some core functions of the *Sámedikkit*, we also find that there is no single institution in Russia that performs these. Representation of the Russian Sámi in international and particularly pan-Sámi affairs is mainly taken care of by AKS and OOSMO; the official voice of the Sámi minority *vis-à-vis* the authorities is the Council of Representatives; and as for a politically and symbolically unifying organ for the Murmansk Region Sámi, there exists at the time of writing no institution which is both democratically representative and politically relevant enough to fill this role.

On the whole, since the collapse of the USSR, the authorities of Murmansk Region have gradually created a more sophisticated system for indigenous participation in policy-making; but the political power of Sámi representatives is still low when compared to the other states that have indigenous Sámi populations, and there are no adequate mechanisms to ensure that the Sámi included in official indigenous governance networks are representative of Murmansk Region's Sámi population.

Abbreviations and shorthand names

AKS: *Associjacija Kol'skikh Saamov* Association of Kola Sámi. Murmansk-City-centred NGO (est.1989). RAIPON member.

Co-ordination Council: *Koordinacjonnyj sovet pri gosudarstvennom oblastnom učreždenii 'Murmanskij oblastnoj centr korennykh maločislennykh narodov Severa'*. Advisory council established by Indigenous Centre, 2006–8. Constituted by representatives of all Sámi civil-society organisations in Murmansk Region.

Congresses: *S"jezdy korennogo maločislennogo naroda Rossijskoj Federatsii (Saamov) proživajuščego v Murmanskoj oblasti*. Sámi congresses. First Congress of elected Sámi delegates held in Olenegorsk, 2008, organised by Indigenous Centre, selected SUPS. 'Second Congress' held in Murmansk City in 2010, organised by non-state actors, elected Sobbar.

Council of Representatives: *Sovet predstavitelej korennykh maločislennykh narodov Severa pri pravitelstve Murmanskoj Oblasti*. Council of *obščina* representatives (est. 2009) by Governor to advise government on Sámi policy.

Indigenous Centre: *Gosudarstvennoje Oblastnoje [Bjudžetnoje] Učreždenije 'Centr korennykh maločislennykh narodov Severa'*. Institution (est. 2004) by regional authorities to assist in creation, co-ordination, and execution of Sámi policy.

Indigenous Issues Committee: *Komitet po delam korennykh maločislennykh narodov Severa*. Committee for Sámi affairs under the government of Murmansk Region, 1992–1997. Replaced by Indigenous Sector.

Indigenous Problems' Committee: *Komitet po problemam korennykh maločislennykh narodov Severa*. Responsible for indigenous governance 2000–2. Merged with other committees in 2002. From 2004, Indigenous Centre new central institution for indigenous governance.

Indigenous Sector: *Otdel po delam korennykh narodov Severa*. Responsible for indigenous governance 1997–2000. Reorganised into Indigenous Problems' Committee.

Initiative Group: *Iniciativnaja gruppa po sozdaniju Parlamenta saami Murmanskoj oblasti*. Initiative group for Russian Sámi Parliament (2008). Worked for realisation of Russian Sámi Parliament and suggested creation of SUPS.

NCA ('Autonomies'): *Nacional'no-kul'turnye avtonomii*. National-cultural autonomies, City-based, non-territorial NGOs (Apatity, Lovozero, Mončegorsk) to protect Sámi culture and identity (first est. 2007).

Obščiny: Kin-/community-based non-commercial membership organisations for indigenous people, aimed at the preservation of traditional lifestyles. First Sámi *obščina* (est. 2002).

OOSMO: *Obščestvennaja organizacija saamov Murmanskoj Oblasti*. NGO of Murmansk Region Sámi. Lovozero-centred NGO (est. 1998).

RAIPON, Russian Association of Indigenous Peoples of the North: *Associjatsija korennykh maločislennykh narodov Severa, Sibiri i Dal'nego Vostoka Rossijskoj Federatsii*. Indigenous NGO umbrella organisation (est. 1990) with headquarters in Moscow. AKS was founding member.

Sám' Nuraš: Russian Sámi youth organisation, (est. 2009).

Sobbar: *Saamskij parlament, Kuèllnègknjoark Sám' Sobbar*. Elected 2010 by 'Second Congress' to represent Russian Sámi.

SUPS; *Sovet upolnomočjonnykh predstavitelej saamov Murmanskoj Oblasti*. Elected 2008 by First Congress to represent Sámi. Replaced by Sobbar 2010

References

2004.murman.ru: *O delakh korennykh maločislennykh narodov Severa Murmanskoj oblasti*: http://2004.murman.ru/power/exepower/depart_comit/departament_zakonoproekt/o_delah.shtml (accessed May 2015).

7x7-journal.ru: *9 avgusta vo vsio m mire otmečajut den' korennykh narodov mira. No v Murmanske*: http://7x7-journal.ru/item/20144 (accessed May 2015).

Aasland, Aa., Berg-Nordlie, M. and Holm-Hansen, J. (2013) 'Hva skjer med det russiske sivilsamfunnet?', *Klassekampen* 6 May 2013.

Alymov, V. K. (2006) 'Om samernas assimilering', in L. Rantala (ed) *Dokument om de ryska samera och Kolahalvön*, Rovaniemi: Lapin yliopistopaino.

Anaya, J. (2011) *Report of the Special Rapporteur on the Rights of Indigenous Peoples, James Anaya*. Addendum. The situation of the Sami people in the Sápmi region of Norway, Sweden and Finland, United Nations Human Rights Council Eighteenth Session, Agenda Item 3.

Arnstein, S. (1969) 'A ladder of citizen participation', *Journal of the American Institute of Planners* 35(4): 216–24.

Barentsobserver.com (2013A) 'Crackdown on RAIPON spurs international concern': http://barentsobserver.com/en/arctic/crackdown-raipon-spurs-international-concern-15-11 (accessed 13 October 2013).

— (2013B) 'Moscow staged RAIPON election thriller': http://barentsobserver.com/en/politics/2013/04/moscow-staged-raipon-election-thriller-03-04 (accessed May 2015).

— (2012C) 'Pomor brotherhood?': http://barentsobserver.com/en/opinion/2012/11/pomor-brotherhood-22-11 (accessed May 2015).

Berg-Nordlie, M. (2011) 'Need and misery in the eastern periphery. Nordic Sámi discourses on the Russian Sámi', *Acta Borealia* 28(1): 19–36.

— (2013) 'The Iron Curtain through Sápmi. Pan-Sámi politics, Nordic cooperation and the Russian Sámi', in K. Andersson (ed.) *L'image du Sápmi II, Études comparées. Textes réunis par Kajsa Andersson. Humanistica Oerebroensia. Artes et linguae*, Örebro: Örebro University.

— (2015a) 'Representasjon i Sápmi. Fire stater, fire tilnærminger til inklusjon av urfolk i samstyring', in B. Bjerkli and P. Selle (eds) *Den Samepolitiske Utviklingen på 2000-tallet*, Oslo: Gyldendal.

— (2015b) 'Two centuries of Russian Sámi policy: arrangements for autonomy and. participation seen in light of Imperial, Soviet and Federal indigenous minority policy 1822–2014', *Acta Borealia* 32(1): 40–67.

Bergh, J. and Saglie, J. (2015) 'Partisystem og skillelinjer i samepolitikken', in B. Bjerkli and. P. Selle (eds) *Samer, Makt og Demokrati. Sametinget og den nye samiske offentligheten*. Oslo: Gyldendal.

Bjerkli, B. and P. Selle (2003) 'Sametinget – kjerneinstitusjonen innenfor den nye samiske offentligheten', in B. Bjerkli and P. Selle (eds) *Samer, Makt og Demokrati. Sametinget og den nye samiske offentligheten*. Oslo: Gyldendal.

Bol'šakova, N. (2005) *Žizn', obyčai i mify kol'skikh saamov v prošlom i nastojaščem*. Murmansk: Murmanskoje Knižnoje Izdatel'stvo.

Broderstad, E. G. (2003) 'Urfolksinnflytelse i en ny europeisk kontekst', in B. Bjerkli and P. Selle (eds.) *Samer, Makt og Demokrati. Sametinget og den nye samiske offentligheten*, Oslo: Gyldendal.

Broderstad, E. G., Hernes, H.-K. and S. Jenssen (2015) 'Konsultasjoner – prinsipper og gjennomføring', in B. Bjerkli and P. Selle (eds) *Samer, Makt og Demokrati. Sametinget og den nye samiske offentligheten*, Oslo: Gyldendal.

Bækken, H. (2009) *Selective law enforcement against Russian NGOs. Pursuing informal interests through formal means*, unpublished Master's thesis, European and American Studies, Faculty of Humanities, University of Oslo.

Davies, J. S. (2011) *Challenging Governance Theory. From network to hegemony*, Bristol: Policy Press.

Docs.pravo.ru (A) *Murmanskaja oblast', Postanovlenie ot 06 janvarja 1993 goda No 4, O struktura administracii Murmanskoj oblasti:* http://docs.pravo. ru/document/view/13258466/?&mode=full (accessed May 2015).

—   (B) *Murmanskaja oblast', Postanovlenie ot 06 sentabrja 1994 goda No 379, Ob utverždenii položenija o komitete po delam korennykh narodov Severa administracii oblasti:* http://docs.pravo.ru/document/ view/13259062/ (accessed May 2015).

—   (C) *Postanovlenie ot 28 fevralja 2000 goda No 10-PP Ob utverždenii položenija o Komitete po problemam korennykh maločislennykh narodov severa administracii Murmanskoj oblasti:* http://docs.pravo.ru/document/ view/13257959/?&line_id=1 (accessed May 2015).

Duma.murman.ru: *Zakon Murmanskoj oblasti No 996-01-3MO 'Ob obščestvennoj palate Murmanskoj oblasti':* http://www.duma.murman. ru/representatives/chamber/ (accessed May 2015).

Falch, T. and P. Selle (2015) 'Staten og Sametinget', in B. Bjerkli and P. Selle (eds) *Den samepolitiske utviklingen på 2000-tallet*, Oslo: Gyldendal.

Federal List of Traditional Places (*Perečen' mest tradicionnogo proživanija i tradicionnoj khozjajsvtvennoj dejatel'nosti KMN RF*): http://giod. consultant.ru/page.aspx?1;1013127 (accessed May 2015).

Finnmarken.no: *Vil ha russisk sameting:* http://www.finnmarken.no/Utenriks/ article4020187.ece (accessed May 2015).

First Congress Document (*Položenije o porjadke organizacii i provedenija pervogo s''jezda korennogo maločislennogo naroda Rossijskoj Federacij (saamov) prozivajuščego v Murmanskoj oblasti*).

FNSSE (2005): *Nordisk samekonvensjon, utkast fra finsk-norsk-svensk-samisk ekspertgruppe, avgitt 26, oktober 2005.*

Gavrilov, S. (2009) *Mnenie delegata S''jezda saamov:* http://saamisups.ucoz.ru/ publ/2-1-0-11. (accessed May 2015).

Gov-Murman.ru (A) *Kratkaja informacija ob obščestvennykh organizacijakh, obščinakh, nacional'nykh preprijatiakh:* http://www.gov-murman.ru/ region/saami/short_info/ (accessed May 2015).

—   (B) *GOBU 'Murmanskij centr narodov severa':* http://www.gov-murman. ru/region/saami/mcns/ (accessed May 2015).

—   (C) *Položenie o koordicionnom sovete pri gosudarstvennom oblastnom učreždenii 'Murmanskij oblastnoj centr korennykh maločislennykh narodov severa':* http://gov-murman.ru/natpers/centre/position/ (accessed May 2015).

—   (D) *Postanovlenie o sovete predstaviteleh korennykh maločislennykh narodov Severa pri pravitel'stve Murmanskoj oblasti:* http://www. gov-murman.ru/region/saami/convocation/ (accessed May 2015).

Gutsol, N. and L. Riabova (2002) 'Russian Sámi and regional development', in Karppi, K. and J. Eriksson (eds) *Conflict and Cooperation in the North*, Umeå: Norrlands Universitetsforlag.

HREOC (2008) *Building a Sustainable National Indigenous Representative Body – Issues for consideration*, Human Rights and Equal Opportunity Commission of the Aboriginal and Torres Strait Islander Social Justice Commissioner.

Infonor (year not given) *Den juridiske gennemgang av Den hvide ren III*.

— (2008) *Avsluttende rapport. UM j.nr.104.N.548.b.1 (12.10.08)*.

Indigenous Centre (2006) *Koordinacjonnij sovet pri gosudarstvennom oblastnom učreždenii 'Murmanskij oblastnoj centr korennykh maločislennykh narodov Severa'*.

— (2011) *Ustav gosudarstvennogo oblastnogo učrezhdenija 'Murmanskij oblastnoj centr korennykh maločislennkh narodov severa'*.

Indigenous Centre Charter: *Ustav gosudarstvennogo oblastnogo učreždenija 'Murmanskij oblastnoj centr korennykh maločislennykh narodov severa'*.

Initiative Group (2008) *Projekt: Položeniye o sovete upolnomochjonnykh predstavitelej saamov murmanskoj oblasti (saamskom parlamente)*.

Hætta, O. H. (2003) 'Urfolks organisering og status 1975–2003', HiF-rapport 2003: 11.

IWGIA (1996) *The Indigenous World 1995–96*, Copenhagen: IWGIA.

Jakovleva, Je. S. (2013) *Informacija E. S. Jakovlevoj, prezidenta Obščestvennoj organizacii Murmanskoj oblasti 'Associacii kol'skikh saamov' na konferencii saamskikh parlamanteriev. Sovet predstavitelej korennykh narodov Severa pri Pravitel'stve Murmanskoj oblasti*.

Josefsen, E. (2008) 'Stat, region og urfolk – Finnmarksloven og politisk makt', in Hernes, H-K. and N. Oskal (eds) *Finnmarksloven*, Oslo: Cappelen Damm.

Josefsen, E., Mörkenstam, U. and Saglie, J. (2015) 'Different institutions within similar states: The Norwegian and Swedish *Sámediggis*', *Ethnopolitics* 14(1): 32–51.

Kalstad, J. A. (2009) *Dorogoj Nadežd. Politika Rossijskogo gosudarstva i položenie saamskogo naroda v Rossii (1864–2003)*, Murmansk: Murmanskoje Knižnoye Izdatel'stvo (based on notes by indicated author, written by I. B. Cirkunov).

Kal'te, Z. M. (1995). 'Saamskiyj parlament: Poslednij šans?', in *Poljarnaya Pravda 18.07.95*.

— (2003) *Politiko-pravovye aspekty razvitija korennogo maločislennogo naroda Rossijskoj Federacii – Saami. Dissertacija na soiskanie učenoj stepeni kandidata političeskikh nauk*, Political science dissertation at the Russian Academy of State Agencies under the President of the Russian Federation, Faculty of National and Federal Relations.

KMNS Law: Federal law *O garantijakh prav korennykh maločislennykh narodov Rossijskoy Federacii*.

Konstantinov, Y. and V. Vladimirova (2006) 'The performative machine: transfer of ownership in a northwest Russian reindeer herding community (Kola Peninsula)', *Nomadic Peoples* 10(2): 166–86.

Krjažkov, V. A. (2010) *Korennye maločislennye narody Severa v Rossijskom prave*, Moskva: Izdatel'stvo NORMA.

— (2012) 'Rossijskoje zakonodatel'stvo o severnykh narodakh i pravoprimenitel'naja praktika: sosjtojanie i perspektivy', *Gosudarstvo i Pravo* 5: 27–35.

Larsson-Kalvemo, A. (1995) *Fighting for Survival. Överlevelsesstrategier i nye omständigheter bland samerna på Kolahalvön*, Hovedfagsoppgave, Sosialantropologi, Universitetet i Tromsø.

Ledeneva, A. V. (2013) *Can Russia Modernise?* Sistema, *power networks and informal governance*, Cambridge: Cambridge University Press.

Lindi, G. E. E. (2005) *Tema: Kvinnebevegelsen*: http://sapmi.uit.no/sapmi/ ExhibitionContainer.do?type=tema (accessed 7 May 2013).

Lovozerocentre.ru: *V Murmanskoj oblasti idjot rabota po sokhraneniju saamskogo jazyka.* http://lovozerocentre.ru/index.php?option=com_ content&view=article&id=106: 2013-08-14-15-28-40&catid=34:center news (accessed 14 October 2013).

LP (1989) *Ustav Associatsii kol'skikh saamov* (*Lovozerskaja Pravda 09.09.1989*).

— (2007) *Natsional'noj kultur'noj avtonomii – byt'!* (*Lovozerskaja Pravda, 30.03.07*).

— (2008) *Sijt sobbar – sto let spustja* (*Lovozerskaja Pravda 26.12.08*)..

Mikkelsen, C. (2010, ed.) *The Indigenous World 2010*, Copenhagen: IWGIA.

Murmansk.news-city.info (A) *Postanovlenie administracii Murmanskoj oblasti ot 06.01.1993 'O strukture administracii Murmanskoj oblasti' (vmeste s 'Perečnem otdelov, upravnelij i komitetov administracii oblasti, finansirujemykh za sčet sredtsvt oblastnogo bjudžeta, s predel'noj čislenost'ju rabontikov'*: http://murmansk.news-city.info/docs/sistemsj/ dok_oeqxei.htm (accessed May 2015).

— (B) *Postanovlenie Administracii Murmanskoj oblasti ot 06.09.1994, N 379 'Ob utverždenii položenija o komitete po delam korennykh narodov severa administracii oblasti'*: http://murmansk.news-city.info/docs/ sistemsb/dok_oeqdoi.htm (accessed May 2015).

— (C) *Rešenie Murmanskogo oblastnogo Soveta ot 27.04.1993 N 79 'O sostojanii raboty po predostavleniju zemel'nykh učastkov i ikh prodaže na territorii oblasti i merakh po eio uskorenieu' (vmeste s 'Položeniem o porjadke vozbuždenija i rassmotrenija khodatajstv o predostavlenii zemel'nykh učastkov')*: http://murmansk.news-city.info/docs/sistemsj/ dok_oeqxwo.htm (accessed May 2015).

— (D) *Postanovlenie gubernatora Murmanskoj oblasti ot 23.06.1997 N 294 'O komitete po delam korennykh narodov severa administracii Murmanskoj oblasti'*: http://murmansk.news-city.info/docs/sistemsy/ dok_oeyozo.htm (accessed May 2015).

— (E) *Postanovlenie Gubernatora Murmanskoj oblasti ot 11.03.2001 N 97-PG 'Ob èkspertno-koordinacionnom sovete po realizacii regional'nykh social'nykh programm v interesakh sem'i i detstva pri acministracii Murmanskoj oblasti'*: http://murmansk.news-city.info/docs/sistemsn/dok_oeygni.htm (accessed May 2015).

— (F) *Postanovlenie Gubernatora Murmanskoj oblasti ot 09.01.2001 N 14-PG 'O predsedatele komiteta po problemam korennykh maločislennykh narodov severa administracii Murmanskoj oblasti'*: http://murmansk.news-city.info/docs/sistemsh/dok_oeyysb.htm (accessed May 2015).

— (G) *Postanovlenie Pravitel'stva Murmanskoj oblasti ot 28.02.200 N 10-PP 'Ob utverždenii položenija o komitete po problemam korennykh maločislennykh narodov severa administracii Murmanskoj oblasti'*: http://murmansk.news-city.info/docs/sistemsh/dok_oeydeb.htm (accessed May 2015).

— (H) *Postanovlenie Administracii Murmanskoj oblasti ot 14.04.1998 N 130 'Ob utverždenii sostava soveta po realizacii regional'nykh social'nykh programm v interesakh sem'i i detstva administracii Murmanskoj oblasti'*: http://murmansk.news-city.info/docs/sistemsy/dok_oeyati.htm (accessed May 2015).

— (I) *Postanovlenie Pravitel'stva Murmanskoj oblasti ot 08.07.2004 N 232-PP /7 'O sozdanii gosudarstvennogo oblastnogo ucreždenija 'Murmanskij oblastnoj centr korennykh maločislennykh narodov severa'*: http://murmansk.news-city.info/docs/sistemsz/dok_ieqasb.htm (accessed May 2015).

Mvestnik.ru: *Gostej potčevali saamskoj ukhoj*: http://www.mvestnik.ru/shwpgn.asp?pid=201308108 (accessed May 2015).

NCA Law: Federal law '*O nacional'no-kultur'noj avtonomii*'.

Nord-news.ru: *Sovet korennykh maločislennykh narodov Severa sovmestno s komitetom rybokhozjaistvennogo kompleksa*: http://www.nord-news.ru/murman_news/2012/04/11/?newsid=28982 (accessed May 2015).

Nrk.no (A) *Kola-samer vil ha eget sameting*: http://img.nrk.no/kanal/nrk_sami_radio/1.6206117 (accessed May 2015).

— (B) *Sterke kvinner uenige om sameting*: http://www.nrk.no/kanal/nrk_sapmi/1.7563483 (accessed May 2015).

— (C)–*Hva skal vi med et Sameting?*: http://nrk.no/kanal/nrk_sapmi/1.7565691 (accessed May 2015) (accessed May 2015).

Nyyssönen, J. (2015) 'Det samiske etablissamentet og motmobiliseringen – konflikter om etniske kategorier i Finland' in Bjerkli, B. and P. Selle (eds) *Den samepolitiske utviklingen på 2000-tallet*, Oslo: Gyldendal.

Obščina Law: Federal law '*Ob obščikh principakh organizacij obščin KMN Severa, Sibiri i Dal'nego Vostoka Rossijskoj Federatsij*.

OOSMO (year not given) *Proyekt 'Saamskiy Parlament Kol'skikh Saamov'*, (project document).

Osipov, A. (2010) 'National cultural autonomy in Russia: a case of symbolic law', *Review of Central and East European Law* 35(1): 27–57.

Overland, I. N. (1999) *Politics and Culture Among the Russian Sami. Leadership, representation and legitimacy*, PhD dissertation, Scott Polar Research Institute, University of Cambridge.

Overland, I. and Berg-Nordlie, M. (2012) *Bridging Divides. Ethno-political leadership among the Russian Sámi*, New York: Berghahn Books.

Pettersen, T. (2014) 'The Sámediggi electoral roll in Norway 1989–2009: basis, growth and geographical shifts', in this volume.

Rantala, L. (2004) *Samerådet 50 år*.

— (2009) *Inlägg i Murmansk 02.10.2009*.

Raipon.info: *Saami*: http://www.raipon.info/index.php/narody/narody-severa-sibiri-i-dalnego-vostoka-rf/252-2009-08-20-13-54-58 (accessed May 2015).

Raipon.org: *Drugie obschestvenniye organizacii KMNSS i DV RF*: http://www.raipon.org/АКМНССиДВРФ/ДругиеобщественныеорганизацииКМHC/tabid/297/Default.aspx (accessed May 2015).

Regnum.ru: *V murmanskoj oblasti skončalsia Nikolaj Bogdanov, èkspert po voprosam saamov*: http://www.regnum.ru/news/1333529.html (accessed May 2013).

Robbins, J. (2011) 'Indigenous representative bodies in Northern Europe and Australia', in G. Minnerup and P. Solberg (eds) *First Worlds, First Nations. Internal colonialism and indigenous self-government in Northern Europe and Australia*, Brighton, Portland, OR and Toronto: Sussex Academic Press.

Røiseland, A. and S. I. Vabo (2012) *Styring og samstyring – governance på norsk*, Bergen: Fagbokforlaget.

Šaršina, N. and Je. Jakovleva (2010) *Pervyj s''jezd saamov Rossii: Doroga k realizatsii vozmožnostey, 2008*: http://www.saminissonforum.org/norsk/?p=315 (accessed May 2015).

Semb, A. J. (2015) 'Internasjonal rett og nasjonal politikk – Finnmarksloven', in B. Bjerkli and P. Selle (eds) *Den samepolitiske utviklingen på 2000-tallet*, Oslo: Gyldendal.

Scheller, E. (2011) 'The Sámi language situation in Russia', *Uralica Helsingensia* 5: 79–96.

Schmidt, L; Guttu, J. and L. Knudtzon (2011) *Medvirkning i planprosessen i Oslo kommune. NIBR-rapport* 2011: 11.

Selle, P. (2011) *Sametingets organisatoriske utfordringer. Ei vurdering*: Bergen/Alta-Álta: Bergen University /Norut Alta – Áltá.

Selle, P. and Strømsnes, K. (2015) 'Sivilsamfunnet og Sametinget som «støvsuger»' in B. Bjerkli and P. Selle (eds) *Den samepolitiske utviklingen på 2000-tallet*, Oslo: Gyldendal.

Skogvang, S. F. (2005) *Samerett. 2. utgave*. Oslo: Universitetsforlaget.

Sovkina, V (2008) *Saamskij Parlament*.

SPR (2008) *Samisk parlamentarisk råds virksomhetsplan 1.11.2008–31.12.2010*.

SR (1980) *Samepolitisk program*.

— (1987) *Samernas XIII konferens. Åre 13.–15.8.1986. Skandinavisk upplaga*.

—   (1994) *Samernas 15. konferens, Helsinki 15.–17.6.1992.*
—   (1997) *Samernas 16. konferens. Murmansk 15.–18.10.1996.*
—   (2013) *The 20th Saami conference 2 to 4 May 2013, Murmansk, Russia, The Kuellnegk Neark Declaration.*
Stammler, F. (2005) 'The *Obščina* movement in Yamal: defending territories to build identities?', in E. Kasten (ed.) *Rebuilding Identities. Pathways to reform in Post-Soviet Siberia*, Berlin: Dietrich Reimer Verlag.
Stepanov, V. (2012) '*Kritičeskij analiz programmy Vserossijskoj perepisi naselenija. 2010.*' *Demoskop Weekly* No. 531–532. http://www. demoscope.ru/weekly/2012/0531/analit01.php.
Stuvøy, K. (2013) 'Stat og sivilt samfunn i postsovjetisk Russland: betydningen av utenlandsk støtte og nye samhandlingsformer', *Nordisk Østforum* 27: 377–400.
SUPS (2008) *Resoljucija Pervogo S"jezda saamov Murmanskoj oblasti,* Saamisups.ucoz.ru: http://saamisups.ucoz.ru/publ/2-1-0-5 (accessed May 2015).
—   (2010) *Resheniye Vtorogo S"yezda korennogo malochislennogo naroda severa Murmanskoy oblasti – Saami.* Saamisups.ucoz.ru: http:// saamisups.ucoz.ru/publ/vtoroj_sezd_saamov_murmanskoj_oblasti/ reshenie/4-1-0-36 (accessed May 2015).
Sørensen, E. and J. Torfing (2009) 'Making governance networks effective and democratic through network governance', *Public Administration* 87(1): 234–258.
Tanner, V. (1929) *Antropogeografiska studier inom Petsamo-området.* I. Skolt- lapparna, Fennia 49: Helsingfors
Tarasenko, A. Dubrovskiy, D. and A. Starodubcev (2011) *Navesti mosty meždu obščestvom i gosudarstvom. Obščestvenno-konsul'tativnye struktury v regionakh Severo-Zapada*, St Peterburg: CNSR.
Torfing, J., Sørensen, E. and Fotel, T. (2009) 'Democratic anchorage of infrastructure governance networks: the case of the Femern Belt Forum', *Planning Theory* 8(3): 282–308.
Törnquist, O. (2009) 'Introduction: the problem is representation!', in O. Törnquist, N. Webster and K. Stokke (eds) *Rethinking Popular Representation*, New York: Palgrave Macmillan.
Utvik, U. K. (1985) *Kolasamene. Fra tsarens undersåtter til sovjetiske borgere*, Masters dissertation, Bergen University.
Vinogradova, S. N. (2005) *Saami kol'skogo poluostrova: osnovnye tendencii sovremennoj žizni.* Apatity: KNC RAN.
Vladimirova, V. (2006) 'Just labor. Labor ethic in a post-Soviet reindeer herding community', *Acta Universitatis Upsaliensis, Uppsala Studies in Cultural Anthropology* 40, Uppsala: Uppsala Universitet.
Wessendorf, K. (2005) (ed.) *An Indigenous Parliament? Realities and perspectives in Russia and the Circumpolar North*, Copenhagen: IWGIA Document No. 116.

Winsvold, M, Stokke, K. B., Klausen, J. E. and Saglie, I. L. (2009) 'Organisational learning and governance in adaption in urban development', in W. N. Agder, I. Lorenzoni and K. O'Brien (eds) *Adapting to Climate Change: Thresholds. Values. Governance.* Cambridge: Cambridge University Press, pp. 476–40.

Interviews

A: Nina Afanas'jeva, AKS-leader (1991–2010), member of Initiative Group, SUPS and Sobbar. Murmansk, 23 November 2009.

B: Nina Afanas'jeva. Murmansk, 1 May 2010.

C: Aleksandr Kobelev, OOSMO leader (1998–2008), member of Initiative Group and SUPS. Lovozero, 26 April 2010.

D: Jelena Jakovleva, AKS leader (2010–present), Initiative Group member, former leader, *obščina* 'Kil'din'. Murmansk, 3 May 2010.

E: Valentina Sovkina, Leader of Initiative Group, SUPS and Sobbar. Lovozero, 26 April 2010.

F: Anna Afanas'jeva, Leader of Sám' Nuraš (2009–10). Murmansk, 22 April 2010.

G: Natal'ja Gavrilova, Leader, Apatity and Regional Sámi NCA. Apatity, 23 April 2010.

H: Andrej Agejev, Leader, Indigenous Centre 2004–9 and Co-ordination Council 2006–8. Murmansk, 22 April 2010.

I: Sámi civil-society activist, spring 2010.

J: Je. Jakovleva. Murmansk, 24 November 2011.

K: Je. Jakovleva. Murmansk, 24 April 2010.

L: Andrej Jakovlev, member *obščina* 'Puaz', Public Chamber, leader Indigenous Council (2011–13). Murmansk, 3 May 2013.

M: Claus Oreskov, aid organisation 'Infonor'. Internet, 26 April 2010.

N: Mončegorsk NCA. Mončegorsk, 24 April 2010.

O: Anna Prakhova, Vice-President RAIPON (1994), elected AKS leader in one of the 1995 elections but did not become leader (*cf,* Overland and Berg-Nordlie 2012), member Initiative Group and SUPS. Murmansk, 5 January 2010.

P: Viktor Ignatienko, Vice-Leader, Indigenous Centre. Murmansk, 22 April 2010.

Q: Sámi civil-society activist, spring 2010 spring 2010.

R: Sámi civil-society activist, spring 2010.

S: Sovkina. Lovozero, 26 November 2009.

T: Nina Šaršina, Delegate, First Congress. Lovozero, 26 November 2009.

U: Je. Jakovleva. Murmansk, 23 April 2013.

V: Nadežda Čuprova, Leader of the Indigenous Centre. Murmansk, 25 April 2013.

W: Dinara Skavronskaja, leader OOSMO (2006–present) and Boris Skavronskij, lawyer for OOSMO. Murmansk, 2 April 2013.

X: Sovkina. Murmansk, 19 April 2013.

Chapter Ten

Semi-Autonomy: Contemporary Challenges for Indigenous Peoples in Brazil

Einar Braathen and Cássio Inglez de Sousa[1]

Introduction

The indigenous peoples in contemporary Brazil are the survivors of a long process of attempted annihilation, resulting from colonisation efforts by the Portuguese. The process was continued by successive Brazilian governments after independence in 1822. Indigenous peoples have been subjected to genocide through the physical elimination of various populations as well as ethnocide through processes of forced assimilation (see Stavenhagen 1991).

According to the 2010 national census, Brazil has a population of 896,900 self-defined indigenous people. The indigenous population has been growing steadily for the past 20 years and the national census data from the year 2000 and 2010 showed an increase of the indigenous population by 11 per cent. This can be attributed both to improvements in data-collection and to natural population growth (Azevedo 2011).[2] In addition, more people are recognising and declaring themselves as indigenous.[3] This is a new and positive development in Brazilian society, especially considering the gloomy prospects under the military dictatorship from 1964 to 1985, when indigenous people were believed to be doomed to extinction.

The big shift in the history of the indigenous people in Brazil came with the new democratic constitution of 1988 (Souza Lima 1995; Cardoso de Oliveira 1996; Baniwa 2006). For the first time, indigenous people obtained the same civic,

1. The authors want to thank Mikkel Berg-Nordlie and Ann Sullivan for detailed comments and Clarisse Carvalho Figueiredo, Ana Lucia Lennert da Silva, Diana Oliveira and Celina Myrann Sørbøe for assistance with different drafts of the article.

2. The national census in 2000 registered 760,000 indigenous citizens in Brazil, of whom 450,000 lived inside the indigenous territories and 310.000 outside. However, pro-indigenous NGOs criticised the methodology of the census and estimated the true total figure to be 1.2 million.

3. In Brazil, the anthropologists refer to *povos indígenas emergentes*, or 're-emerging indigenous peoples' when describing people who, at a given historical moment, ceased to recognise themselves as indigenous but who, in a new historical context, reaffirm their indigenous identity. In Latin America, ethno-historians define these processes as 'ethnogenesis', through which indigenous peoples create or recreate themselves as distinct, non-western cultures (Corr and Vieira Powers 2012). In Brazil, recent processes of ethno-genesis have taken place in various regions, above all in the north-east.

political, economic and social rights as everybody else in Brazil. Furthermore, the 1988 constitution guaranteed to grant special protection to indigenous people, their cultures and their livelihoods. The *Terras Indígenas* (Indigenous Lands) were established, with exclusive rights of residence and use of the natural resources for indigenous communities. By the end of the 1990s, an intensive process of territorial delimitation had been carried out (Santilli 1999), resulting in nearly 600 Indigenous Lands being established. Today, these territories cover 12.5 per cent of the Brazilian territory (106.7 million ha), including almost one-fourth of the Amazonian regions. According to the 2010 census, 517,400 people or 57.7 per cent of the total indigenous population in Brazil reside in these Indigenous Lands (ISA 2012).

The establishment of the Indigenous Lands and their occupation by indigenous communities is providing a sense of self-determination or semi-autonomy. The indigenous people enjoy exclusive occupancy rights but not administrative sovereignty over the Indigenous Lands, as the territory is owned by the Brazilian state and not the communities themselves (Inglez de Sousa, 2010a). While the indigenous people inhabiting these territories have exclusive surface usage rights in order to continue and maintain their traditional ways of life and practices, they face restrictions regarding some economic activities, such as tourism, forest-management and large-scale agriculture. They cannot exploit the subterranean resources (such as minerals), because these are owned and controlled by the Brazilian state, which determines exploration and exploitation of these resources.

There are several problems with the semi-autonomy of the indigenous peoples. Although indigenous social and political organisations are recognised by the Brazilian state, no formal governance structure has been established for the Indigenous Lands. There has been no devolution of authority from the Brazilian state to indigenous groups or indigenous representatives to allow them to govern their Indigenous Lands. The day-to-day decisions regarding land-management are made by traditional leaders and communities but governing authority remains with the state. The relationship with the state is fragmented, based on *ad hoc* arrangements with a range of sectoral government institutions, such as the National Indian Foundation (FUNAI), the health ministry, the education ministry, regional and local governments, the environmental agency (IBAMA) and so on. This generates multi-level governance arrangements with very complex decision-making processes.

Although indigenous organisations and associations have flourished since the 1980s, they are not formally recognised by the Brazilian state as legitimate representatives of the indigenous people living in a specific territory (Souza Lima 2010). Nevertheless, since 2003 there have been important political-institutional changes. In 2007, the federal government created the National Council for Indigenous Policies (*Conselho Nacional de Políticas Indígenas*, CNPI). It consists of representatives from government, pro-indigenous NGOs and indigenous regional organisations. In 2008, CNPI initiated discussions to design a National Policy for the Environmental and Territorial Management of Indigenous

Territories (PNGATI), resulting in what is known as the Federal President Decree 7747 of 2012. The PNGATI is governed by a national committee and managed by regional and local committees; and each committee has representatives from indigenous organisations. These indigenous representatives are not elected in any formal sense; rather, they are appointed by the northern, north-east, south and south-east regional indigenous organisations.[4]

Another important process to be highlighted started in 2012, when the Brazilian Government established practical procedures to implement the policy for Previous Consultation and the Free Prior and Informed Consent (FPIC), one of the most important statements of United Nations Declaration on the Rights of Indigenous Peoples (UNDRIP 2007) and Convention 169 of the International Labour Organization. The establishment of FPIC has been a key demand from indigenous peoples to gain them more participation in decision-making processes and more autonomy (Inglez de Sousa and Vaz Ribeiro 2013).

This chapter will discuss the emergence of the new and complex system for indigenous self-organisation and representation in Brazil. First, it will provide a historical and geographical background to give a contextual and political understanding of contemporary developments. Second, the issue of territorial control will be discussed, including the demarcation of indigenous territories and the evolution of state policies that have allowed for this process. The institutional fragmentation of the indigenous relationship with the Brazilian state is emphasised, along with lack of capacity and sustainability characterising the Indigenous Lands.[5] The ambiguity and limits of indigenous territorial autonomy in Brazil today demonstrate the semi-autonomous position of indigenous groups on the Indigenous Lands.

Third, the article will address some of the current political challenges faced by indigenous peoples. The democratisation of Brazil in the post-military rule era led to the new constitution of 1988 and was accompanied by a new indigenous movement creating a myriad of organisations and associations. After a period of politicised mobilisation, the indigenous organisations became more concerned with day-to-day management of projects related to health, education and protection of the Indigenous Lands. However, a new generation of well educated indigenous leaders has emerged, with a better understanding of pan-ethnic[6] issues than previous generations. A new wave of endogenous political activism has emerged the last years. On the one hand, it is linked to resistance against federal policies related to infrastructural, hydropower and mining development. On the other,

---

4.   COIAB in the northern region of Brazil, APOINME in the north-east, ARPINSUL in the south and ARPINSUDESTE in the south-east.

5.   'Indigenous Land' (in singular), or *Terra Indígena* in Portuguese, refers to the general legal category of an official and specific, demarcated territory. Indigenous Lands (in plural) refers to the established and existing units of this legal category.

6.   By 'pan-ethnic' issues and politics, we refer to the political association of distinct indigenous groups, with a differentiated social, cultural and historical background, to act as an interest group in interaction with the Brazilian state.

engagement with the federal government is developing in order to co-ordinate service delivery and policies related to the indigenous population. The indigenous population has restructured political-organisational relations both internally and with the federal state.

Historical and geographical background

The indigenous population in Brazil is very diverse in terms of culture, livelihood and environment and history of contact with the Brazilian national society. The Socio-Environmental Institute (*Instituto Socio-Ambiental*, ISA) identifies more than 230 ethnic groups and over 180 languages (ISA 2012). There are important variations between indigenous groups in terms of their size. The largest groups, such as the Guarani, Yanomami, Kaingang, Terena and Tikuna, each have more than 20,000 members. Smaller groups can range from a few hundreds to fewer than 10 members (ISA 2012). Overall, there is an evident population growth but some of the very small indigenous groups are under serious threat of extinction.

The Brazilian regions have different compositions of indigenous groups, with some inhabiting territories across borders between Brazil and neighbouring countries. The majority of the population is concentrated in the north (Amazonas) and north-east regions, in which 38 and 25 per cent of the indigenous peoples live, respectively (IBGE 2012).While most indigenous peoples in the north live inside Indigenous Lands, the same cannot be said about other regions. In the south-east, for example, over 80 per cent of the region's indigenous people live outside indigenous territories.

Many of these demographic and geographic variations have historical explanations, as the Portuguese colonisation and the consolidation of territorial control by post-colonial Brazilian governments did not occur uniformly across regions (Souza Lima 1995). Indigenous populations living along the Brazilian coast and in the north-east and south-east regions were the first ones to be occupied by the Portuguese in the sixteenth and seventeenth centuries. In the south, indigenous peoples were especially confronted by Germans, Italians and other immigrants in the nineteenth century. In the Amazon region, the Portuguese occupation process started with the navigation of the big rivers during the sixteenth century. Another intense effort in the northern region occurred with the national integration projects of the twentieth century, which gained special momentum under the military dictatorship from 1964–1985. The military government sought to construct road networks and other infrastructure in the Amazonian territories in order to boost economic growth. It also attempted to colonise the area by providing land to landless farmers and low-income groups from other parts of Brazil. In addition to spreading diseases that devastated indigenous populations, this re-colonisation process threatened to deprive the indigenous peoples of territories and natural resources that had nurtured their cultures for generations (Cardoso de Oliveira 1996).

Many indigenous groups resisted the colonial encroachment into their territories and, by the 1970s and 1980s, they were being supported by anthropologists, the Catholic Church, national and even international NGOs and a growing environmentalist movement emerging from urban Brazilian society. The indigenous people's struggle for survival became part of the huge pro-democracy and human rights movement that brought the dictatorship down in 1985, culminating in the new constitution in 1988.

The indigenous and the state (I): The issue of territorial control

When the Indian Protection Service (*Serviço de Proteção ao Índio*, SPI) was created in 1910, the national government's position towards indigenous peoples was based on a 'guardianship' principle. Since indigenous people were considered 'relatively disabled' they did not enjoy full citizenship rights and duties. The government's role to protect them and act on their behalf was delegated to the Indian Protection Service (SPI). Indigenous policies were guided by assimilation strategies that aimed at incorporating the indigenous population into mainstream society and the national economy, transforming them into a labour force for farming and cattle-raising activities. This *assimilacionismo* policy had a major impact on land-management. The indigenous territories demarcated during this period were usually very small and were established on the assumption that the indigenous peoples would be assimilated. Government policy actively opposed the traditional lifestyle of the people and refused to support their traditional culture, values, economy and social organisation.

In 1967, the Indian Protection Service (SPI) was replaced by the National Indian Foundation (*Fundação Nacional do Índio*, FUNAI). Despite this institutional change, the guardianship and assimilation policies remained in place until the late 1980s (Cardoso de Oliveira 1996; Oliveira Filho 1998). Additionally, indigenous policies also became aligned with the military government's policy of 'developmentalism' (*desenvolvimentismo*), which placed a particular emphasis on the economic integration of Amazonia. FUNAI's role was to 'pacify' the indigenous peoples and pave the way for large development projects, such as the construction of hydroelectric power plants, roads, and mining industries. The policies that FUNAI promoted and implemented were a series of initiatives aimed at developing large-scale economic activities, such as logging and mining in indigenous territories.

From a legal perspective, the 1988 Brazilian Constitution represented a paradigmatic shift in the government's policies towards indigenous people.[7] Reflecting the international trend set by organisations such as the United Nations and the International Labour Organization towards recognition of indigenous rights, the new Constitution acknowledged indigenous socio-cultural diversity and set forth a number of specific rights and policies for indigenous people. The constitution recognises that the 'Indians' were the first and natural habitants of Brazilian territory and Article 231 declares that they have an aboriginal right to the

---

7. In particular, Articles 231 and 232.

territories traditionally occupied by indigenous peoples.[8] Santilli (1999) argues that Article 231 is the key article that recognises indigenous rights through including the right to the land and to 'the environmental resources necessary for the well-being and physical and cultural reproduction' of the indigenous peoples.[9] Hence, it provides indigenous people with a mechanism to formalise the delimitation of Indigenous Lands, where the rivers, lakes and soils are for 'the exclusive use by the indigenous peoples' who inhabit these territories.[10] The Federal President Decree 1775 of 1996 established clear procedures for the creation of Indigenous Lands, boundary-demarcation, ratification and registration. It stressed the importance of ensuring indigenous participation during the demarcation stage; anthropological reports have played a key role in highlighting indigenous perceptions and lifestyles during this process (Santilli 1999).

According to Little (2002), the legal definition of Indigenous Land has instituted a new land category, namely land 'for collective use', in contraposition both to 'private' land with private ownership and 'public' land. The latter belongs to the Brazilian state, thus belonging, in theory, to all Brazilians. However, although the Indigenous Lands are not owned by the indigenous peoples but by the Brazilian federal state, the land is 'inalienable' and cannot be sold.[11] The federal state also retains ownership of the subterranean resources, such as minerals (Inglez de Sousa 2010a). Hence, indigenous people enjoy semi-autonomy and not full sovereignty over the indigenous territories.

In addition to acknowledging indigenous claims to land, the Constitution recognises indigenous socio-cultural diversity and establishes a series of rights and public policies especially for the indigenous peoples. It shifts the policy direction, at least legally, from the integrationist and assimilationist vision towards the government becoming the guardian of indigenous people's rights. Several initiatives focus on 'sustainable ethno-development', which are policies linked to economic activities, income-generation and community-development based on respect for indigenous culture and lifestyle, yet incorporating new consumption patterns.

Indigenous Lands: New problems

Many challenges surround the Indigenous Lands, as a modern attempt to nurture and re-establish the indigenous peoples physically and culturally. In this section, three current challenges will be presented. The first challenge is in spatial terms; it refers to the size and sustainability of the Indigenous Lands. The territories have to be large enough to secure the physical survival

---

8. Paragraph 1 in Article 231 of the constitution states '*o direito originário*', which we have translated as 'the aboriginal right'.
9. This is stated in Paragraph 1, Article 231 of the Constitution.
10. Paragraph 2, Article 231 of the Constitution.
11. Paragraph 4, Article 231 of the Constitution.

and cultural reproduction of the inhabitants. This is made more difficult by territorial fragmentation, in which one indigenous group might be spread out over several Indigenous Lands.

A second challenge is the allocation of administrative and political responsibilities for service delivery to the indigenous territories. The presence of a repressive-assimilative state had to be replaced with institutions that are truly indigenously controlled; new and improved relationships with the outside world must be established. The challenge is not only to reduce environmental and other threats to indigenous ways of life but also to secure human resources and organisational capacities – institutional management skills – to see the indigenous peoples thrive.

A final important challenge comes from outside, namely the impacts of large-scale industrial exploitation, such as agro-business (large-scale and monoculture agriculture), hydro-power dams, mining, railways and roads on Indigenous Lands. These have significant impact on indigenous territories and communities, not only on the environment but also in social, economic and cultural terms (Inglez de Sousa and Vaz Ribeiro 2013).

Demarcation of sustainable Indigenous Lands

During the first half of the twentieth century, indigenous peoples were located in what were known as 'Indian Reserves'. The area of these reserves was constantly reduced in order to liberate land for commercial farming. The aim of the Brazilian government at the time was to expand the country's cattle production and sugar-cane plantations (Grünber 2006). The size of each cattle farm was allowed to be 3600 hectares (36 km^2). Indigenous people were forced to adapt to the government's farming objectives. This policy had a particularly hard impact on the Guaraní Indians.[12] Around 38,000 tribal members living in 30 separate indigenous reserves, which averaged 1000 hectares, were affected (Grünber, 2006).

Traditional land and their natural resources are fundamental to indigenous peoples' social and cultural survival. Hunting and gathering require vast areas of (rain) forests. Hence, an important issue has been to expand the size of the Indigenous Lands, to make them large enough to maintain traditional indigenous livelihoods. The Xingú Indigenous Park, established in 1961, is considered an appropriate model for an Indigenous Territory. The Park is 2.8 million hectares (28,000 km^2), with a population of approximately 4,000 people who live in villages averaging about 100 people.[13] Hence, the establishment of the Xingú Indigenous Park is considered a turning point for indigenous land delimitation (Inglez de Souza and Braathen 2010).

---

12. The Guaraní-Ñandeva and Guaraní-Kaiowá groups.

13. The population of Xingú Indigenous Park is grouped in 14 indigenous groups, each with a distinct language. They belong to the four main indigenous language groups in Brazil: Tupi, Aruak, Karib and Jê.

Institutional fragmentation

Prior to 1988, *FUNAI* (*Fundação Nacional do Índio*) was the sole responsible agency for indigenous public policies and the only entity providing welfare and social services to indigenous populations (healthcare, education, capacity-building programmes and law enforcement, among others). The 1988 constitution dissolved this type of institutional monopoly (see Souza Lima 2010). After 1988, FUNAI's duties were distributed among several government actors: the ministry of health, the ministry of education, the ministry of environment, the ministry of agrarian development, the ministry of justice and others. The ministries often delegated tasks to more technical agencies, such as the National Health Foundation (*Fundação Nacional de Saúde*, FUNASA). In many services such as health and education, the federal agencies were assisted by the sub-national states and municipalities. However, these public-sector bodies were usually poorly co-ordinated and, for many years, the quality and coverage of their services left a lot to be desired. During the same period, many NGOs and international institutions intensified their co-operation with indigenous peoples, at the same time that indigenous organisations and associations were flourishing. During the 1990s, several sustainable programmes were developed to support indigenous peoples.

FUNAI survived, with tasks limited to assistance in the delimitation and surveillance of the borders of the Indigenous Lands. FUNAI was, nevertheless, also given the general task of co-ordinating the governmental indigenous policy. The Indigenous Lands have not had the status of being legal persons, which would centralise the management of each of them. The Indigenous Lands have geographical boundaries clearly defined by law and the internal affairs of the Indigenous Lands are supposed to be under control of the indigenous peoples, as stated by Articles 231 and 232 of the federal constitution. No external agencies are allowed to enter without the consent of indigenous peoples. Still, the lack of governing bodies has made real control by indigenous peoples elusive. The constitutional recognition of the social and political organisation of indigenous peoples has not been accompanied by their administrative and managerial recognition. The indigenous communities cannot make decisions and definitions that are binding for any government bodies.

The fragmentation of 'indigenist' public policies has been criticised by many indigenous activists, such as Valéria Paye Pereira, from the Kaxuyana people:

> Some projects in the indigenous territories were executed in dispersed ways and with delays of until 10 years. There were a lot of uncoordinated actions. Everybody could make the same thing or over again I don't know how many times … . People from the state were never worried about the lack of coordination (Inglez de Sousa 2010b: 209).

An indigenous land is not a closed territory, although it has boundaries. It maintains relations of strong interdependence with its immediate social and environmental surroundings and with its more distant political-institutional surroundings. The Kayapó people, who call themselves Mebengokrê, show examples of this. They are 6000 individuals who inhabit several Indigenous Lands in the states of Mato Grosso and Pará, in the southern and eastern parts of Amazonia. They left their semi-nomadic way of life and settled down in permanent villages, due to their dependence on services from outside, in education, health, pensions and transport, and in order to get access to markets and other modern urban services. In this context, the Kayapó expanded their relations with regional and national institutions. In addition to FUNAI, they established relationships with the federal health agency FUNASA, various municipalities in the region, the state governments, regional economic agents (large commercial farmers, loggers, miners), environmental and pro-indigenous NGOs and several other institutions (see Jerozolimski *et al.*, 2011). Some Kayapó communities became involved in the exploration of gold and timber, while others preferred more sustainable practices. They have developed in different directions and, at the same time, there has been no decision-making and governing centre that could establish clear guidance for all the communities.

In this situation, many NGOs and indigenous organisations had to compensate for the lack of public action, and they played a vital role in innovating more participatory approaches in favour of indigenous peoples in welfare-provision, land-management, revenue-generation and capacity-building. Still, the NGOs could not mend the lack of public-policy co-ordination. This lack of public action was underpinned by the neo-liberal doctrines dominating Brazilian public policy since the 1990s, encouraging the involvement of the private sector and NGOs in delivering public goods.

As a result, even if many institutional actors managed to co-operate, their joint interventions emphasised micro projects, or project-based development assistance. An example was PDPI (The Demonstration Projects of the Indigenous Peoples) sponsored by the Brazilian Ministry of Environment.[14] Large scale public programmes were not on the agenda. On the other hand, as the piloting interventions needed to have a strong experimenting and learning orientation, it was perhaps not yet time for large-scale programmes.

Lack of capacity and sustainability

Project-based interventions seemed to be what the indigenous communities themselves asked for. In the 1990s, Brazil saw a proliferation of indigenous associations and organisations within the Indigenous Lands. These associations were formed to present the demands of the communities to the Brazilian state; and to address concrete problems of the indigenous communities. They sought technical and financial assistance from state agencies to projects under community control. However, a common problem for these associations was their lack of

---

14. The PDPI has supported around 70 projects for sustainable economy, cultural appreciation, institutional strengthening and capacity-building since 2002. It spent the equivalent of almost 20 million USD and attended 175 indigenous peoples in 20 states.

familiarity with the state bureaucracy. They knew little about how to manage financial resources according to the bureaucratic rules of the state. There was much trial-and-error. There were even indigenous peoples without anyone who could read or write Portuguese, so the ability to write applications and obtain funds for projects was unevenly distributed (Ingles Souza, 2010).

While NGOs and projects could help developing the organisational capacity of indigenous peoples, there were structural constraints that could only be addressed by political action at the federal level. The main structural problem was the limited size of most Indigenous Lands. The largest indigenous territories are in the Amazon region, where they cover one-fourth of the surface. However, many indigenous territories are so small, particularly in the south, that their resident groups are unable to maintain their livelihoods based solely on traditional means of resource-management, farming and extraction. Hence, outside the Amazon region, the territorial question is the critical one. The territory of the Indigenous Lands need to expand to become sustainable.

The sustainability challenge is linked not only to the limited natural-resource base of each Indigenous Land but also to the environmental-economic management of areas surrounding the Indigenous Lands. One obvious example is large-scale agricultural activities leading to deforestation, pollution and reduced groundwater level, affecting indigenous territories directly. Another example is large dams and hydropower projects undertaken in the Amazon region, such as the Belo Monte project at the Xingú River. Indigenous communities are displaced by the construction of dams and the bio-diversity and ecology of neighbouring Indigenous Lands might be impacted by hydrological changes in a macro region.

There are specific procedures for the socio-environmental impact-assessment studies and 'mitigation and compensation plans' related to indigenous lands and communities, which includes consultation processes. These procedures were consolidated at an inter-ministerial meeting, resulting in the resolution *Portaria Interministerial 419*, in which FUNAI was given the responsibility of evaluating the impact and measures for indigenous lands, based on anthropological reports of impact assessments. However, these procedures do not seem to be enough to ensure effective participation of indigenous peoples in the decision-making processes for big projects at earlier stages, with reference to a much larger scale than the single Indigenous Land area. This is the reason why the design of practical implementation procedures for 'free prior and informed consent' (FPIC) is considered a priority for many indigenous leaders and their supporters (Inglez de Sousa and Vaz Ribeiro 2013).

These challenges have increased with the new policy of large-scale state interventions to promote economic growth, the so-called 'neo-developmentalism', which has characterised the governments of Luis Ignácio Lula da Silva (2003–10) and Dilma Rousseff (2011–). The next section will argue that indigenous peoples have experienced some improvements with these two governments. However, it remains to be seen if the pro-growth policies become adjusted to pro-indigenous policies.

The indigenous and the state (II): A new partnership?

Indigenous self-organisation and representativeness

Appreciating their social and cultural diversity is a key to understanding indigenous peoples. The indigenous peoples who live within an Indigenous Land often have different forms of social and political organisation. While generically classified as 'indigenous', these peoples cover an extremely broad and diverse range of human societies. Some of the groups live in large villages or communities and have strong leaders and a centralised power structure; while others have extremely decentralised leadership, living in small groups scattered all over an Indigenous Land. Some have only recently established contact with other ethnic groups and the outside world.[15] This makes decision-making processes complex. Frequently, there are conflicts and disagreements on how to manage their territories among the indigenous peoples themselves. In these cases, there are no clear principles for how to proceed to a final resolution, especially when the contested issue has implications for public policies.

During the 1970s, FUNAI commonly designated the indigenous spokespersons or representatives of the different indigenous territories and regions. Oliveira Filho (1989) presented a rich ethnography of the relationship between an ethnic group and FUNAI, describing in detail the figure of the indigenous 'captain' or spokesperson. This person did not necessarily represent an indigenous people in a legitimate way. In many cases, the 'captains' chosen were not the traditional indigenous leaders; rather, individuals with greater knowledge of Portuguese were favoured by FUNAI, to facilitate dialogue. At other times, the choice of 'captains' was a result of deliberate strategies to undermine traditional leaders who resisted state authority.

Prior to the new federal constitution of 1988, the indigenous peoples had not been considered citizens on equal terms because the Brazilian state understood them as 'semi-capable' persons in need of protection. As the state apparatus handling the indigenous population was fragmented after 1988, the indigenous groups began to establish a wide range of relationships with state and non-governmental Brazilian social actors. Thereby, the indigenous peoples formed their own associations and representative institutions. Together, these are known as the 'indigenous movement' (Oliveira Filho 1998).

An indigenous view of the new movement

Gersen Luciano dos Santos Baniwa, an indigenous anthropologist from the Baniwa's people in the Amazonas, has contributed valuable reflections on the indigenous movement, indigenous organisations, traditional indigenous leaders and contemporary political leaders (Baniwa 2006). He defines the 'indigenous

---

15. The study of the relationship between indigenous peoples and the national society is named the study of *inter-ethnic contact*. The book of Roberto Cardoso de Oliveira is recognised as a major milestone in this area (Cardoso de Oliveira 1996).

movement' as a set of actions, activities, events, strategies and encounters between people, communities and indigenous organisations that gather and articulate to defend their interests and their rights within the national society, surpassing previous conflicts and tensions. The current organised indigenous movement originated in the 1970s. Today, groups that had waged wars among themselves until a few decades ago work together within the indigenous movement for the defence of their rights.

The process of forming an indigenous movement has been difficult and complex. In addition to overcoming past conflicts and tensions, often dormant but with the potential to awaken, indigenous people have the difficult task of creating a common agenda. Creating unity of action among the variety of groups, realities, interests and aspirations is a big challenge. The indigenous organisations were created when the movement realised that the dialogue with the state, the state bureaucracy and agents of the national society was difficult due to the lack of recognition of the diversity of indigenous social and political organisation. The state, in general, can only engage with models, patterns and bureaucratic organisations. In order to make a dialogue with the state bureaucracy possible, the indigenous peoples adopted this bureaucratic model – formal organisation with legal identity and other protocols. This incorporation does not necessarily mean cultural 'loss' or weakening but is an assimilation of an external model with the purpose of improving the quality of the lives of indigenous people.

Gersen Baniwa also makes the differentiation between two general political categories: 'traditional leaders' and 'modern political leaders'. The traditional leaders are the responsible for the internal leadership in the indigenous villages and among the indigenous peoples inside their territory. They play the traditional role as social and political leaders. However, in some cases, they do not conduct their association's management and external political representation at the state level.

For Baniwa, traditional leaders have a role in '… representing, coordinating, articulating and defending the interests of segments of indigenous peoples. They … have an inherited responsibility, passed on for generations and passed naturally from the social and political dynamics prevailing in every people' (Baniwa 2006: 65). Therefore, according to Baniwa, they are the leaders legitimised by the internal social structures of indigenous peoples.

On the other hand, there are the indigenous modern political leaders,[16] who are organised to make the dialogue within the indigenous movement and representative organisations. They usually 'perform specific functions as leaders of organizations, intermediaries and interlocutors between communities and institutions, local, regional, national and international community' (Baniwa 2006: 65) and hold dialogues directly with the non-indigenous world. Traditional leaders can also exercise political leadership, because these roles are not mutually exclusive. 'In the reality, traditional leaders and political leaders coexist and try to coordinate their actions and representations jointly, not always an easy task.' (Baniwa 2006: 66).

---

16. It is worth emphasising that Baniwa is not referring to democratically elected leaders. His notion of 'modern political' leaders refers to people in charge of the contact with the outside world.

The new organisations

Ever since they were created, indigenous organisations and their leaders have assumed the role of indigenous interlocutors in intercultural dialogues with non-indigenous entities; these might be representatives of the Brazilian government or other non-indigenous sectors of national or international society. In recent years, these organisations have increasingly shifted their activities from the grassroots level to working with the administration of projects and programmes. According to Matos (2006: 37–8),

> indigenous organizations have become less political, dealing less with wider political activism and more with management and execution of projects, including actions of state responsibility such as projects related to indigenous health and the protection of indigenous lands.

The indigenous organisations and their councils, unions, co-ordination offices and so on must register themselves in the General Register of Juridical Entities (*Cadastro Geral de Pessoas Jurídicas*) in order to become an institution recognised by the Brazilian government. In general, they imitate the organisational-structural forms of the larger Brazilian society, with the formation of boards elected by vote at meetings. In legal terms, they are voluntary civil society organisations. In other words, they do not exercise any public authority in the management of Indigenous Lands, even if, on some occasions and in some situations, these organisations enjoy political recognition by the Brazilian state as representing indigenous interests and peoples.

In the first years after 1988, it was common to form organisations, or associations, that connected all communities and indigenous groups in an Indigenous Land as a network. However, divisions, conflicts and difficulties of internal management eventually led to a proliferation of various associations within one Indigenous Land. An example is the Wajãpi Amapá people. In the 1990s, they founded 'Apina' – the Council of Wajãpi Villages. This council linked all the ethnic sub-groups and its main focus was the territorial delimitation of their Indigenous Land. As the association gathered all Wajãpi villages, there was political recognition of the representativeness of the institution. Over the years, however, a part of the Wajãpi decided to form another association (Apiwata). After that, other, more localised associations were also founded (Braathen *et al.* 2007).

The same occurs at the regional and national level. The indigenous organisations continue to be voluntary entities, forming an indigenous civil society. There is no formal or institutional recognition of their representation, only political recognition. In other words, there are no statutes or regulations that formally delegate the responsibility of or authority to represent the indigenous peoples and Indigenous Lands to these organisations. Nonetheless, in their everyday dialogue and discussions with indigenous peoples, they have been recognized as *de facto* representatives of their groups. These organisations are consulted in decision-making processes and are also requested by the state to nominate representatives for the governmental Councils and Technical Chambers (Conselhos e Câmaras Técnicas), among other bodies.

This is the case, for example, of the COIAB – the Co-ordination of Indigenous Organisations of the Brazilian Amazon (*Coordenação das Organizações Indígenas da Amazônia Brasileira*), founded in 1989 and embodying a long and vast history of struggles and achievements of indigenous rights. It co-ordinates dozens of grassroots organisations in the Brazilian Amazon, has political recognition from the Brazilian government and is included in decision-making and policy-making. Therefore, one can observe an institutionalisation of the role of COIAB as a *de facto* (but not *de jure*) representative of indigenous organisations.

At the federal (all-Brazilian) level is the Network of the Indigenous Peoples of Brazil (*Articulação dos Povos Indígenas do Brasil*, APIB). It has experienced a development similar to that of COIAB, with an increasing political recognition by the federal state as a representative of the indigenous peoples of Brazil. APIB is composed by the various regional indigenous organisations (Souza Lima 2010):

- The network of indigenous peoples in the north-east and the states of Minas Gerais and Espirito Santo (*Articulação dos Povos Indígenas do Nordeste, Minas Gerais e Espírito Santo*, APOINME).
- The network of indigenous peoples of the Pantanal region (*Articulação dos Povos Indígenas do Pantanal e Região*, ARPIPAN).
- The network of indigenous peoples in the south-east (*Articulação dos Povos Indígenas do Sudeste*, ARPINSUDESTE).
- The network of indigenous peoples in the south (*Articulação dos Povos Indígenas do Sul*, ARPINSUL).
- The large assembly of the Guarani people (*Grande Assembléia do Povo Guarani*, ATY GUASSÚ, from the Mato Grosso do Sul province).
- The Co-ordination of Indigenous Organisations of the Brazilian Amazon (COIAB).

These organisations have a regional approach and gather many sub-regional, local and smaller ethnic organisations. The regional networks incorporate a bureaucratic organisational structure, with an elected co-ordinating body (secretariat), a board and a general assembly. Their members are appointed by sub-regional organisations, which usually also have elected co-ordinators, and specific set-ups for the sub-region. The regional-territorial and socio-cultural differences led to a large variety of local organisations. Some of them represent only one ethnic group; others represent various groups. Some of them are related to only one Indigenous Land, while others gather representatives from many. In sum, the range of sub-regional organisations is extremely diverse.

Nevertheless, the annual gathering *Acampamento Terra Livre* (the 'Free Land Camp') has become the most important assembly of indigenous leaders in Brazil. In 2004, it gathered 200 participants from 33 peoples, and in some of the subsequent camps more than 1000 leaders from more than 200 peoples have participated. The gatherings deal with policies in single sectors, such as education and health; major conflict issues, such as the government's hydropower projects and policies for economic growth; as well as overall issues related to bodies and mechanisms for effective and democratic participation of the indigenous peoples in Brazilian policy-making. The camps have accompanied the new dialogues with the federal government. These dialogues have resulted in the establishment of the National Commission for Indigenous Policies, CNPI.

The CNPI was established in March 2006 and is composed of 12 representatives from the government (three from the President's Office, three from the Ministry of Justice and six from other ministries), 20 indigenous representatives from the different regions in the country (ten of whom have the right to vote) and two representatives from civil-society entities, thus ensuring voting parity between government and non-government representatives. CNPI has thematic sub-committees for policy areas such as Indigenous Lands, education, health, (economic) ethno-development and legislation. CNPI proposes directives and priorities for the 'indigenist'[17] national policy, monitors the actions of federal bodies working closely with indigenous peoples and accompanies parliamentary activities.

The Free Land Camp pressed for the CNPI council to be 'deliberative' (with real influence for indigenous representatives) and not merely 'consultative'.[18] The Free Land Camps have become important supplements to the permanent inter-ethnic structures – in particular, the Network of the Indigenous Peoples of Brazil (APIB) (Souza Lima, 2010) previously mentioned.

Pro-indigenous NGOs, national and international, have been important in the struggle for indigenous constitutional rights and in basic service-delivery for the survival of the indigenous communities. The NGOs have supported indigenous empowerment and pioneered 'ethno-development' (sustainable economic development based on indigenous knowledge of natural-resource management) projects. However, gradually indigenous organisations have emerged to deal directly with the government to improve their own rights and welfare situation. The support of the NGOs is still important, but their role has become increasingly complementary to that of the indigenous organisations.

Government responses

The Brazilian federal state has a very complex structure, making it hard for the indigenous movement to influence public policies. There are three government tiers (municipal, state and federal union) as well as meticulous check-and-balance arrangements between legislative, executive and judicial authorities. As mentioned earlier, the links between the state and the indigenous peoples became extremely fragmented after 1988. However, thanks to indigenous mobilisations and changes of government policies, new relations have developed between the indigenous population and the federal state. First, the policies are more holistic – they link various policy areas that were formerly fragmented and disassociated. Second, they build on the participation of indigenous representatives, although

---

17. The category 'indigenist' refers to state policies related to indigenous peoples.

18. 'Deliberative' in Brazilian political-juridical jargon means that a committee or council has the authority to make decisions in the areas stated by the law, in contrast to 'consultative' bodies, which lack this authority.

such participation is not 'deliberative' – it lacks real decision-making and veto rights for the civil-society representatives. In most cases, participation is only consultative (advisory) (Inglez de Sousa and Vaz Ribeiro 2013). FUNAI hosted a national conference of indigenous peoples in 2006, leading to a consultation process around a new Statute of Indigenous Peoples in 2009. It has, however, not yet been designated for implementation.

In 2009, the federal Ministry of Education organised a national conference for indigenous education. The conference proposed a policy to establish ethno-educational territories in order to transcend the differences in education contents offered by different municipalities or states serving one and the same indigenous people. The training, employment and active managerial involvement of indigenous teachers are key elements in this policy. It remains to be seen how effective the implementation is. Still, the indigenous vernacular has become the instruction language in most of the indigenous schools.

The Ministry of Health has organised similar national conferences for indigenous health. The ministry has a federal sub-system for health services to the indigenous population, organised in special districts, each with a multidisciplinary health team, a council with indigenous representatives and contacts in each village.

In spite of the importance of these government responses, a challenge is fragmentation and lack of co-ordination between the different public policy areas; this can be witnessed in the lack of common geographical scales and territorial units of implementation. The regional co-ordinating offices within FUNAI do not correspond to the same indigenous people as those defined by the Special Indigenous Health Districts (*Distritos Sanitários Especiais Indígenas*) of the Ministry of Health, which, in turn, are different from the areas defined for the ethno-educational territories. These territorial-administrative units reflect specific institutional dynamics and are not congruent with the Indigenous Lands. On the one hand, this might be good for the work in each sector (FUNAI, education, health). On the other hand, it generates disconnection between the institutional bodies, posing major difficulties for the indigenous to follow and influence their activities.

The most important response from the government, however, was the creation of the National Commission for Indigenous Policies, CNPI, in 2006. Based on previous programmes for 'ethno-development' and food security (such as *Carteira Indigena*), the CNPI launched the National Policy for the Environmental and Territorial Management of Indigenous Territories, PNGATI, in 2008.[19] The PNGATI deals directly with the environmental and territorial management of the Indigenous Lands in Brazil. Its main goal is to guarantee and promote the protection, recuperation, conservation and use of sustainable natural resources in the Indigenous Lands. One of the main implementation tools used by the PNGATI is the Plan of Territorial and Environmental Management in Indigenous Lands.

---

19. The following information is based on the authors' own interviews but also on public information accessible on http://sites.google.com/site/PNGATI/). We have especially used 'Document to support consultation with indigenous peoples'.

By recognizing the importance of the indigenous peoples' role and the respect for the existing rules and legislations, these plans aim for the social and cultural sustainability of the indigenous peoples and the establishment of agreements and deals between the communities living in the Indigenous Lands.

Still, the lacunae in the Indigenous Lands management structures stimulated the discussion and definition of a national policy for the environmental and territorial management of indigenous territories in 2007. A long process of dialogue between indigenous representatives, government and specialists was concluded on June 5, 2012, through the President Decree 7747. The general objective of the PNGATI was formulated in these words:

> … to guarantee and promote the protection, recuperation, conservation and sustainable use of the natural resources in the Indigenous Lands and territories, by securing the integrity of the indigenous heritage, the improvement of the quality of life and the full conditions for physical and cultural reproduction of the present and future generations of indigenous peoples, respecting their autonomy and own forms of territorial and environmental management.[20]

Besides emphasising the importance of the socio-cultural aspects related to territorial management, the idea and general objective of PNGATI thus highlights the need to implement mechanisms for participation of the indigenous peoples in decision-making processes. PNGATI defined the organs with guaranteed indigenous participation:

- The National Commission for Indigenous Policy – CNPI.
- The National Conference of PNGATI.
- The National Deliberative Committee of PNGATI.
- Regional committees of PNGATI.
- Local committees of PNGATI linked to a particular Indigenous Land.

The indigenous participants are nominated by the regional member organisations of APIB, which we have listed earlier.

Some specific objectives of PNGATI were announced, in which the principal guidelines were made concrete:

- Protection of indigenous territories and their resources.
- Governance and indigenous participation.
- Regulation of the surroundings of the indigenous territories.
- The relationships between indigenous territories, parks or units of conservation, and protected areas.
- Indigenous peoples in voluntary isolation and by the national frontiers.
- Prevention and reparation of damage.
- Environmental licensing of public works and activities that potentially might pollute indigenous territories and their surroundings.
- Sustainable use of resources and indigenous productive initiatives.

---

20. *See* previous footnote.

- Intellectual property and genetic heritage.
- Capacity-building and training for the implementation of PNGATI.
- Financial resources and general dispositions.

The PNGATI reinforces the political dimension of territorial management. The political dimension stands out in terms of indigenous participation in the decision-making processes connected to PNGATI, as well as in the necessity of capacity-building and training envisaged by the policy.

Half of the members of the national deliberative committee, regional committees and local committees controlling PNGATI are people nominated by the indigenous civic organisations at the national, regional and local levels. If there are more indigenous organisations than seats for indigenous people in these committees, the heads of the indigenous organisations come together to suggest joint candidates.

Indigenous representatives also participate in councils for policies that are not particularly 'indigenous' but are important for indigenous peoples: the National Council for the Environment (CONAMA); the National Council for Food Security and Nutrition (CONSEA); and the Council for Genetic Patrimony (CEGEN), among others. Although the majority of these councils only play advisory roles, they have given voices to the indigenous peoples in an emerging Brazilian welfare state characterised by direct citizen participation in the formulation and implementation of policies.

The indigenous representatives on these structures are mostly nominated by the regional indigenous organisations described earlier.

Despite some improvements, the last years have also seen many threats to indigenous peoples' rights, with direct impact on their semi-autonomy. The dialogue between federal government and indigenous movement has decreased, reversing a positive trend observed after the making of the Constitution of 1988. Several recent initiatives can lead to reversal of indigenous conquests. The major threat is related to the demarcation processes of indigenous territories. There is a proposal to amend the constitution (*Projeto de Emenda Constitucional,* 'PEC 215'), with the intention of transferring the responsibility for approval of Indigenous Lands from FUNAI to the federal legislative power (the National Congress), where the anti-indigenous interests, headed by politicians connected with the agro-business lobby, are in a majority. This proposal follows pressures on the Brazilian government, mainly from the agro-business sector, to stop new processes of Indigenous Land demarcation (Inglez de Sousa and Vaz Ribeiro 2013). Another law proposal ('PL 1610') is intended to regulate mining inside indigenous lands. This proposal clearly limits the consultation process with affected indigenous peoples.

Concluding remarks

In hindsight, the new Federal Constitution of 1988 marked a revolutionary divide in the history of the indigenous peoples of Brazil. Colonialism, centralism and authoritarianism were overthrown. The achievement of a comprehensive set of indigenous rights, including the right to establish Indigenous Lands, created an effective trend of decolonisation, decentralisation and democratisation in the relationship between the indigenous population and the state. The principles of state 'guardianship', westernised 'assimilation' and 'development' have been replaced by indigenous self-organisation and goals of sustainable 'ethno-development'.

However, the large majority of the almost 600 Indigenous Lands that emerged were too small and lacked the organisational-managerial capacities and resource endowments to become self-sustainable territories. The post-1988 federal state offered only an extremely fragmented institutional structure to support the Indigenous Lands, which depended on human and financial resources from the outside world to survive. National and international NGOs substituted to some extent for the service-delivery duties of the state.

This fragmentation led to conflict within ethnic groups and Indigenous Lands. These conflicts often centred on trivial issues such as the location of health-centres and organisational headquarters, or on the choice of the preferred city outside the Indigenous Land for access to modern services and state agencies. At a larger scale, there have been important regional differences between the indigenous peoples. For example, in the southern and south-eastern regions of Brazil, contact with the white man was established earlier, the genocide and 'assimilation' policies went deeper, and the recent indigenous territories have turned out smaller than in the Amazon region. In the latter, the natural resource base is richer, more diverse and more intact, and resistance to infrastructural (such as roads) and hydropower projects has been stronger. Therefore, it has not been easy for the various peoples to agree on a common indigenous agenda.

Nevertheless, the most important development since 1988 is the opening of spaces for broad-based political mobilisation, across ethnic lines and beyond local indigenous territories.

A proper sense of citizenship has been evolving among the indigenous peoples, following emancipation from paternalistic guardianship. The first steps of democratic self-organisation and self-management have been taken (Souza Lima 2010).

In this process, the indigenous population has restructured its political-organisational relations, both internally and with the federal state. The indigenous peoples, some of them enemies in the past, realised that a stronger political alliance across ethnicities was necessary to face new challenges related to the wider national society. Besides, they realized that new knowledge was needed: skilled leaders, but also indigenous teachers, lawyers, health professionals, environmental specialists, organisational managers, negotiators and many others.

By the beginning of the new millennium, an indigenous education system was in place and had fostered a younger and more educated group within the indigenous peoples, such as school teachers. The indigenous movement became vitalised and more pan-ethnic in its outlook, as demonstrated by the annual 'Free Land Camps' held since 2004.

An emerging Brazilian welfare state, characterised by direct citizen/'user' participation in the formulation and implementation of policies, has started to include the indigenous population as well. In 2007, the National Commission for Indigenous Policies (CNPI) was established, with federal government and indigenous representatives, and this committee has started to implement an ambitious policy for improved environmental and territorial management in Indigenous Territories (PNGATI).

However, the indigenous territories outside the Amazon region remain too small for sustainable ethno-development. Moreover, the Indigenous Lands belong to the federal state and, while the indigenous peoples inhabiting them have the exclusive right to use the surface of the land, the subterranean resources (such as minerals) are federal-state property. Hence, the indigenous peoples enjoy semi-autonomy and not full sovereignty over the indigenous territories. This had the potential to generate conflict with the federal state on key economic issues. In this situation, the indigenous organisations realised they had to keep up some creative and strategic alliances with non-indigenous entities: national NGOs, international organisations, and certain federal government institutions that were not connected to from economic policies.

The governments of Luis Inácio Lula da Silva (2003–10) and his successor Dilma Rousseff have emphasised industrialism and *neo-desenvolvimentismo* ('neo-developmentalism'). This policy has led to the implementation of large projects for hydropower generation, mining and other economic purposes, particularly in the Amazon region. The most emblematic one has been the Belo Monte project by the Xingú River, building the third largest hydropower plant in the world. These endeavours tend to undermine territorial and other rights of the indigenous peoples and they bring into question the commitment of the Brazilian government to its own policy for consultation and Free Prior and Informed Consent (FPIC). Hence, the capacity for pan-ethnic mobilisation, solidarity and pro-active policy formulation will be key issues in the future indigenous politics of Brazil.

The recent anti-indigenous initiatives represent a real threat to the indigenous peoples in Brazil. These initiatives could lead to the reversal of many indigenous achievements in political, legal and territorial arenas. The already limited autonomy of the indigenous peoples could become even more restricted. Still, it is important to note that the indigenous peoples, through their leaders and supporters, mobilise strongly against attempts to undermine their achievements from the 1980s on. They demonstrate their will to create proper autonomy combined with real participation in the decision-making processes in federal Brazil.

References

Azevedo, M. M. (2011) 'O censo 2010 e os povos indígenas', *Povos Indígenas no Brasil*, São Paulo: Instituto Socio-Ambiental.

Baniwa, G. J. dos Santos Luciano (2006) *O Índio Brasileiro: O que você precisa saber sobre o índio brasileiro de hoje*, Rio de Janeiro, Brasília: Trilhas de Conhecimentos/LACED; MEC/SECAD, 2006; UNESCO.

Braathen, E., Wiig, H., Haug, M. and Lundeberg, H (2007) *Development Cooperation through Norwegian NGOs in South America*, Study 2/2007. Oslo: Norad.

Cardoso de Oliveira, R. (1996) *Os Índios e o Mudo dos Brancos,* Editora Unicamp: Campinas.

Corr, R. and Vieira Powers, K. (2012) 'Ethnogenesis, ethnicity and "cultural refusal": the case of the Salasacas in Highland Ecuador', *Latin American Research Review* 47, Special Issue: 4–30.

Grünber, F. P. (2006) 'A relação com a terra', in *Povos Indígenas no Brasil,* 2001–2005, São Paulo: Instituto Socioambiental.

IBGE (2012) 'Característica gerais dos Indígenas', *Censo Demográfico 2010,* Rio de Janeiro: Instituto Brasileiro de Geografia e Estatística.

Inglez de Sousa, C. and Braathen, E. (2010) 'Avaliação do Programa Xingú do Instituto Socioambiental', [Evaluation of the Xingú programme in Amazon Brazil], *NIBR Project Report Series, 2010*: 10, Oslo: Norwegian Institute for Urban and Regional Research.

Inglez de Sousa, C. (2010a) 'Dimensão política da gestão territorial', in Inglez de Sousa *et al.* (eds), *Povos Indígenas: Projetos e desenvolvimento II,* Brasília: Paralelo 15, Rio de Janeiro: Laced.

— (2010b) 'Perspectiva indígena sobre projetos, desenvolvimento e povos indígenas. Entrevista com Valéria Paye Pereira Kaxuyana e Euclides Pereira Macuxi', in Inglez de Sousa *et al.* (eds), *Povos Indígenas: Projetos e desenvolvimento II,* Brasília, Paralelo 15, Rio de Janeiro: Laced.

Inglez de Sousa, C. and Ribeiro de Almeida, F. (eds, 2013) 'Gestão territorial em Terras Indígenas no Brasil', *Coleção Educação Para Todos* 39(6), Série Vias dos Saberes, Brasilia: Ministério da Educação, Secretaria de Educação Continuada, Alfabetização, Diversidade e Inclusão.

ISA (2012) 'Quadro geral dos povos', *Povos Indígenas no Brasil,* São Paulo: Instituto Socioambiental: http://pib.socioambiental.org/pt/c/0/1/2/populacao-indigena-no-brasil (accessed 6 December 2012).

Jerozolimski, A., Ribeiro, M. B. N., Ingles de Sousa, C. Noronha and Turner, T. (2011) 'Cisões recentes e mobilidade das comunidades Kayapó', in *Povos Indígenas no Brasil 2006 –2010,* São Paulo: Instituto Socioambiental.

Little, P. (2002) 'Territórios sociais e povos tradicionais no Brasil. Por uma antropologia da territorialidade', *Série Antropologia 322,* Brasilia: UNB.

Matos, M. H. O. (2006) *Rumos do movimento indígena no Brasil contemporâneo: experiências exemplares no Vale do Javari,* unpublished doctoral thesis, Antropologia Social, Campinas: UNICAMP.

Oliveira Filho, J. P. de (1989) *O Nosso Governo. Os Ticuna e o regime tutelar,* MCT, CNPq. Rio de Janeiro: Editora Marco Zero.

Oliveira Filho, J. P. de (ed., 1998) *Indigenismo e Territorialização. Poderes, rotinas e saberes coloniais no Brasil contemporâneo,* Rio de Janeiro: Editora Contra Capa.

Santilli, M. (1999) 'Natureza e situação da demarcação das Terras Indígenas no Brasil', in C. Kasburg and M. Gramkow (eds), *Demarcando Terras Indígenas. Experiências e desafios de um projeto de parceria,* Brasília: FUNAI; PPTAL; GTZ.

Souza Lima, A. C. (1995) *Um Grande Cerco de Paz. Poder tutelar, indianidade e formação do Estado no Brasil,* Petrópolis: Editora Vozes.

Souza Lima, A. C. (2010) 'Povos Indígenas no Brasil contemporâneo: de tutelados a "organizados"?', in Inglez de Sousa *et al.* (eds), *Povos Indígenas: Projetos e desenvolvimento II*, Brasília: Paralelo 15; Rio de Janeiro: Laced.

Stavenhagen, Rodolfo (1991) 'Ethnocide ou ethno-dévelopment: la nouveau défi', in D. Perrot (ed.) *La fiction et la feinte, développment et peoples autochtones*, Ethnies 13, Paris: Survival International.

PART III

INDIGENOUS REPRESENTATION – CONCRETE CONFLICTS

Chapter Eleven

The Devil Never Left: Indigeneity and Protest in Morales' Bolivia

John-Andrew McNeish[1]

Introduction

In September 2011, Bolivian police raided an encampment of several hundred indigenous peoples from the lowlands gathered just outside Yucumo to protest government plans to build a road through their territory. '*La Chaparina*',[2] as the raid is known, is now widely recognised as sparking the most significant[3] crisis of public confidence in the current Bolivian government since its coming to power in 2006.[4] The brutality of the raid was surprising in a country in which, in contrast to the rest of Latin America, such events are rare. Moreover, its purpose of disbanding an indigenous protest aimed at stopping the construction of a road through the Isoboro Sécure National Park and Indigenous Territory (TIPNIS), appeared to contradict the image and supposed aspiration of the Morales government as a defender of both the rights of indigenous peoples and of nature. Indeed, as the controversy surrounding the raid and protest spread, it became evident that indigenous peoples in Bolivia were not only in conflict with the state but also at loggerheads amongst themselves with regards to the sides chosen and positions they expressed. As this chapter highlights, to explore, the TIPNIS struggle uncovered the complex and often contradictory dynamics of indigeneity in Bolivia.

When Evo Morales Ayma entered the presidential palace (known as the Burnt Palace because of its role as the focus of earlier protest and confrontations), the indigenous majority of the Bolivian population celebrated the moment as marking the end of over 500 years of discrimination. Morales' residency of the palace was widely seen by non-elites in Bolivia as marking the completion of a revolution, the final arrival of long-awaited liberty and the beginning of an era in which their

---

1. A version of this text was published in the *Journal of Latin American and Caribbean Ethnic Studies* (*LACES*), July 2013, 8(2): 221–42.

2. The name commonly used in media coverage and discussion to describe the location of the raid.

3. The other major political crisis faced by the Morales government was the controversy surrounding the hike in gas prices, or *Gasolinazo*, in February 2011.

4. Morales' public support was registered as dropping to 37% (down 7%) in the month following the police raid. See https://www.zcomm.org/zblogs/bolivia-dilemmas-turmoil-transformation-and-solidarity-by-kevin-young/ (accessed 5 December 2014).

interests would be listened to and respected. Morales is now in his third term in office and his government is widely recognised as responsible for a long list of reforms. The historical political hegemony of the white elite has gone; the country's mineral and hydrocarbon wealth has been nationalised; and a new constitution and regime of social policy exists. This has resulted in the formalisation and expansion of political and social rights, particularly those of indigenous peoples.

Widespread recognition has been given by a diverse set of international organisations, including the World Bank and the UN Economic Commission for Latin America, to the successful impact of many social reforms introduced by the Morales' Movement for Socialism on the country's previous, and persisting, indices of poverty. This includes the payment of social subsidies drawn from hydrocarbon rents to marginalised sectors of the population. Despite approval from neo-liberal institutions, the leadership in Bolivia has also made clear its opposition to US imperialism and, together with other countries in the region, has attempted to forge a new socialist alternative to neo-liberalism through the ALBA[5] project. In the new guise of the 'pluri-national state', the Bolivian administration is also recognised for its alternative position in international climate policy debates. By drawing on indigenous cosmology, the Morales administration attempted to establish a 'peoples' model that recognises the rights of 'Mother Earth'.[6] The *Chaparina* raid made it evident, however, that whilst 'a process of change' was taking place, it was far from what many people, indigenous and otherwise, in the country wanted or expected.

Despite the quite obviously radical nature of political, economic and social change in Bolivia, it has become increasingly evident in recent years that large sectors of the very community that reforms should have favoured remain, counter-intuitively, dissatisfied with the process of change. Whilst initially supportive of political transformation, many indigenous communities and movements in the country argue that they have been let down by the Morales government – and say their patience has now run out.

Indigenous leaders and organisations in the highlands and lowlands of the country highlight that – even though the government talks of their rights and respect for 'Mother Earth', in its effort to secure resources for public spending – a significant expansion of infrastructure and extractive industries is taking place; and this threatens the basis of their livelihoods and hard-won autonomy.[7] Constitutional recognition is granted in the pluri-national state to legal pluralism and indigenous autonomy; in practice, however, indigenous rights and existing regulations demanding free, prior consent and social and environmental impact studies before infrastructure and extractive activities are carried out are being

---

5. Bolivarian Alternative for Latin America and the Caribbean.

6. Bolivia enacted a new law enshrining the legal rights of nature, the Law of Mother Earth and Integral Development for Living Well, in October 2012.

7. Based on my informal conversations with leaders from both highland and lowland indigenous organisations taking part in the TIPNIS march.

ignored. Indigenous actors are also concerned with increasing government authoritarianism and the direct interference of the executive in civil-society organisations. Recognising these contradictions, indigenous communities have lost patience with the government and mounted new campaigns, blockades and marches in opposition to the government's plans. Although lacking the levels of violence seen in Peru, Brazil or Chile, serious confrontations sparking militancy and clashes with the police have occurred in Bolivia over the last few years. This disappointment is also increasingly evident in the changing political alliances and conclusions of a series of national and international analysts.[8]

Responding to this economic and social picture, intellectuals from Bolivia and abroad have widely broadcast the message that nothing has really changed in Bolivia from neo-liberal times (see, for example, Wanderley 2011, 2008; Webber 2011; Madrid 2011). Unconvinced by claims of Bolivia's difference, several authors have recently linked contestation in the country to what they call a larger system of neo-extractivism in Latin America. Bebbington (2009, 2011), for example, has linked these events in Bolivia with a continent-wide push to open frontiers for extracting hydrocarbons, mining, producing bio-fuels, harvesting timber and investing in agro-industry. It is argued that the progressive governments of Bolivia and Ecuador are just as likely as Peru's to tell activists and indigenous groups to get out of the way of national priorities; just as likely to allow extractive industry into fragile and protected ecologies; and just as determined to convince indigenous peoples that extractive industry is good for them too, without fulfilling their rights.

Whilst recognising substantial ideological differences between Andean governments, Gudynas argues that Bolivia belongs to a group of 'neo-extractivist' countries. As such, whilst re-emphasising the role of the state and the redistribution of surplus to the population, Bolivia repeats the negative environmental and social impacts of the old extractivism (2010a, 2010b). Whilst recognising the impact of social reform and effort to change the basis for environmental governance, Gudynas questions the continuing anthropocentrism of the Bolivian government's leftist emphasis on progress and modernity in its development policies (2010). Gudynas' ecological reading of current Bolivian policy is also one that is clearly shared by many of the organisations and networks that support the TIPNIS protest in Bolivia.[9] Environmentalist groups argue that Bolivia's drive for development is in conformity with the Initiative for Integration of Regional Infrastructure of South America (IIRSA), a pan-South American agreement signed in 2000.[10] Many of the TIPNIS campaign posters and documents produced by the environmental movement contain images clearly depicting a face-off between indigenous ecology and

---

8. See, for example, Postero's return from a position of 'post-neoliberalism' (2006) to one of renewed neo-liberalism (2010).

9. See, for example, http://www.fobomade.org.bo/art-1272 (accessed 5 December 2014).

10. See http://www.fobomade.org.bo/art-1943 and http://www.fobomade.org.bo/art-19432 (accessed 5 December 2014).

the 'developmentalism' of the Bolivian government and other Latin American powers.[11] The road-building project on which the protest was built is taken as a motif of wider environmental destruction, in which tractors, chainsaws and government forces are visualised as cutting into the vibrant natural environment of trees, tropical animals and indigenous peoples (sometimes painted blue to draw attention to popular parallels with the Navi in the Hollywood film *Avatar*).

By highlighting the persistence of European ideological models of development and the linkages of Bolivian extraction and related infrastructure construction with the wider expansion and violence of extractive economies throughout the Americas, the authors offer important reflections on the possible causes of recent tensions in the country. However, whilst undoubtedly relevant, their macro-level analysis misses a great deal of the complexity of the politics and important social dynamics of these events. Indeed, in this chapter I aim to demonstrate that detailed qualitative analysis of the TIPNIS case reveals that indigenous communities' oppositional stances on extractive politics cannot be taken for granted. The chapter contains empirical details drawn from ethnographic research, semi-structured interviews and secondary sources conducted and collected in the period 2010–13.[12]

Close-up study of the TIPNIS protest reveals the reality and violence of the political disagreements currently taking place. Moreover, it also reveals a more nuanced and dynamic picture of relationships between indigenous themselves and with the state; and also of their relationships to extractivism and development. The TIPNIS protest, and others like it, not only involve a larger spectrum of interests than currently acknowledged but demonstrate internal conflicts and tensions between indigenous people. Recent events surrounding the TIPNIS controversy, and Bolivian historical development more generally, reveal the ambiguity of indigeneity and the existence of a complex matrix of contrasting, overlapping and – at times – conflicting demands. Moreover, it reveals some of the internal logics and contradictions of a government position that claims to protect Mother Earth whilst significantly expanding the exploitation of natural resources. It also shows the cynicism of the political right in harnessing indigenous protests against development projects to capture votes and support. In this chapter, different readings of the TIPNIS controversy and it significance are discussed. Indeed, it is argued that we need to revisit assumptions about the identity and interests of indigenous peoples in Bolivia, as elsewhere, through attention to empirical and historical details, in order to fully understand the aspirations and demands of indigenous communities and individuals in the country.

---

11. See, for example, the campaign poster on this web-site: http://www.tipnisesvida.net (accessed 5 December 2014)

12. Together with a Bolivian colleague, I spent a month researching community justice and gender relations within the northern part of the TIPNIS in May 2010. Results of this research are now published in McNeish and Seider (2013) *Gender Justice and Legal Pluralities: Latin American and African perspectives*, London and New York: Routledge. In the period 2011–13, several research trips have been made to Bolivia on behalf of several research projects.

The TIPNIS protest

On 15 August 2011, 2000 marchers left the city of Trinidad, the lowland regional capital of the department of Beni, to follow a route that would take them 66 days and 600 km of walking through heavy rain and burning sun to reach the capital city, La Paz. The central demand on which the protest march was founded was the cessation of a road-building project planned to go through the Isobore Sécure National Park and Indigenous Territory (*Territorio Indígena y Parque Nacional Isiboro Sécure*, TIPNIS). The TIPNIS is a triangular piece of land covering 1.2 million hectares, straddling the southern part of the department of Beni and the northern part of Cochabamba. The area was declared a national park in 1965 and, in 2009, the Mojeño-Ignaciano, Yuracaré and Chimán indigenous groups living[13] in the area received legal title to territory (known as *territorio indígena originario campesino*[14], TIOC), amounting to over a million hectares.

Formally, integration and development were the two arguments that the Morales' government gave as their reasons why Tramo II of the Villa Tunari–San Ignacio de Moxos road (300 km) should be built. Bolivia is little developed in terms of road infrastructure and the government argued that the road would create a physical connection between the Andes and Amazonia. The planned road will link Trinidad to Cochabamba, complementing another road being built from La Paz to Trinidad by way of San Borja.

What was not stated as a reason for this national policy was that there are a host of other interests that impinge on the park's territorial integrity, which local people recognise as motivating the government's decision to build a road. From the 1970s onwards, Aymara and Quechua *campesino* (peasant) colonisers from the Altiplano and high valleys began to settle in the area south of the park, close to Cochabamba and adjacent to the coca-producing Chapare area. They began to produce cacao, bananas, cassava, maize, citrus fruits and coca. With time, their numbers increased and pressure on the lands of the natural reserve grew. From 1992, leaders of the indigenous peoples and coca-producers were involved in marking out the boundaries between the reserve and indigenous lands on one hand and the area occupied by the colonisers on the other. Indeed, Evo Morales (now president), as a leader of the coca-producers, was involved in early agreements between the two groups. A 'red line' was drawn marking the boundary, the colonisers occupying the part marked to the south of the reserve, called *Polígono 7*. Though some indigenous groups remain in this area, it is now mainly populated by 20,000 colonising families (some 100,000 people), organised in agrarian trade unions: they belong to the *Federación del Trópico*, one of the six federations of coca-producers of the Chapare area. Dividing the land into individual lots, these *colonos* have a distinct manner of land-use compared to the communitarian structures of land-use applied by the communities within the park area.

---

13. In 2001, according to the most recent census (INE), there were 12,388 indigenous people living in the area.
14. Indigenous, autochthonous, peasant territory.

To the west of the park territory, several blocks[15] of natural gas have been identified and, under earlier governments, contracts were signed with the Spanish corporation Repsol for the exploitation of these fields. Under the terms of the current nationalised oil and gas industry, these contracts have been transferred to the Bolivian-Venezuelan joint venture, Petro-Andina (YPFB-PDVSA). Whilst on the one hand the national oil and gas company states[16] that it currently has no dates for when these reserves will be accessed, there is, nonetheless, recognition that currently exploited fields will not be sufficient to meet the demands of both domestic consumption of energy and international agreements for the sale of gas to Brazil and Argentina. According to a report produced by the La Paz-based research institute CEDLA,[17] a third of the park area has now been marked out in government development plans as areas for oil and gas production.[18] The opening of new oil and gas reserves is also seen as the only way of ensuring that there are sufficient state funds to cover the cost of the package of social policies, including the pension programme started in 2005. There is therefore a policy-driven demand to expand current levels of production and to look for new fields that can be exploited.[19] The road would, as many environmental organisations in the country suggest, be an important first step in ensuring access to currently isolated areas where these reserves are found.

The government claimed that the road project, and other planned developments in connection with it, would all take place in conformity with the national legal norms and protections governing environmental and social impacts. The 2009 constitution clearly states the general principles for processes of prior consultation, making it obligatory for the state to carry out pre-project consultations with indigenous peoples and their organisations when non-renewable natural resources on their lands are to be exploited. It is supposed to ensure that they will benefit from such activities. However, in line with international agreements and the Bolivian constitution itself, the recommendations that may arise from the process of consultation are not necessarily binding. The Hydrocarbons Law of 2005 (and the regulations guiding it) lays down the legal requirement for consultation in the case of oil and gas exploitation; and the proposed new mining legislation (currently under discussion) also includes prior consultation. Still, the details of how to carry out such consultations have yet to be clarified. Moreover, in the case of the TIPNIS, the local indigenous populations pointed out that no prior consultation exercise had been carried out.

---

15. i.e. mapped areas of oil and gas reserves.

16. Interview, September 2011.

17. This has been further supported in new statements by Morales at the start of his third administration.

18. See http://www.cedla.org (accessed 5 December 2014).

19. Under the current administration, 42 new areas of hydrocarbon exploitation have been approved. In expanding from 11 to 22 million hectares, the area under use for oil and gas extraction in Bolivia's nine Departments is doubled in size. See http://www.fobomade.org.bo/art-1678 (accessed 5 December 2014).

Recognising that the government's actions masked undesired impacts and contradicted official statements on promises of integration and development, the communities of the TIPNIS drew on their connection with CIDOB, the principal umbrella organisation for lowland indigenous peoples, to organise opposition to the road project. The protest platform grew as the 34 other indigenous organisations in the lowlands of the country added their support. CONAMAQ, the principal indigenous organisation from the highlands; the national human-rights ombudsman; and a group of environmental- and human-rights-oriented non-governmental organisations all agreed to join the inhabitants of the TIPNIS on the march. In the minds of these organisations, the threat posed to the TIPNIS by the road was symptomatic of the threats they also faced as a result of the careless planning of other infrastructure, extractive and development projects nationally.[20] In particular, the Asamblea Pueblo Guaraní (APG), the principal organisation representing the Guaraní indigenous communities, saw the TIPNIS march as a means to further their campaign against government plans to restart oil and gas extraction in the Aguaragüe Park in Southern Tarija.[21]

Unexpected outcomes

The march continued for over 40 days before its free passage was blocked by a counter-protest of coca-growers, *colonos* (colonisers), on the road between San Borja and Yucomo. Claiming fears of a violent confrontation between the march and the coca-farmers, the government sent over 500 police to the area to 'keep the peace'. The government also claimed that it had evidence of connections between the indigenous leaders of the march and other interests wanting to destabilise the country and destroy the government's campaign for a 'process of change'.[22] Links were publicised by the government between the leaders of the march, environmental organisations, political opposition groups and the US Embassy. The government sent ministers to negotiate with the leaders of the march but, because they refused to touch upon the route of the road, all these efforts failed.[23] Returning from abroad, the president appeared to be trying to split the marchers by flying to different communities within the park area to discuss the issue of the road there. The marchers stood firm: they would continue to La Paz and not go along with what they saw as a crude effort to further divide their community. Moreover, the leaders were resolute that there could be no solution to the conflict until the president invited the leaders of the TIPNIS to sit down with him within the Burnt Palace.

---

20. Interview with FOBOMADE, 22 September 2011.

21. See http://constituyentesoberana.org/3/noticias/tierra/082011/080811_1.pdf (accessed 5 May 2013).

22. See http://www.lostiempos.com/diario/actualidad/economia/20110821/el-presidente-acusa-a-indigenas-del-tipnis-de-comunicarse-con-la-embajada_138630_283795.html (accessed 5 December 2014).

23. I was informed of this during my visit to the march.

The day before the police raid on the camp, the foreign minister was sent in a final effort to negotiate with the marchers. Whilst attempting to build rapport with the protesters on the basis of his own ethnicity, the foreign minister also refused to discuss the course of the road. This decision resulted in a group of female protesters taking him by the arm and forcibly marching him several km towards the police line stretching across the road in front of the *colono* blockade, to make him understand what the march had cost them. This was reported in the Bolivian press as the 'kidnapping' of the minister. Responding to this event in the press, the leader of the principal highland indigenous peasant confederation (CSUTCB), Roberto Coraite, a steward of the ruling party's interests, used this event to denounce the lowland indigenous protesters as 'savages'.[24] This press angle clearly angered the authorities and, in a last desperate effort to rid itself of a thorny obstacle to its plans for modernist development, the police were given a new assignment. From keeping the peace, the mission of the police turned to breaking the spirit of the march by force.

Following the extensive media coverage, including images and reports from the police raid, there was a massive public outcry in Bolivia in support of the TIPNIS march. In many of the main towns and cities of the country, the streets filled with protestors expressing the disgust of individual associations and union organisations with the government action. From a high of 70 per cent popularity in January 2010 polls, Morales's approval rating plunged to an average 35 per cent across the major cities of La Paz, El Alto, Cochabamba and Santa Cruz by mid October 2011.[25] Counter-protests, in which many of the country's main roads were blocked, were also organised by indigenous communities in the highlands and lowlands of the country. The human rights ombudsman and opposition parties tried to launch a legal action against the government and a series of international organisations, including the Organization of American States (OEA), made statements condemning the police raid. The hundreds of detained protesters from the camp were freed from captivity in the regional airport of Rurrenabaque by a massive turnout of militant support. Following this, the protesters regrouped and continued their march on the capital. They arrived to a hero's welcome in the city of La Paz on 19 October.

Clearly surprised by the public outcry and embarrassed by the scenes of bloodshed and aggression that the national media had captured during the raid – but also reluctant to assume personal responsibility – President Morales held a press conference in which he apologised for the violence and promised that an investigation would be held into who was responsible for its instigation. The vice-minister of the interior, Marcos Farfán, immediately denied any involvement in giving the order, as did the minister, Sacha Llorenti. Despite his initial denial Llorenti, resigned from office[26] shortly after; later, evidence strongly indicated

---

24. See http://www.laprensa.com.bo/diario/actualidad/bolivia/20110906/roberto-coraite-de-la-csutcb-afirmo-que-desea-que-la-carretera-evite-que_5690_9859.html (accessed 5 December 2014).

25. See http://www.isj.org.uk/?id=780 (accessed 5 December 2014).

26. He was given a new role in the Bolivian diplomatic corps.

his role in ordering the raid. The newly appointed minister of defence, Cecilie Chacón, also resigned, stating her desire to separate herself from the irresponsible actions of the government and police in connection with the raid.[27] The Brazilian Development Bank (BNDES) withdrew its financial support for the road. The government officially suspended all activity on the road project.

Following a series of meetings between the protesters and the president in the presidential palace, the government agreed to pass a legal decree (*ley corta*) on 24 October 2011, guaranteeing that the Villa Tunari–San Ignacio de Moxos road would not pass through the TIPNIS territory. Furthermore, the law state that, from now on, the TIPNIS territory would be protected by the state as an 'intangible' territory that is, effectively making the territory out of bounds for all forms of future state or development projects. On the day he signed the decree, President Morales stated that he thought that he had been 'living up to his national responsibilities, but recognised that this might have been wrong'. He ended with one final comment: 'time would tell'.[28]

Continuing controversies

From all ostensible indications the passing of the decree of intangibility confirmed the success of the protest march and vindicated the TIPNIS platform. However, just days after the passing of the new decree, the indigenous leaders who had been involved in the march publicly claimed that by categorising the park as intangible the government had managed to secure its revenge against the indigenous protestors.[29] The intangible designation would restrict *all* the productive activities that could be carried out in the park.[30] The indigenous protesters argued that the stipulation of intangibility should only apply to external third parties or *terceros*, that is, actors who are not indigenous to the area, such as peasants entering the area or other external commercial interests. The government denied the claims that the new labelling of the territory was meant to imprison the TIPNIS and stated that it was a valid response to the demands presented to them at the negotiating table. The government also urged the indigenous leaders behind the march to explain to their own people in TIPNIS what the formal demands they presented to the government entailed.[31]

In contrast to the information provided by supporting environmental organisations and analysts, the indigenous leaders stated that their protest was not intended to stop all development projects in their territory indefinitely but rather

---

27. See http://www.isj.org.uk/id=780 (accessed 5 December 2014).

28. See http://www.lostiempos.com/diario/actualidad/economia/20111025/el-presidente-promulga-la-ley-corta-del-tipnis_146889_303848.html (accessed 5 December 2014).

29. See http://www.eju.tv/2011/11/trampa-evo-saca-del-tipnis-actividades-econmicas-indgenas-ven-una-venganza-poltica/ (accessed 5 December 2014).

30. The controlled hunting of caiman and the gathering of cocoa beans and brazil nuts.

31. See http://www.eju.tv/2011/11/trampa-evo-saca-del-tipnis-actividades-econmicas-indgenas-ven-una-venganza-poltica/ (accessed 5 December 2014).

to oppose the irresponsible building of a highway that, given its proposed route would clearly not benefit local communities in the TIPNIS (because of distance and lack of connection to many of the communities).[32] As was made clear to me during a research visit to the TIPNIS in 2010, community leaders proposed to the government that the road should rather follow the route of the River Sécure, along which most of the local communities are located. They argued that such a route would help connect them to necessary services and markets outside of their territory but, at the same time, allow greater protection of the majority of the park – including areas that are sacred and environmentally sensitive. Johnny, an Osomomo leader who had taken part in the protest, reported to Al Jazeera that:

> if they build it correctly, so that it skirts the reserve, a road could be a good thing. For example, we have very few health supplies and doctors here and it could help keep our children healthy.[33]

Unfortunately, as a result of the government's refusal to enter into dialogue on these points, its failure to respect the law regarding impact studies, to carry out genuine consultation and its signing of a contract with a Brazilian company to go ahead with the project, the demands of the protest had become increasingly recalcitrant. Indeed, the indigenous leadership for the TIPNIS represented by the sub-central (one of three indigenous governing authorities in the territory and holder of the communal land title) concluded by rejecting the road entirely. Whilst protection of the natural environment was important to the marchers, this was not expressed as a value in its own right but rather as a point used to reinforce the issues they saw as priorities, that is, the defence of territory and autonomy, with biodiversity following after. For example, asked about the cause of the march, Emilio Nosa, president of the sub-central of Sécure (TIPNIS) responded to me in an interview on the day of the *la Chaparina* that:

> The defense of the territorial autonomy of the TIPNIS comes first. This is the spearhead [*punto de lanza*] of the march. We are defending our rights against what we see is a slow crime. The road threatens our culture, customs and the biodiversity of the territory.

Stopping the road was therefore a genuine priority of the protesters but autonomy and rights were considered crucial. Indeed, another fifteen additional demands were listed by the time the march arrived in La Paz. These points not only highlighted the wider interest of the population of the TIPNIS but the influence of other indigenous lowland organisations. The local leadership of the TIPNIS sub-central received support from the umbrella organisation of the lowlands indigenous peoples (CIDOB) to start the march, and they were joined

---

32. This was repeated several times during my fieldwork in the TIPNIS in 2010.

33. Al Jazeera and agencies, 'Bolivia's Morales suspends road project': http://www.aljazeera.com/news/americas/2011/09/2011930181931356216.html (accessed 15 December 2014).

by representatives from eleven of the regional indigenous organisations from Chaco, the Amazon and western Bolivia, the highland indigenous organisation CONAMAQ and a group of environmental and human-rights oriented NGOs.

As the march picked up media coverage, other organisations and individuals also joined the march. Autonomy, control and protection of indigenous territories (TCOs) were the central issues these groups named as the reasons for this growing support. The environmental flag was raised, on one hand to protect the livelihoods of the communities living in the park dependent on the use of natural resources and on the other hand for the park's extraordinary biological diversity (402 species of plants, 714 species of animals) and fresh water reservoirs in the Bolivian Amazon.

The additional 15 demands also show that the marchers' interests stretched well beyond environmental protection, to livelihood concerns and economic interests. A number of the demands related specifically to development concerns amongst indigenous communities in the lowlands (housing, health, education and the census). The demands also include requests for state-sponsored plans for appropriate economic production, follow-up on land reform, legal frameworks for the forest sector, consultation and the role of the media. The women in the march were especially concerned with education and health issues, which also included better access to these services in remote areas (Sotto Wattara 2012).

Direct compensation to indigenous territories, from climate mitigation projects or a carbon fund, was also amongst the demands listed by the marchers. Indigenous leaders viewed the claim as being related to their claims for collective titles to land and autonomy (providing an income source to protect their territories from illegal logging and other destructive activities) and support to sustainable livelihood activities (such as non-timber-related income activities, like the collection of Brazil nuts). However, the government saw the demand as a threat to the international position taken by Bolivia against carbon markets and offsets in projects related to reducing emissions from deforestation and forest degradation (REDD); they accused the indigenous organisations from the lowlands of being traitorous in their promotion of what the president called the 'trans nationalization and privatization of the forests'.[34]

As well as highlighting the different platforms and interests within the TIPNIS campaign itself, the government also questioned how representative the leadership of the march was of community interests. They revealed that, of the 66 communities within the TIPNIS, only ten participated in the march. During the protest march and the efforts by the president to return negotiation to the park areas, the media revealed that there was serious fragmentation amongst the communities that make up the TIPNIS population (itself made up of three different peoples with different organisational and political structures). Many of the communities and leaders of the TIPNIS were willing to meet with the government and voice their support for the road project during government efforts to derail the march by holding negotiations in the park. Much is made here of the

---

34. See http://www.fobomade.org.bo/art-1943 (accessed 5 December 2014).

fact that much of the road had already been built and that what was at stake was only the remaining 50 km. Indeed, 21 indigenous communities with 12 living in the south of the TIPNIS indigenous territory and another nine in Poligono 7 banded together to form the Indigenous Council of the South (CONISUR). They mounted their own march to La Paz in favour of the government's road-building project in December 2011.[35] Critical questions were, in turn, asked by the leaders of the TIPNIS march about the apparent material support that the government granted the CONISUR march that reached the capital before the 1 January 2012.

It was these signs of disagreement within the TIPNIS and clear disagreement on the issue of the road and wider concerns with development that the government claimed must be cleared up by a return to the issue of consultation. In February 2012, the Movement for Socialism (MAS) government passed new legislation to guarantee consultation on proposals for the construction of a road through the Isiboro-Sécure National Park and Indigenous Territory (TIPNIS). The official stance is that the new law was an attempt to make amends for a previous lack of consultation with indigenous communities over the project, despite being glaringly at odds with the government's previous support for the intangibility decree. The consultation was to be completed within 120 days and cover three main themes: whether the TIPNIS should remain 'intangible'; whether the proposed road through the area should be constructed; and what measures should be taken to prevent illegal settlements in the TIPNIS. Despite the official timetable for the consultation, no clear conclusion was reached until December 2012.

The government claimed that the results of the four-plus-month process (which started late, on July 29) represented a 'triumph of representative democracy', and a successful outcome of Bolivia's first experience with the 'consulta previa' for indigenous communities that is mandated by the new constitution and by international law.[36] In contrast, for indigenous, environmental, and human-rights groups concerned about the adverse effects of the road, the outcome of the consulta was seen as a foregone conclusion, in favour of what President Evo Morales was determined to achieve.[37] The national media began asking about the government's decision to grant contracts for the construction of the road before the consultation exercise was over, as well as about the legality of granting the contract to two construction companies with direct links to the coca-growers associations.[38] In these accounts, the government's deception, manipulation, and co-optation casts doubt on the final results.

Fernando Vargas, head of the TIPNIS subcentral, insists that at least 30 communities rejected the consulta. In many cases, he argues, the official consulta

---

35. See http://www.boliviainfoforum.org.uk/news-detail.asp?id=101 (accessed 5 December 2014).

36. See https://www.nacla.org/blog/2012/12/13/bolivia-end-road-tipnis-consulta (accessed 5 December 2014).

37. See 'Indígenas ponen en duda los resultados de la consulta' In Pagina Siete 23/10/12 (accessed 5 December 2014).

38. See 'Empresa de cocaleros hará el tramo 1 de la vía por el TIPNIS' in Pagina Siete 11/10/12 (accessed 5 December 2014).

included only a minority of residents and took place without the sanction of indigenous authorities. He also claimed that people were misled about the intentions of the consultation due to its wording, which stressed developmental benefits, such as improved access to health, education and infrastructure and not the route of the road.[39] Indeed, in conjunction with the formal conclusion of the *consulta*, the government has promised to create an integral development plan for the TIPNIS, emphasising sustainable development projects – where an ecological highway is only one element of a plan to deliver basic services such as education, health, and transportation, and protection against land encroachments and exploitation of natural resources. Community support for development projects, he argues, was taken as an endorsement of the road.

Vargas's claims of government manipulation of the consultation exercise has also provided some further credibility to the findings in December 2012 of a 15-member commission representing the Catholic Church and the Permanent Assembly of Human Rights in Bolivia (APDHB), in association with the Inter-American Federation of Human Rights (FIDH). Of the 36 communities visited, they reported, 30 reject the proposed road, three accept it, and three have conditioned their acceptance on further study and/or changes in the route.[40] These conclusions directly contradict official consultation reports that argue that 80 per cent of the 69 communities included in the official consultation process support the road. The commission also concluded that the consultation process did not conform to standards for prior consultation established by national and international law. It failed to respect collective indigenous decision-making norms, with some meetings held in the absence of traditional authorities or even outside the community. It did not provide information on the road's potential environmental, social, economic, and cultural impacts, necessary to achieve informed consent. It is also claimed in the report that the government's delivery of community benefits and promises of development and services in conjunction with the consultation severely compromised the integrity of the process. The strategy used by the government had divided communities and families and created interfamilial pressures which, in some cases, amounted to intimidation.

In an effort to mark indigenous discontent with the consultation exercise and the government's attitude towards the future development of the TIPNIS and lowlands, Pedro Nuni, previously a deputy for ruling party MAS, ran as an independent candidate in the Benian provincial election in an attempt to protest the manner in which the TIPNIS consultation had taken place. Despite only gaining little over 3 per cent of the vote in the election, Nuni was nonetheless offered the newly proposed position of governor in the TIPNIS territory.[41]

---

39. See https://www.nacla.org/print/8726 (accessed 5 December 2014).

40. See https://www.nacla.org/print/8726 (accessed 5 December 2014).

41. See http://www.la-razon.com/nacional/Gobernador-Beni-Pedro-Subgobernacion-TIPNIS_0_1774622583.html (accessed 5 December 2014).

Indigeneity and extraction in Bolivia

To date, most analysis of these events has focused on the role and response of the government to the TIPNIS march. Indeed, coverage of events by the media, environmental organisations and other NGOs, and by Bolivian and foreign analysts has largely been aimed at criticising the response of and action taken by the Morales government.[42] Little attention has been given to the complex interests of the marchers, local communities and regional interests described above. Moreover the constantly repeated message is that the government's muddled handling of the TIPNIS affair, in terms of failing to guarantee the security of the protest marchers, in its apparent manipulation of the law and in its corporate connections with coca-growers and peasant farmers, are all reminiscent of earlier right-wing governments. This message is not only repeated by academics and analysts (Wanderley 2011; Webber 2011) but by individuals with key positions in Bolivian public life. For example, writing in an opinion column following his resignation from the post of minister for the environment, Alejandro Almaraz wrote:

> The attitude of the Morales government in relation to the indigenous march in defence of the TIPNIS has converted into a mechanical wheel that reproduces in fine detail the discourse, methods and ideology of the governments of the neoliberal right when they were provoked by marches and indigenous mobilisation.[43]

Similarly Pablo Salon, former ambassador for Bolivia at the UN and Coordinator of the World People's Conference on Climate Change and the Rights of Mother Earth, wrote in an open letter:

> There must be coherence between what we do and what we say. One cannot speak of defending Mother Earth and at the same time promote the construction of a road that will harm Mother Earth, doesn't respect indigenous rights and violates human rights in an 'unforgiveable' way.[44]

Rather than being seen as an isolated event, the raid at Yucumo and the TIPNIS march is seen as part of a general trend in which, despite its rhetoric, the government has failed to leave behind the country's historic baggage of inequality and a *rentier* economy. Roberto Laserna a prominent academic advocate of market liberalism in Bolivia, has posed the question 'what has changed in the last few years?' His answer:

---

42. See, for example: http://www.isj.org.uk/?id=780 and http://www.bolpress.com/art.php?Cod=2012050713 (accessed 5 December 2014).

43. See http://www.paginasiete.bo/2011-09-12/Opinion/Destacados/14Opi00112-09-11-P720110912LUN. aspx (accessed 5 December 2014).

44. See http://www.upsidedownworld.org/main/bolivia-archives-31/3247-tipnis-march-in-bolivia-a-letter-to-evo-morales-from-pablo-solon (accessed 5 December 2014).

A lot, if one observes the process in terms of its discourses and symbols and maintains a short-term perspective. But very little if one is attentive to structural conditions and observes the economic and social tendencies with a longer-term view.[45]

Over the last nine years (i.e. since 2006), the Morales government has placed great emphasis on its aim to end exploitative privatisation through a return to national ownership of the mineral and hydrocarbon resources on which the national economy depends; and it has vehemently voiced opposition to the application of market-based models in international climate policy debates. Widely publicised efforts have also been made to draw rhetorically on indigenous cosmology, to establish an alternative 'peoples' model of development that recognises the rights of Mother Earth. National development policy is now supposed to express in practice the Aymaran philosophical moral value of *suma q'amaña*, or 'living well'. In brief, the indigenous concept of 'living well' means having all of one's basic needs met, while existing in harmony with the natural world, as opposed to 'living better' by seeking to amass more and more material goods at the expense of others and the environment. Many intellectuals in Bolivia, such as Laserna, above, question if this indigenous morality is really being put into practice; and the TIPNIS case has repeatedly been highlighted as representing the gap between rhetoric and practice. Kevin Young, writing in a blog for Znet, highlights the protest march organised by the Bolivian Central Workers Union in October 2011. The main labour confederation, the COB, called for a one-day general strike in support of the TIPNIS protestors. The protesters' slogans indicate anger at Morales's failure to comply with his own rhetoric, referring to the president as a 'traitor' and bidding 'farewell to the process of change[46]'. They accuse the government of being a tool of Brazilian 'sub-imperialism' for succumbing to the pressures of the Brazilian government and the Brazilian company OAS, which is contracted to fund the highway's construction.

This critical questioning of whether 'business is continuing as usual' in Bolivia is valid, but to date few well researched efforts have been made to consider the balance of concrete political outcomes *v* policy failures in the country. Moreover, and the issue this chapter focuses on, critical study by both leftist and rightist analysts (Webber 2012; Laserna 2012) of the TIPNIS controversy has also relied on a series of over-simplified assumptions about the class and identity interests of those involved in the march. Analysis of the controversy has largely fallen into one of two parallel critical narratives. On the one hand, the TIPNIS protest is described as the action of a rural proletariat resisting the overly controlling

---

45. See Robinson, William I., 2011, 'Latin America's Left at the Crossroads', *Al Jazeera* (14 September), http://www.aljazeera.com/indepth/opinion/2011/09/2011913141540508756. html (accessed 5 December 2014).

46. The protestors chanted: *Evo decía, Que todo cambiaría, Mentira,mentira, La misma porquería.*

actions of an exploitative state (Webber 2012; Saavedra 2012). On the other hand, the protest is interpreted as an environmental campaign in which indigenous peoples and environmentalists are seen confronting the state together to secure a sustainable way of life.[47] Both of these reductive narratives have dangerous unintended consequences in terms of being easily co-opted as part of the basis for the political right to argue its case in opposition to the 'process for change'. In this action, these narratives are transformed as part of a useful liberal 'rights-based' discourse, which requires action to protect marginalised and indigenous rights. This is proposed alongside a rejection of the operation of customary forms of values and justice, on the basis that these conflict with individual citizenship rights. These narratives also ignore or deny the dissonance of interests within the TIPNIS protest and the kinds of contradictions detailed above in terms of the debate surrounding the 'intangibility' of territory; they deny the wider complex historical realities of identity-formation more generally within the country. Most crucial to reconsidering these relationships and to exploding renewed stereotypes, there is a need to highlight the particular historic linkages of Bolivian indigenous communities to extractive industries and global commodity markets, and the manner in which national economic and political transformations have squeezed ethnic and class identities together.

From the era of European conquest to the present day, Bolivia's natural-resource wealth has determined its link to both international markets and its destiny as site of periodic social and political contestation (Nash 1993). Throughout colonial, republican and modern history, the Bolivian economy (formal and informal) has remained largely dependent on the export of a limited range of non-renewable[48] and renewable[49] commodities. Whilst there is no space in this article to go into any depth on this history and its linkages to the particular formations of identity in the country, it is important to note that the lowlands – often thought to have a separate history – and the highlands were drawn together into this history. I agree with Fabricant and Gustafson (2011: 8) that there is a need to recognise the articulations across spaces that have occurred in Bolivia and which, through their economic and social pressures, left both the Andean highlands and the eastern lowlands embedded both politically and culturally in each other. The TIPNIS is a space where, as a result of population movements necessitated by a wider political economic history, the cultural logics of the highlands and the lowlands collide.

In the 1980s and 1990s, the ushering in of structural adjustment – following an inflationary crisis in a new democratic period – allowed the return of the extractive industries to private (and often foreign) ownership and control.

---

47. See, for example, http://www.eju.tv/2011/08/la-defensa-de-los-derechos-de-la-madre-tierra-en-el-tipnis/ and http://e360.yale.edu/feature/in_bolivia_a_battle_over_a_highway_and_a_way_of_life/2566/ (accessed 5 December 2014).

48. Silver, gold, tin, zinc, iron, oil, natural gas.

49. Timber, coca, soya, cashews.

In 1996, the state withdrew from an operational role and signed over the industry to the private sector, through shared-risk contracts for upstream activities and authorised private transport and refining concessions (Miranda 2008). Privatisation and the search for economic efficiency led to drastic cuts in the national workforce of miners and oil workers and had serious impact on labour rights and union membership. Tens of thousands of indigenous-*campesinos* from the highlands of the country were forced to move to the valley and lowland areas of the country in search of either work or land. In the process, highland forms of organisation and values, the *ayllu*[50] and union, were transferred to new contexts in which they were set in tension with lowland ideas and traditions of community leadership and land-use. At this time, resettlement and the rapid expansion of agri-industry was encouraged in lowlands departments by Bolivian governments. Soya production and cattle-raising in Santa Cruz rapidly expanded to become key elements in the national economy.

Parallel to these developments in the formal economy, coca-production was established in the Chapare and soared in value and importance for migrant producers dependent on an even-faster-growing informal economy. With the tremendous expansion of agricultural development, lowland indigenous populations experienced a wave of land invasions and a series of threats to their personal and community security. In reaction, new organisations representing lowland indigenous interests and rights were established and protest marches organised. In 1991 the communities of the TIPNIS organised the first march for 'territory and dignity', which not only won legal recognition from the government of their status as an indigenous territory but was highly influential in bringing about a series of legal and constitutional changes recognising the rights and diverse interests of indigenous communities throughout the country (see McNeish and Arteaga Böhrt 2013). This march, and the continuing militancy of the TIPNIS, is also widely cited as an event marking the start of the gradual transformation of the country into its current form as a pluri-national state.

In the TIPNIS, we can see the coming together of these connecting but conflicting trajectories. Migrant coca-growing *campesinos*, cattle ranchers, and local indigenous populations have all been touched by Bolivia's wider political economy. This is a political economy, which whilst changing, remains heavily reliant on processes of extraction. As a result, all have been forced to grasp and build a relationship to an extractivist state but, as a result of different histories, exhibit contrasting internal sectoral dynamics, in terms of whether they privilege class or ethnic identity: class is more important to coca-farmers than it is to indigenous populations, for whom ethnic identity is a stronger trope.

A closer look at the TIPNIS case emphasises the nuances of indigenous positions in the present. Here, blood is clearly being spilt because of differences of opinion and understandings of the natural environment. However, if we look closer at the demands of TIPNIS protesters and consider the other interests that surrounded the

---

50. The Andean form of community organisation and membership.

march, we end up with a different picture from what has commonly been assumed to be the case by external analysts, environmental interest groups and the political opposition, who formed an alliance with the marchers. The fragmentation within the ranks of the marchers, as well as the confrontation with the coca-growers and government forces described above, indicate the way in which expressions of indigeneity in this event are marked by contrasting historical experiences. Indeed, they highlight contrasting histories of linkages to government and commodity markets. Historical experiences have meant that different sectors of the population refer to different points on a sliding scale between class and ethnic identification.

The devil never left

Current interpretations of indigenous peoples' responses to extractive projects appear to have forgotten, or ignored a history of debate within anthropology and the wider social sciences. In this earlier anthropology indigenous practice and thought were understood by scholars to be connected to processes of globalisation and development. Here, it is perhaps important to remember the work of Taussig (1983), as well as the debates that followed his ground-breaking work *The Devil and Commodity Fetishism in Latin America* (1983). Discussing the symbolism of money and ritual payments in the Andean context, Taussig argued that 'devil contracts' – votive offerings in cane fields of Colombia and the mines of Bolivia – should be seen as a question of resistance and not just a way to accumulate capital.

Grounding his analysis in Marxist theory, Taussig argued that the fetishisation of evil, in the image of the devil, mediated the conflict between pre-capitalist and capitalist modes of objectifying the human condition. Whilst Taussig made an important contribution to the study of these ritual pacts in his recognition of the global connections between indigenous practice and the global commodities market, what is also of interest here is the debate that followed his seminal work. Various scholars, including Harris (1995) highlighted that, whilst ground-breaking in its form, Taussig's characterisation of the devil pacts reflected a dualistic and oppositional thinking in anthropology that simply divides 'traditional' from 'modern' capitalist economies.

Harris (1995) stressed that the appearance of money in an economy in which circulation was previously organised on some other basis has often been assumed to initiate a teleological sequence of changes in which the values attached to collective interests are destroyed and replaced by accumulation for individual gain. This, was not, she noted, in reality a clear-cut or unambiguous form of change; nor should it be conceptualised in a way that reflects European thought, that is, in which money itself comes to be seen as evil and unnatural (Harris 1995: 302). It is important to emphasise that in the Andes, ritual payments are made not only to the devil, for example as the owner of mines (Nash 1979; Taussig 1983), but also to *pachamama*[51] and the *apus*;[52] and that these are important in a range of different social relationships and rites of passage.

---

51. Mother Earth.

52. The spirits of the ancestors alive in different aspects of the natural landscape.

What is worthwhile to dust off from this earlier debate is its recognition that, as with money, the meaning and use of resources, commodities and the market are similarly transformed and contentious in indigenous thought. Indigenous peoples express genuinely organic *eco-sophies* (ecological philosophies) that draw on both their physical and cosmological linkages to the natural environment. However, because of histories that are local, national and global we cannot assume, as analysts and the media have done, that a simple division of rationalities or of understandings about the use of the environment exists. Even accepting that different peoples construct the relationship between society and nature differently (Descola 1996), the commonly expressed assumptions – as seen in the reporting, analysis and environmental and oppositional mobilisation of support for the TIPNIS march – of entirely distinct and conflicting cultural categories of thought about the natural environment – are out of step with the materiality of historical and political experiences (Bakker and Bridge 2006; Swyngedow 1996).

Drawing on ideas of a 'cosmo-politics' initially developed by Latour (1993) and Stenger (2005), de la Cadena argues that 'participating in more than one and less than two socio-natural worlds, indigenous politicians are inevitably hybrid, usually shamelessly so' (2010: 353). Recognising that a cosmo-politics opens up an understanding of politics to one based on hybrid positions demands a recognition of power disputes that not only take place within a singular world but where there is the possibility of *pluri-versal* (Rancière 1995) adversarial relations, in which both humans and nature (the cosmos) interact. In the TIPNIS case, we can see the coming together of connected but also conflicting 'cosmo-politics' or resource sovereignties. Here, blood was being spilled because of differences of opinion, understandings and relationships with the natural environment. However, if we look closer at the demands of the TIPNIS protesters and consider the range of interests that surround the march, we end up with a different picture from that commonly assumed by external analysts or environmental interest groups and the political opposition.

In daily practice, tradition and resistance are required by the circumstances of global economic pressures to be balanced with a discussion about state-formation, modernity and exploitation. Whilst regional campaigns for cultural recognition have secured the constitutional recognition of rights to identity and autonomy, the essentialised and concessional terms in which these processes have been won have had the unintended consequence of reducing the spaces available to indigenous organisations to negotiate the further expansion of political and economic rights (Engle 2010). Moreover, as this chapter means to convey, the essentialised characterisation of indigenous peoples' interests also threatens to close down the possibility of recognising and learning from a more nuanced understanding of the way in which they are at once tied to similar historical processes and differentially understand the linkages between development and environment.

In this light, whilst the Bolivian vice-president's recently published (Garcia-Linera 2012) analysis of the conservative manipulation of fractures in the Bolivian popular movements and the need for the state to confront patrimonial interests may have some evidence to support it, it is also patronising in its assumption that the state has a right to veto the agency and efforts of lowland Amazonian communities, such as those in the TIPNIS, to imagine their own futures. The details of the TIPNIS case and other cases of 'resource sovereignty' the bracketing together of peoples' relationships to nature and resources with historically moulded political claims to resources and territory (McNeish and Logan 2012), make it clear that indigenous communities consciously engage with the complex contradictions of their development and identity. Indeed, in a situation in which stable traditional modes of production and subsistence come into contact with the apparent quick gains of legal and illegal extraction, it should be unsurprising that contrasting aspirations and demands are expressed – and that many of these are without progressive 'guarantees' (Cadena and Stern 2007: 4). However, it should also be noted that amongst the clamour of indigenous people's ideas and proposals there is also awareness, based on experience, that displacement from their lands or territories would threaten both their personal and community's security. It is for this reason that, whilst disagreements rage, autonomy and sovereignty over territory and, in particular, communal title, return as the principal concerns of indigenous peoples such as those in the TIPNIS, in their encounter with extractive and development activity.

Conclusion

In this chapter I have highlighted that the TIPNIS controversy not only led to the violence of *la Chaparina* and a political crisis in which the government's claims to be pursuing decolonisation and sustainable development have been shown to be hollow; it also revealed anew the complex dynamics of indigeneity in the country. Recent years have demonstrated that whilst significant changes have been made in social policy and the legal protection of both indigenous peoples and the environment, the Bolivian government's retention of an extractive economic model has meant that earlier tensions related to land and identity have remained. These tensions have, as described above, led to a series of difficult and at times violent clashes between local populations and state forces, and resulted in a wave of political activity with the energy to destabilise government planning. In this chapter, I have described one of these recent confrontations, the TIPNIS controversy, and demonstrated its links to wider processes; I have also questioned the manner in which other analysts and organisations have chosen to interpret the interests involved in such processes.

In recounting the history of the TIPNIS protest, I have demonstrated that local communities' positioning in opposition to a road project was far from straightforward. As I have shown above, there are significantly different opinions, both within the TIPNIS areas and without, with regards to future development. Other indigenous groups, in addition to people from the TIPNIS, also used the act of opposing the road as a means to force negotiation with the government on a series of other development issues. These included alternative productive uses of the territory. Moreover, the oppositional position adopted by the leadership of the three ethnic groups within the TIPNIS territory was not adopted by all of the territory's population.

Whilst it is partially true that the TIPNIS protest represented a marginalised indigenous population with a militant concern for the environment, their history and current relationships to the state and environment do not follow neat distinctions. Indigeneity in Bolivia, as elsewhere, does not follow neat categorisation. This chapter highlights the development of the extractive industry in Bolivia and the manner in which indigenous communities have become embedded in its development and capital consumption. I have argued that common mistakes made by external observers are to assume clear relationships between class and ethnicity or to see the clashes over the TIPNIS as a signs of solidarity between indigenous peoples and environmentalists in the outright rejection of government plans and of the Morales government. On the basis of this history, but also recent actions and statements of indigenous leaders, it is argued that assumptions about the operation of neatly contrasting values and ideas about nature and its exploitation are misleading.

As I demonstrate above, in the TIPNIS controversy there is a more complex reality and interplay of interests than those that would simply match assumed, or easily co-opted, class or ethnic interests. This does not mean that these assumed interests do not exist. Rather it demands recognition of an extension of previously supposed grammars of race, rights, identity and territory in the country – the TIPNIS protest reveals a poly-vocality of perceptions of and claims to development at all levels of Bolivia. Moreover, we should recognise here that the TIPNIS is as much tied to material concerns as it is competing cultural and epistemic models for reshaping political, social and economic orders. If territorial orders during the neo-liberal era were reshaped to facilitate trade liberalisation and market-oriented accumulation (with labour flexibility and rural dispossession), the reconstitution of a sovereign developmentalist state and the recognition of the country's indigenous majority have fueled a new array of re-mappings emerging both from official policy and from social movement struggle (Fabricant and Gustafson 2011: 3).

In contrast to the assumptions of media reports and academic writing, the chapter reveals the existence of a complex matrix of contrasting, overlapping and at times conflicting demands and interests within the indigenous communities involved in the march. As such, the chapter repeats the emphasis of earlier work regarding the key role of diverse social forces, in contrast to institutional and economic models, in determining the outcome and stability of resource governance (McNeish and Logan 2012). It argues that recognition of this ambiguity and multiplicity is important not only for providing a realistic characterisation of recent events and helping to avoid repeated violence but for creating opportunity for real concerns and challenges to come to the fore. Here, a position of protagonism, not resistance, is also revealed, in which protest becomes a mechanism for multiple actors to balance the pressures and possibilities of development with claims for continued self-determination. Importantly self-determination here is not only thought of in terms of rights of participation and consultation but in terms of settling a combination of social, material and territorial claims.

References

Arze, C. (2004) 'El referendum del gas y la nacionalización', La Paz, Bolivia: *CEDLA Informe* No. 7.

Bakker, K. and Bridge, G. (2006) 'Material worlds? Resource geographies and the "matter of nature"', *Progress in Human Geography* 30(5): 5–27.

Bebbington, A. (2009) 'The new extraction: rewriting the political ecology of the Andes?', *NACLA Report on the Americas* 42(5), Sept/Oct: 12–24.

Bebbington, A. and Bebbington, D. (2011) 'An Andean avatar: post-neoliberal and neoliberal strategies for securing the unobtainable', *New Political Economy* 15(4): 131–45.

Brysk, A. (1996) 'Turning weakness into strength: the internationalization of Indian rights', *Latin American Perspectives* 23(2), Spring: 38–57.

Cannesa, A. (2012) *Intimate Indigeneities: Race, sex and history in the small spaces of Andean life*, Durham and London: Duke University Press.

Cadena, M. and Starn, O. (2007) 'Introduction', in M. Cadena and O. Starn (eds) *Indigenous Experience Today*, Oxford and New York: Berg.

Conklin, B. A. and Graham, L. R. (2009) 'The shifting middle ground: Amazonian Indians and eco-politics', *American Anthropologist* 97(4): 695–710.

Descola, P. (1996) *In the Society of Nature. A native ecology in Amazonia*, Cambridge: Cambridge University Press.

Engle, K. (2010) *The Elusive Promise of Indigenous Development: Rights, culture, strategy*, Durham and London: Duke University Press.

Fabricant, N. and Gustafsen, B. (2011) (eds) *Remapping Bolivia: Resources, territory, and indigeneity in a plurinational state*, Santa Fe: School for Advanced Research Press.

Garcia-Linera, A. (2012) *Geopolítica de la Amazonia: Poder hacendal-patrimonial y acumulación capitalista*, La Paz, Bolivia: Vice-Presidencia de la Republica de Bolivia.

Gudynas, E. (2010a) 'The new extractivism of the 21st century: ten urgent theses about extractivism in relation to current South American progressivism', Americas Policy Program Report, Washington, DC: Center for International Policy.

Gudynas, E. (2010b) 'Si eres tan progresista ¿Por qué destruyes la naturaleza? Neo-extractivismo, izquierda y alternativas', *Ecuador Debate* 79: 61–81, Quito: CAAP.

Hall, S. (1996) 'Who needs identity?', in Hall and de Gay (eds) *Questions of Cultural Identity*, Sage: London.

Harris, O. (1995) 'Ethnic identity and market relations: Indians and Mestizos in the Andes', in B. Larson, O. Harris and E. Tendeter (eds), *Ethnicity, Markets and Migration in the Andes: At the crossroads of history and anthropology*, Durham and London: Duke University Press.

Kohl, B. and Farthing, L. (2006) *Impasse in Bolivia: Neoliberal hegemony and popular resistance*, London and New York: Zed Books.

Lee Van Cott, D. (2008) *Radical Democracy in the Andes*, Cambridge: Cambridge University Press.

Madrid, R. (2011) 'Bolivia: origins and policies of the Movimiento al Socialismo', in S. Levitsky and K. Roberts (eds) *The Resurgence of the Latin American Left*, Baltimore, MD: Johns Hopkins University Press.

McNeish, J. (2006) 'Stones on the road: the politics of participation and the generation of crisis in Bolivia', *Bulletin of Latin American Research* 25(2): 220–40.

McNeish, J. and Arteaga Böhrt, A. (2013) 'An accumulated rage: legal pluralism and gender justice in Bolivia', in R. Sieder and J. McNeish (eds) *Gender Justice and Legal Pluralities: Latin American and African perspectives*, Oxford and New York: Routledge.

McNeish, J. and Logan, O. (2012) *Studies on the Socio-Economics of Oil and Gas*, London and New York: Pluto Press.

Miranda, C. (2008) 'Gas and its importance to the Bolivian economy', in Crabtree, J. and Whitehead, L. (eds) *Unresolved Tensions: Bolivia past and present*, Pittsburgh, PA: University of Pittsburgh Press.

Nasdasdy, P. (2006) 'Transcending the debate over the ecologically noble Indian: indigenous peoples and environmentalism', *Ethnohistory* 52(2): 291–331.

Nash, J. (1993) *We Eat the Mines and the Mines Eat Us: Dependency and exploitation in Bolivian tin mines*, New York: Colombia University Press.

Orgáz Garcia, M. (2005) *La Nacionalización del Gas. Economía, politica y geopolitical de la 3ra nacionalización de los hydrocarburos en Bolivia*, La Paz, Bolivia: C&C Editores.

Postero, N. (2010) 'The struggle to create a radical democracy in Bolivia', *Latin American Research Review* 45, Special Issue, Actually Existing Democracies: 59–78.

Redford, K. (1991) 'The ecologically noble savage', *Orion* 9: 24–9.

Taussig, M. (1983) *The Devil and Commodity Fetishism in South America*, Chapel Hill, NC: University of North Carolina Press.

Saavedra, J. L (2012) 'A un año de la represión gubernamental en Chaparina', *Nueva Cronica y Buen Gobierno*, 111, September: 4–5.

Sieder, R. and McNeish, J. (2013) *Gender Justice and Legal Pluralities: Latin American and African perspectives*, Routledge: London and NY.

Sotto Watara, A. (2012) *'Para que no se pierda la historia': Diario de la VIII Marcha Indígena por la Defensa del TIPNIS y los Territorios Indígenas*, La Paz, Bolivia: CIPCA.

Swyngedouw, E. (1996) 'The city as hybrid: on nature, *Regeneracimiento* and the production of the Spanish waterscape 1890–1930', *Annals of the Association of American Geographers* 89: 443–65.

Wanderley, F. (2008) 'Beyond gas: between the narrow based and broad based economy', in J. Crabtree and L. Whitehead (eds) *Unresolved Tensions: Bolivia past and present*, Pittsburgh, PA: University of Pittsburgh Press.

—   (2011) 'The economy of the extractive industries', *Revista: Harvard Review of Latin American Studies*: http://www.drclas.harvard.edu/publications/revistaonline/fall-2011/economy-extractive-industries (accessed 29 May 2015).

—   (2008) 'Beyond gas: between the narrow based and broad based economy', in J. Crabtree and L. Whitehead (eds) *Unresolved Tensions: Bolivia past and present*, Pittsburgh, PA: University of Pittsburgh Press.

Weismantel, M. (2001) *Cholas and Pishtacos: Stories of race and sex in the Andes*, Chicago, IL: University of Chicago Press.

Webber, J. (2011) *From Rebellion to Reform in Bolivia: Class struggle, indigenous liberation, and the politics of Evo Morales*, Chicago, IL: Haymarket Books.

Chapter Twelve

Indigenous Rights, Political Mobilisation and Indigenous Control over Development: Natural-Gas Processing in Western Australia

Ciaran O'Faircheallaigh

Introduction

Since the early 1970s, there has been a trend towards growing formal recognition of indigenous rights in international forums and in many states with significant indigenous populations. Given that the continued possession and control of their ancestral lands is central to the survival and wellbeing of indigenous peoples, recognition of indigenous interests in land and sea has been central to the movement for recognition of indigenous rights. In the international arena, the principle of Indigenous Free Prior Informed Consent (IFPIC), which asserts that indigenous peoples must decide whether development occurs on their ancestral estates, and the nature of any development that does occur, has increasingly been reflected in international treaties and declarations, including the International Convention on Biodiversity (2002) and the UN Declaration on the Rights of Indigenous People (2007). At the national level, constitutional enactments or legislation providing for recognition of indigenous rights in land has been introduced in countries as diverse as Australia, Canada, New Zealand, the Philippines, Nicaragua and Colombia.

This growing recognition of indigenous rights has required widespread political mobilisation by indigenous peoples and their allies at both international and national levels (Attwood and Markus 1999; Corntassel 2007; Morgan 2004; Muehlebach 2003). The focus of this paper is on another area of indigenous political mobilisation that required to ensure that formal recognition of rights translates into indigenous control over commercial development 'on the ground'. There are a number of reasons why this might not occur. First, many international instruments that enshrine recognition of indigenous rights, including the UN Declaration, are not legally binding on states; governments anxious to secure the economic benefits of development may ignore them in practice (Baluarte 2004). Second, national legislation recognising indigenous rights may do little more than create opportunities to negotiate with state agencies and developers regarding the terms on which development may occur; political mobilisation is essential if indigenous groups are to make effective use of those opportunities (O'Faircheallaigh 2007). Third, non-state parties such as business interests and environmental groups may seek to constrain the ability of indigenous peoples to control what happens on their ancestral lands and indigenous landowners may need to mobilise to counter such attempts. Finally, and more generally, the process of recognising indigenous rights is not linear and cumulative but dynamic and subject to reversal; and indigenous political mobilisation is required to consolidate existing gains and to resist attempts to 'roll back' recognition of indigenous rights (Baluarte 2004; Corntassel 2007; Morgan 2004).

This chapter focuses on indigenous political mobilisation in the context of one of Australia's largest proposed resource projects, the establishment of an Industrial Precinct for processing natural gas into liquefied natural gas (LNG) in the Kimberley region of Western Australia. It documents the successful mobilisation of Kimberley Aboriginal 'traditional owners'[1] and their regional organisation, the Kimberley Land Council (KLC), to grasp the opportunities offered by a policy commitment of the Australian Labor Party state government: to apply the principle of IFPIC to the selection of a site for the LNG Precinct, in 2006–8. This policy was reversed by a newly-elected Liberal-National Party Government in late 2008, which threatened to use its compulsory acquisition powers to acquire land for the LNG Precinct if traditional owners did not agree to its development. The paper discusses the efforts of Aboriginal traditional owners and the KLC to maintain the principle of IFPIC in an increasingly hostile and complex political environment, in which a pro-development state government, business interests, environmental groups and local tourism operators opposed to the LNG Precinct all sought to deny the right of traditional owners to have the final say over development on their ancestral lands. An important part of this discussion involves the way in which tensions within the Aboriginal group fanned by this rising political hostility threatened the political efficacy of the KLC and traditional owners.

The chapter illustrates the extent to which ongoing indigenous political mobilisation is essential if formal recognition of indigenous rights is to translate into greater indigenous control of development on indigenous lands, and the critical role of indigenous political organisation in this regard. It also shows how indigenous political mobilisation is affected by, and generates, interacting sets of politics at many levels, from the micro-politics of inter-group conflict to global contests around recognition of indigenous rights.

The next section provides essential context by introducing the Kimberley region and its indigenous peoples and providing a brief background on the proposed LNG Precinct. The following sections outline the successful mobilisation of Kimberley indigenous people during 2006–8 and the countervailing pressure exerted against their attempts at achieving control over development on their traditional lands during 2008–11. The chapter highlights the enormous obstacles indigenous people face, despite growing legal recognition of their rights, in determining whether or in what form development should occur on their ancestral lands.

---

1. The term 'traditional owners' is used in Australia to describe those indigenous people who have primary affiliations with, and responsibility for, areas of land and water and the cultural and spiritual sites they contain.

The Kimberley region and the proposed LNG Precinct

The Kimberley region (*see* Map 12.1) occupies some 424,000 sq km in the north-west of Western Australia. Its population is around 41,000, some one-third of which is Aboriginal. Like many indigenous peoples, Kimberley Aboriginal people suffer serious economic and social disadvantage. Opportunities for wage employment are scarce; incomes are well below the national average; and access to education, healthcare, housing and other human services are limited. On the other hand, many traditional owners have maintained their connections to 'country'[2] and are still able to obtain a large part of their food requirements from their traditional lands; while Aboriginal cultural and social values and practices remain vibrant (KLC 2010a: 46–50). Kimberley Aboriginal people established the KLC in 1978 to provide a regional political platform from which they could oppose the uncontrolled development being promoted by the Government of Western Australia (WA) and, over the following decades, the KLC established a strong presence as a regional grassroots indigenous organisation with a significant national profile (KLC 2011a).

In 1992, Australia's High Court, in its *Mabo* decision, recognised the existence of inherent indigenous rights in land pre-dating white settlement in 1788. *Mabo* was given legislative effect by the Commonwealth Native Title Act 1993 (NTA), which created a system through which eligible indigenous people could claim native title and established processes for judicial determination of claims. The NTA also provided for the establishment of Native Title Representative Bodies (NTRBs), which would assist native-title claimants to lodge and pursue their claims (Bartlett 2004). The KLC was designated as the NTRB for Kimberley and so added statutory functions under the NTA to its existing role as a grassroots representative body.

Today, over half of the Kimberley is recognised as native-title land and a number of additional claims are at an advanced stage (KLC 2011b). Recognition of native title does not allow Aboriginal people to control development but rather confers on them a 'right to negotiate' in relation to proposed commercial development on their lands. Agreements negotiated with developers and/or the state authorities can provide for sharing of project revenues and/or landowner equity in projects; employment and business-development programmes to benefit Aboriginal people; and measures to protect cultural heritage and the environment. The KLC has supported traditional owners in negotiating a series of agreements for major mining, agricultural and other projects (KLC 2011c). If native-title holders oppose development in principle, or are unable to reach agreement on terms, the developer can refer the matter to a government statutory authority, the National Native Title Tribunal, which determines whether, and on what conditions, project proponents may be granted the interests they require to allow a project to proceed.

2. The unity of land, sea, sites, knowledge, law, culture and people is often expressed by Kimberley (and other) Aboriginal people through the use of a single English word, 'country', to refer to all of them.

Conservative Liberal-National Party Governments in Western Australia have been overtly hostile to the recognition of native title. The WA Government introduced legislation in 1994, eventually deemed unconstitutional by Australia's High Court, to prevent the Commonwealth NTA from applying in WA. Liberal National Party Governments have opposed native-title claims, including claims in the Kimberley region, as a matter of principle, and have spent many millions of dollars fighting claims in the courts (Bartlett 2004: 35–6, 42–3).

The Browse Basin is an extensive marine trough which lies between 250 and 500 km off the Kimberley coast (*see* Map 12.1). Starting in the 1970s, reserves of natural gas were located in the Basin by a succession of Australian and multinational companies, including Australia's largest energy company, Woodside Energy Ltd ('Woodside'), Shell, Chevron, BP, and Inpex Ltd, in which the Japanese state is the largest shareholder. It is estimated that the Browse Basin holds some 25 per cent of Australia's recoverable natural gas reserves; and new discoveries continue to be made.

By 2005, rising energy prices and improvements in offshore technology had enhanced the commercial viability of the Browse gas fields. The natural gas would have to be piped ashore for processing into liquefied natural gas (LNG) and by-product liquid petroleum gas (LPG) and condensate (light crude), for export to Asian and other markets. Woodside identified Wilson Point on the Dampier Peninsula north of the tourist town of Broome as a possible location for processing gas from three fields (Torosa, Brecknock and Calliance) it had located some 300 km north of Broome (*see* Map 12.1). While the gas reserves themselves are offshore and not subject to native title, the establishment of an LNG plant onshore would require the grant of interests in land subject to native-title claims; and so Woodside approached the KLC and the traditional owners of Wilson Point to initiate negotiations. Senior traditional owners indicated to Woodside that they were not prepared to enter negotiations at that point and Woodside's CEO stated that Woodside would not proceed with the project against the wishes of the traditional owners.

Inpex Ltd was also seeking a site to process gas from its Ichthys field and identified the Maret Islands, off the north Kimberley coast, as its preferred location. During 2006–7, the KLC and traditional owners for the Maret Islands negotiated with Inpex but were unable to reach an agreement. In addition, environmental studies undertaken by Inpex and cultural heritage work undertaken by traditional owners and the KLC raised serious issues regarding the suitability of the Marets as a site for LNG processing.

The site selection process and the traditional owner task force

In 2006, the (Labor) WA government decided that, rather than have individual proponents identify and develop their own sites for LNG plants along the Kimberley coast, the government would seek a single location for an 'LNG Precinct', where processing of all gas from the Browse Basin would occur, an approach expected to minimise the environmental and cultural impacts of processing. The then

Map 12.1: Kimberley Region, Browse Basin and short-listed sites for LNG Precinct

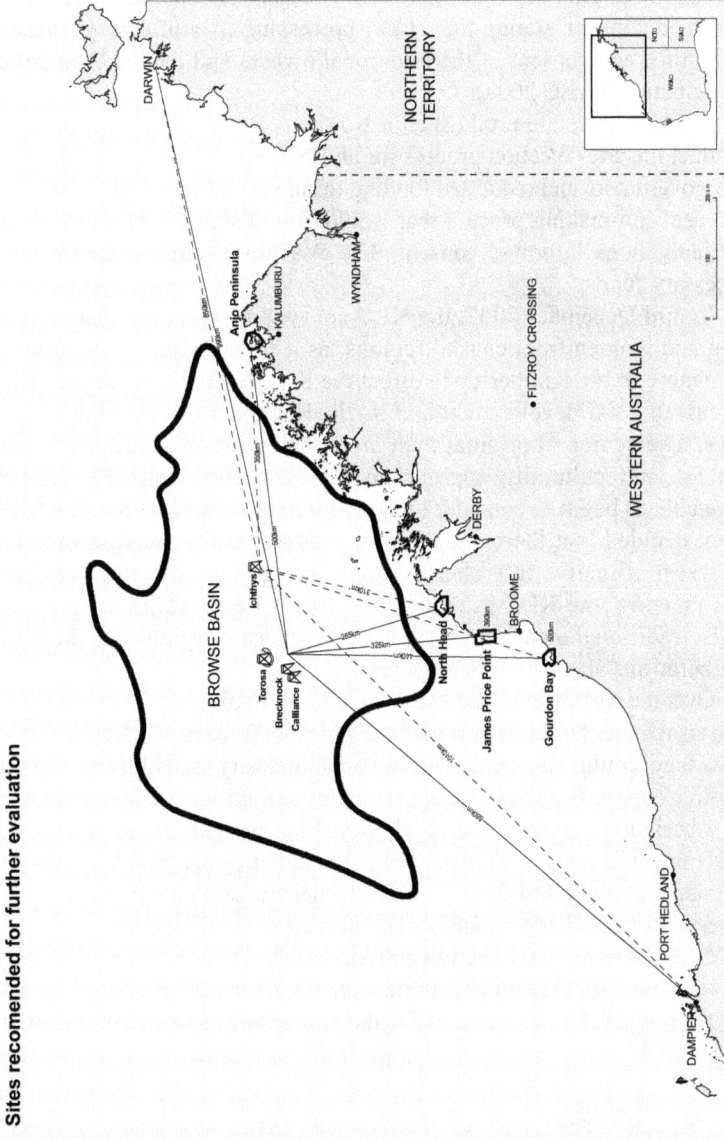

Source: Department of State Development Western Australia

Western Australian Premier, Alan Carpenter, stated that LNG development in the Kimberley would not proceed unless it created significant economic and social benefits for Aboriginal people and unless it had the support of Kimberley traditional owners (Carpenter 2006). The deputy premier and minister for state development reiterated this position in February 2008 and indicated the need for informed consent, stating that 'LNG processing ... will only go ahead with the fully informed consent of the traditional owners and their substantial economic participation' (ABC 2008).

In 2007, the state established a Northern Development Taskforce (NDT) to conduct the site-selection process for an LNG Precinct. The KLC approached the WA government and requested funding to support a traditional-owner consultation and decision-making process that would give practical effect to the state's need for indigenous informed consent. The WA government agreed to provide the necessary funds.[3]

In mid December 2007, the KLC convened a meeting of senior Aboriginal men and women from coastal regions, as well as senior 'cultural bosses' from elsewhere in the Kimberley to direct the KLC on how to proceed. The meeting discussed LNG development and its likely impacts in the Kimberley over two days. The senior Aboriginal men and women present outlined a consultation process and culturally appropriate representative structures, and drafted a timetable to begin to consider the Government's proposal for an LNG Precinct. They decided that there should be a Traditional Owner Taskforce (TOTF) to represent all native-title claims groups along the Kimberley coast. Following this meeting, the KLC established a Senior Leadership Group to advise and assist traditional owners of the Kimberley coastal regions and the KLC in their deliberations about gas development.

Over the wet season (December–February), traditional owners of the Kimberley coastal regions began to consider the potential impact of LNG development and how they could effectively engage with industry and government to achieve positive outcomes and realise opportunities to improve socio-economic conditions for Aboriginal people in the Kimberley. In January 2008, the KLC and the WA government formalised a Financial Assistance Agreement (FAA), pursuant to which the state committed to fund the KLC to undertake a comprehensive consultation process with Kimberley traditional owners about LNG development.

On 6 February 2008, the WA and Australian governments signed an agreement that provided for the two governments to jointly conduct strategic assessments of the proposed LNG Precinct under the Commonwealth Environment Protection

---

3. This section of the paper draws on relevant parts of a KLC Aboriginal Social Impact Assessment Report, which is publicly available (KLC 2010a). That report drew, in turn, on a confidential report to the KLC regarding traditional-owner involvement in the LNG Precinct site-selection process: Kim Doohan and Ciaran O'Faircheallaigh, 'Hydrocarbon processing in the Kimberley region: laying the foundations for an Aboriginal Social Impact Assessment', Broome, December 2008. Any confidential information contained in relevant sections of this latter report is not included here.

and Biodiversity Conservation Act 1999 and WA Environmental Protection Act 1986 (WA). The strategic assessments would conclude with a decision or decisions by the relevant government ministers that:

a. the LNG Precinct as described in the Plan for the LNG Precinct could proceed as proposed;
b. the LNG Precinct could proceed subject to modifications of the original Plan and/or the imposition of conditions on the development; or
c. the proposed development could not proceed.

Unlike previous environmental assessments conducted under state and Commonwealth legislation, the terms of reference (ToR) for the strategic assessments required a major focus on impacts on indigenous peoples and culture, and on how these impacts would be managed. The strategic assessment report that would provide the basis for ministerial decisions on the proposed LNG Precinct would have to include 'a comprehensive analysis of the potential impacts of the plan [for the LNG Precinct] on indigenous people'; 'a description of the potential impacts, including socio-economic impacts, of the Plan on Indigenous people'; and details of 'the specific measures intended to avoid, minimise and mitigate for the potential environmental and Indigenous impacts of the Plan' (ToR Clauses 7 and 9). As discussed later in the paper, the strategic assessments represented another significant avenue through which Kimberley Aboriginal people would mobilise in seeking to influence LNG development.

In mid February 2008, a further meeting of senior Aboriginal men and women confirmed the KLC's Senior Leadership Group in its role, in accordance with appropriate cultural practices, including separate men's and women's meetings and consensus decision-making. Some more senior men and women were added to the group. The Senior Leadership Group would provide advice and leadership to the KLC's consultation process and attend meetings with coastal native-title claim groups. The KLC was instructed to:

•   undertake a consultative process with all traditional owners with native-title claims along the Kimberley coast;
•   facilitate selection of representatives for a TOTF equivalent of the established state government's NDT; and
•   gain as much information from as many sources as possible concerning proposed gas development in the Kimberley.

The area of the Kimberley coast within which the state was seeking a single suitable location for an LNG Precinct encompasses parts of the traditional country of 15 different native-title claim groups. Senior Aboriginal men and women took the position that all those groups had to be consulted, for two reasons. First, they recognised that the proposed LNG development is a massive long-life project and that its impacts, positive and negative, would be highly significant, be felt widely and have intergenerational effects. The second arose from the bonds and commitments inherent in the cultural form that pervades the Kimberley, the *wunan*. The *wunan* can be viewed as an overarching foundational practice of local and regional indigenous governance, like a blueprint for living. It embodies a range of social relations that joins together large numbers of people over vast areas of land. It has binding, moral, ritual, economic and supportive elements, which were often called on during the process of forming the TOTF and during TOTF meetings, as a mediating and reaffirming practice, one considered to be greater than local groups, or even larger native title groups, and to encompass 'the Kimberley' (Doohan 2007: Chapter 7). To be consistent with the principles of the *wunan*, decision-making in relation to LNG development would have to be inclusive and involve mutual support between all of the native title groups involved.

The KLC commenced a series of meetings involving all 15 Kimberley coastal native title groups. The meetings discussed the limited information about LNG development then at hand, what LNG development might mean for the Kimberley, both positive and negative, and how the KLC's consultation process was intended to work; they sought advice, suggestions, questions and direction from traditional owners and aimed to establish what was important for them. Each native-title claim group was invited to consider the selection of four representatives to form the TOTF and how the TOTF should function, including how it should report back to native-title claim group members. The TOTF was established in May 2008, following a series of (Cultural) Bloc meetings, which brought together clusters of related native-title groups. At these meetings, the KLC provided traditional owners with details of the possible locations being considered for development. Further information and advice was also provided regarding gas processing and its likely cultural, social, economic and environmental impacts; and regarding some of the potential benefits of development, including, for example, equity participation, employment and training, business opportunities and education.

At the meetings each native-title claim group selected four representatives to participate in the work of the TOTF. Formal instructions from the native-title claim group members to the KLC to act on their behalf were affirmed by each native-title claim group. During the Bloc meetings the roles and rules of the TOTF were discussed, clarified and endorsed. Of critical importance and consistent with traditional decision-making practices, it was decided that the TOTF members could not make decisions on behalf of their native-title groups; nor could they make decisions about whether to agree to the locating of a LNG hub in the Kimberley or on their traditional land and sea country. Any of these decisions would need to go back to the whole native-title claim group for an area being considered as a suitable location. TOTF members were selected to ensure the integrity of the consultation and information delivered by the TOTF and the KLC project team members; to act as a conduit for the flow of information to and from the larger native-title claim group membership; and to provide a mechanism through which the native-title claim groups would support each other, whatever decision individual groups made about LNG development on their traditional country.

Managing what became a large group with members from all over the Kimberley was a major logistical exercise and an indication of the respect and attention paid to the cultural processes that Aboriginal men and women insisted must happen. It was also an expensive exercise in terms of funding and energy, given the costs and level of administrative organisation required to move more than 60 people from throughout the Kimberley using small aircraft, vehicles and buses, to meet the very demanding meeting timetable. But the establishment and management of the TOTF process reaffirmed Kimberley Aboriginal people's cultural practices and their right to make decisions about their country, in the context of contemporary large-scale resource development.

The initial TOTF meetings were conducted every second week, with Monday and Friday allocated as travel days. All meetings were held in Broome to simplify logistics and ensure adequate space and facilities for the large group of participants. This was a demanding schedule, especially as the majority of TOTF members had to travel to Broome to attend meetings, some for long distances. The TOTF meetings continued until September 2008, when only four potential LNG Precinct sites remained, which the TOTF recommended for further consideration (*see below*).

Throughout the meetings, the members of the TOTF engaged in exchanges with government, non-government and industry visitors, all of whom presented information and responded to questions concerning the proposed LNG development. At each TOTF meeting an agenda was set, minutes were recorded, key issues and tasks to be undertaken were highlighted and questions unanswered or requiring further elaboration and detail were noted. These records formed the basis for preparing TOTF newsletters that were presented at the following meeting as a record of the meeting as well as the basis for discussion within families and the wider native-title claim groups.

Between July and August 2008, the KLC met with relevant native-title claim groups to determine which of the remaining 11 locations chosen for further consideration by the NDT, from 42 original possible locations, could remain in the site-selection process. Traditional owners for these proposed locations participated in a number of scientific and engineering studies, in collaboration with the NDT. As the process unfolded, a number of traditional-owner groups withdrew their land and sea country from consideration as potential sites, though these decisions were not made public until the four remaining locations were made known on 10 September 2008 (*see below*). In some cases, traditional owners withdrew sites because multiple potential sites existed in their land and sea country and they only wished a single site to be considered. In other cases they withdrew sites because of their serious concerns about the potential impact of a Precinct on the environment and on their cultural and economic lives. The NDT site-selection processes also removed some of these same sites from consideration due to environmental and/ or technical considerations.

The process of information-provision and the ability of traditional owners to decide which sites would and would not continue to be considered highlights the application of the principle of IFPIC through the TOTF process. It represents a significant achievement in terms of translating recognition of indigenous rights into control over development 'on the ground'. That achievement reflects, in turn, the extensive political mobilisation undertaken by the KLC and Kimberley traditional owners.

In July 2008, a state election was called and, six weeks later, the election was held. During this period, it was unclear whether the NDT process and the TOTF would continue and, if it did not, what would replace it. Nonetheless the KLC and TOTF continued to meet and progress the consultations and decision-making about LNG development and possible Precinct locations. The TOTF also continued, despite the uncertainty, to engage in formal meetings with the four native-title claim groups that had decided to leave the locations within their traditional country for further consideration. These groups reaffirmed instructions to the KLC to leave their locations in the process, to seek further detailed information and to continue the consultation processes. By early September 2008 and, before the results of the state government elections were finalised, the TOTF formally announced the remaining four locations still being considered by traditional owners: Anjo Peninsula, North Head, Quondong to James Price Point and Gourdon Bay (*see* Map 12.1).

Following the establishment of the Liberal National State Government on 13 September 2008 and the lack of certainty or engagement with the new government, the KLC and the TOTF were confronted with very serious financial and political considerations. In an effort to retain the TOTF process in some form, and in light of the funding and process uncertainty, the TOTF members and the KLC decided to reduce the active participation of TOTF members to those involved with the remaining four potential locations (the 'TOTF (4)').

The new premier, Colin Barnett, announced on 15 October 2008 that it was unacceptable for government to, in his words, give 'a right of veto to local Aboriginal people expressed in the following terms, that projects would not go ahead unless there was informed consent by Aboriginal people' (Government of Western Australia 2008a). The state government indicated that while it would consult with traditional owners regarding measures for impact-mitigation and community benefits, the existing site-selection process would be discontinued.

Funding under the FAA was sufficient to allow the KLC and the TOTF (4) to continue to conduct meetings in November and early December but failure to secure further funding jeopardised any future TOTF or native-title claim group meetings after a Karajarri native-title claim group meeting on 16 December 2008. At this meeting, the traditional owners decided to remove the Gourdon Bay location from consideration, following their interpretation of newly released NDT environmental survey results and their own body of traditional ecological knowledge.

In summary, the site-selection process conducted between December 2007 and September 2008 embodied the principle of IFPIC to a substantial degree. In particular, a number of traditional-owner groups were able to take informed decisions as to whether or not their land and sea country would continue to be considered as potential LNG Precinct sites. However the change of government in September 2008 changed the landscape fundamentally and presented the KLC and traditional owners with major problems in maintaining IFPIC.

Resistance to indigenous control: compulsory acquisition and the LNG Precinct 'Heads of Agreement'

As noted above, on 15 October 2008 the newly elected Liberal National Party Government reversed the former state government's policy position on indigenous consent. In December 2008, the state, after receiving advice on the short-listed sites from the WA Environmental Protection Agency, announced James Price Point as its preferred site for the development of the LNG Precinct. The premier indicated that compulsory acquisition powers under the WA Public Works Act 1902 would be used to acquire land needed for LNG processing facilities if traditional owners failed to reach agreement with the state for location of the Precinct at James Price Point. He indicated that he would allow a period of three months ending on 31 March 2009 for the negotiation of a Key Terms Agreement or Heads of Agreement between the state, traditional owners and Woodside, that would provide traditional-owner consent for the LNG Precinct to proceed. If this was not achieved, the process of compulsory acquisition would be initiated (O'Brien 2008; Government of Western Australia 2008b). As detailed below, the James Price Point site was subject to a native-title claim combining the Goolarabooloo and Jabirr Jabirr people. It was this combined group whose consent would be required.

Changes in state policy on traditional-owner consent and the state's position on the timing of negotiations altered the basis of indigenous participation in relation to the proposed LNG Precinct in fundamental ways. Previously, indigenous participation was centred on the question of whether or not an LNG Precinct site could be found that met relevant engineering, technical and environmental requirements and whose selection as the LNG Precinct site also had the support of traditional owners for the area concerned. Now the central issue was how negative impacts associated with a choice of site made by the state without indigenous consent could be minimised, while at the same time allowing traditional owners and other affected indigenous people to share in the benefits of development.

Another basic change resulted from the imposition of very tight time frames on the negotiation process. The three months nominally allowed by the premier for negotiation of a Heads of Agreement contrasts with the several years taken to reach an equivalent point in similar negotiations for less complex projects.[4] This resulted in a situation in which the KLC and Goolarabooloo and Jabirr Jabirr (GJJ) traditional owners would be negotiating under enormous pressure, especially as the premier's deadline for conclusion of a Key Terms Agreement approached.

While the Premier had indicated a willingness to engage in negotiations with the GJJ, the KLC was seriously hampered in establishing an appropriate representative structure and in preparing for negotiations by the absence of any agreed framework for engaging with the state and Woodside or any funding to support negotiations. (A formal funding agreement with the state was not

---

4. Cases in which it took several years to reach key terms agreement in ILUA negotiations include the Argyle Diamonds Ltd ILUA (Western Australia) and the Western Cape Communities Co-existence Agreement (Queensland).

finalised until 11 March 2009). Partly for this reason, the first formal negotiation meeting did not occur until 26 February 2009. This left only five weeks (later extended to seven weeks, on the basis that a final agreement could be reached by 15 April 2009) for the KLC and the GJJ to negotiate a Key Terms Agreement for one of the largest and most complex industrial projects that has been the subject of negotiations involving indigenous people in Australia. This situation appears to be fundamentally inconsistent with the requirements for IFPIC.[5]

On 19 and 20 February 2009, a meeting of the GJJ native-title claim group authorised the KLC to act on their behalf in relation to LNG development and unanimously endorsed motions that:

a.   traditional owners would enter into negotiations with the state and Woodside for a Key Terms Agreement about a LNG processing facility on their country, if the KLC and traditional owners were properly resourced to do so; and

b.   a traditional owner Negotiation Committee (TONC) was authorised to negotiate the Key Terms Agreement, subject to authorisation by the traditional owners. The KLC was authorised to act for and on behalf of traditional owners on LNG matters.

The meeting nominated members of a TONC to represent the Goolarabooloo/ Jabirr Jabirr native-title claim group in negotiations with the state and Woodside. Over the following weeks, the TONC and the KLC met formally on a number of occasions with the state and Woodside, while technical teams from the KLC, the state and Woodside continued discussions in the periods between these meetings. The state and Woodside presented positions across a range of relevant issues but did not present fully developed proposals until towards the end of the seven-week period. The TONC and KLC put forward counter-proposals to positions put by the state and Woodside and, in addition, made repeated representations to the state and Woodside that the state should not threaten them with, or resort to, compulsory acquisition.

On 14 and 15 April 2009, the KLC held a meeting of the GJJ native-title claim group to consider the current offers from the state and Woodside in relation to establishment of an LNG Precinct at James Price Point; to facilitate a decision by the GJJ claimants on whether to accept the offers, sign a 'Heads of Agreement' providing consent to the location of an LNG Precinct in the area of James Price Point; and to continue negotiations towards a comprehensive Indigenous Land Use Agreement under the Native Title Act, which would give final legal form to the offers and the GJJ consent. The alternative was to refuse the offers, conclude negotiations and face the threat of compulsory acquisition. At the end of the second day of the meeting, the GJJ made a decision that the KLC should, on their behalf, enter into the Heads of Agreement. Members of

---

5.   This account of events leading to the KLC's signing of the LNG Precinct Heads of Agreement is based on a publicly available report prepared by the author for the KLC (KLC 2010b).

an extended family associated with the Goolarabooloo group left the meeting before a decision was taken and subsequently expressed their opposition to the outcome (*see below*).

The 'Heads of Agreement' is confidential, but it provides for:

- agreement on the area where proposed LNG Precinct will be located;
- transfer to the traditional owners of freehold land equivalent in area to the land needed for the LNG Precinct;
- financial benefits provided by Woodside both to the traditional owners of James Price Point and to a Kimberley regional fund;
- substantial financial commitments by the WA government;
- broad principles and some key commitments on indigenous training, employment, and business-development opportunities;
- participation of traditional owners in environmental and cultural heritage management.

The traditional owners were not successful in achieving some outcomes from the negotiations that they had established as prerequisites for an acceptable agreement. In addition, they accepted only reluctantly certain components of the Heads of Agreement. However, the traditional owners determined that the agreement they had negotiated was the best that could be achieved under the circumstances and that it was preferable to the outcomes likely to be achieved if the state proceeded with compulsory acquisition of the Precinct site. One important consideration in this regard was that the Heads of Agreement allowed them a major and continuing role in the selection of a specific site for the LNG Precinct and in determining the location of Precinct components within that site; in the ongoing management of the Precinct as it was developed; while it is operating; and when it is eventually decommissioned and rehabilitated. For the traditional owners, such a role was essential if they were to fulfil their obligations to look after their land and sea country, including cultural sites. There was no certainty that they would have any significant role in project-design or -management if the state acquired the LNG Precinct by compulsory acquisition. The Heads of Agreement also included a commitment to an agreement between the state and traditional owners to exclude LNG development elsewhere on the Kimberley coast and to provide for the return of the LNG precinct to the traditional owners at the end of the project life (KLC 2010b).

The process leading to the signing of the Heads of Agreement clearly departs from the principle of IFPIC in important respects. Traditional-owner consent was not given freely, because it was given under the threat of compulsory acquisition, within time-frames that were unduly and severely truncated and in the context of a lack of any continued funding for the TONC to meet or for the KLC to provide support for traditional owners after 31 March 2009 (or, later, after 15 April 2009). It was only partially informed because, while the TONC did have access to a range of information and advice, it did not have access to critical information regarding the proposed LNG Precinct, particularly regarding potential environmental impacts. During the meetings leading to the signing of the Heads of Agreement, traditional owners and the KLC frequently brought to the attention of Woodside and the state the limited information available to them, including the specific location of the Precinct and its layout; details of its operation including, in particular, use of water resources and any emission of noxious gases; critical aspects of its environmental impact, for instance, as a result of dredging; the nature of the workforce and the location of worker accommodation; and the timing of development.

The Heads of Agreement were given detailed and legally binding expression in a series of agreements concluded between the GJJ, the KLC, the state and Woodside in June 2011.[6]

Because of constraints of confidentiality, it is not possible to discuss Woodside's role, as lead proponent for the LNG Precinct, in the negotiations surrounding the Heads of Agreement or in the state's reversal of its policy on indigenous consent. However, Woodside is on the public record as supporting the state's initiation of the compulsory acquisition process in September 2010. The company stated that compulsory acquisition maintained the opportunity for a negotiated outcome to be secured while, at the same time, it would 'provide a greater deal of certainty for the development' (AAP 2010). Senior traditional owners believe that the state government was, in fact, responding to pressure from Woodside in initiating the compulsory acquisition process. For example, Frank Parriman, co-chair of the TONC, stated:

> I believe a lot of this stuff was orchestrated by Woodside – my anger is at Woodside more than the Premier. They [Woodside] want this project and they're prepared to do anything to get it. But [Mr Barnett] should have had enough courage to stand up to Woodside and say you do the right thing by Aboriginal people and we'll be right. Instead, he's happy to knock down Aboriginal people – and he knows he's going to get public support, because it's easy to knock the old blackfella down. He's prepared to take land from us – he's not prepared to stand up to the company (cited in Prior 2010).

Threats to indigenous political mobilisation: 'black politics'; 'green politics'

Following the signing of the Heads of Agreement, serious and protracted internal conflict, expressed in part through ongoing litigation, emerged within the GJJ native-title claim group and between sections of the group and the KLC. This was to have a profound impact on the prospects for ongoing indigenous political mobilisation. A brief history of the GJJ native-title claim is essential background to an understanding of this development.

During the 1930s, an Aboriginal man, Paddy Roe, and his wife came to live in Jabirr Jabirr country; both were members of other native-title groups. Roe

---

6.   It is rare for such agreements to be publicly available but in this case they are (State of Western Australia *et al.* 2011a; State of Western Australia *et al.* 2011b; State of Western Australia and Goolarabooloo Jabirr Jabirr Peoples 2011).

was admitted to some cultural knowledge by Jabirr Jabirr elders but the extent and significance of this knowledge, and the degree to which this knowledge was also passed on to others, is contested. In July 1994, shortly after the passage of the Native Title Act 1993, Roe's grandson, Joseph Roe, lodged a native-title claim over part of what became the GJJ native-title claim, with himself as the native-title applicant (*see below* for a discussion of this role). Jabirr Jabirr people opposed this claim on the basis of their exclusion from it and, in October 1995, after mediation facilitated by the KLC, they were added to the Goolarabooloo claim (Federal Court of Australia 2011: 33). This claim was re-registered in 1999 as the Goolarabooloo Jabirr Jabirr native-title claim, to meet a new registration test required by 1998 amendments to the NTA. Joseph Roe remained as a named applicant and a second applicant was added. Little occurred to progress the claim over the following decade but it became the focus of considerable attention as a result of the proposal to establish the LNG Precinct.

The position of named applicant is of considerable significance under the NTA. Named applicants are responsible for directing conduct of the claim and for giving instructions to the NTRB. A process is provided for a native-title claim group to remove named applicants if they exceed their authority or are no longer acting in the interests of the claim group but, unless they are removed, an NTRB is required to take instructions from them, even if consultation with the wider native-title group indicates support for an alternative course of action (Federal Court of Australia 2010: 14). On this basis, and claiming that his status as a 'Law Boss' also conferred on him a central role in decision-making in relation to proposed developments on the GJJ claim area, Roe argued that the KLC's decision to sign the Heads of Agreement against his opposition and, on the basis of approval by the majority of people attending the meeting of 14–15 April 2009, was unsound (Federal Court of Australia 2010, 8). Roe initiated action in the Federal Court of Australia in April 2010 to challenge the validity of the meetings in February and April 2009, which authorised the formation of the TONC, and the KLC's signing of the Heads of Agreement, and to restrain the KLC from acting on behalf of the GJJ claim group on the native-title claim or in negotiations concerning the LNG Precinct. Additional matters came before the court as a result of the second named applicant's unwillingness to support Roe's course of action and of a decision by a GJJ native-title claim group meeting in August 2010 to replace Joseph Roe as a named applicant. The Jabirr Jabirr members of the claim group took the position that Roe was not descended from Jabirr Jabirr ancestors, and had not been adopted into the native-title group, and so could not be a member of the group (Federal Court of Australia 2011: 31). The Court has found against Roe in these proceedings (Federal Court of Australia 2010, 2011).

It is impossible to overestimate the impact of this conflict and the associated litigation on indigenous political mobilisation around the LNG Precinct. The litigation has consumed extensive resources in terms of money, time, human skills and emotional energy, both for members of the native-title claim group and the KLC.[7] These resources could otherwise have been deployed in pursing positive outcomes from negotiations and from the Strategic Assessment process (*see below*). The conflict has, according to the executive director of the KLC, Wayne Bergmann, 'undermined the power and authority of the KLC to negotiate' (cited in Barrass 2010). In addition, the conflict has been a major – and at times the only – focal point for media coverage of LNG-related issues. For example, when the conflict spilt into the public domain after a claim-group meeting in April 2010, it drew scores of reports in print and electronic media. The media's focus on the conflict makes it difficult to ensure coverage of other issues critical to the achievement of positive outcomes for indigenous people and makes it harder to mobilise public and stakeholder support in pursuit of these outcomes.

In addition, in communicating with the GJJ native-title claim group, the KLC was forced to focus on resolution of matters related to the claim and, in order to have any prospect of achieving a resolution, to avoid discussing the politically sensitive LNG Precinct. While the KLC continued to work closely with the TONC, this situation seriously hampered its ability to secure mobilisation of the wider native-title claim group in support of positive outcomes from the negotiations and the strategic assessment process. Finally, the existence of the conflict has been used by the government of Western Australia to raise questions regarding the 'mandate' of the KLC and the TONC and to justify the initiation of a compulsory acquisition process in September 2010 (Government of Western Australia 2010), which, in turn, threatens to undermine the indigenous negotiating position (*see below*).

The scope for and efficacy of indigenous political mobilisation was also greatly affected by the actions of environmental groups and high-profile individuals opposed to LNG development in the Kimberley. Some larger environmental groups, such as the Australian Conservation Foundation and the World Wildlife Fund, while opposing the location of LNG processing on the Kimberley coast in principle, accepted the right of traditional owners to make decisions about proposed developments on their traditional country. Other groups, such as the Wilderness Society and a Broome-based alliance of environmentalists and local tourist operators called 'Save the Kimberley', vehemently opposed the location of an LNG Precinct at James Price Point and denied the right of traditional owners to have the final say about development on their traditional country (Save the Kimberley 2012a; Wilderness Society 2012a). A number of high-profile individuals – including musicians Missy Higgins and John Butler, actor Michael Catton and former federal court judge Murray Wilcox – also publicly opposed the development. In Broome, individual opponents regularly posted anti-LNG notices around town; put graffiti on the KLC office; vandalised the

---

7. For a specific illustration of the extent of resources the KLC has had to devote to resolution of the claim issues, see, for example, the Federal Court's summary of preparations for the August 2010 claim-group meeting: (Federal Court of Australia 2011: 16–20).

KLC Executive Director's vehicle; and regularly confronted KLC staff and traditional owners at public events and in private settings such as shopping centres (Burrell 2010; Laurie 2010).

This opposition, particularly its local component, caused considerable distress to the Aboriginal people involved (Bergmann 2010; Laurie 2010). It also threatened to undermine the legitimacy of their decision to support development of an LNG Precinct, especially as the environmental groups and local opponents failed to acknowledge that coastal traditional-owner groups had, in fact, protected sites that were regarded both by themselves and by scientists as considerably more sensitive, environmentally and culturally, than James Price Point (Bergmann 2010). Typical of numerous statements ignoring this fact and questioning the legitimacy of decisions by traditional owners is the following by the musician Missy Higgins in a 'Save the Kimberley' video clip:

> The only people who are saying it [the LNG Precinct] is the right thing to do have dollar signs flashing around their heads. And if that's your only way of justifying it, then I'm sorry that's just wrong (cited in Laurie 2010: 35).

What rendered this opposition to the LNG Precinct much more potent from the point of view of the KLC and Jabirr Jabirr people was that these environmental groups and high-profile individuals provided extensive support and encouragement to Joseph Roe – despite the fact that Roe was not opposed to the establishment of an LNG Precinct or to gas development more generally but only to the specific location proposed for the Precinct.[8] They assisted in financing his legal action; John Butler, for instance, donated part of the value of ticket sales from his national concert tour in 2010. They provided extensive coverage to and support for Roe's position on websites and in the media. For instance, Roe appeared on stage with John Butler and Wilcox hosted media events in Sydney and supported Roe and criticised the KLC on the Australian Broadcasting Corporation's flagship current affairs programme, 4 Corners. Wilcox also provided legal advice (ABC 2010; Burrell 2010; Laurie 2010; Save the Kimberley 2012b). The national leader of the Greens party, Bob Brown, visited James Price Point with Roe in October 2010, where he 'planted his feet in the ground' and vowed to fight the development (McGough 2010).

This support for Roe continues (Save the Kimberley 2012a; Wilderness Society 2012a) even after the Federal Court dismissed his action against the KLC, the GJJ native-title claim group voted by a majority of three to one to replace him as a native-title applicant and the Federal Court gave legal effect to this decision (Federal Court of Australia 2011: 19–20, 44). According to Wayne Bergmann, the environmental groups have engaged in a 'new paternalism', seeking to pit the 'noble savage' (in the form of Joseph Roe) against the 'greedy blackfella' (in the form of the KLC and the Jabirr Jabirr):

---

8. Roe expressed this position very clearly, for instance, in an interview with the ABC's 4 Corners programme (ABC 2010).

This new paternalism underpins the actions of individual green activists ... who have played politics in our communities and helped split native title groups ... 'Save the Kimberley' and the Wilderness Society are pretending to champion the Indigenous cause in order to bolster their own positions and credibility ... There are all these people who make throwaway lines about 'selling out'. I don't see any of these people ... knocking on my door and saying, 'What can we do about the homeless people in Broome? or the high suicide rates or the people on dialysis machines' (cited in Laurie 2010: 36).

Ongoing political mobilisation

The Jabirr Jabirr traditional owners and the KLC have continued to mobilise in the defence of the right of traditional owners to control development at James Price Point. At one level, they engaged in extensive negotiations with the state and with Woodside, seeking to obtain as much control as possible over how the LNG Precinct is developed and operated, to ensure that any negative impacts are minimised and positive opportunities maximised. They have consistently lobbied state and federal politicians and senior government officials in pursuit of these goals. At another level, they have sought to use the media to maximum effect, for instance, to fight against the threat of compulsory acquisition. This is not an easy task, requiring as it does the communication of complex narratives to journalists and their potential audiences: these narratives encompass indigenous rights; the cultural obligations of traditional owners; the native-title claim process; protection of the environment; the desire of traditional owners to improve their living conditions; compulsory acquisition; state and federal government policies; and the actions of environmental groups. The KLC and traditional owners have, however, enjoyed some success – gaining, for instance, extensive and often favourable media coverage in response to the WA premier's initiation of the compulsory acquisition process in September 2010 (see, for example, Jones 2010; Murphy and Manning 2010; Taylor 2010).

The KLC and Kimberley traditional owners have also sought to use the strategic assessment process, briefly outlined earlier, to influence outcomes in relation to LNG development. In particular, the KLC negotiated with the state government that the KLC would manage the studies required to address the indigenous components of the terms of reference for the strategic assessment. It prepared a six-volume Indigenous Impacts Report, which documents in detail the expected cultural, social, and economic impact of an LNG Precinct on traditional owners and other affected indigenous people and includes numerous recommendations for management arrangements designed to minimise negative impacts and maximise indigenous opportunities (KLC 2010c). The KLC is using both representations to relevant government ministers and senior officials and the public submission process in relation to the Draft Strategic Assessment Report to press for these recommendations to be the basis for enforceable management arrangements accompanying any Government approval of an LNG Precinct. At the time of writing, the federal minister for the environment had yet to release his response to the Draft Strategic Assessment Report; and so the final outcome of these ongoing efforts at indigenous mobilisation remains to be seen.

Conclusion

This chapter highlights the opportunities created by recognition of indigenous rights, the extent of the indigenous political mobilisation required to convert this recognition into control over development on indigenous lands and the strength and tenacity of the resistance that indigenous people encounter from the state, business and opposing political groups in seeking to achieve that control.

In response to the WA state government's short-lived policy of accepting the need for indigenous consent to LNG development in the Kimberley, the KLC and traditional owners combined customary law with 'modern' forms of representation, communication and organisation to gain a real measure of control over development. As a result, a number of traditional-owner groups were able to decide that development should not occur on their traditional lands. These decisions survived the subsequent policy reversal by the WA government and they represent a major achievement for the groups involved and for the other traditional owners and the KLC, who supported their decisions. The central role of the KLC in securing the resources to support the TOTF site-selection process and in helping traditional owners to mobilise around the opportunity provided by the WA Government's policy commitment to indigenous consent, highlights the absolutely central role of indigenous political organisation. The role of the TOTF in supporting individual traditional-owner groups emphasises the importance of indigenous political unity.

The forms of political mobilisation used by Kimberley Aboriginal people emphasised use of state-sponsored planning, impact assessment and regulatory processes; they also relied largely on provision of government funding. This stands in contrast to forms of mobilisation involving direct opposition to state and developers' plans and decisions and, in some cases, involving violence – described, for example, by McNeish in this volume in relation to Bolivia (see also Evans *et al.* 2002; Oxfam America 2009). Kimberley Aboriginal people avoided the costs, including death and injury, often associated with direct confrontation with the state, while at the same time gaining substantial control over development and securing a share of its benefits. In addition, given the remoteness, size and sparse Aboriginal population of the Kimberley region, it would have been difficult for the KLC to support traditional-owner mobilisation in the absence of external funding. On the other hand, reliance on state funding creates a crucial vulnerability, because there is always the possibility that the state may, as WA did in October 2008, refuse to renew funding and so seriously undermine continued political mobilisation. It is also the case that regulatory regimes can create obstacles as well as opportunities for indigenous political mobilisation, as illustrated by Western Australia's use of the threat of invoking compulsory acquisition powers to pressure the GJJ into negotiating an agreement for the LNG Precinct.

More broadly, events since the change in government in WA in September 2008 emphasise the fragility of government policy commitments and the strength of the forces that can mobilise to resist indigenous control over development. Faced with compulsory acquisition, serious time pressures and limited information, the GJJ native-title claim group decided to sign an in-principle agreement that provided their consent for an LNG Precinct on their traditional country and offered them, and Kimberley Aboriginal people, significant benefits and an ongoing role in the planning and management of the LNG Precinct. Their decision caused division within the GJJ native title group and was met with widespread resistance from environmental and other groups opposed to LNG development. The combination of the two created formidable problems for the KLC and the Jabirr Jabirr traditional owners in continuing to mobilise around ongoing negotiations with the state government and commercial proponents. The KLC and the traditional owners continue to use the means they have available, including the media, political lobbying, and the regulatory avenues provided by the strategic assessment process, to pursue their goal of ensuring traditional-owner control of development on indigenous land. Whatever the eventual outcome, the difficulty of achieving this goal, despite the growing international recognition of indigenous right, is all too clear. A final point is that the complexity of the political forces that mobilised around the LNG Precinct proposal, and the divisions that emerged among indigenous people, illustrates McNeish's point (in this volume) regarding the contrasting, overlapping and at times conflicting demands and interests that surround indigenous resource contestation.

Appendix: explanation of abbreviations

GJJ	Gollarabooloo Jabirr Jabirr Native-title claim Group, the entity representing native-title claimants for the area of the proposed Kimberley LNG Precinct at James Price Point.
IFPIC	The principle of Indigenous Free Prior Informed Consent, which asserts that indigenous people should be able to determine whether and in what form development should occur on their ancestral lands, without duress, in possession of relevant information regarding the proposed development, and in advance of any actions by state authorities or developers.
KLC	Kimberley Land Council, a grassroots organisation representing Kimberley Aboriginals, established in 1979, and exercising statutory functions as a Native Title Representative Body under the NTA.
LNG	Liquefied Natural Gas, natural gas that has been liquefied at very low temperature to enable its transport by sea.
NDT	Northern Development Taskforce, body established by the Government of Western Australia to recommend a site for a single common user LNG facility on the Kimberley coast.

NTA   Native Title Act 1993, Australian federal legislation that provides for the recognition of indigenous rights in land that survive the process of colonisation and confers a 'right to negotiate' on native-title claimants and holders in relation to proposed developments.

NTRB   Native Title Representative Body, a legal entity responsible for assisting indigenous Australians to establish and exercise native title rights under the *NTA*.

TONC   Traditional Owner Negotiating Committee, formed in February 2008 to represent the Goolarabooloo/Jabirr Jabirr native-title claim group in negotiations with WA and Woodside regarding the proposed LNG Precinct at James Price Point.

ToR   Terms of Reference for the joint WA and Australian Government Strategic Assessments of the proposed Kimberley LNG Precinct under the Commonwealth Environment Protection and Biodiversity Conservation Act 1999 and WA Environmental Protection Act 1986.

TOTF   Traditional Owner Task Force, the representative body established by the KLC on the instructions of Kimberley cultural leaders to ensure that the site-selection process for a Kimberley LNG Precinct reflected Kimberley cultural values and the principle of IFPIC.

TOTF (4) TOTF representing the four native title groups which still had potential LNG Precinct sites under consideration after withdrawal of WA Liberal Government support for the site-selection process in September 2008.

WA   The State of Western Australia.

References

AAP (2010) 'Woodside says Browse LNG on track', AAP Newswire 2 September: http://news.theage.com.au/breaking-news-business/woodside-says-browse-lng-on-track-20100902-14p1g.html (accessed 27 March 2012).

ABC (Australian Broadcasting Commission) (2008) 'Minister accuses Opposition of ignoring Kimberley concerns', ABC News Online, 28 February: http://www.abc.net.au/news/2008-02-28/minister-accuses-opposition-of-ignoring-kimberley/1057358 (accessed 29 May 2015).

ABC (2010) *Rush for Riches: 4 Corners 21 June 2010*: http://www.abc.net.au/4corners/content/2010/s2929919.htm (accessed 21 March 2011).

Attwood, B. (2003) *Rights for Aborigines*, Sydney: Allen and Unwin.

Baluarte, D. C. (2004) 'Balancing indigenous rights and a state's right to develop', *Sustainable Development Law and Policy* 4(2): 9–15.

Barrass, T. (2010) 'Barnett to force land gas deal on Kimberley Land Council', *Australian*, 26 August: http://www.theaustralian.com.au/news/nation/barnett-to-force-gas-land-deal-on-kimberly-land-council/story-e6frg6nf-1225910123051 (accessed 27 March 2012) .

Bartlett, R. (2004), *Native Title in Australia*, Chatswood: LexisNexis Butterworths.

Bergmann, W. (2010) 'Greens should not force poverty on traditional owners', *Australian*, 5 April: http://www.theaustralian.com.au/news/opinion/ greens-should-not-force-poverty-on-traditional-owners/story-e6frg6zo-1225849632605 (accessed 27 March 2012).

Burrell, A. (2010) 'Court challenge threatens $30 bn Woodside plant', *Australian*, 6 April: http://www.theaustralian.com.au/business/ mining-energy/court-challenge-threatens-30bn-woodside-plant/story-e6frg9df-1225850083335 (accessed 27 March 2012).

Carpenter A. (2006) 'West Kimberley onshore liquefied natural gas processing facilities: statement by Premier', Legislative Assembly, Western Australia, 21 November: http://www.parliament.wa.gov.au/Hansard%5Chansard. nsf/0/17abc1a733076925c82575700032596a/$FILE/A37%20S1%20 20061121%20p8443c-8443c.pdf (accessed 29 May 2015).

Corntassel, J. (2007) 'Partnership in action? Indigenous political mobilization and co-optation during the first UN Indigenous Decade', *Human Rights Quarterly* 29: 137–66.

Doohan, H. (2007) *'Making things come good': aborigines and miners at Argyle*, unpublished PhD thesis, Sydney: Macquarie University.

Evans, G., Goodman, J. and Lansbury, N. (eds) (2002) *Moving Mountains: Communities confront mining and globalisation*, London: Zed Books.

Federal Court of Australia (2010) *Roe v Kimberley Land Council Aboriginal Corporation* [2010] FCA 809 (2 August 2010): http://www.austlii.edu. au/au/cases/cth/FCA/2010/809.html (accessed 27 March 2012).

Federal Court of Australia (2011) *Roe v State of Western Australia (No 2)* [2011] FCA 102 (15 February 2011): http://www.austlii.edu.au/au/cases/cth/ FCA/2011/102.html (accessed 27 March 2012).

Government of Western Australia (2008a) 'Premier Colin Barnett: interview transcript: report of the Northern Development Taskforce, 15 October 2008', Perth: Department of the Premier and Cabinet, Government Media Office.

— (2008b) 'Liberal-National Government makes decision on LNG precinct', Perth: Department of the Premier and Cabinet: http:// www.mediastatements.wa.gov.au/Lists/statements/DispForm. aspx?ID=131095 (accessed 27 March 2012).

— (2010) 'State Government to trigger land acquisition process for LNG Precinct', Perth: Department of the Premier and Cabinet: http:// www.mediastatements.wa.gov.au/Pages/Results.aspx?ItemID=133948 (accessed 27 March 2012).

Jones, L. (2010) 'Land acquisition risk to gas project', *Adelaide Advertiser,* 3 September.

KLC (2010a) *Kimberley LNG Precinct Strategic Assessment Indigenous Impacts Report Volume 3: Aboriginal social impact assessment*: http://www.dsd. wa.gov.au/documents/Appendix_E-3.pdf (accessed 27 March 2012).

—   (2010b) *Kimberley LNG Precinct Strategic Assessment Indigenous Impacts Report Volume 2: Traditional owner consent and indigenous community consultation*: http://www.dsd.wa.gov.au/documents/ Appendix_E-2.pdf (accessed 27 March 2012).

—   (2010c) *Kimberley LNG Precinct Strategic Assessment Indigenous Impacts Report:* six volumes: http://www.klc.org.au/2010/12/09/james-price-point-indigenous-impacts-report-released/ (accessed 27 March 2012).

—   (2011a) *History*: http://www.klc.org.au/about/history/ (accessed 27 March 2012).

—   (2011b) *Native Title*: http://www.klc.org.au/native-title/ (accessed 27 March 2012).

—   (2011c) *Agreements*: http://www.klc.org.au/agreements/ (accessed 27 March 2012).

Laurie, V. (2010) 'Dividing the territory', *The Monthly*, October: 32–8.

McGough, P. (2010) 'Brown makes a stand against proposed "biggest gas plant on the planet"', *Sydney Morning Herald*, 14 October: http://www. smh.com.au/environment/conservation/brown-makes-a-stand-against-proposed-biggest-gas-plant-on-the-planet-20101013-16k49.html (accessed 27 March 2012).

Morgan, R. (2004) 'Advancing indigenous rights at the United Nations: strategic framing and its impacts on the normative development of international law', *Social Legal Studies* 13(4): 481–500.

Muehlebach, A. (2003) 'What self in self-determination? Notes from the frontiers of transnational indigenous activism', *Identities: Global Studies in Culture and Power* 10(2): 241–68.

Murphy, M. and Manning, P. (2010) 'Land grab stoush hits Woodside', *Sydney Morning Herald*, 3 September: http://www.smh.com.au/ business/land-grab-stoush-hits-woodside-20100902-14rs3.html (accessed 27 March 2012).

O'Brien, A. (2008) 'I'll take native title land: Barnett', *Australian*, 11 December: http://www.theaustralian.news.com.au/story/0,25197,24782899-5013945,00.html (accessed 27 March 2012).

O'Brien, A. (2010) 'Woodside land move to be felt "around the world"', *Australian*, 3 September: http://www.theaustralian.com.au/national-affairs/woodside-land-move-to-be-felt-around-world/story-fn59niix-1225913520232 (accessed 27 March 2012).

O'Faircheallaigh, C. (2007) ' "Unreasonable and extraordinary constraints": native title, markets and the real economy', *Australian Indigenous Law Review* 11(3): 18–42.

Oxfam America (2009) *Mining Conflicts in Peru: Condition critical*, Boston, MA: Oxfam America MA.

Prior, F. (2010) 'Traditional owners focus anger at Woodside', *West Australian*, 9 September: http://au.news.yahoo.com/thewest/a/-/breaking/7913975/traditional-owners-focus-anger-at-woodside/ (accessed 27 March 2012).

Save the Kimberley (2012a) 'Welcome to Save the Kimberley': http://www.savethekimberley.com/wp/ (accessed 27 March 2012).

— (2012b) 'Save The Kimberley – On Tour With the John Butler Trio': http://www.savethekimberley.com/wp/2010/08/29/save-the-kimberley-on-tour-with-the-john-butler-trio/ (accessed 27 March 2012).

State of Western Australia, Goolarabooloo Jabirr Jabirr Peoples, Woodside Energy Limited, Broome Port Authority, LandCorp (2011a) *Browse LNG Precinct Project Agreement*: http://www.dsd.wa.gov.au/documents/Project_Agreement_web.pdf (accessed 27 March 2012).

State of Western Australia, Minister for Lands, Conservation Commission of Western Australia, Kimberley Land Council, Woodside Energy Limited (2011b) *Browse LNG Precinct Regional Benefits Agreement*: http://www.dsd.wa.gov.au/documents/Regional_Benefits_Agreement_web.pdf (accessed 27 March 2012).

State of Western Australia and Goolarabooloo Jabirr Jabirr Peoples (2011) *Browse (Land) Agreement*: http://www.dsd.wa.gov.au/documents/Land_Agreement_web.pdf (accessed 27 March 2012).

Wilderness Society (2012a) 'Help save the Kimberley': http://www.wilderness.org.au/campaigns/kimberley/ (accessed 27 March 2012).

Wilderness Society (2012b) 'TV ad opposing Kimberley industrial site': http://www.wilderness.org.au/campaigns/kimberley/your-help-vital-to-stop-polluting-industry-destroying-the-kimberley-coast/ (accessed 27 March 2012).

Index

Entries in italics refer to figures.

www.ingramcontent.com/pod-product-compliance
Lightning Source LLC
Chambersburg PA
CBHW072049020426
42334CB00017B/1439

* 9 7 8 1 7 8 5 5 2 2 3 5 2 *